Time Out

Budapest

www.timeout.com

FOR SALE

WITHDRAWN
FROM STOCK

Time Out Digital Ltd

Tel: +44 (0)20 7813 3000

Fax: +44 (0)20 7813 6001

Email: guides@timeout.com

Published by Time Out Digital Ltd, a wholly owned subsidiary

of Time Out Group Ltd. Time Out and the Time Out logo are

trademarks of Time Out Group Ltd.

© **Time Out Group Ltd 2015**

Previous editions 1996, 1998, 1999, 2003, 2005, 2007, 2011.

10 9 8 7 6 5 4 3 2 1

This edition first published in Great Britain in 2015 by Ebury Publishing.

20 Vauxhall Bridge Road, London SW1V 2SA

Ebury Publishing is part of the Penguin Random House group of companies

whose addresses can be found at global.penguinrandomhouse.com

Distributed in the US and Latin America by Publishers Group West

For further distribution details, see www.timeout.com.

A CIP catalogue record for this book is available from the British Library.

Printed and bound in China by Leo Paper Products Ltd.

While every effort has been made by the author(s) and the publisher to

ensure that the information contained in this guide is accurate and up to

date as at the date of publication, they accept no responsibility or liability

in contract, tort, negligence, breach of statutory duty or otherwise for any

inconvenience, loss, damage, costs or expenses of any nature whatsoever

incurred or suffered by anyone as a result of any advice or information

contained in this guide (except to the extent that such liability may not

be excluded or limited as a matter of law). Before travelling, it is advisable

to check all information locally, including without limitation, information

on transport, accommodation, shopping and eating out. Anyone using this

guide is entirely responsible for their own health, well-being and belongings

and care should always be exercised while travelling.

All rights reserved. No part of this publication may be reproduced, stored in

a retrieval system, or transmitted in any form or by any means, electronic,

mechanical, photocopying, recording or otherwise, without prior permission

from the copyright owners.

Penguin Random House is committed to a sustainable future for our

business, our readers and our planet. This book is made from Forest

Stewardship Council® certified paper.

Time Out Digital Ltd
4th Floor
125 Shaftesbury Avenue
London WC2H 8AD
United Kingdom
Tel: +44 (0)20 7813 3000
Fax: +44 (0)20 7813 6001
Email: guides@timeout.com
www.timeout.com

Published by Time Out Digital Ltd, a wholly owned subsidiary of Time Out Group Ltd. Time Out and the Time Out logo are trademarks of Time Out Group Ltd.

© **Time Out Group Ltd 2015**
Previous editions 1996, 1998, 1999, 2003, 2005, 2007, 2011.

10 9 8 7 6 5 4 3 2 1

This edition first published in Great Britain in 2015 by Ebury Publishing.
20 Vauxhall Bridge Road, London SW1V 2SA

Ebury Publishing is part of the Penguin Random House group of companies whose addresses can be found at global.penguinrandomhouse.com

Distributed in the US and Latin America by Publishers Group West (1-510-809-3700)

For further distribution details, see www.timeout.com.

ISBN: 978-1-90504-298-2

A CIP catalogue record for this book is available from the British Library.

Printed and bound in China by Leo Paper Products Ltd.

Contents

44

64

85

176

219

Budapest

Editorial
Editor Peterjon Cresswell
Copy Editor Dominic Earle
Proofreader John Shandy Watson

Editorial Director Sarah Guy
Group Finance Manager Margaret Wright

Design
Senior Designer Kei Ishimaru
Designer Darryl Bell
Group Commercial Senior Designer Jason Tansley

Picture Desk
Picture Editor Jael Marschner
Deputy Picture Editor Ben Rowe
Picture Researcher Lizzy Owen

Advertising
Managing Director St John Betteridge

Marketing
Senior Publishing Brand Manager Luthfa Begum
Head of Circulation Dan Collins

Production
Production Controller Katie Mulhern-Bhudia

Time Out Group
Founder Tony Elliott
Chief Executive Officer Tim Arthur
Managing Director Europe Noel Penzer
Publisher Alex Batho

Contributors
Budapest Today Matthew Higginson. **Explore** Peterjon Cresswell (*Restaurants* Tom Popper). **Gay & Lesbian** Andrea Giuliano. **Nightlife** Aniko Fenyvesi. **History** Matthew Higginson, Peterjon Cresswell. **Baths** Matthew Higginson.

The Editor would like to thank all contributors to previous editions of *Time Out Budapest*, whose work forms the basis for parts of this book.

Maps JS Graphics Ltd (john@jsgraphics.co.uk). The Óbuda map is based on data supplied by © OpenStreetMap contributors (www.openstreetmap.org).

Cover and pull-out map photography Emilie Chaix/Getty Images

Back Cover Photography Clockwise from top left: S-F/Shutterstock.com, Tupungato/Shutterstock.com, Denis Bychkov/ Shutterstock.com, Time Out Budapest, Ana del Castillo/Shutterstock.com

Photography pages 2/3 Aleksey Morozov/Shutterstock.com; 4/5, 44 (top) Dziewul/Shutterstock.com; 5 (top), 16/17, 19, 21, 27 (bottom), 64, 114, 118, 122, 123, 202, 203, 205 Fumie Suzuki; 5 (middle left), 176 Klagyivik Viktor/ Shutterstock.com; 7 ilolab/Shutterstock.com; 10/11, 22/23 (top), 25, 46/47, 112 S-F/Shutterstock.com; 12, pull-out map Emi Cristea/Shutterstock.com; 13 (top), 48, 235 (top), 242/243 Tupungato/Shutterstock.com; 13 (bottom) Anibal Trejo/Shutterstock.com; 20, 191 Szilas/Wikimedia Commons; 22/23 (bottom), 27 (top) Derzsi Elekes Andor/ Wikimedia Commons; 23, 24 (top) Asaf Eliason/Shutterstock.com; 24 (bottom), 37, 61 Peterjon Cresswell; 26 (bottom) paul malaianu/Shutterstock.com; 27 (middle right) Hernadi Levente Haaralamposz; 27 (middle left) www.soosbertalan. com; 28/29 GTS Productions/Shutterstock.com; 30, 32 Mohai Balázs; 33 Takacs Szabolcs/Shutterstock.com; 34/35 (top) Canoneer/Shutterstock.com; 35 Nataliya Nazarova/Shutterstock.com; 36 SKYART KFT; 36/37 MattPhoto; 38/39 Gabor Barkanyi/Shutterstock.com; 40 Balazs Toth/Shutterstock.com; 40/41 Rudy Balasko/Shutterstock.com; 42 (top), 109 (right) posztos/Shutterstock.com; 42 (bottom) Mr. Sergey Olegovich/Shutterstock.com; 44 (bottom) conejota/ Shutterstock.com; 46, 114/115, pull-out map Felix Lipov/Shutterstock.com; 50 Oleksandr Berezko/Shutterstock.com; 51, 74/75, 126 photo.ua/Shutterstock.com; 54 redoctober/Wikimedia Commons; 54/55 Bokic Bojan/Shutterstock. com; 56 Chad Bontrager/Shutterstock.com; 57 Ferran Cornellà/Wikimedia Commons; 62, 81 Pecold/Shutterstock. com; 65, 141 Botond Horvath/Shutterstock.com; 68, 68/69, 76, 79, 166 (top), 184/185, 204 Hungarian Tourism; 74 dsajo/Shutterstock.com; 80 Snóbli Iván/Wikimedia Commons; 84 belizar/Shutterstock.com; 86, 106 Yelkrokoyade/ Wikimedia Commons; 86/87 Alex A Belov/Shutterstock.com; 88, pull-out map Oleksiy Mark/Shutterstock.com; 92 karnizz/Shutterstock.com; 94 (top) Illustratedjc/Wikimedia Commons; 94 (bottom) Goran Bogicevic/Shutterstock.com; 96 Peter Egyed; 97 S.Varga Ilona - ALionphoto; 98 Annto/Shutterstock.com; 98/99 Konstantin Tronin/Shutterstock. com; 100 Capa Center; 109 (left) Sonia Alves-Polidori/Shutterstock.com; 124 dimbar76/Shutterstock.com; 126/127 mmsz/Shutterstock.com; 129 Beroesz/Wikimedia Commons; 134 Balazs_Glodi; 136 sarkao/Shutterstock.com; 138/139 Palace of Arts - Budapest, Gábor Kotschy; 140 netopaek/Shutterstock.com; 142 Budapest Spas cPlc.; 144 Nemeth Daniel; 148, 149 np/Shutterstock.com; 153, 156, 158 Time Out Budapest; 157 Erika Pereszlényi; 161 (top) Marton Nemenyi; 161 (middle and bottom) Vica Fekete; 163 Mark Somay; 164 gordoneszter; 166 (bottom) Ana del Castillo/Shutterstock.com; 167 Zsuzsa Petã; 169 Denis Bychkov/Shutterstock.com; 170/171, 179 andras_csontos/ Shutterstock.com; 172 pgaborphotos/Shutterstock.com; 181 Nightman1965/Shutterstock.com; 181 Nightman1965/ Shutterstock.com; 183 Zsolnay Heritage Management Nonprofit Kft.; 186/187 Gamma-Keystone/Getty Images; 188 Robert Jakatics/Shutterstock.com; 189 Hektor Múlich/Wikimedia Commons; 190 Kyrien/Shutterstock.com; 193 Imagno/Austrian Archives/Getty Images; 195 Wikimedia Commons ; 199 AP Photo/MTI, Szilard Koszticsak; 200/201 MarKord/Shutterstock.com; 206/207, 217 (bottom) AD Photography; 208, 220 (bottom right) Adam Parker; 215 Paul Thuysbaert Photography; 235 (bottom) Fanfo/Shutterstock.com

The following images were supplied by the featured establishments: 5 (middle right and bottom), 11, 14, 15, 22, 26 (top), 34/35 (bottom), 52, 53, 63, 67, 73, 83, 85, 90, 105, 119, 120, 145, 146, 147, 150, 151, 152, 154, 155, 160, 165, 209, 210, 211, 213, 214, 217 (top), 218, 219, 220 (top and bottom left), 222

About the Guide

GETTING AROUND

Each sightseeing chapter contains a street map of the area marked with the locations of sights and museums (❶), restaurants (❶), cafés and bars (❶) and shops (❶). There are also street maps of Budapest at the back of the book, along with an overview map of the city. In addition, there is a detachable fold-out street map.

THE ESSENTIALS

For practical information, including visas, disabled access, emergency numbers, lost property, websites and local transport, see the Essential Information section. It begins on page 206.

THE LISTINGS

Addresses, phone numbers, websites, transport information, hours and prices are all included in our listings, as are selected other facilities. All were checked and correct at press time. However, business owners can alter their arrangements at any time, and fluctuating economic conditions can cause prices to change rapidly.

The very best venues, the must-sees and must-dos in every category, have been marked with a red star (★). In the sightseeing chapters, we've also marked venues with free admission with a FREE symbol.

THE LANGUAGE

Many local under-40s can speak some English. The older generation will have a smattering of German. Signs in the metro stations have English translations, but you'll have to learn as you go in shops, restaurants, places of entertainment and offices. You'll find a primer on page 234, along with some help with restaurants on page 235.

PHONE NUMBERS

The area code for Budapest is 1. You don't need to use the code when calling from within Budapest; simply dial the number as listed in this guide. To call other places around Hungary from Budapest, or to call Budapest from the rest of the country, you have to dial 06 first, wait for the second tone, and then follow with the code and number. To call Hungary from abroad, dial 36 and then 1 for Budapest. For a provincial Hungarian town or a Hungarian mobile from abroad, dial 36 then the number with no initial 06. For more on phones, see page 232.

FEEDBACK

We welcome feedback on this guide, both on the venues we've included and on any other locations that you'd like to see featured in future editions. Please email us at guides@timeout.com.

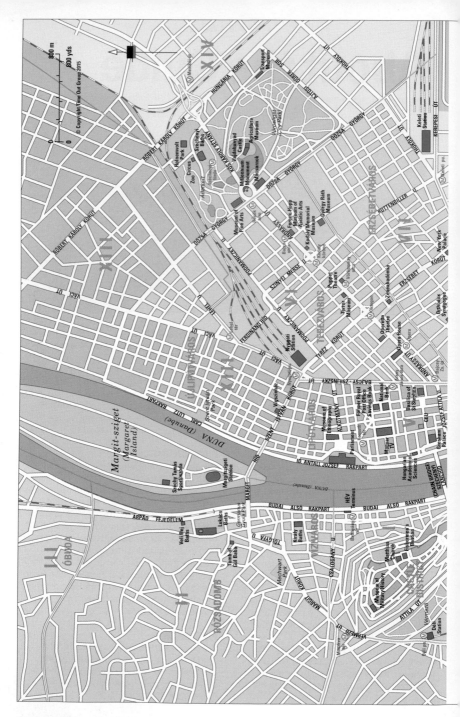

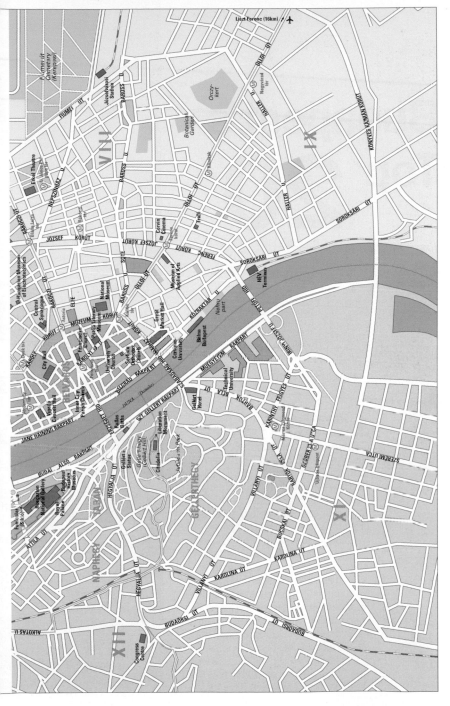

Liszt Ferenc (16km)

VIII

IX

XI

XII

Hungarian Museum of Electrotechnics
Central Synagogue
Franciscan Church
City Hall
ELTE
MÚZEUM
Petőfi Literary Museum
National Museum
Great Market Hall
Museum of Applied Arts
Serbian Orthodox Church
University Church
Inner City Parish Church
Vigadó Concert Hall
Budai Vigadó
Rác Baths
Hungarian National Gallery
Royal Palace
Budapest History Museum
Gellért Statue
Citadella
Liberation Monument
Gellért Hotel
Technical University
Corvinus University
Corvin Cinema
Erkel Theatre
Józsefvárosi Stadion
Botanical Garden
Orczy-kert
HÉV Terminus
Congress Centre

ÜLLŐI ÚT
BAROSS U.
FIUMEI ÚT
RÁKÓCZI ÚT
NÉPSZÍNHÁZ U.
JÓZSEF KÖRÚT
JÓZSEF KÖRÚT
FERENC KÖRÚT
SOROKSÁRI ÚT
SOROKSÁRI ÚT
VÁGÓHÍD U.
HALLER U.
KÖNYVES KÁLMÁN KÖRÚT
ÜLLŐI ÚT
KÁROLY KÖRÚT
KÁLVIN TÉR
KÁROLYI U.
BELGRÁD RAKPART
SZABADSÁG HÍD
BUDAI ALSÓ RAKPART
JANE HAINING RAKPART
DUNA (Danube)
SZT. GELLÉRT RAKPART
MŰEGYETEM RAKPART
Nehru part
KÖZRAKTÁR U.
BÉLA BARTÓK
BÁRTÓK BÉLA ÚT
KARINTHY FRIGYES ÚT
DOMBÓVÁRI ÚT
VÁSÁRTELEK
BOCSKAI ÚT
VILLÁNYI ÚT
KAROLINA ÚT
KAROLINA ÚT
BUDAÖRSI ÚT
HEGYALJA ÚT
ATTILA ÚT
ALKOTÁS U.
NAPHEGY
TABÁN
GELLÉRTHEGY
PETŐFI HÍD
IRINYI JÓZSEF U.
SZEREMI UTCA

Budapest's Top 20

From railways to ruin bars, we count down the capital's finest.

1 Royal Palace
(page 48)

Gazing over the city from atop Castle Hill, the Royal Palace is invariably every tourist's first port of call. Also known as Buda Castle, this historic landmark was most recently rebuilt after World War II. As part of that 30-year-long process, previously unseen medieval remains were found, some of which are now on display in the Budapest History Museum. This is one of two major attractions housed here. The other is the Hungarian National Gallery, a labyrinthine collection of paintings, sculptures and graphics covering the history of the nation up to the 20th century. The rest of the complex looks much as Habsburg Empress Maria Theresa planned it in the 1700s, after the Siege of Buda destroyed what was left of the Renaissance palace in 1686.

2 Széchenyi Baths
(page 205)

The picture-postcard shot of Budapest is the one of old locals playing chess in the waters of the Széchenyi Baths, with the ornate bathhouse as a backdrop. Recently renovated, the 'Szécsa' is atmospheric all year round. In winter, steam surrounds the warm natural waters of one of three outdoor pools, ice and snow piled up around. In summer, it's a fun-filled lido, families spending all day around the waters. Inside are saunas and pools of varying temperatures, with massage treatments also available. There's also a terrace restaurant, a whirlpool for the kids and a lane pool. Couples can take a private cabin to change in before and after.

3 Szimpla kert
(page 158)

These days, Budapest is well known for more than just spas and Habsburg architecture. Ruin bars, *romkocsma*, are another of the city's must-see attractions. Originally, these were set up in the ruined courtyards of residential houses around the inner neighbourhoods of Pest – specifically District VII. And the Szimpla kert, in Kazinczy utca, was the bar that started it all off in the early 2000s with a tumbledown courtyard filled with skip-found furniture, plus a projection screen on the side of an adjoining house, bars in every nook and cranny, and DJ decks.

4 Chain Bridge
(page 44)

Strung across the Danube like the necklace of a countess, the iconic Chain Bridge was the first permanent crossing over the river between Buda and Pest. It was conceived by Anglophile Count István Széchenyi after being unable to cross the frozen Danube to attend his father's funeral. Admiring the great bridges across the Thames, most notably at Hammersmith and Marlow, Széchenyi hired their engineer, William Tierney Clark, to design one for Budapest. Clark in turn had his namesake, Scotsman Adam Clark, to stay in Hungary to see the project through. Stay he did, marrying a Hungarian and preventing the Austrians from blowing up the bridge before it was due to open. By then, Széchenyi had been committed to an asylum – and never saw his bridge unveiled in 1849.

5 Margaret Island
(page 45)

Margaret Island is the green lung of the Hungarian capital, spread out along the Danube halfway between Buda and Pest, and closed to traffic apart from pedalos, cycles and the 26 bus. The city's best-loved lido, the Palatinus, and the Alfréd Hajós swimming pool are among the attractions at the island's southern tip – further along, you'll find a petting zoo, a Japanese garden, an open-air concert stage, tennis courts and a number of open-air bars and restaurants in summer.

6 Sziget
(page 31)

If there's one thing that has put Budapest on the map, it's the week-long Sziget music festival. Begun in 1993, Sziget aimed to revive two concepts: Socialist-era holiday camps and the alternative music scene that developed out of the Communist stranglehold on youth culture. Both had disappeared with the change of system in 1989. In choosing

to name a festival after its island (*'sziget'*) location, by a forgotten stretch of boat workshops north of town, the organisers found a winning concept. Keeping prices affordable (you could see Bowie for a fiver in 1997), the Sziget team also brought in games, sport, film and theatre. Throw in transport by boat, bars at every turn, and recent big-name acts such as Prince, the Killers and Dizzee Rascal, and you have a perfect week of wanton fun.

7 Funicular
(page 50)

It only lasts two minutes, but the funicular is the perfect opportunity to gain an overview of all of Pest's sights in one go. From Clark Ádám tér on the Buda side of Chain Bridge, the two-carriage *sikló* climbs the hillside, passing beneath a series of footbridges along the way. Below, the glory of Pest spreads out beyond the Danube. From the top, it's a short stroll to the Royal Palace and the historic sights of Castle Hill.

8 Franz Liszt Music Academy
(page 167)

Looking stately after a €45-million overhaul, the Franz Liszt Music Academy is the stand-out venue for classical concerts. The establishment was founded by Liszt himself at his then residence in 1875. It later moved to nearby Andrássy út, then, in 1907, to this art nouveau masterpiece. All the greats of Hungarian music have worked here – Bartók, Kodály and Dohnányi. Famous alumni include Sir Georg Solti, whose statue now stands outside – near one of Liszt himself, who worked here until his death in 1886.

9 Parliament
(page 93)

Inaugurated, incomplete, for the Hungarian Millennial celebrations of 1896, Parliament was created when Budapest was twin capital of Austro-Hungary. It was the largest parliament building in the world, and heavy with symbolism. Imre Steindl designed the building to be exactly 96 metres (315 feet) tall – to mark the events of 1896. Its neo-Gothic exterior dominates a graceful bend in the Danube. Steindl went blind and died in 1902, shortly before the building was fully completed. Within two decades, Hungary had lost its empire.

10 Tram 2
(page 224)

Running from Rákóczi Bridge in the south to Margaret Bridge in the north, tram 2 trundles along the Pest embankment, passing Budapest's major bridges along the way. For the price of a transport ticket (less than €1), passengers are treated to a jaw-dropping view of both halves of the Hungarian capital – the grand sights of Buda on one side, the five-star hotel façades and fin-de-siècle landmarks of Pest on the other.

11 Basilica of St Stephen
(page 88)

Dominating the skyline of Lipótváros, the Basilica of St Stephen is named after the first king of Hungary. Designed in

1845 but not completed until 60 years later, the Basilica was redesigned halfway through its construction so that it was exactly 96 metres (315 feet) tall – to mark the Hungarian millennial celebrations of 1896. St Stephen is honoured here each 20 August when his mummified right hand, usually on display in its own side chapel, is paraded outside. Huge bells fill the two towers, accessed by lift or stairs for panoramic views of Budapest and the river.

12 House of Terror (page 109)

Budapest's most controversial major attraction is effective because it's set in the very location where the terrible events it describes took place. This one-time family villa on a corner of Andrássy út was first used by the right-wing Arrow Cross to interrogate and torture political opponents. Then, after World War II, the Communist secret police, the ÁVO, moved in. Reconfigured as an award-winning museum in 2002, the House of Terror displays video interviews, original artefacts and actual torture cells to tell the building's dark history.

13 Great Synagogue (page 116)

Located at the gateway to the Jewish Quarter, the Great Synagogue is one of the world's largest. It was created in Moorish style, with two exotic towers rising up over a complex also containing a Jewish museum, a memorial park and, unusually for a synagogue, a cemetery. Inside, the Great Synagogue can accommodate 3,000 worshippers in separate men's and women's galleries. The memorial park – named after the Budapest-based Swedish diplomat Raoul Wallenberg, who saved many Jews in World War II – is crowned by Imre Varga's poignant representation of a weeping willow, the names of wartime victims inscribed on each of its leaves.

14 A38 (page 158)

Moored near Petőfi Bridge, atmospheric A38 is Budapest's leading spot for live music. It's an old Ukrainian cargo ship, transformed into a party venue with a permanent Danube view. It's not just for gigs, either – DJ nights, exhibitions, literary evenings, book launches and film festivals have all been held here. Recent sets have included Dutch nu-jazz, Berlin techno and Balkan party sounds.

15 Danube cruises (page 25)

There are various ways to cruise the Danube. The easiest is to take one of many of the sightseeing boats that leave from Vigadó tér, a short walk from Vörösmarty tér. These take an hour to glide up to Margaret Bridge, down again to Petőfi Bridge and back up to Vigadó tér. Most also run in the evenings, when the bridges are illuminated – which is when the pricier dinner-dance boats set off, perhaps with a gypsy band or jazz trio on board. Perhaps the best idea of all is to sail to Szentendre or further up the Danube Bend to Visegrád or Esztergom, doable in a day, ideally coming back just as the bridges are lighting up.

18 Children's Railway
(page 143)

A rare popular hangover of Communism, the narrow-gauge Children's Railway was one of many built around the former Eastern bloc to teach youngsters how to run a railroad. Budapest's, which runs through the lush hills and valleys of Buda, is the longest. Originally named the Pioneer Railway after the scouts who manned it, the Gyermekvasút still runs for 11 kilometres (seven miles) from Széchenyi-hegy to Hüvösvölgy. As under Kádár, it's grown-ups who are actually behind the controls.

19 New York Café – Boscolo Budapest
(page 125)

The grandest of Budapest's grand fin-de-siècle coffeehouses, the New York was the talk of the town when it opened in 1894. Alajos Hauszmann's sumptuous creation was awash with marble, bronze and silk, topped by Venetian chandeliers. A sorry tourist trap after World War II, the New York building was converted into a five-star hotel in 2006. Designer Adam A Tihany seems to have relished the chance to recreate Hauszmann's masterpiece.

16 Ecseri piac
(page 137)

Open every day, but busiest and best at weekends, Ecseri is Budapest's finest flea market. Spread across a large site in south Pest, Ecseri is loosely divided into areas for furniture, household items, paintings, ornaments and, arguably best of all, random junk from Communist Europe. Czechoslovak toy cars, Soviet army hats, East German cameras – they'll all be here.

17 Citadella
(page 57)

Set atop Gellért Hill, Citadella is the prosaic (and currently closed) fortress built by the Austrians after the War of Independence in 1848-49. Here, up at 235 metres (770 feet), the whole city is spread out before you. The main viewing points are the Liberty Statue and the fenced-off vantage point close by, a favourite photo op with newlyweds.

20 National Museum
(page 128)

A historic landmark in more ways than one, the National Museum lends its name to this section of the Kiskörút close to the city centre. When Sándor Petőfi needed a stage to read out his poem 'Nemzeti dal' to urge compatriots to stand up against Vienna in 1848, he chose these steps. The museum had only just moved to Mihály Pollack's grand neoclassical edifice, where today the history of Hungary is told in two entertaining sections, divided by the end of the Ottomans in 1686.

Budapest Today

The beating heart of Hungary.

TEXT: MATTHEW HIGGINSON

A modern, sophisticated capital of 1.8 million people – a fifth of Hungary's population – Budapest is the centre of government, business, mass media, culture and entertainment, generating 38 per cent of the national economic output. But this oversized city is really an anachronism. Its heft and grand architecture are a relic of its role as dual capital in the Austro-Hungarian monarchy, where Budapest served a country that was more than double the size it is today. To paraphrase Gloria Swanson in *Sunset Boulevard*, Budapest is still big – it's the country that got small.

Indeed, this beautiful, fascinating old city frequently serves as a cut-price cinema stand-in for larger, more influential European cities such as Moscow, Berlin or Rome. In reality, enduring while pretending to be something, somewhere else may be Budapest's greatest skill, and certainly this gloriously decadent, cosmopolitan city appears at odds with the parochial conservatism espoused by its current mayor and national government.

VICTORY FOR FIDESZ

Budapest is European at heart, its kinship with Paris and Vienna expressed most vividly through their shared belle époque architecture. But the country's current ruling Fidesz-KDNP coalition is deeply mistrusting of its continental counterparts. After a landslide victory in the general election of 2014, the Fidesz campaign in the subsequent European elections was distilled into a single phrase: 'Send a message to Brussels!' Never fully elucidated, this was to be taken as a war cry – Hungary was its own man, and Prime Minister Viktor Orbán's government would not be told what to do by the leftist gravy-train policy wonks of Strasbourg. With no credible opposition apart from radical right-wing party Jobbik, Fidesz walked the Euro elections, leaving those Budapesters who embraced EU accession as a confident stride away from the exile of the socialist era confused and worried.

THANK YOU, BRUSSELS

The fall-out from the 2008 global financial crisis was felt keenly in Budapest construction projects. Overnight, speculative property gambles predicated on forecasts of rising disposable incomes collapsed in a pit of bad money and broken dreams. A walk around downtown will reveal empty plots of land once slated for new offices and housing, but now home to rottweilers on chains and security guards in caravans. The tap of government spending was also turned off as the nation and the city sought to balance budgets.

Budapest's mayor, István Tarlós, a Fidesz-approved independent, is a fiscal and social conservative. He has overseen belt-tightening in almost every sector, making European money in the form of transfers from the EU Cohesion Fund the only game in town. Without largesse from Brussels, there would have been no metro line 4 (see p19 **Budapest's Fabulous Folly**), no renovation and beautification of the 47/49 tram line on Károly körút in District V, no refit of Parliament's Kossuth tér and environs, no refurb of Széll Kálmán tér, and no large-scale pedestrianisation of the city centre.

In early 2015, Tarlós announced that Budapest would receive up to a further €1.3 billion in EU funding over the next seven years, which would help pay for the desperately needed renovation of metro line 3, complete the extension of tram line 1, and enable the completion of a tram service linking Újpalota in north-east Budapest with Baross tér in District VIII. The message Budapest should be sending to Brussels is one of heartfelt gratitude.

WHITE ELEPHANTS

EU money hasn't always been used wisely, though. The refurbishing of neo-Renaissance Várkert Bazár at the foot of Castle Hill is a notable cock-up. Designed by Miklós Ybl – Hungary's Christopher Wren, the building complex was built between 1875 and 1883. Badly damaged in World War II, it fell into disrepair in the early 1990s and was left to rot. To date, its on/off renovation has cost around €30 million, the lion's share being EU money. The beauty of the original design is not in doubt – nor is the craftsmanship on display in the refit – but the city still appears unsure why it did the work, and what it should do with the resulting white elephant, which sits largely empty and redundant.

There has also been controversy over the funding for the new home of the Office of the Prime Minister – adjacent to Sándor-palota, the official residence of the president of Hungary, atop Castle Hill. Coveting the view, the PM tried unsuccessfully to move his office to Sándor-palota during his first administration (1998-2002). In 2014, his huge electoral majority made things a little easier, and the old Carmelite Courtyard/National Dance Theatre complex was duly appropriated. Beethoven might have played at the theatre in 1800, but Fidesz has little time for high culture, and the resident dance company was forced to find a new home. There has been no consultation with local residents and plans have been designated a national security secret, meaning that the taxpayers footing the bill have no idea what they're buying. Quizzed on the eventual cost, László L Simon, parliamentary secretary of state for the PM's Office, said: 'It will cost a lot of money, but it will also serve the joy of every one of us.'

MONUMENTAL INSENSITIVITY

In summer 2014, the government unveiled a memorial in central Szabadság tér (Freedom Square) to the suffering caused by the 1944 Nazi occupation of Hungary. National and international outrage had delayed its construction, and the statue – which depicts

BUDAPEST'S FABULOUS FOLLY
Controversial metro line 4 opens.

An unwanted hangover from the previous regime, burdened by controversy and an over-running budget, Budapest's metro line 4 was eventually unveiled by Prime Minister Viktor Órbán in March 2014. This link between south Buda and east Pest, which mainly follows the line of already popular bus and tram routes, had been rubber-stamped well over a decade previously. Delayed 17 times thereafter and built at an estimated cost of €1.5 billion, the 7.4-kilometre (4.6-mile) M4 line consists of ten swish new stations, bookended by the rail hubs of Kelenföld in south Buda and Keleti in Pest.

To say it had been derided during its construction would be an understatement. Footage on YouTube from a secret camera fixed to a gap in the fence around one of the construction sites showed workmen idly kicking a football about during long summer lunch breaks. The year that the maligned line was eventually ready, its construction company, French-based Alstom, was charged by the UK's Serious Fraud Office with alleged corrupt practices when gaining transportation contracts in three countries. In December 2014, the firm agreed to pay a $772 million fine set by the US Justice Department for violations of foreign bribery laws – the largest fine ever charged in such circumstances.

But by then, Budapest's line 4 was already open, with the public given free access for the few first days. Two generations removed from the drab, Soviet-built metro in place since the 1970s, M4 serves smart, strikingly bold stations. US-based online architectural magazine *Architizer* immediately showered Budapest's Spora Architects with awards for its adjacent stations of Szent Gellért tér and Fővám tér, just across the river.

In fact, the contrast between rusty line M3, out of action at weekends throughout the winter of 2014-15, and green-coded M4 could not be more striking. Just change lines at Kálvin tér to see for yourself. A flashing striplight along facing platforms indicates when a train is arriving from either direction – though the departure boards are clear enough on timing. Well lit, with swift escalators and long carriages free of interlinking doors, both the stations and trains are passenger friendly and easy on the eye.

What happens next is unclear. The original plan under the previous administration of mayor Gábor Demszky was for the line to continue to Rákospalota, District XV, through under-served District XIV. Without this extension – now extremely doubtful since EU funding has been refused – line 4 is an expensive folly: an award-winning, state-of-the-art way to get from Kelenföld to Keleti in 13 minutes, rather than the 25 minutes it would have taken on the 7 bus the year before the line opened.

Memorial to the suffering caused by the 1944 Nazi occupation of Hungary, Szabadság tér. See p16.

A NÉMET MEGSZÁLLÁS ÁLDOZATAINAK EMLÉKMŰVE

the archangel Gabriel, a symbol of Hungary, being slain by the eagle of Germany – had to be finished under cover of night and behind a cordon of heavily armed riot police.

For months, protesters had thwarted its completion, during which the ill-conceived piece of public art had become an impromptu site of resistance and a shrine to memory – relatives of those lost to the Holocaust had attached photographs to the security railings, and, at the time of writing, stones and other mementoes (a pair of glasses, an old suitcase) remain. Critics say the government is attempting to homogenise the suffering of Hungarian citizens in World War II with the Holocaust, while simultaneously airbrushing out the nation's direct role in sending 437,000 Hungarian Jews to the Nazi death camps. In protest, Randolph L Braham, Professor Emeritus at the City University of New York – the world's foremost authority on the Hungarian Holocaust and himself a survivor – returned his Honorary Order of Merit of the Republic of Hungary and forbade any use of his name in connection with the Holocaust Information Centre in Budapest.

The 1944 Memorial furore must be seen in the context of a recent outbreak of revisionism. In 2012, a bust of Hungary's fascist wartime leader Admiral Miklós Horthy – a figure for whom Orbán has expressed admiration – was inaugurated in Csókakő, a small village an hour from Budapest. Next, the town square in Gyömrő was renamed in Horthy's honour (a decision reversed in 2014) and the Reformed College of Debrecen

affixed a blue plaque honouring its former pupil. At the same time, several Horthy-era writers made it back on to the national school curriculum, including József Nyírő, an unapologetic Nazi supporter.

In the interwar years, Horthy's Hungary was known as 'the land of three million beggars'. In a nation of nine million, that equated to one in three supposedly living in poverty. According to the European Commission's Eurostat figures, the percentage of the population deemed 'severely materially deprived' in 2008 was 18 per cent in both Poland and Hungary. By 2013, the rate in Hungary had risen to 27 per cent, while Poland's had fallen to 12 per cent. Today, despite overall positive GDP growth, more and more Hungarians are slipping through the net and into the abyss, as social spending is cut and welfare is tied to controversial *közmunka* 'workfare' schemes. The programme has slashed unemployment, but pays less than the minimum wage – critics say it's a return to the economics of the workhouse. Watching hordes of unfortunate litter-collectors shuffle around Budapest in orange hi-viz jackets, it's hard to see how the scheme is equipping anyone with transferable skills or nurturing an appetite for a return to the workforce, which are the ruling party's two main claims for the programme.

TOURIST TOWN

While the *közmunkások* clean the streets, traffic is being driven out of downtown by pedestrian zoning, and dedicated bike lanes abound. According to Budapest's pro-bike

Critical Mass movement, cyclist numbers in the capital are up tenfold since 2004. Such is the success of Critical Mass that the organisation hung up its bike clips in 2013, stating it had met its goals.

In the inner city, Budapest feels like a proper European capital. Wealthy travellers are back and well catered for at the superbly renovated five-star landmarks of the Habsburg era – the Corinthia Grand Hotel Royal, the Four Seasons Gresham Palace and the Boscolo (formerly the New York Palace). Spa hotels abound, as do high-end restaurants and grand coffeehouses. For the younger crowd, newly fashionable District VII survived an attack on opening hours from the local council, and is now a party warren of hipster bars, artisanal *gelateria* and pop-up bistros complete with waiters sporting beards and full-sleeve tattoos, straight out of the Lower East Side.

The city council, through its Valuable Heritage Protection Assistance programme, has been giving grants to finance renovations of buildings around town since 1993. The result is that previously blighted areas such as District IX north of the Nagykörút are now home to social housing, landscaped parks and new amenities. But this transformation hasn't touched everywhere equally. A trip from verdant, affluent Rózsadomb in Buda down to District VIII in Pest, a distance of no more than a few miles, provides a vivid illustration of the increasing gap between rich and poor.

LOOKING TO THE FUTURE

The unification of the cities of Buda, Pest and Óbuda took place in 1873. In the 140-odd years since its creation, the city was at the core of the collapse of the Habsburg and Soviet empires, and had unenviable front-row seats for the rise and fall of the Third Reich. This is a place where history is so close you can put your finger in the bullet holes. But it's a city that endures and reinvents itself.

A significant makeover of the Városliget (City Park) and the Fine Arts Museum at Hősök tere (Heroes' Square) is planned, and more funds (mainly from the EU) will be pumped into the more depressed and decrepit areas of Districts VIII and IX. Having bid unsuccessfully for the Olympic Games of 1920, 1936 and 1960, Budapest is trying again for 2024. Co-hosting of football's Euro 2020 is already assured and a new national stadium is being constructed (see *p129* **2020 Vision**).

There is a deeply antagonistic relationship between Budapest and its current bullying, corrupt political and fiscal overlords, but the capital has outlived all those that have tried to constrain her, and will likely do so again.

Mazel Tov, District VII.

Itineraries

*Plot your perfect trip
to the capital with our
step-by-step planner.*

9AM

1PM

Day 1

9AM There's no better way to start the day than on the leafy terrace of the **Gerlóczy Kávéház** (*p82*), blissfully pastoral while still being at the heart of the downtown action. You can pore over your sightseeing schedule while tucking into a hearty Hungarian omelette – you'll need the energy. From here, stroll over to the main shopping street of Váci utca, across the main square of Vörösmarty tér and towards **Chain Bridge** (*p44*).

10AM After taking a gander at the landmark art nouveau **Gresham Palace** (*p217*), now a luxury Four Seasons hotel, stroll across the Danube by its most venerable and beautiful crossing, taking in the bridges on either side. With Elizabeth Bridge and Szabadság Bridge to the left, and Margaret Bridge to the right, walk straight ahead towards Castle Hill rising up before you. You'll arrive at Clark Ádám tér, named after the heroic Scottish engineer who saved the Chain Bridge from demolition by Habsburg

2.30PM

3PM

forces. From the square, the **Funicular** (p50) chugs up to the **Royal Palace** (p48), which houses the **Budapest History Museum** (p48) and the **National Gallery** (p50), with its extensive history of Hungarian art.

1PM Close to the Royal Palace, **Matthias Church** (p52) and nearby **Fisherman's Bastion** (p51) – both the work of fin-de-siècle architect Frigyes Schulek – are must-see sights. One has its roots in the glory of Renaissance Buda, the other is a faux-historic confection but has outstanding views of the Danube and Pest beyond. Immediately below, steps run back down to river level – and the **Lánchíd Söröző** (p64), a homely introduction to Hungarian cuisine for lunch.

2.30PM After a morning of walking, it may be time to hop on the 19 tram, which runs along the Buda embankment. To the right, you'll see the revamped and recently reopened **Várkert Bazár** (p60), created by Miklós Ybl

of Opera House fame – it's lovely to look at, but has yet to develop its potential as a cultural venue. The tram then passes the equally revamped **Rudas Baths** (p204), with a panoramic rooftop pool, before reaching the most famous hotel (and baths) in town, the **Gellért** (p204). A mid-afternoon coffee and cake behind its stunning art nouveau façade, and you're ready for the last stretch of sightseeing for the day.

3PM Frequent trams 47 and 49 clatter over Szabadság Bridge from Gellért tér. On the Pest side, the **Great Market Hall** (p137) is both a tourist attraction and a one-stop shop for Hungarian souvenirs. Don't overload yourself too much, though, because the last port of call for the day, one tram stop or ten minutes' walk away, is the **National Museum** (p128). Steeped in a history of its own – it was here that poet Sándor Petőfi read his 'National Song' to kick-start the revolution of 1848 – the museum should provide a good hour's entertainment.

Clockwise from left: **Várkert Bazár**; **Gerlóczy Kávéház**; **Fisherman's Bastion**; **Great Market Hall**.

9AM

Day 2

9AM Grand and historic, the café at the **Danubius Hotel Astoria** (*p215*) allows you to breakfast in splendour while contemplating what the day holds. With Budapest's most scenic baths at the end of it, you should pack your costume in your daysack. Next, step out and cross the busy junction named after the hotel. Five minutes' walk away stands the **Great Synagogue** (*p116*). Its twin onion domes rising overhead, this Moorish revivalist landmark needs a good hour or so to admire, taking in the architecture, history, Heroes' Temple, cemetery and memorial park.

11AM As well as being a designer store, workshop and gallery, nearby **Printa** (*p121*) is also a café, allowing you to enjoy a strong mid-morning brew and browse the funky merchandise. Note the T-shirts bearing customised

maps of buzzing District VII. Walking past the **Rumbach Sebestyén utca Synagogue** (*p116*) diagonally opposite – its impressive façade fronting an inactive place of worship – you'll reach Király utca and nearby **Gozsdu udvar** (*p118*). If it's Sunday, you might find this six-section passageway lined with the artisanal GOUBA market. The rest of the week, the shoulder-to-shoulder bars, restaurants and shops will be busy.

NOON Wandering around District VII, up Dob utca and crossing Klauzál tér, you quickly appreciate the thriving Jewish culture around you – and perhaps what life would have been like here before World War II. On the other side of Klauzál tér is Akacfa utca. There, **Mazel Tov** (*p122*) provides excellent Med street food from midday at weekends – note the ruin-bar surroundings, echoing the after-dark atmosphere of

11AM

similar nightspots on Kazinczy, Wesselényi and Király. On weekdays, there are plenty of other lunchtime options – **Spinoza** and **Macesz Huszár** (for both, see *p119*) on Dob utca are known for the quality of their Jewish cuisine.

2PM After lunch, head to the Nagykörút, the ring road linking the main districts of Pest. Veering left, you'll pass the five-star **Corinthia Grand Hotel Royal** (*p221*), the site of Budapest's first cinema. Further on is Oktogon, where

3.30PM

Clockwise from left: **Great Synagogue**; **Heroes' Square**; **Printa.**

the Nagykörút crosses the showcase boulevard of Andrássy út. Stroll Andrássy back towards the centre, and you'll pass the theatre quarter of Nagymező utca, then the **Opera House** (*p100*); take the avenue north and, at the second block up, you'll see –announced in reverse stencilled letters – the **House of Terror** (p109). One of Budapest's most gripping attractions, the Terror Háza is located at the address where the events it describes took place. Here, the Communist secret police (the ÁVO) tortured its victims. Original artefacts and recorded interviews relate these grim events in fascinating but terrifying detail.

3.30PM Afterwards, you'll need a change of scene. Back outside, either enjoy a 15-minute stroll up grand, tree-lined Andrássy út, towards the diplomatic quarter and **Heroes' Square**

(Hősök tere; *p111*) – or take the M1 metro; the line was the first underground railway in continental Europe. Created for the Hungarian millennial celebrations in 1896, Heroes' Square is dominated by a colonnade that depicts key figures from the Magyar conquest of 896 onwards. On one side, the **Museum of Fine Arts** (*p111*) is Budapest's main home for European art, with a particular focus on Spanish masters. On the other side, the **Palace of Arts** (*p113*) houses temporary exhibitions, and should attract more visitors as the Museum of Fine Arts is being overhauled until 2018.

4.30PM Behind Heroes' Square is **Városliget**, the City Park (*p111*), where many of the 1896 celebrations took place. Past the ice rink, you'll see Vajdahunyad Castle, a Disney-style recreation also built for 1896. Veer left, and the ornate building ahead of you is the **Széchenyi Baths** (*p205*). These are Budapest's most tourist-friendly, with three large outdoor pools and an indoor complex of saunas, steam rooms and thermal baths. In summer,

the Széchenyi doubles up as a lido; in winter, bathers lounge in the warm water as the snow falls around them. Either way, it means hours of relaxation. Late afternoon is a good time to arrive as the baths stay open until 10pm, with the moonlight creating a magical atmosphere.

Guided tours

As well as **Tourinform** (V.Sütő utca 2, 438 8080, www. tourinform.hu), **Discover Budapest** (VI.Lázár utca 16, 269 3843, www.discover budapest.com) is an excellent one-stop shop for information about tours around the city, particularly offbeat ones. Segway tours (Ft15,000) can be booked from here.

BOAT TOURS
Legenda
Pier 7, V.Vigadó tér (317 2203, www.legenda.hu). Tram 2. **Departures** *Summer* throughout the day. *Winter* 2pm daily. **Admission** Ft3,900-Ft5,500; Ft3,500-Ft4,400 reductions. **Map** p249 D5.
All kinds of jaunts up the Danube, from the standard Duna Bella sightseeing hop up to Margaret Island and

Top: **City cycle tours**. Bottom: **City Tour Hop-on Hop-off bus**.

back (1hr) to candlelit dinners and party boats.

Mahart Passnave
Passnave Pier 6, V. Vigadó tér (484 4013, 318 1223, www. mahartpassnave.hu). Tram 2. **Departures** *May, June, Sept-late Oct* 10am-9pm daily. *July, Aug* 10am-10pm daily. *Late Oct-early Jan* hourly 11am-6pm daily. *Mid Mar-Apr* hourly 11am-7pm daily. **Tickets** Ft2,990; Ft2,490 reductions. **Map** p249 D5.
Along with standard treks up the Danube, Mahart lays on various sightseeing tours around Budapest, including bearably cheesy dinner-and-dance trips (Ft8,990; Ft4,490 reductions) – the bridges at night are magical.

River Ride
V. Széchenyi tér 7-8 (332 2555, www.riverride.com). Tram 2, or bus 16, 105. **Departures** *Apr-Oct* 10am, noon, 3pm, 5pm daily. *Nov-Mar* 11am, 1pm, 3pm daily. **Tickets** Ft8,500; Ft6,000 reductions; free under-6s. **Map** p246 D4.

A big, yellow amphibious bus shows passengers the streets of Budapest before dramatically splashing into the Danube for a floating tour.

BUS TOURS
City Tour Hop-on Hop-off
Main office: VI. Andrássy út 2 (374 7050, www.citytour.hu). **Departures** 3-7 times daily. **Tickets** Ft3,000; Ft2,500 reductions; free under-6s. **Map** p249 D5.
These red buses (some are open-top) make three stops around the capital. Tickets are valid for 24 hours and include a boat ride. English commentary available.

EUrama
Hotel InterContinental, V. Apáczai Csere János utca 12-14 (327 6690, www.eurama.hu). Tram 2. **Departures** *Summer* 10am, 11am, 2.30pm daily. *Winter* 10am, 2.30pm daily. **Tickets** Ft5,000; Ft2,500 reductions; free under-6s. **Map** p249 D5.
The standard city tour is two hours long , but there are other themed versions.

CYCLE TOURS
Budapestbike
VII. Wesselényi utca 13 (06 30 944 5533, www.budapest bike.hu). M1, M2, M3 Deák tér, or tram 47, 49. **Map** p249 F5.
This friendly young firm hires out bikes and also runs cycle tours. As well as a tour of city sights (Ft7,000), there's one of rock venues (Ft11,000), Szentendre (Ft9,000) and various others.

WALKING TOURS
Beyond Budapest
06 20 332 5489, www. beyondbudapest.hu. M3, M4 Kálvin tér. **Departures** vary. **Admission** (1-6 people) from €75/tour.
Alternative walking tours of Budapest's gritty, fascinating District VIII. Themed tours include the palace quarter, hidden Jewish sites and edgier art galleries. Most tours are conducted in English; departure points include the National Museum, VIII. Gutenberg tér and VIII. Kálmán Mikszáth tér.

Multigo Tours
II. Frankel Leó út 51-53 (323 0791, 06 70 282 0710, www.multigotours.com). Bus 86. **Departures** vary. **Tickets** vary.
Tours include Buda caves, Jewish heritage sites and art nouveau Budapest, among others. Multigo also puts together regional tours of five or ten days.

UniqueBudapest
06 30 210 9486, www.unique budapest.com. **Departures** vary. **Tickets** vary.
Walking tours focusing on art nouveau villas and palaces, the mysteries of Buda Castle, and so on.

BUDAPEST BY NIGHT
The city comes to life after dark.

NIGHT AT THE MUSEUM

Budapest comes to life after dark. With a full public-transport infrastructure – including the 6 tram running through the night down the Nagykörut – and affordable taxis, visitors can explore the city at its most buzzy. If you have to choose any time to do it, then it would be the **Night of Museums** (*p31*), on or close to midsummer. Most of Budapest's historic attractions put on special displays, programmes or demonstrations, accessed with one all-round ticket, and accessible by buses that shuttle between venues. Closing time is generally 2.30am.

BATH TIME

Every weekend, the newly renovated **Rudas Baths** (*p204*) open to men and women until 4am, though the rooftop panoramic pool remains off-limits until the following morning. Just up the Danube past Margaret Bridge, the **Lukács Baths** (*p204*) are currently hosting spa DJ party Magic Bath until 3am on Saturday nights. Meanwhile, over in Pest, in the City Park, the **Széchenyi Baths** (*p205*) operate until 10pm – or open up again at 6am, shortly after many of the bars in District VII have seen the last reveller off the premises.

DRINK IN THE VIEWS

Certain venues lend themselves to certain times of the night. Though you'll pay a modest admission fee later on, you may want to catch sunset on the roof terrace of the **Corvintető** (*p153*), cocktail in hand. Alternatively, on Andrássy út, the **360 Bar** (*p104*) atop the ornate Párisi Nagyáruház also offers rooftop views and DJ tunes from May to September. For Danube vistas, the **A38** boat (*p158*) is not only a gig venue but a restaurant too – you can enjoy a meal and sundowner without having to pay admission for the night. If you fancy staying on the Buda side, though, chances are you'll catch something worth listening to here.

PEST PARTY

Pest is party central. Between Király utca and Dob utca, **Gozsdu udvar** (*p118*) is now livelier than ever and lined with at least a dozen bars and clubs. Exit either way and you'll find plenty of other options along Kazinczy utca, parallel to Gozsdu udvar, many also serving food until late. Halfway between Király and Dob utca, a small pedestrianised strip includes **400**, **Pirítós** and **Félix Hélix** (for all, *see p120*). The night might then take you over to Akácfa utca, Wesselényi utca or Kertész utca – not knowing your next move is part of the fun.

Diary

Seasonal celebrations –
plus the biggest music
festival in the region.

Hungarians are big on festivals and tradition. The largest event of the year is the Sziget festival, a week of rock, world and electronic music, film, theatre and scores of side events that takes place on an otherwise empty island in the Danube. Back in town, there are major cultural festivals in spring and autumn: the autumn event has recently been rebranded Café Budapest Contemporary Arts, while the Budapest Spring Festival remains the annual highbrow highlight. The biggest sporting event in the calendar is the Grand Prix, held each year in August. Certain holidays are linked to landmark events in Hungarian history, such as 23 October (Remembrance Day) and 15 March (Revolution Day). Christmas is a stay-at-home family affair – only bars and restaurants in major hotels stay open, while the rest of the city shuts down completely for two days solid by noon on Christmas Eve. New Year's Eve is a street party, with big crowds gathering in the main squares.

Budapest Spring Festival.

Spring

Revolution Day

Date 15 Mar.

Revolution Day commemorates poet Sándor Petőfi reciting his 'Nemzeti Dal' ('National Song') on the steps of Budapest's National Museum in 1848, an event that is commonly considered to have launched the national revolution. Gatherings at Petőfi's statue were against the law until 1990; nowadays, an official ceremony is held near the statue and the city gets decked out in red, white and green. Speeches are given, music is performed and many locals wear cockades in national colours on their lapels.

Budapest Spring Festival

555 3000, 486 3311, www.btf.hu.

Date 2wks Apr.

The Budapest Spring Festival (Budapesti Tavaszi Fesztivál) is the most prestigious event in the Hungarian arts calendar. A smattering of internationally renowned talent from the world of classical music – plus local orchestras and classical music stars – provide a fortnight of concerts. It's also a showcase for art and drama. Some 36 venues across the city act as hosts.

Easter Monday

The most drunken occasion in a calendar soaked with them, Easter Monday is when menfolk go

PUBLIC HOLIDAYS

New Year's Day
1 Jan

Revolution Day
15 March

Easter Sunday

Easter Monday

May Day
1 May

Whit Monday

St Stephen's Day
20 Aug

Remembrance Day
23 Oct

Christmas
25, 26 December

ISLAND LIFE

Sziget is Hungary's biggest festival – and its greatest export.

With an annual attendance of more than 400,000, **Sziget** (*see p31*) is the biggest music festival in the region and provides the kind of promotion opportunities that money can't buy, with tens of thousands of foreigners attending the five-day bash. As a result, savvy Sziget organisers have linked up with city authorities to provide free entry to certain museums and baths around town. Now, not only is an island north of Budapest packed for a week in August, but some city-centre attractions are too.

Ironically, it was current cheerless Budapest mayor, right-wing István Tarlós, who originally tried to have the festival closed down when he was mayor of surrounding District III.

Started in 1993, Sziget aimed to revive two concepts: Socialist-era holiday camps and the alternative music scene that developed out of the Communist stranglehold on youth culture. Both had disappeared with the change of system in 1989. Keeping prices affordable – in 1997, you could see Bowie for a fiver – the Sziget team also brought in other entertainment to complement the music. As the big names kept coming – Prince stepped in a few days after the untimely death of Amy Winehouse in 2011 – so word spread around Europe.

Sziget's USP is its location. Instead of some field in the city suburbs, Sziget occupies an island, Óbuda-sziget, accessed by a bar-equipped boat that ferries festival-goers up the Danube from the Pest side of Margaret Bridge. It feels like a cross between a holiday camp and Glastonbury, with attractions such as street theatre, family-friendly games, sport, cinema, dance areas and stalls. Plus, of course, several music stages. All told, there are some 50 sideshows to choose from, including fortune tellers, random entertainers, counsellors, therapists, teachers and spiritual advisers of every stripe. There's even a wedding tent on site – one year someone married his beer.

For those coming by boat, admission is included in the price of the ticket bought on the day. For those arriving by HÉV train to Filatorigát, there's a definite sense of crossing the Rubicon as you buy your day ticket from the booth and traverse the metal footbridge to an oasis of wanton fun. Everyone is totally up for it. Drinking is dangerously cheap (one local beer company wins the rights to provide inexpensive ale), everyone's body clock is set to 24/7 and monogamy goes out of the window. For those with a weekly ticket, this is normality for five days and five longer nights. When you've had enough, HÉV trains run around the clock, as well as three night buses, and the stand for taxis is well regulated – you shouldn't have to wait more than ten minutes in the queue to fall into one.

door-to-door indulging in the pagan rite of *locsolkodás* – spraying women with cheap perfume and getting a large *pálinka* (fruit brandy) in return.

Titanic International Film Festival
Uránia Nemzeti Filmszínház, VIII.Rákóczi út 21 (www.titanicfilmfest.hu). **Date** mid Apr.
Arthouse and cult movies from around the world, screened across nine days at three cinemas in town. *See also p147.*

Budapest Dance Festival
Nemzeti Táncszínház Értekesítési csoportja (201 4407, www.budapesttancfesztival.hu). **Date** 1wk late Apr/early May.
Timed to coincide with International Dance Day (29 April), the BDF holds its performances at the Palace of Arts (MÜPA; *see p168*). The event sees organisers invite a couple of dance troupes from abroad – New Spanish Ballet from Rojas y Rodriguez was the stand-out in 2015 – as well as providing a showcase for up-and-coming dancers from Hungary, such as Szeged Contemporary Dance.

May Day
Date 1 May.
No longer a forced wave at medal-festooned leaders along Dózsa György út, May Day still brings people out for entertainment in the city's parks. Open-air May Day (Majális) events from pre-Communist days are organised in village squares around Hungary, while more recent additions include a rock festival on the open-air Tabán stage in Buda. There's also a big party, with a sausage barbecue, in the City Park. EU accession is marked with flag-waving and fireworks the night before.

Summer

Danube Carnival
240 5553, 06 20 314 2062, www.dunakarneval.hu. **Date** 3wks June.
Celebrating its 20th anniversary in 2015, the three-week Danube Carnival involves performances by some 2,000 artists from 20 countries. Concerts, dance and sundry international entertainment take place in 17 venues across Budapest, including the Erkel Theatre (*see p165*), Várkert Bazár (*see p60*) and Vörösmarty tér, destination for the carnival parade that rolls across the Chain Bridge one Sunday in mid June.

Night of Museums
06 20 282 8338, www.muzej.hu. **Date** June.
Running over the night closest to midsummer, Múzeumok Éjszakája sees nearly all the museums in town opening their doors and laying on events from the afternoon of one day to 2.30am the next morning. Along with special exhibitions and demonstrations at venues as diverse as the Hospital in the Rock (*see*

p52), the Museum of Applied Arts (*see p136*) and the House of Terror (*see p109*), the Night of Museums gives visitors the chance to see Budapest's lovely old neon lit up at the Museum of Electrotechnics (*see p119*). One ticket (Ft1,500, Ft600 reductions, free under-6s), covers all entries; there are special bus services between more distant places.

Budapest Pride
www.budapestpride.hu. **Date** early July.
A week-long celebration of lesbian, gay, bisexual and transgender culture, culminating in the Pride Parade through the city, usually on the first Saturday in July. *See also p148.*

★ Balaton Sound
Zamárdi (372 0650, www.sziget.hu/balatonsound). **Admission** Day pass €50. *Festival pass* €150.
Date 5 days July.
With an international profile almost as high as sister festival Sziget, Balaton Sound brings top international names in electronic music and hip hop to the shores of Lake Balaton. Some 100,000 music lovers head to Zamárdi for sessions by the likes of David Guetta, Sven Väth and Felix Da Housecat. Bus tickets from Budapest and accommodation can be bought from the festival website – the fastest regular train takes 1hr 40mins from Budapest Kelenföld. There's plenty of private accommodation around Zamárdi and nearby Szántód. *Photo p32.*

Hungarian Formula One Grand Prix
Hungaroring, Mogyoród (www.hungaroinfo.com). **Date** late July.
The long established Hungarian Grand Prix, the biggest event in the country's sporting calendar, is always held in the sweltering heat of summer. The city fills up with F1 fans, creating trade for hotels, restaurants and sex clubs. The course is at Mogyoród, 20km (12 miles) north-east of Budapest. The Hungaroring track has recently been adapted to make the race more exciting, and improvements have been made to the press, VIP and pit areas. Those paying top dollar sit in the Super Silver Grandstand, above the start/finish line.

★ Sziget
Óbudai-sziget (372 0650, www.sziget.hu). **Admission** 1-day pass Ft18,000. 5-day pass Ft72,000. 7-day pass Ft80,000. **Date** 1wk Aug.
See p30 **Island Life.**

St Stephen's Day
Date 20 Aug.
Hungarians celebrate their founding father in some considerable style. The right hand of St Stephen, inside a reliquary, is taken on a strange religious procession in front of the basilica. Military parades, plus flying and skydiving demonstrations, provide entertainment during the day. In the evening, cruise boats and river-view restaurants are all booked up

Left: **Balaton Sound**. *See p31*. Right: **Busójárás**.

weeks in advance to get the best view of the fire-works display over the Danube. Downtown streets are packed with all generations of Hungarians waving the red, white and green.

Jewish Summer Festival
Tourism & Cultural Centre of the Jewish Community of Budapest, VII.Síp utca 12 (413 5531, www.zsidonyarfesztival.hu). **Date** 1wk late Aug/early Sept.
Inaugurated in 1998, the Jewish Summer Festival comprises a week of Jewish theatre, art and concerts, mainly in District VII. The musical performances include classical, jazz and klezmer.

Autumn

★ Buda Castle Wine Festival
203 8507, www.winefestival.hu. **Date** 5 days Sept.
Hungary's leading wine producers descend on Buda Castle for five days to woo major buyers, with concerts and folk dancing overlooking the Danube and hills of Buda. Tickets, for one or five days, allow entry to all shows, along with a free glass to sample the many domestic wines on offer.

National Gallop
www.vagta.hu. **Date** 3 days Sept.
The Nemzeti Vágta celebrates Hungary's long equine tradition. Races, shows and reconstructions of battle scenes take place at Heroes' Square over a three-day weekend, with dance performances, live music and traditional Hungarian cuisine. Prizes are given for winning riders in different categories.

Budapest Design Week
www.designweek.hu. **Date** 1wk late Sept-early Oct.
This event showcases Hungarian designers from the worlds of fashion, interiors and engineering. Some 70 stores offer discounts, workshops and opportunities to meet local creatives.

Café Budapest Contemporary Arts Festival
www.cafebudapestfest.hu. **Date** 2wks Oct.
The former Autumn Festival has been rejuvenated as Café Budapest, a couple of weeks of contemporary art, dance, film and music at venues such as Trafó (*see p162*), A38 (*see p158*) and the Palace of Arts (*see p168*). Performers in 2014 included Nina Hagen, Laurie Anderson, Cirque Le Roux and Tiger Lillies.

Art Market Budapest
Millenáris Park, II.Kis Rókus utca 16-20 (www.artmarketbudapest.hu). **Date** 4 days Oct.
Established in 2011, this four-day contemporary art fair at Millenáris Park introduces some 20,000 visitors to works by exhibitors from 20 countries, with the emphasis on Hungary and the region. A recent innovation has been Art Photo Budapest, the only photo fair of its kind in central and eastern Europe.

Budapest International Marathon
www.budapestmarathon.com. **Date** 2nd Sun in Oct.
Some 3,000 competitors take part, a third of them from abroad. Budapest's generally flat topography and pretty scenery – the race starts in Heroes' Square, heads down Andrássy út and takes in the Danube embankment – make it one of the most popular on the marathon circuit.

Hungarian Film Week
Cinema City MOM Park, XII.Alkotás út 53 (www.cinemacity.hu, www.filmhet.hu). **Date** mid Oct.
Hungarian Film Week (Magyar Filmhét) made a welcome return to the scene in 2014. *See also p147.*

Remembrance Day
Date 23 Oct.
The anniversary of the 1956 Uprising is a national day of mourning. Wreath-laying ceremonies take place at plot 301 of Új köz Cemetery, where 1956 leader Imre Nagy was secretly buried after his execution, and doleful documentaries are broadcast on TV.

them to be good, *virgács* – small *Krampusz* puppets hung on a gilded tree branch – are also left out.

Christmas
Date 25, 26 Dec.
The traditional meal is carp, devoured on Christmas Eve, when modest present-giving takes place, thanks to the secret work of Jézuska. The city closes for three days from noon on 24 December. Some hotel bars and restaurants stay open, but otherwise tourists should leave any seasonal visit to Budapest until New Year's Eve.

New Year's Eve
Date 31 Dec.
New Year's Eve (Szilveszter) is when everyone takes to the streets in style. After the national anthem has boomed out at midnight, it's champers, kisses and fireworks. Public transport runs all night, and most bars and restaurants lay on some kind of special event. Merriment continues into the next day when *kocsonya* (pork jelly) wobbles its way into people's hangovers.

Mangalica Festival
V. Szabadság tér (www.mangalicafesztival.hu).
Date early Feb.
This event has grown with the revival of the Mangalica itself, a domestic breed of pig renowned for the quality of its meat (*see p84* **Pig in Clover**). Producers offer Mangalica in all kinds of guises, alongside other artisanal products such as cheeses, honey and oils.

Busójárás
Mohács, 210km south of Budapest (www.mohacsi busojaras.hu). **Date** mid Feb.
Near the border with Croatia, Mohács is where Hungary lost arguably the most vital battle in its history, against the Turks in 1526. As if to ward off any lingering evil spirits, and to welcome the coming of spring, the annual pagan festival held here is the liveliest and most colourful event to take place in the provinces. During the six-day carnival, menfolk in frightening masks and woolly cloaks parade around town, some arriving in rowing boats along the Danube. A giant bonfire is set up in the main square, surrounded by music stages and food stalls.

Fat Thursday
Various venues (www.torkoscsutortok.itthon.hu).
Date mid Feb/early Mar.
Fat Thursday (Torkos Csütörtök), held the day after Ash Wednesday, gives diners the chance to visit some of the best restaurants in town without having to pay through the nose. On one single Thursday, more than 300 establishments in Budapest offer their full menu – lunch or dinner, with drinks – at half price. Naturally, tables at the city's most renowned restaurants get booked early, so check the website well in advance.

All Saints' Day
Date 1 Nov.
While Halloween has been rather slow to catch on in Hungary, the traditional Christian holiday for remembering friends, family and relatives no longer with us is Halottak Napja. Large crowds wander the cemeteries all afternoon and into the evening to leave flowers and burn candles before the Day of the Dead.

Winter

Anilogue Budapest International Animation Festival
Uránia Nemzeti Filmszínház, VIII. Rákóczi út 21 (www.anilogue.com). **Date** Nov.
Anilogue is Hungary's largest animated film festival. *See also p147.*

★ Negyed7Negyed8
www.negyed7negyed8.hu. **Date** early Dec.
This alternative festival celebrates the Jewish seasonal celebrations of Hanukkah with parties, concerts, exhibitions, films and culinary events. Venues involved include Csiga (*see p133*), Fekete Kutya (*see p123*) and Auróra (*see p153*).

Mikulás (St Nicholas' Day)
Date 6 Dec.
On the eve of 6 December, children put their shoes out on the window sill for Santa (*Télapó*) to fill to the laces with chocolates, fruit and small presents. For Hungarians, this is the only seasonal appearance of the man in red. He is assisted by *Krampusz*, the bogeyman, a threat to naughty children. To remind

Budapest's Best

There's something for everyone with our hand-picked highlights.

Sightseeing

VIEWS

Fisherman's Bastion p51
The Danube spread out right below you.
Citadella p57
Panoramic backdrop for many a photo.
Elizabeth Lookout Tower p65
Favourite vista of a favoured Habsburg empress.
Tomb of Gül Baba p66
Gaze on the slopes of Rózsadomb (Rose Hill), named after the mausoleum's permanent resident (known as 'Father of the Roses').
Libegő p65
Take a chairlift ride into the Buda Hills.

Funicular p50
Short, sweet and spectacular.
Sziget Eye p76
Ride the big wheel.

ART

Ludwig Museum p136
The city's main modern and contemporary showcase.
Hungarian National Gallery p50
A millennium of Hungarian art.
Kiscelli Museum p72
Bucolic setting for famous Magyar painters.
Vasarely Museum p72
The father of op art.
Museum of Applied Arts p136
Budapest by design.

Clockwise
from left:
**Hungarian
National
Museum**;
Funicular;
**Margaret
Island**.

HISTORY
**Budapest History
Museum** p48
How the city came to be.
**Museum of Military
History** p52
Battles, wars and campaigns.
**Holocaust Memorial
Center** p135
Intelligently conceived
and fascinating.
House of Terror p109
The horrors of 1956
revisited.
**Hungarian National
Museum** p128
From prehistory to the
present day.

OUTDOORS
Margaret Island p45
Verdant escape surrounded
by the Danube.
Városliget p111
Budapest's City Park, dotted
with major attractions.

CHILDREN
Zoo p140
An ornate residence for
every species – and a
funhouse too.
Palace of Wonders p141
Science the fun way.
Tropicarium p141
Watch the sharks glide by.

Aqua Park p141
Slides, chutes, pools
and wave machines.
Capital Circus p143
Keeping it old-school.

Eating &
Drinking

BLOW-OUTS
Costes p136
Groundbreaking Michelin-
starred cuisine.
Gundel p113
The most legendary
restaurant in Budapest.
Nobu p78
De Niro brings the
world-beating Peruvian-
Japanese kitchen to town.
**Bábel Budapest
Étterem** p81
New venue for György
Lörincz and team.

GLOBAL
**Pampas Argentin
Steakhouse** p82
The finest cuts, sizzled
as you wish.
Arany Kaviár p66
The cuisine of the Tsars.
Mazel Tov p122
Street food of the Levant.

Fuji p66
Wonderfully fresh sushi and
sashimi – at a price.
Dang Muoi Pho Bistro p104
Authentic Vietnamese in the
heart of the theatre district.
Ristorante Krizia p104
Mediterranean warmth and
authentic own-made pasta.
Taj Mahal p110
Tandoori delights and
Goan specialities.

LOCAL
Réti Sas Vendéglő p60
Barely changed since 1934.
Horgásztanya p63
The Hungary of catfish stew
and lazy riverbanks.
Fülemüle p132
Classic Jewish cuisine –
goose a go-go.
Kádár Étkezde p122
Cheap, honest and
unchanged since Kádár.
Múzeum p132
Serving Habsburg dishes
since 1885.

BARS
Boutiq' Bar p104
Budapest's best bet
for cocktails.
Caledonia p105
The kind of place that gives
expat pubs a good name.
360 Bar p104
Rooftop cocktails and jazzy
tunes as the sun goes down.
Lánchíd Söröző p64
Rock 'n' roll haunt by Chain
Bridge – now with food.
Gresham Bar p217
Go on, spoil yourself.
You're on holiday!
Pántlika p113
All the *pálinka* that's fit
to drink.
Bambi Presszó p63
Authentically retro spot
with prices to match.
Félix Hélix p120
Hopping spot in a
happening bar hub.

Aznap p123
Craft beers, bare-brick
decor and football on TV.
Fekete Kutya p123
Buzzing boozer in the
heart of District VII.

Shopping

GIFTS & SOUVENIRS
Bomo Art Budapest p83
Handcrafted stationery with
echoes of the Golden Age.
Printa Akadémia p121
Screen prints, sassy togs
and funky paraphernalia.
**Rododendron Art
& Design** p85
Notebooks, phone cases
and wearable works of art.

BOOKS & MUSIC
Alexandra Könyvesház p107
Huge bookstore in a prime
location, with a stunning
café to boot.
Rózsavölgyi Zeneműbolt p79
Lovely old emporium for
records and sheet music.

Központi Antikvárium p84
Shelves and shelves of
second-hand literary treats.
Laci Bácsi Lemezboltja p124
Vital vinyl across the decades.

FASHION
Heaven Store p79
All the leading designers
under one roof.
Náray Tamás p107
Designer to the stars.
Aiaié p61
Randomly inspired bespoke
pieces by Zsanett Hegedűs.

Clockwise
from left:
**Ecseri piac;
Boutiq' Bar;
Doboz.**

Anda Emilia p82
Stand-out couture
collections.
Tisza Cipő p121
Wear Hungary's answer to
Adidas, circa 1975.
Retrock Deluxe p107
Edgy, urban clothes for a
streetwise clientele.
WonderLab p85
Concept store, creative
workshop and fave hangout
for designers.
Garden Studio p83
Devised by fashionistas,
frequented by urban creatives.
Nanushka p79
Sophisticated womenswear
by the queen of cool cotton.

MARKETS
Great Market Hall p137
Budapest's landmark
food bazaar.
Fény utcai piac p67
Popular purveyor of
organic produce.
Ecseri piac p137
The daddy of all post-
Communist flea markets.

FOOD & DRINK
Bortársaság p64
Best for wine – with savvy
staff on hand.
Balaton Ízlező p83
Lakeside treats, bottled,
jarred and wrapped.
Culinaris p111
Top-notch grocers who know
their onions.
Szalámibolt p85
Its name means Salami Shop.
You need search no longer.

Nightlife

CLUBS
Corvintető p153
Rooftop capers after dark.
Doboz p155
Dance all night in a
soundproofed box.
Szimpla kert p158
The don of all ruin bars.

MUSIC
A38 p158
Music ahoy on this old
cargo ship.
Dürer kert p160
Home of the loud and the
leather-clad.
Roham p162
Keeping the alternative
music scene alive.

Arts

FESTIVALS
Sziget p31
Central Europe's biggest and
best music bash.
**Café Budapest Contemporary
Arts Festival** p32
Dance, film, music and art
across two weeks.
Hungarian Film Week p32
Revived celebration of
Magyar celluloid.
Balaton Sound p31
Electronic music festival
by Hungary's biggest lake.

FILM
**Uránia Nemzeti
Filmszínház** p146
Grab a balcony seat amid
fin-de-siècle furnishings.
Buda Bed Cinema p144
Watch films while you recline.
Puskin p146
Classic film palace dating
back to 1926.

OPERA & BALLET
**Hungarian State Opera
House** p166
Landmark jewel on
Andrássy út.
Erkel Theatre p165
Second home of the
National Ballet Company.

Explore

The Danube & Bridges

The Danube is integral to Budapest's history and economy, and provides the city's most beautiful scenery. Celts first settled this stretch of the river, at mineral springs near today's Óbuda Island. They called it Ak-Ink ('Plentiful Water'), which became Aquincum after the Romans chased them out in the first century AD. A small fortress over the river, Contra Aquincum, served as an outpost, but it wasn't until Count István Széchenyi built the Chain Bridge 1,800 years later that a permanent crossing was established between what would become Buda and Pest. Part of Óbuda Island stages the hugely popular Sziget music festival during the summer, which attracts star names and serious crowds. Almost touching Óbuda's southern tip is Margaret Island, the city's central green getaway. This delightful pleasure garden is most easily accessed via pretty Margaret Bridge.

Margaret Island.

Don't Miss

1 Chain Bridge This iconic crossing is the city's most majestic sight (p44).

2 Margaret Island Green getaway in the heart of the city (p45).

3 Palatinus Strand Much-loved summer lido (p45).

4 Holdudvar Terrace diner by day, party central by night (p45).

5 Margaret Bridge An overhaul has returned the bridge to its 19th-century glory (p44).

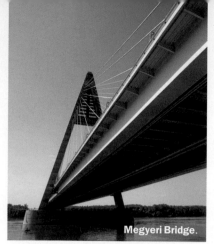

Megyeri Bridge.

ALONG THE DANUBE

Always present in the panorama from Buda's hills, the mighty Danube beckons as you stroll down any Pest street that leads towards the embankment. Snatches of the river appear between rows of buildings, the light changing as you approach. Contrary to Strauss legend, the Danube isn't blue, sadly, but a dull, muddy brown. By the time it passes swiftly through Budapest, it's heavily polluted.

An afterthought in Vienna, underused in Bratislava, the Danube divides and defines Budapest. Boats and hydrofoils connect all three capitals, setting off from the quay at downtown Vigado tér, five minutes' walk from focal Vörösmarty tér in the heart of the Hungarian capital. Sightseeing boats also dock here, day and night. This is the river at its narrowest, less than 300 metres (1,000 feet) across, the historic sights of Buda seemingly

within touching distance. All of the eight bridges (and one railway bridge) that carry traffic over the river are short enough to cross on foot in a matter of minutes. Strolling along the river, taking selfies on the embankment and stopping in the middle of any bridge (*híd*) for a memorable view feature highly on first-time visitors' must-do lists.

Alternatively, try and get a window seat on the 2 tram, which hugs the Pest embankment from Rákóczi Bridge in the south to Margaret Bridge in the north. It takes you past major sights such as the Great Market Hall, the hotel-lined Duna Korzó, the Gresham Palace and Parliament, all built with the river in mind and in view. Trams also serve the Buda embankment but, given the recently introduced **Bubi** municipal bike-sharing scheme (*see p223*), it seems rather a shame not to take advantage of the riverside cycle lanes that run past picturesque Margaret Island up towards Szentendre.

Several bars and restaurants overlook the river, but there are only a handful of actual floating venues. The most notable is the **A38** boat (*see p158*), a major restaurant, gallery and nightlife venue moored near Petőfi Bridge. Other floating restaurants cluster between Elizabeth Bridge and Chain Bridge, close to the city centre.

THE BRIDGES

The capital's northernmost crossing, **Megyeri Bridge** (Megyeri híd), is also the longest and most recent. Sweeping over the southern tip of Szentendre Island, it features a series of A-shaped pylons, which look stunning when illuminated at night. The bridge opened in 2008 to connect the outer fringe of Óbuda with the burgeoning suburban town of Dunakeszi. It also forms part of the M0 motorway circling the city, Budapest's equivalent of London's M25.

Margaret Bridge.

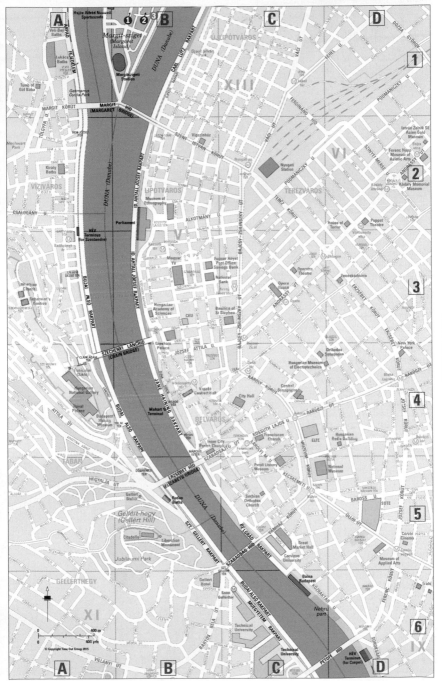

EXPLORE

Chain Bridge.

The next crossing down, **Árpád Bridge** (Árpad híd), is huge, prosaic and constantly busy, linking the districts of Óbuda and Újpest as it passes over the northern tip of Margaret Island. The bridge is part of the important 1 tram's route, currently part of a two-year renovation project.

The southern tip of Margaret Island is served by **Margaret Bridge** (Margit híd), built by the French in the 1870s. It was overhauled in 2010, when elegant lighting was installed, resonant with the era in which it was built. Forked in the middle to allow pedestrians to step off the bridge on to the island, Margaret Bridge forms part of the Nagykörút, the ring road that snakes through the main districts of Pest. Along it runs the world's busiest tramline, used by the 4 and 6 trams, which stop at three points on Margaret Bridge, one of which is midway, by the island itself.

The **Chain Bridge** (Lánchíd) was commissioned by anglophile Count István Széchenyi, whose foresight created much of general civic benefit in Hungary during the first half of the 19th century. The Chain Bridge was the first permanent crossing between Buda and Pest, conceived by Széchenyi when freezing waters prevented him from traversing the river by pontoon to attend his father's funeral. He asked Bristol-born engineer William Tierney Clark to design a bridge similar to the ones he had built over the Thames at Hammersmith and Marlow. Scotsman Adam Clark (no relation) was employed to look after the project in situ – a plaque stands at his former residence near the river at I.Ybl Miklós tér 6. The roundabout on the Buda side of the bridge is also named after him. Adam Clark is revered in Hungary, not only for taking a Hungarian wife and having three children here, but also for preventing the Austrians from blowing up the nearly completed bridge during the War of Independence in 1848-49. The Chain Bridge was opened on 20 November 1849, by which time poor Széchenyi had been placed in

an asylum near Vienna. It was reopened exactly a century later, having been rebuilt after retreating Nazis blew up all of Budapest's bridges in 1945.

Elizabeth Bridge (Erzsébet híd) is the post-war replacement for the original single-span construction built in 1903 and destroyed in 1945. This sweeping 1960s suspension bridge was the last one to be reopened after the war.

Linking the Kiskörút with Gellért tér, **Szabadság Bridge** (Szabadság híd) features an appealing criss-cross of sturdy green girders, topped with golden-coloured mythical *turul* birds. On the Buda side, a plaque remembers the Aeroexpress hydroplane, which whisked high-paying visitors between Vienna, Lake Balaton and the Gellért Hotel during the 1920s.

Further south, on the lower stretch of the Nagykörút, is ordinary-looking **Petőfi Bridge** (Petőfi híd). Like Rákóczi Bridge to the south of it, Petőfi is long, full of fast-moving traffic and of little interest to visitors.

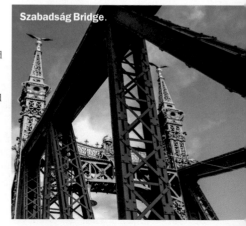

Szabadság Bridge.

The southernmost bridge for traffic, **Rákóczi Bridge** (Rákóczi híd), until recently known as Lágymányosi, was opened in 1995. Nearby, on the Pest side, is a waterfront cultural complex built for the new millennium, which is home to the **Palace of Arts** and the **National Theatre** (for both, *see p168*). Alongside, Közvágóhíd is not a bridge, but rather it's a transport hub that forms the southern terminus of the 2 tram, a 20-minute journey from Margaret Bridge at the other end of the line.

MARGARET ISLAND

Car-free **Margaret Island** (Margitsziget) is the city's main recreation area. The remains of a 13th-century Dominican church and convent – the former home of Princess Margit, after whom the island is named – can be spotted alongside a UNESCO-protected water tower and exhibition space. Following 19th-century landscaping work and the extension of Margaret Bridge in 1901, a spa, hotel and sports facilities were opened amid the 10,000 trees dotted across the island.

There's a five-kilometre (three-mile) jogging track, several seasonal clubs and restaurants, two spa hotels (including the **Danubius Health Spa Resort Margitsziget**; *see p209*), and two swimming pools, the **Hajós Alfréd Nemzeti Sportuszoda** and **Palatinus Strand**. Hajós Alfréd, named after Hungary's first Olympic champion, who won swimming gold at the inaugural 1896 Games in a freezing Aegean Sea, has staged two European Swimming Championships and two European Water Polo Championships in recent years. It's also part of Budapest's bid, officially announced in February 2015, to stage the 2024 Olympics.

Other island attractions include a recently renovated Japanese garden, a water fountain (popular for wedding photos), a petting zoo and an open-air concert stage, the **Margitszigeti Szabadtéri Színpad** (*see p167*). Cycle and pedalo hire, and tennis courts, provide further outdoor entertainment.

Restaurants

★ Holdudvar

Casino kert, XIII. Margitsziget (236 0155, www. holdudvar.net). Tram 4, 6, or bus 26. **Open** *Apr-Sept* 11am-11pm daily. Closed Oct-Mar. **Main courses** Ft2,100-Ft4,300. **Map** p43 B1 ❶ **Hungarian/international**

This popular summer-only venue is a convivial terrace restaurant by day, doubling up as a bar and nightclub after dark. In a timeless atmosphere engendered by the fin-de-siècle former casino and verdant grounds it occupies, the Holdudvar ('Moon Courtyard') intersperses Hungarian classics with

top-notch pasta dishes. Tuck into beetroot gnocchi with gorgonzola sauce, traditional Alföldi goulash or duck breast with cherry sauce. It's worth stopping by just for dessert – the fig and apple pie with apricot cream is divine. A grill bar sets up once the venue fills with drinkers and clubbers.

▶ *The late-night Holdudvar stays open until 5am for post-dinner dancing.*

Széchenyi Étterem

Danubius Grand Hotel Margitsziget, XIII. Margitsziget (889 4700, www.danubiushotels. com). Tram 4, 6, or bus 26. **Open** 7-10am, noon-3pm, 6-11pm daily. **Main courses** Ft3,900-Ft6,900. **Map** p43 B1 ❷ **Hungarian**

The restaurant of the Danubius Grand Hotel has a beautiful setting, in a tree-shaded garden on Margaret Island. Fancier (and pricier) than average Hungarian and 'wellness' dishes are on offer, as well as all-you-can-eat buffet lunches and dinners. Don't be put off by the gypsy band that occasionally plays in the garden – the menu here is decent, hearty Hungarian fare, from the goulash soup starter right through to the venison stew. Also look out for the cold fruit soup to start or finish.

▶ *The Széchenyi Étterem is attached to the Danubius Grand, one of the finest spa hotels in town (see p209).*

Cafés & Bars

Sziget Champs Beergarden

XIII. Margitsziget, Sirály Csónakház (06 20 471 0029, www.champssziget.hu). Tram 4, 6, or bus 26. **Open** *May-Sept* noon-midnight daily. Closed Oct-Apr. **Map** p43 B1 ❸

The outdoor Sziget Champs Beergarden serves up a mix of beer and big-screen sport. Facing the Pest embankment, near the southern tip of Margaret Island, Champs has a long bar counter and a large terrace space perfectly suited to relaxed sports gawping. Standard bar food and affordable cocktails complement draught beers such as Slovak Zlaty Bazant and Edelweiss.

EXPLORE

The Castle District

Castle Hill (Várhegy) is the city's top attraction and an essential stop on the Budapest tourist trail. Aside from the obvious major landmarks – the Royal Palace complex, Matthias Church and Fisherman's Bastion – the narrow streets and open squares that straddle this 60-metre (200-foot) hill also contain plenty of museums, from appealing oddities to national institutions such as the Széchényi Library and National Gallery, along with assorted churches, mansions and statues. Practically every building, as the ubiquitous stone plaques with their Hungarian-only inscriptions indicate, seems to have been declared a *műemlék* (historic monument). As this UNESCO-protected area is neatly contained on the top of a hill, tourists have their own playground, isolated from the rest of the city – though a smattering of locals still have their old homes here.

Funicular

Don't Miss

1 Funicular Glide up Castle Hill in style (p50).

2 Matthias Church Signature gingerbread roof atop a neo-Gothic rebuild (p52).

3 Budapest History Museum Medieval finds, modern rarities (p48).

4 Hungarian National Gallery Centuries of Magyar masterpieces (p50).

5 Ruszwurm Cukrászda Tasty treats in historic surroundings (p53).

Hungarian National Gallery. *See p50.*

BUDA PALACE & AROUND

You have to hold a permit, or be staying at the **Hilton Budapest** (*see p209*), to bring a car into the Castle District. Tourists arrive by coach, by the regular diminutive Várbusz that pootles up from Széll Kálmán tér, or by clip-clopping horse and carriage steered by traditionally costumed coachmen (available for hire at Szentháromság tér). Alternatively, for a nominal fee, a public elevator leads here from Dózsa György tér.

A more romantic way to ascend the hill is via the **funicular**. Its lower entrance is located on Clark Ádám tér, which is named after the Scottish engineer who supervised the construction of the nearby Chain Bridge. Later, Clark built the Tunnel (Alagút) running under Castle Hill. On this same square stands the **Zero Kilometre Stone**, the point from which all distances from the city are measured.

The top terminus of the funicular is presided over by an early 20th-century bronze statue by Gyula Donáth of the *turul*, a huge mythical bird. According to local legend, this protector of the Hungarian nation flew with the invading Magyar tribes, carrying the sword of Attila the Hun. The *turul* is a common motif on key fin-de-siècle Budapest structures. Breathtaking views of the Danube and Pest spread out below.

The strategic setting of the flat, rocky promontory of **Castle Hill** has seen it fought over for centuries. Evidence of the most recent attack on the castle, during the last desperate battles between the Nazis and Soviets, can be seen at Disz tér in the wrecked stump of the former Ministry of Defence, still bullet-pocked from the fighting in 1945. Buda Castle has been destroyed and rebuilt so many times that little of historic note remains.

Still, the past does manage to peek through the reconstruction: Baroque façades on Úri utca often include Gothic windows and doorframes;

reconstructed merchants' houses can be found at Tárnok utca 14 and 16; and distinctive *sedilias* – seats for servants inside gateways – can be seen at Országház utca 9 and 20, and at Szentháromság utca 5 and 7.

The centrepiece of Castle Hill, though, is the huge **Royal Palace**, a post-war reconstruction of an architectural hotchpotch from the 18th, 19th and 20th centuries, with several wings and interconnecting courtyards. Under the reign of King Mátyás (1458-90), the Royal Palace reached its apogee. Mátyás's Renaissance-style court featured hot and cold running water and fountains that spouted wine. Partially wrecked during the Turkish siege of 1541, the area was completely laid waste when it was recaptured from the Turks in 1686. Empress Maria Theresa had a new 203-room palace built in the late 18th century. This was badly damaged in the 1848-49 War of Independence, then rebuilt and expanded in neo-Baroque style by Miklós Ybl and Alajos Hauszmann.

Buda Castle was destroyed in World War II, and it took 30 years to return it to the simpler state you see today, a complex housing the **Hungarian National Gallery**, the **National Széchényi Library** and the **Budapest History Museum**.

Sights & Museums

Budapest History Museum

Budapesti Történeti Múzeum
I.Szent György tér 2, Buda Palace, Wing E (487 8800, www.btm.hu). Várbusz from M2 Széll Kálmán tér, or bus 16. **Open** *Mar-Oct* 10am-6pm Tue-Sun. *Nov-Feb* 10am-4pm Tue-Sun. **Admission** Ft1,300; Ft650 reductions. **No credit cards. Map** p49 D5 ❶
Beginning with the earliest tribal settlements, illustrations, artefacts and excavation photographs trace Budapest's development to the present day. With documentation in English, displays focus on key symbols through the ages, such as Charles of

Time Out Budapest

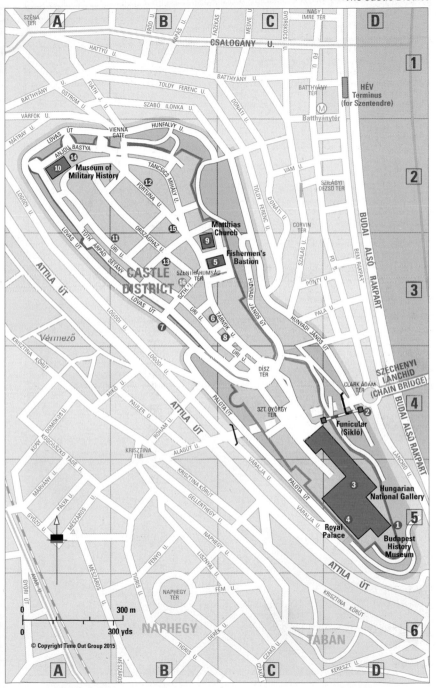

SZÉNA TÉR · A · CSALOGÁNY U. · B · FAZEKAS · MEDVE U. · C · GYORSKOCS · NAGY IMRE TÉR · D

HATTYÚ U. · ERŐD U. · KAPÁS U. · 1

FŐ U. · BATTHYÁNY U. · BATTHYÁNY TÉR · HÉV Terminus (for Szentendre)

TOLDY FERENC U. · DONÁTI U. · M Batthyányi tér

BATTHYÁNY U. · OSTROM U. · FÁTH J. U. · SZABÓ ILONKA U. · VÁM U. · SZILÁGYI DEZSŐ TÉR · 2

VÁRFOK U. · HUNFALVY U. · TOLDY FERENC U. · DONÁTI U.

MÁTRAY U. · LOVAS ÚT · VIENNA GATE · ANJOU BASTYA · 10 · Museum of Military History · 12 · FORTUNA U. · TÁNCSICS MIHÁLY U. · CORVIN TÉR

BÉM RAKPART · BUDAI ALSÓ RAKPART

11 · ORSZÁGHÁZ U. · 15 · Matthias Church · 9 · Fishermen's Bastion · 5 · SZALAG U. · FŐ U. · 3

TÓTH ÁRPÁD SÉTÁNY · ÚRI U. · 13 · SZENTHÁROMSÁG TÉR · 16 · SZT. U. · HUNYADI JÁNOS ÚT · PÁLA U. · DŐNTY U.

CASTLE DISTRICT · LOVAS ÚT · ÚRI U. · 6 · TÁRNOK U. · 8 · ÚRI U. · HUNYADI JÁNOS ÚT

ATTILA ÚT · Vérmező · LOGODI U. · 7 · LOGODI U. · DÍSZ TÉR · CLARK ÁDÁM TÉR · SZÉCHENYI LÁNCHÍD (CHAIN BRIDGE)

KRISZTINA KÖRÚT · MIKÓ U. · PAULER U. · ROHAM U. · PALOTA ÚT · SZT. GYÖRGY TÉR · Funicular (Siklo) · 2

KRPY DOMOKOS U. · KOSCIUSZKO TADÉ U. · KRISZTINA TÉR · ALAGÚT U. · KRISZTINA KÖRÚT · VÁRALJA U. · PALOTA ÚT · VÁRALJA U. · 3 · Hungarian National Gallery

MÁRVÁNY U. · PÁLYA U. · GELLÉRTHEGY U. · 4 · Royal Palace · 1 · Budapest History Museum · 5

GYŐZŐ U. · MÉSZÁROS U. · NAPHEGY U. · FENYŐ U. · LISZNYAI U. · ATTILA ÚT

GYŐRI ÚT · AVAR U. · MÉSZÁROS U. · TIGRIS U. · NAPHEGY TÉR · FÉM U. · KRISZTINA KÖRÚT

0 300 m · 0 300 yds · NAPHEGY · TIGRIS U. · DERÉK U. · TABÁN · 6

© Copyright Time Out Group 2015

A · B · CZAKÓ U. · C · KERESZT U. · D

EXPLORE

Lothringen's Triumphal Arch to celebrate the defeat of the Ottomans, and red drapes from May Day 1919 during the short-lived Hungarian Soviet Republic. Modern Budapest is illustrated through the contemporary architecture of József Finta and organic villas and yurt houses created by Imre Makovecz, who died in 2011. A dark room is full of ghoulish Gothic statues unearthed at Buda Castle, some of which pre-date King Mátyás.

▶ *The Budapest History Museum has two other branches, both in Óbuda: the Kiscelli Museum (see p72) and the Aquincum Museum (see p70).*

Funicular
Sikló
I.Clark Ádám tér (201 9128, www.bkv.hu/hu/ siklojegy). Tram 19, or bus 16, 86, 105. **Open** 7.30am-10pm daily. Closed every 2nd Mon. **Admission** *Single* Ft1,200; Ft700 reductions. *Return* Ft1,800; Ft1,100 reductions. **Map** p49 D4 ❷
The funicular crawls up the side of Castle Hill in two minutes, offering a wonderful view of the Danube and Pest on the way up. Originally built in 1870 to provide cheap transport for clerks working in the Castle District – in the days when it was a hub of municipal offices rather than museums – the first funicular was powered by a steam engine. It was restored and electrified in 1986. Cars run up and down every five to ten minutes.

Hungarian National Gallery
Magyar Nemzeti Galéria
I.Szent György tér 2, Buda Palace, Wings A, B, C, D (06 20 439 7325, 06 20 439 7331, www.mng.hu). Várbusz from M2 Széll Kálmán tér, or bus 16. **Open** 10am-6pm Tue-Sun. **Admission** Ft1,400. *Temporary exhibitions* varies. **Map** p49 D5 ❸
This vast museum attempts to chronicle Magyar art since the birth of the nation. To fully appreciate all the paintings, sculptures, ecclesiastical art, medallions and graphics would require more than one visit. The two collections considered the most important are 15th- and 16th-century winged altarpieces, and mid 19th- to early 20th-century art. Most of the work here derives from major European movements, including classicism, impressionism, Fauvism and art nouveau. There are depictions of Hungarian history by Viktor Madarász and lively sculptures of Hungarian peasants by Miklós Izsó. Mihály Munkácsy's paintings are considered a vital contribution to Hungarian art, especially his *Yawning Journeyman* (1868). Also noteworthy are the many works of impressionist József Rippl-Rónai, Hungary's Whistler (he even painted his mother), and great early 20th-century painters such as symbolists Lajos Guláscy and János Vaszary, mad self-taught genius Tivadar Kosztka Csontváry, and the sad figure of István Farkas, a Jew murdered at the end of the war. For a small fee, a guide can take you round the Palatine Crypt under the museum, built in 1715 as part of the Habsburg palace reconstruction. Occasionally, another wing opens for temporary contemporary shows. *Photo p48.*

National Széchényi Library
Országos Széchényi Könyvtár
I.Szent György tér 2, Buda Palace, Wing F (224 3700, www.oszk.hu). Várbusz from M2 Széll Kálmán tér, or bus 16. **Open** 9am-8pm Tue-Sat. **Admission** varies. **No credit cards. Map** p49 D5 ❹
The seven-storey National Széchényi Library houses five million books, manuscripts, papers, newspapers and journals – anything, in fact, related to Hungary or published in Hungarian anywhere in the world. To browse or research, bring a passport and ask for English-speaking staff. The building is named after Count Ferenc Széchényi (father of 19th-century reformer István), who donated his library to the state

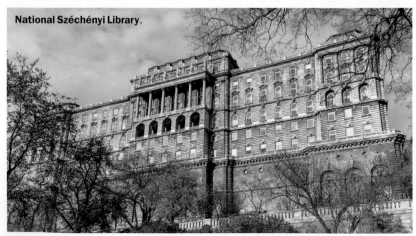

National Széchényi Library.

Fisherman's Bastion.

in 1802. The institution is also home to the Corviniani, a collection of books and manuscripts that belonged to King Mátyás, who owned one of the largest library collections in Renaissance Europe. Sadly, these are rarely displayed.

AROUND CASTLE HILL

At the same time as Buda Castle was being rebuilt in the late 1800s, Frigyes Schulek set about the reconstruction of **Matthias Church** and the erection of **Fisherman's Bastion** nearby. Strolling away towards Szentháromság tér, you'll pass the **Golden Eagle Pharmaceutical Museum**. On the parallel street of Úri utca, the **Labyrinth** makes use of the extensive network of caves still found here. Also on Úri utca stands the appealingly antiquated **Telephone Museum**

Where Úri utca and Szentháromság utca meet stands the equestrian statue of the hussar András Hadik, a favourite of Maria Theresa and later governor of Transylvania. Pre-exam engineering students still consider it good luck to rub the testicles of Hadik's horse. Around the corner, on Hess András tér – named after the man who printed the first Hungarian book on the same square – is the **Red Hedgehog House** (Vörös Sünház), which dates back at least as far as 1390. Once apparently owned by a nobleman whose coat of arms was the hedgehog, it's now a private residence with several flats. Nearby is the **Ruszwurm**, the city's oldest pastry shop (*cukrászda*) and a tourist haven.

The Castle District's streets still follow medieval lines and are protected by a series of gates. At the northern end, between the Vienna Gate (Bécsi kapu) and the Memorial to the last Pasha of Buda and the Anjou Bastion, stands the **Museum of Military History** in a former 18th-century barracks.

Across from it is the site of the **Church of St Mary Magdalene** (Mária Magdolna templom), where Magyar Christians worshipped when

Matthias Church was used by Buda's German population. All but the tower and gate were pulled down after the destruction of World War II. Next to the Museum of Military History, a large neo-Gothic building with decorative roof tiles houses the **National Archives**.

Along the western ramparts is Tóth Árpád sétány, the promenade overlooking **Vérmező**, a pretty park. The park was given its name, Blood Meadow, after a mass execution of Hungarian rebel leaders by the Habsburgs in 1795. The view, beautiful at sunset under the chestnut trees, extends westwards over the rolling Buda Hills. Relatively tourist-free, this street is where the few citizens who actually live in the Castle District come to stroll. Immediately below, running parallel to the promenade and accessed via its steep steps, Lovas utca contains the **Hospital in the Rock** (Sziklakórház), a reconstruction of the military hospital that operated here during the Battle of Budapest in late 1944 and early 1945.

Sights & Museums

FREE Fisherman's Bastion
Halászbástya
I. Várhegy (458 3000). Várbusz from M2 Széll Kálmán tér, or bus 16. **Open** 24hrs daily. *Upper Towers* mid Mar-Apr 9am-7pm daily. May-mid Oct 9am-8pm. **Admission** free. *Upper Towers* Ft700; Ft350 reductions. **No credit cards. Map** p49 B3 ⑤
Just as he romanticised Matthias Church, so architect Frigyes Schulek conceived this panoramic confection. Guarded by a statue of St Stephen on horseback, this neo-Romanesque vantage point comprises seven turrets, one for each of the original Hungarian tribes. The Upper Towers open for seven months of the year and carry a nominal entrance fee.

Golden Eagle Pharmaceutical Museum
Arany Sas Patikamúzeum
I. Tárnok utca 18 (375 9772). Várbusz from M2 Széll Kálmán tér, or bus 16. **Open** *Mid Mar-Oct*

Baltazár.

10.30am-6pm Tue-Sun. *Nov-mid Mar* 10.30am-4pm Tue-Sun. **Admission** Ft500; Ft250 reductions. **No credit cards. Map** p49 B3 **6**
Located in a 15th-century house, one of the oldest on Castle Hill, the Golden Eagle Pharmaceutical Museum is a curious little diversion. Exhibits include a reconstruction of an alchemist's laboratory and mummy powder from Transylvania, believed to cure epilepsy.

Hospital in the Rock
Sziklakórház
I.Lovas utca 4C (06 70 701 0101, www. sziklakorhaz.eu). Várbusz from M2 Széll Kálmán tér, or bus 16. **Open** 10am-8pm daily. **Admission** (with guide) Ft3,600; Ft1,800 reductions. **No credit cards. Map** p49 B3 **7**
It's a shame that this attraction is so expensive – you can only visit as part of an hourly English-speaking tour. Converted into a museum, this part of Buda Castle's cave network was where combatants in the Battle of Budapest were treated during the terrible winter of 1944-45. It was later used as a nuclear bunker and listening station during the Cold War. Its previous functions are explained by means of original artefacts and wax models.

Labyrinth
Labirintus
I.Úri utca 9 (312 9097, www.labirintus.eu). Várbusz from M2 Széll Kálmán tér, or bus 16. **Open** 10am-7.30pm daily. **Admission** Ft2,000; Ft600-Ft1,500 reductions. **No credit cards. Map** p49 C3 **8**
Controversially closed down, expropriated and reopened by the authorities in 2011, this popular if somewhat kitsch tourist attraction comprises a series of faux historic waxworks in the authentic setting of the Buda Castle caves. Dracula, aka Vlad III 'The Impaler', was a prisoner of King Mátyás here in 1462, a fact the Labyrinth management is keen to play up. It also conducts oil-lamp tours of the museum every day at 6pm.

★ Matthias Church
Mátyás templom
I.Országház utca 14 (489 0716, www.matyastemplom.hu). Várbusz from M2 Széll Kálmán tér, or bus 16. **Open** 9am-5pm Mon-Fri; 9am-noon Sat; 1-5pm Sun. **Admission** Ft1,400; Ft1,000 reductions. **No credit cards. Map** p49 B3 **9**
Named after Good King Mátyás, who was twice married here, this neo-Gothic landmark dominates tourist central. Parts of the structure still date from the 13th century, but most of it was reconstructed in the 19th century. Converted into the Great Mosque by Buda's Turkish rulers in 1541, the building suffered terribly during a six-week siege in 1686, when Vienna took it back from Istanbul. Some 200 years later, architect Frigyes Schulek returned to the original 13th-century plan but added his own decorative details, such as the gargoyle-bedecked stone spire. The interior is brightly coloured, almost playful, as is the gingerbread-house roofing. These are Zsolnay tiles, made from frost-resistant pyrogranite. On summer evenings, the church hosts classical concerts.

Museum of Military History
Hadtörténeti Múzeum
I.Kápisztrán tér 2-4 (325 1600, www.militaria.hu). Várbusz from M2 Széll Kálmán tér, or bus 16. **Open** *May-Sept* 10am-6pm Tue-Sun. *Oct-Apr* 10am-4pm Tue-Sun. **Admission** Ft1,500; Ft750 reductions. **No credit cards. Map** p49 A2 **10**
This museum covers 1,000 years of Hungary in conflict. On the first floor, the two World Wars are given particular focus in a permanent exhibition entitled 'From the Piave to the Don, from the Don to the Danube'. The Piave refers to the breakthrough in 1917 that led to the collapse of the Austro-Hungarian Empire. Note the models of sad Hungarian soldiers sitting in a train wagon. Maps of troop movements help the visitor understand the lie of the land, most notably the Russian Front at the Don in 1942-43. This is strikingly illustrated with model soldiers – few would envy being a Hungarian private at that time. The Battle of Budapest is also brought vividly to life.

EXPLORE

Telephone Museum
Telefónia Múzeum
*I.Úri utca 49 (201 8857, www.posztamuseum.hu).
Várbusz from M2 Széll Kálmán tér, or bus 16.* **Open**
10am-4pm Tue-Sun. **Admission** Ft500; Ft250
reductions. **No credit cards. Map** p49 B3 ⓫
Old switchboards and telephones are described
here in wonderfully useless Hunglish. Which is a
shame, because Hungary's own pioneer, Tivadar
Puskás, merits further investigation. He was a
major influence on Thomas Edison and invented
the telephone exchange.

Restaurants

21 Magyar Vendéglő
*I.Fortuna utca 21 (202 2113, www.21restaurant.
hu). Várbusz from M2 Széll Kálmán tér.* **Open**
11am-midnight daily. **Main courses** Ft2,760-
Ft5,780. **Map** p49 B2 ⓬ **Hungarian**
This modern eaterie, serving superb contemporary
takes on traditional Hungarian cuisine, is reason
alone to come to the Castle District. Go for local
standards such as Hortobágy pancake stuffed with
chicken, or goose liver. There's also a specials board
with daily and seasonal offerings.

★ Alabárdos Étterem
*I.Országház utca 2 (356 0851, www.alabardos.hu).
Várbusz from M2 Széll Kálmán tér, or bus 16.*
Open 7-11pm Mon-Fri; noon-3pm, 7-11pm Sat.
Main courses Ft1,800-Ft8,900. **Map** p49 B3
⓭ **Hungarian**
Alabárdos Étterem combines progressive Magyar
dishes and wonderful service. The mock medieval
decor suits the touristy location, but fortunately
what's on the plate is a far classier act. Among
the choices grouped under the loose heading of
'traditional' are the likes of Lake Balaton pike fillet
marinated with citrus, grilled duck liver and saddle
of deer with juniper.

21 Magyar Vendéglő.

★ Baltazár
*I.Országház utca 31 (300 7050, www.baltazar
budapest.com). Várbusz from M2 Széll Kálmán tér,
or bus 16.* **Open** 7.30am-midnight daily. **Main
courses** Ft2,760-Ft8,960. **Map** p49 A2 ⓮ **Grill**
This new venue is a top-notch grill restaurant,
wine bar and 11-room boutique hotel (*see p210*)
in one. Chef Zsolt Litauszki makes brilliant use
of the Josper charcoal grill and prime beef from
South Dakota to provide gourmet street food and
Hungarian grilled favourites. Pork and duck are
sourced from small batch and family suppliers in
southern Hungary. The wine list is outstanding and
there's a terrace for summer dining.

Vár: a Speiz
*I.Hess András tér 6 (488 7416, www.varaspeiz.hu).
Várbusz from M2 Széll Kálmán tér.* **Open** 11am-
11pm daily. **Main courses** Ft2,990-Ft8,900.
Map p49 B2 ⓯ **Hungarian**
This bistro serves excellent renditions of Hungarian
classics plus fishy favourites such as grilled salmon
with caramelised puréed cauliflower. The chef is
Árpád Kovács, who worked with Károly Rudits at
the late lamented LouLou when the current Speiz
owner opened it back in the 1990s.

Cafés & Bars

Ruszwurm Cukrászda
*I.Szentháromság utca 7 (375 5284, www.
ruszwurm.hu). Várbusz from M2 Széll Kálmán
tér, or bus 16.* **Open** 10am-7pm Mon-Fri; 10am-
7.30pm Sat, Sun. **Map** p49 B3 ⓰
Founded in 1827, Hungary's oldest *cukrászda* (café-
cum-pastry shop) has a warm interior that retains
some of the 1840s Empire-style cherrywood fittings.
Its history and location are a hit with the tourist
crowds, and the handful of tables, inside and along
the pavement, are often full. The kitchen produces
masterful pastries, freshly made ice-cream and delicious *pogácsa* scones.

EXPLORE

Riverside & Green Buda

EXPLORE

Quiet garden neighbourhoods amid rolling hills make Buda a great place to live, and a pleasant place to visit. Beyond the immediate tourist attractions of the Castle District, Buda offers terrace restaurants, visible history, scenic riverside strolls and hikes in the hills. Castle and Gellért hills carve up central Buda into a patchwork of separate areas, while below lie the old quarters of Tabán and Víziváros, lined with Ottoman-era spas such as the Rudas and the Király. The area loses its definition around the two transport hubs of Széll Kálmán tér, currently being revamped, and Móricz Zsigmond körtér. 'Móricz Zsiga' is on the new No.4 metro line, connecting south Buda with Pest. Beyond urban Buda, smart residential districts amble up into still higher hills – leafy, lined with villas and laced with excellent walking opportunities.

Tomb of Gül Baba.

Don't Miss

1 Citadella Best hilltop vantage point in Budapest, crowned by the Liberty Statue (p57).

2 Tomb of Gül Baba Ornate evidence of Turkish Budapest (p66).

3 Church of St Anne Baroque at its best, with an in-house café (p62).

4 Gellért Baths Classic inside and out, attached to a landmark hotel (p56).

5 Chairlift Head through the trees to the upper slopes of János-hegy (p65).

TABÁN, GELLÉRT HILL & SOUTH BUDA

The quiet, shady park of **Tabán** lies between the twin heights of Castle and Gellért hills. The area was once a disreputable quarter inhabited by Serbs, Greeks and Gypsies – most of whom made their living on the river – until the Horthy government levelled it in the 1930s. Likened somewhat romantically to Montmartre, back then Tabán was also the haunt of artists and writers, including Antal Szerb, who lobbied in vain against its demolition. Even in recent years, the Tabán Museum, and restaurants such as Tabáni Kakas and Tabáni Terász, have all closed – only a modest flea market, the **Tabáni Bolhapiac**, carries the neighbourhood name.

One of the sites that wasn't levelled now houses the **Várkert Casino**, originally a pumphouse for the Royal Palace. It was designed in neo-Renaissance style by Miklós Ybl, whose statue stands in front. The square here is also named after him, and marks the blurry border between Tabán and Víziváros, the mainly waterside district that runs north from here.

This is also where you'll find the **Semmelweis Museum**, named after the influential 19th-century doctor who was born here. It stands near the end of the **Várkert Bazár**, originally created by Ybl. This hillside 'Castle Garden' of criss-crossing balustraded pathways was a sad ruin until it was renovated and reopened in 2014.

Before its demise, the Várkert was known as the Buda Youth Park, a regular venue for open-air concerts in the 1960s and '70s. In a similar vein, the Tabán Fesztivál of free live music, staged on nearby parkland every May Day, keeps alive the spirit of an area that has all but disappeared from living memory.

This stretch of the Danube is rich in natural springs and lined with spas, including the **Gellért**, **Veli Bej** and nearby **Lukács** (for all, see pp204-205). The **Rudas** (see p204) was overhauled and unveiled in 2014. Yet to reopen, though impressively renovated as a baths and hotel, the Ottoman-era **Rácz** remains locked in long-term bureaucratic wrangling. Many older locals still refer to the green area around it as 'Eszperantó Park', after a 1966 language conference there; a stone commemorates the event. With Hungarian so impenetrable, Esperanto was encouraged here before and after the war. Leading local Esperantists include financier George Soros and astronaut Bertalan Farkas. Writer Frigyes Karinthy headed the Hungarian association before his death in 1938.

Gellért Hill is named after the Venetian missionary, Gerard Sagredo, who helped convert Hungary to Christianity in the 11th century. In a pagan uprising, he was thrown down this slope into the Danube. He's commemorated with a

Cave Church.

statue and an artificial waterfall, created in 1904 to mark the country's first Christian martyr.

The nearby landmark **Danubius Hotel Gellért** (see p211), the destination de choix during Budapest's Silver Age between the wars, was built around its equally famous spa baths. Its art nouveau façade still echoes the days of the Grand Tour. Outside, an arch-topped fountain is designed to represent the city's eight natural springs. There's even a water feature in the newly built Gellért tér metro station opposite, a bright example of modern design on the new No.4 line.

From here, the metro and the 49 tram run to the main station of south Buda, Kelenföld. Beyond Kelenföld, the main roads funnel into the motorway for Lake Balaton and Vienna. Before this motorway forks, the old road south, Balatoni út, just inside the city limits, leads to **Memento Park**, the resting place for Budapest's Communist statuary. At nearby Budatétény, close to the river, the huge Campona mall complex also contains the child-friendly attractions of the **Csodák Palotája** (Palace of Wonders) and the **Tropicarium**, a shark-filled oceanarium (for both, see p140).

Back at the Gellért, opposite the entrance to the spa at the start of Kelenhegyi út, a short path leads to the unusual attraction of the **Cave Church**. Above, 230-metre (750-foot) Gellért Hill can be reached via a steep climb up a series of steps and paths – which also zigzag up from the Gellért Statue on the other side of the hill. Alternatively, the 27 bus runs from further up Kelenhegyi út. With Budapest falling away dramatically before you, you finally reach the destination visible from all over the city: the **Liberty Statue**. It dominates **Citadella**, the hilltop fortress built by the Austrians after the Uprising of 1848-49.

Sights & Museums

Cave Church

Sziklatemplom

XI.Gellérthegy (06 20 775 2472, www.szikla templom.hu). M4 Gellért tér, or tram 19, 47, 49. **Open** 9.30am-7.30pm Mon-Sat. **Admission** Ft600; Ft500 reductions. **No credit cards.** **Map** p59 G4 **❶**

The Cave Church, founded by the monks of St Paul in the 1920s, is the only one of Gellért Hill's many caves used as a place of worship. After 1945, the Communist Party jailed the monks, and the cave was boarded up until 1989. It now offers curious visitors a somewhat spooky experience.

FREE Citadella

XI.Gellérthegy. Bus 27. **Map** p59 G3 **❷**

Citadella is the fortress that spreads out across the top of Gellért Hill, topped by the Liberty Statue. It was constructed by notorious Habsburg commander Julius Jacob von Haynau to assert Habsburg authority after the Hungarian uprising of 1848-49. Its commanding position put the city within easy target range – but the Dual Monarchy agreement of 1867 meant that its guns were never fired. Today, its attraction is purely panoramic – the modest museum within is still under long-term renovation.

FREE Liberty Statue

Felszabadulási Emlékmű

XI.Gellérthegy. Bus 27. **Map** p59 G3 **❸**

Perched above Citadella and visible from all over the city, this 14m (45ft) statue depicts Lady Liberty hoisting a palm frond over her head. It was built to mark liberation from Nazi rule by the Red Army in 1945 and is a rare surviving example of Soviet statuary in Budapest. The bronze soldiers in dramatic poses that ran around its base have been moved, like many monuments from that era, to Memento Park (*see below*).

★ Memento Park

XXII.Balatoni út (424 7500, www.memento.hu). M4 Kelenföld pu, then bus 101, 150. **Open** 10am-dusk daily. **Admission** Ft1,500; Ft1,000 reductions. **Map** p59 H1 **❹**

Inventively revamped by Ákos Eleőd, the former Statue Park is a surprisingly popular attraction despite its location on the very outskirts of the Hungarian capital. Essentially a junkyard for some 40 of Budapest's Communist-era monuments – including Marx, Stalin and a rare likeness of 1919 leader Béla Kun – Memento Park has branched out to screen spy-training films (with English subtitles) of the time. An exhibition focuses on popular uprisings across the old Eastern bloc, to put the momentous years of 1956 and 1989 here into focus. The Commie-kitsch gift shop does a roaring trade. A tour bus (Ft4,900 incl admission/Ft3,675 online) leaves from M1, M2, M3 Deák tér at 11am daily.

Semmelweis Museum of Medical History

Semmelweis Orvostörténeti Múzeum

I.Apród utca 1-3 (375 3533, www.semmelweis. museum.hu). Tram 19, 41, or bus 86. **Open** *Apr- Oct* 10.30am-6pm Tue-Sun. *Nov-Mar* 10.30am-4pm

EXPLORE

Memento Park.

EXPLORE

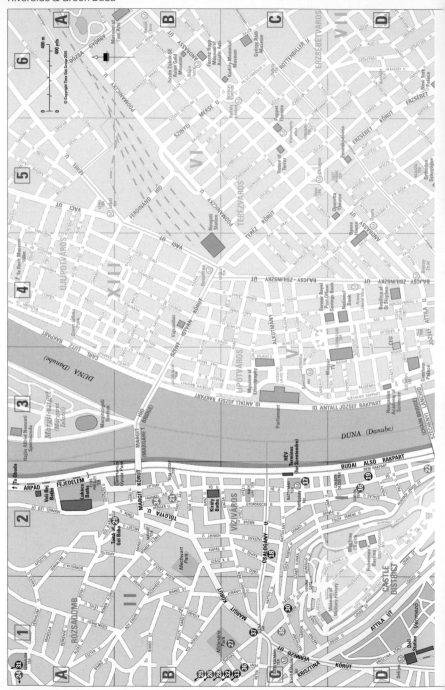

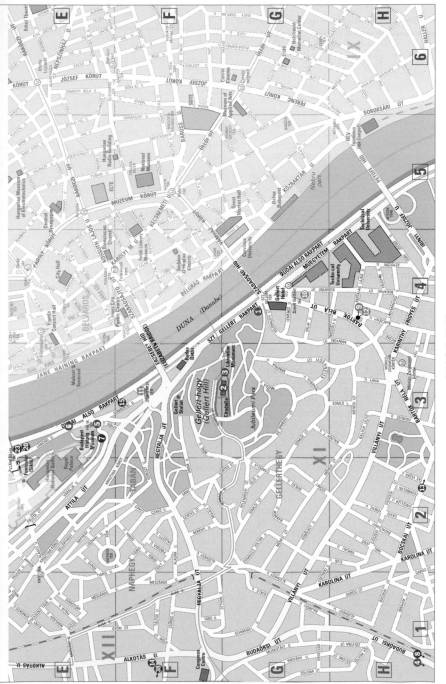

EXPLORE

EXPLORE

ESCAPE FROM BUDAPEST

Break out on your mini-break.

These days, Budapest is many people's favourite getaway – in more ways than one. The Hungarian capital, known for its soothing spa baths and rocking ruin bars, is offering visitors another unique attraction: escape houses.

Escape houses are games for up to five people in which the participants use their collective skills of logic and deduction to find clues, crack codes and break out of a room in which they have been trapped. There's a time limit, usually 60 minutes, and a theme to each game.

'The first game-makers were inspired by similar games on the internet,' said Szinti Polgár, who devised her own escape house in a quiet, residential area of Buda. 'These first computer games were Japanese. Someone decided to create a real-life version in Budapest. Everyone thought he was mad but it was a great success.'

Since then, 50 houses have been set up across Budapest, with various themes (ancient Egypt, medieval Europe and so on). Although the trend is slowly catching on elsewhere, Budapest, with its high-ceilinged flats, cheap rents and empty properties, abounds with escape houses. Plus, games of logic are nothing new to Hungary, home of the Rubik's Cube and crazy chess champions.

Polgár's own **BezárLak** (XI.Szováta utca 2B (36 30 923 5739, www.szabadulj.hu), comprises two room games: one is themed around poker, the other science. Numbered codes are hidden in nooks, around pictures and between book spines. As a computer clock ticks ominously down from 1:00:00, the magic three numbers allow you to open padlocks, find keys, follow laser lights and fish out magnets. Groups may ask for advice – their activity being monitored from outside, reality TV-style, by the games master – but their sense of achievement is greater if they escape without help.

Signs are given in English and Hungarian, with universal iconography provided. Degrees of difficulty are indicated for each particular game. The minimum age is 14, although younger kids can be involved in a mainly adult group.

Tue-Fri; 10am-6pm Sat, Sun. **Admission** Ft700; Ft350 reductions. **No credit cards**. **Map** p59 E3 ❺
Named after the Hungarian doctor who was born in this building, the Semmelweis Museum of Medical History traces the development of healing in the west, with particular focus on the equipment and achievements that characterised Hungarian medicine during the 19th century. Semmelweis himself became known as the 'mothers' saviour' because he realised that doctors who'd just performed an autopsy should wash their hands before moving on to deliver babies.

▶ *The museum also oversees the Arany Sas Patikamúzeum (see p51) in the Castle District.*

Várkert Bazár

I.Ybl Miklós tér (225 0310, www.varkertbazar.hu). Tram 19, 41, or bus 86. **Open** 10am-6pm Tue-Sun. *Garden* 10am-midnight daily. **Admission** *Exhibition* Ft1,800; Ft900 reductions. *South Palace* Ft1,500; Ft750 reductions. *Garden* free. **No credit cards. Map** p59 E3 ❻
Partly reopened in 2014, the Várkert Bazár is essentially an elegant pleasure garden that rolls down the lower slopes of Castle Hill, landscaped with a series of balustraded walkways. Architect Miklós Ybl, also responsible for the Várkert Casino opposite, took eight years to create it – though disrepair forced its closure almost exactly 100 years after Ybl completed it. Immediately before 1984, it was known as the Budai Youth Park (or BIP), one of the best-loved open-air music venues of the Socialist era. Entrance to the garden and grounds is free; the long-running exhibition in the main hall and lesser shows in the South Palace have an admission charge. Other events spaces and a stage are yet to be fully utilised.

Restaurants

Aranyszarvas

I.Szarvas tér 1 (375 6451, http://aranyszarvas.hu). Tram 18, or bus 5, 86, 178. **Open** noon-11pm daily. **Main courses** Ft2,500-Ft4,900. **Map** p59 E3 ❼ **Hungarian**
There's been an inn here since the early 1700s, but not since the literary set frequented the place a century later has so much attention been lavished on the Golden Deer. The reason is chef Gábor Mogyorósi, who cooks up wonderfully inventive Hungarian cuisine (think veal tongue, trout and duck liver) in stylish surroundings. A handy location on the Buda side of Elizabeth Bridge also helps.

★ Réti Sas Vendéglő

XI.Rimaszombati út 7 (310 2914). M4 Kelenföld pu, or tram 19, 49, or bus 139. **Open** noon-11pm Tue-Sat; noon-6pm Sun. **Main courses** Ft800-Ft1,600. **No credit cards. Map** p59 H1 ❽ **Hungarian**

Once upon a time, Budapest was full of little local hostelries. Sadly, though, places such as Réti Sas, tucked away behind Kelenföld station, are now rare. Changed little since 1934 – you almost expect the prices to be in pre-war *pengő* – Réti Sas comprises a traditional wooden interior and bucolic, shaded terrace, plus an extension for the many busy evenings. A comprehensive, meat-heavy menu covers all domestic favourites, portions are huge and prices may as well be in *pengő*. To reach it, head down the platform tunnel at Kelenföld. At the other end, turn right up the staircase and keep walking beside the rails – after a couple of minutes, there'll be a path leading off and a green Borsodi beer sign on the right.

Tabáni Bolhapiac. *See p62.*

Cafés & Bars

Hadik
XI.Bartók Béla út 36 (279 0290, www.hadik kavehaz.blog.hu). Tram 18, 19, 47, 49. **Open** 9am-11pm daily. **Map** p59 H4 ❾
Located in the same building as Szatyor Bár (*see below*), the Hadik harks back to Budapest's golden age. Its literary legacy – writer Frigyes Karinthy was a regular – is honoured by a plaque outside and a mural of famous Hungarian wordsmiths within. In the century between its inauguration and extensive renovation, the coffeehouse has embraced modern tastes to offer roasted nut latte, wines from the Légli, Bolyki and Gál stables, and a weekly-changing menu. The huge terrace spilling over into Gárdonyi tér is a real boon in summer.

Libella
XI.Budafoki út 7 (950 4994). M4 Gellért tér, or tram 18, 47, 49, or bus 86. **Open** 8am-1am Mon-Fri; 10am-1am Sat; noon-1am Sun. **No credit cards**. **Map** p59 G4 ❿
Round the corner from the Gellért Hotel and near a main university, the Libella is a big hit with a young, music-savvy crowd – this is a good place to find flyers for nightlife events. The cosy interior fills quickly by late afternoon.

Platán Eszpresszó
I.Döbrentei tér 2 (06 20 361 2287). Tram 18, 19, 41, or bus 5, 86. **Open** 11am-11pm daily. **No credit cards**. **Map** p59 F3 ⓫
A mixed crowd of alternative slackers, tourists and locals gaze on the Danube from this terrace on the Buda riverbank in a scenic neighbourhood. Set near the flyover of Elizabeth Bridge, the terrace is shaded by the lovely old plane tree (*platán*) that gives the place its name.
▶ *After Platán, head to the nearby Rom kert club (www.rudasromkert.hu) for a late-night party.*

Szatyor Bár
XI.Bartók Béla út 36 (279 0290, www.szatyorbar. blog.hu). Tram 18, 19, 47, 49. **Open** noon-1am Mon-Fri; 2pm-1am Sat, Sun. **Map** p59 H4 ⓬

Adjoining the historic Hadik literary coffeehouse (*see left*), the wantonly funky 'Carrier Bag' bar attracts a different crowd. Socialist-retro decor characterises the expansive interior – the walls, floor and ceiling are crammed with pictures, statues and murals. The tables on the ground floor and in the upstairs loft space fill up most nights. Cocktails complement a fine selection of affordable bar food.

Shops

★ Aiaié
District XI (06 30 906 3109, www.aiaie.wordpress. com). **Open** by appt. **Fashion**
The bespoke designs of MOME-graduate Zsanett Hegedűs can be commissioned by consultation and fitting at her private atelier in south Buda. Sparky but timeless womenswear, menswear and outfits for weddings or other social occasions are Zsanett's stock in trade. Every couple of years, she also comes up with a collection inspired at random – for Vancouver, and 'Shadowgraph', it was Bauhaus design and classic pre-war Hungarian photography. The name? It's an opulent island in Homer's *Odyssey*.

Allee
XI.Október 23a utca 8-10 (372 7208, www.allee. hu). M4 Újbuda-központ, or tram 4, 18, 47, 49. **Open** 10am-9pm Mon-Sat; 10am-7pm Sun. **Map** p59 H3 ⓭ **Mall**
Now served by a metro station on the No.4 line, the modestly sized Allee mall provides a more pleasant, less hectic experience than Buda competitors such as Mammut or MOM Park. It has a cinema, plus shops such as Marks & Spencer and Zara, a large Interspar hypermarket downstairs and a two-floor Libri bookshop. Alongside, Fehérvári úti piac is one of the city's largest indoor food markets; seasonal stalls selling artisanal items are set up between the mall and market.

EXPLORE

MOM Park
*XII.Alkotás utca 53 (487 5500, www.mompark.hu).
Tram 61.* **Open** 7am-midnight Mon-Sat; 8am-
midnight Sun. **Map** p59 F1 ⓩ **Mall**
This large mall contains more than 100 shops,
including iCentre for Apple goods, Bortársaság for
wine and Szamos for marzipan. There's a six-screen
multiplex cinema too.

Tabáni Bolhapiac
*I.Döbrentei utca 10 (06 30 622 0869). Tram 19,
41, or bus 86.* **Open** 10am-7pm daily. **No credit
cards. Map** p59 F3 ⓯ **Antiques**
Opened in March 2014, this friendly emporium is part
car boot sale, part antiques shop. Paintings, crockery,
sewing machines, postcards and little figurines await
the curious visitor, who may have to step over a docile
Alsatian to gain entry. *Photo p61.*

VÍZIVÁROS

From the north-east side of the Castle District,
the ancient streets of **Víziváros** (Water Town)
cascade down towards the Danube. This
neighbourhood stretches along the river, from
Clark Ádám tér by the Chain Bridge, past
Batthyány tér, towards Margaret Bridge.

One of Budapest's oldest districts, Víziváros
centres around narrow Fő utca ('Main Street'),
built in Roman times. Leading off it, street
names – Ponty utca ('Carp Street'), Halász utca
('Fisherman's Street') – reflect the riverside
activities that used to take place here. Today,
the tree-shaded thoroughfare along the Danube
provides some of Budapest's more pleasant
strolls or cycle rides.

On the other side of Fő utca, in the pretty
square of Corvin tér, the **Budai Vigadó &
Hungarian Heritage House** is both an archive
and home of the Hungarian State Folk Ensemble.
Further up Fő utca, Batthyány tér is the area's
centrepiece, a pedestrianised square that serves
as a transport hub, with buses linking up with the
southern terminal of the HÉV suburban rail line
to Szentendre. Fringed by 18th- and 19th-century
architecture – including the **Church of St Anne**
and a former market hall – the square offers a fine
view of Parliament across the river.

North along Fő utca, at Nos.70-72, is the
Military Court of Justice, used as a prison and
headquarters by the Gestapo in the early 1940s
and the secret police in the Stalinist 1950s. Here,
Imre Nagy and associates were tried in secret and
condemned to death after the 1956 revolution.
Just a block away are the **Király Baths** (*see
p204*), a leftover from the Turkish days – note
the Ottoman façade and cupola.

The street ends at Bem tér, with its statue of
General József Bem, the Polish general who led the
Hungarian army in the War of Independence in
1848. His aide-de-camp was national poet Sándor

Church of St Anne.

Petőfi, whose verse is engraved on the pedestal.
On 23 October 1956, this small square was the site
of a massive student demonstration against
Soviet rule, held in sympathy with political
changes in Poland at the time. Thousands of
angry workers also joined in. This would be the
beginning of the Uprising that lasted a week and
finished with Nagy's fateful trial.

Sights & Museums

Budai Vigadó & Hungarian
Heritage House
*I.Corvin tér 8 (225 6049, www.heritagehouse.hu).
Tram 19, or bus 86.* **Open** *Documentation centre*
early Sept-mid July 11am-5pm Mon; 10am-4pm
Tue; 11am-6pm Thur; 10am-3pm Fri. Closed
mid July-early Sept.
Exhibition hall *I.Szilágyi Dezső tér 6 (201 8734).*
Box office 8.30am-4.30pm Mon-Thur; 8.30am-
2pm Fri. **Tickets** varies. **Map** p58 D2 ⓰
This renovated neoclassical building decked in
ostentatious statuary is the home of the Hungarian
State Folk Ensemble. Founded in 1951, the HSFE
presents stage adaptions of Magyar music, dance
and folk plays. The centre is also a library and
archive, allowing visitors to peruse, and buy copies
of, a large collection of audio and video field recordings of Hungarian folk music and dance.

FREE Church of St Anne
Szent Anna templom
*I.Batthyány tér 7 (201 6364, www.felsovizivaros.
plebania.hu). M2 Batthyány tér, or tram 19, 41.*
Services 6.30am, 5/6pm Mon-Fri; 8am, 6pm Sat;
7.30am, 9am, 10am, 11am, 6pm Sun. **Admission**
free. **Map** p58 C2 ⓱

EXPLORE

Construction of Szent Anna, one of Hungary's finest Baroque buildings, began in 1740. Máté Nepauer, one of the most prominent exponents of the genre, oversaw its completion in 1805. The façade is crowned by the eye-in-the-triangle symbol of the Trinity, while Faith, Hope and Charity loiter around the front door. The theatricality of the interior is typical of the style. Larger-than-life statues are frozen in performance on the High Altar, framed by black marble columns representing the Temple of Jerusalem. In the former presbytery next door is the atmospheric Angelika café (225 1653, www. angelikacafe.hu), with an interior illuminated by the glow of stained-glass windows and a cool shaded terrace outside.

Restaurants

Csalogány 26
I.Csalogány utca 26 (201 7892, www.csalogany26. hu). Bus 11, 39. **Open** noon 3pm, 7-10pm Tue-Sat. **Main courses** Ft2,000-Ft4,500. **Map** p58 C2 ⑱ **Hungarian/Modern European**
Five years after this restaurant was all the rage, it's still turning out light, contemporary dishes to a pretty high standard. The food is sourced locally or created on the premises as much as possible. Mains might include the likes of seabass with lentil stew, red-wine risotto with cod or Magyar Tarka beef goulash. Presentation and service are both superb.

Horgásztanya
I.Fő utca 27 (212 3780, www.horgasztanya vendeglo.hu). Tram 19, 41, or bus 86. **Open** noon-midnight daily. **Main courses** Ft890-Ft3,290. **No credit cards. Map** p58 D2 ⑲ **Fish**
Succinctly described in the Budapest Pocket Guide of 1959 as 'fish restaurant, closed on Tuesdays, no dancing', the Fisherman's Rest is still serving Danubian delights more than half a century later.

Set right in the heart of Víziváros, the Horgásztanya offers pleasant river views from its terrace. The decent fish soups come in several varieties (carp, catfish, Tisza) and sizes (cup, pot, bowl), while the freshwater fish platter for two features pike-perch, catfish, carp and sterlet.
▶ More piscine treats are served at the Szeged Vendéglő (XI.Bartók Béla út 1, 209 1688), round the corner from the Gellért Hotel.

★ Zona Budapest
I.Lánchíd utca 7-9 (06 30 422 5981, www.zona budapest.hu). **Open** noon-midnight Tue-Sat. **Main courses** Ft4,500-Ft7,500. **Map** p59 E3 ⑳ **International**
The latest venue from the Baldaszti Group, Zona is a hit thanks to poaching chef Krisztián Huszár from the renowned downtown MÁK Bisztró. Having earned his stripes under Michelin-starred Martín Berasategui in the Basque Country, Huszár brings Iberian and Gallic touches to the table. The menu of some half-a-dozen dishes changes daily, with five- and six-course dinners offered at Ft14,900 and Ft17,900 respectively. The extensive wine list is mainly but not exclusively Hungarian, and it's worth coming a little early and parking yourself at the separate bar counter – not least to enjoy the Chain Bridge location.
▶ The ambitious Baldaszti Group (www.baldaszti. com) has just opened Nomuri, a restaurant and event venue, at V.Sas utca 15.

Cafés & Bars

Bambi Presszó
II.Frankel Leó út 2-4 (212 3171). Bus 86. **Open** 7am-10pm Mon-Fri; 9am-10pm Sat, Sun. **No credit cards. Map** p58 B2 ㉑
Preserved in time, 1965 at a guess, the Bambi is a classic example of a Commie-era presszó, the cafés

EXPLORE

Zona Budapest.

that replaced the elegant pre-war coffeehouses. The wide terrace has a view (just) of the Danube, but the star here is the authentic decor from yesteryear. Equally attractive are the prices, not much more than €1 for a half-litre of domestic beer and less than €2 for Debreczeni sausage, served by a seen-it-all waitress in timeless mules. Card schools and *totó* betting chat provide casual entertainment.

★ Lánchíd Söröző

I.Fő utca 4 (214 3144, www.lanchidsorozo.hu). Tram 19, 41, or bus 16, 86, 105. **Open** 11am-1am daily. **Map** p58 D2 ㉒

Expanded to feature an honest Hungarian kitchen, a larger adjoining dining room and a tasteful gallery space for private hire, the Lánchíd remains a cosy neighbourhood bar with an agreeably retro character. Autographed gig posters and photos of the genial owners beside BB King and John Mayall testify to lives dedicated to rock music and hospitality. Old radios, rare black-and-white shots of Budapest and checked tablecloths complete the picture. Regulars and the many repeat customers from overseas sup on draught Staropramen dark and light, taking advantage of sun-catching pavement tables in summer. The Chain Bridge that gave the bar its name is but a few steps away.

Shops

★ Bortársaság

I.Lánchíd utca 5 (225 1702, www.bortarsasag. hu). Tram 19, 41, or bus 16, 86, 105. **Open** 10am-9pm Mon-Fri; 10am-7pm Sat. **Map** p59 E3 ㉓ **Food & drink**

The largest outlet of this successful chain of wine shops is right by Chain Bridge. Some 75 domestic winemakers are on show – let the knowledgeable staff direct you. As well as regular tastings, Bortársaság can arrange home delivery to anywhere in Hungary (Ft2,550, free for orders over Ft15,000). **Other locations** throughout the city.

TURKISH & NORTH BUDA

Heading north from Bem tér, you come to the northern section of the Nagykörút at the Buda foot of Margaret Bridge. From here, you can walk up Mecset ('Mosque') utca, or climb the steep, cobbled medieval street of Gül Baba utca and come to the **Tomb of Gül Baba**. The most visible reminder of Turkish Buda, this is the last resting place of the so-called 'Father of the Roses'. An associate of Sultan Süleyman the Magnificent, Gül Baba lent his name to surrounding 'Rose Hill', Rózsadomb, Budapest's most exclusive residential area.

From Margaret Bridge, the Nagykörút runs past the **Mammut** mall and to the tram terminal and transport hub of Széll Kálmán tér (until recently known as Moszkva tér). Also until recently, the square's centrepiece was a Socialist-era station building, the look of which reflected its erstwhile Soviet-friendly name, 'Moscow'. In trying to distance Hungary from its post-war past, the current right-wing government has been changing place names across Budapest – Kálmán Széll was the pre-war name of the square, in honour of a former Prime Minister. A Ft5.3 billion rebuild here will run into 2016 and cause transport chaos in the meantime. The new look will complement the millennial concept of the nearby **Millenáris** complex, a patriotically tinged rebuild of a large industrial space conceived by the Fidesz party when they were last in power.

Chairlift

Elizabeth Lookout Tower

From around Széll Kálmán tér, public transport leaves for the hilly reaches of green Buda. The 5 bus takes you to Pasarét, a leafy neighbourhood dotted with notable Bauhaus architecture. As well as a number of villas on Pasaréti út, Vienna-born architect Gyula Rimanóczy also designed Szent Antal Church and the bus terminal that gracefully fringe the roundabout of Pasaréti tér. A little further along, the Bauhaus-inspired estate of Napraforgó utca has 22 houses, each by a different architect; these were built in the 1930s. The architects' names are listed on a monument in a pleasant, bench-lined square adjoining Napraforgó utca halfway along. Another Bauhaus-style structure uphill from Pasaréti tér is the former home of Imre Nagy, ill-fated prime minister during the 1956 Uprising. It's now the **Nagy Imre Memorial Museum**. Also within a ten-minute climb is **Béla Bartók Memorial House**, in the composer's former residence.

Before it veers off to Pasarét, the 5 bus runs along Szilágyi Erzsébet fasor and pretty Városmajor. This is where you find the terminus of the *fogaskerekű*, the cog-wheel railway that climbs through Buda's leafy heights. Buda is not only the domain of bikers and hikers – it is also served by a number of eccentric conveyances. Devised in the same way as the rack rails that were opening up the Alpine slopes to tourists, the cog-wheel railway originally ran through Buda to Zugliget in the Buda Hills. Today's *fogaskerekű*, officially tram 60 of Budapest's transport network, terminates at Széchenyi Hill. There it intersects with the terminus of the 11km-long (seven-mile) **Children's Railway** (Gyermekvasút; *see p143*), a five-minute walk down Golfpálya út – maybe longer if you stop for a drink at the Kőbüfé Söröző.

From Szilágyi Erzsébet fasor, the 102 bus forks off to climb up Zugligeti út to terminate at the Libegő, the **chairlift**. It's a short, steep hike to the top of János-hegy, at nearly 530 metres (1,740 feet) Buda's tallest hill. From the chairlift station, it's an calf-crunching ten-minute hike to the **Elizabeth Lookout Tower**, a popular panoramic spot, with a strudel (*rétes*) hut and a restaurant in an old ski-house. Alternatively, you can take the Children's Railway one stop from Széchenyi-hegy to Normafa, also on the 21 bus route from Széll Kálmán tér.

Sights & Museums

Béla Bartók Memorial House
Bartók Béla Emlékház
II.Csalán utca 29 (394 2100, www.bartokmuseum. hu). Bus 5. **Open** *Jan, Feb* 10am-4pm Tue-Sun. *Mar-Dec* 10am-5pm Tue-Sun. **Admission** Ft1,200; Ft600 reductions. **No credit cards. Map** p58 A1 ㉔
Built in 1924, this elegant house was the composer's last residence in Hungary, and was converted into a museum in 1981 on the centenary of his birth. Bartók composed here in the 1930s before fleeing to America. Artefacts from his travels around Transylvania are the highlights, including a fob watch metronome. Concerts are given in the 120-seat hall upstairs, and in the garden in summer.

Chairlift
Libegő
XII.Zugligeti út 97 (394 3764, www.bkk.hu). Bus 102. **Open** *Jan, Nov, Dec* 10am-3.30pm daily. *Feb, last wk Oct* 10am-4pm daily. *Mar, first 3wks Oct* 10am-5pm daily. *Apr, Sept* 10am-6pm daily. *May-Aug* 10am-7pm daily. Closed every 2nd Mon. **Tickets** Ft1,000/Ft1,400 return; Ft600/800 reductions. **No credit cards. Map** p58 C1 ㉕
Built in 1970 to whisk people from the gentle slope of Zugliget up to the highest hill in Budapest, János-hegy, the chairlift climbs more than 260m (850ft) on its 15-minute journey. Overall it's a pretty gentle experience, and you'll soon find yourself waving to passengers in their two-seater chairs passing in the opposite direction. The top terminal is crying out for a café or restaurant – but you'll have to make do with a snack-bar kiosk.

FREE Elizabeth Lookout Tower
Erzsébet kilátó
XII.János-hegy (224 5900, www.hegyvidek.hu). Libegő. **Open** 8am-dusk daily. **Admission** free. **Map** p58 C1 ㉖
Standing atop Budapest's highest point of 528m (1,730ft) – on a clear day, you can almost see Slovakia – the Elizabeth Lookout Tower is named after beloved Princess Elizabeth, wife of Habsburg emperor Franz Josef. 'Sissi' first walked here in 1882 and so admired the view that a suitably ornate structure was commissioned to replace the wooden one

EXPLORE

IN THE KNOW DOWN TIME

Buda isn't just about hills. Caves are another attraction, with hourly tours laid on at **Szemlőhegy** (II.Pusztaszeri út 35, 325 6001, closed Tue) and **Pálvölgy** (II. Szépvölgyi út 162, 325 9505, closed Mon), both part of the **Duna-Ipoly National Park** (www.dunaipoly.hu) that stretches all the way up to Visegrád and Esztergom near the Slovak border.

Cafer, aka Gül Baba, was a Turkish dervish saint, a personal companion of Sultan Süleyman the Magnificent and a member of the Bektashi order. He came to be known as 'Father of the Roses' and, according to legend, introduced the flower to Budapest, giving the name Rózsadomb (Rose Hill) to the area panoramically spread beyond. The mausoleum is the northernmost active centre of pilgrimage for Bektashi Muslims – the walls are covered in verses inscribed by the Turkish traveller Evliya Tselebi in 1663. The mausoleum was renovated by the Turkish government, since when plenty of appreciative Turkish visitors have signed the visitors' book.

that stood here. If it looks a little like the Fisherman's Bastion in the Castle District, that's because the same architect, Frigyes Schulek, designed both. Opened in 1910, the tower comprises four levels, the top reached by 100 winding steps. The nearest stops for the Children's Railway or city bus network are a good 15-minute walk away – the chairlift is the best option by public transport.

Millenáris Park
II.Kis Rókus utca 16-20 (336 4000, www.millenaris.hu). M2 Széll Kálmán tér, or tram 4, 6. **Open** Park 6am-11pm daily. Exhibitions varies. Concerts varies. **Map** p58 C1 ㉗
The Millenáris Park and events centre was established on the site of the old Ganz foundry and factory to mark the millennium of the crowning of St Stephen, which explains the patriotic exhibitions and overall design. The complex is shaped like a microcosm of Hungary, with a pool intended to symbolise Lake Balaton, and a tiny cornfield and grape arbour standing for the various agricultural regions. Inside, attractions include the currently popular 'Invisible Exhibition', showing what life is like for the blind. It's a good venue for concerts by mainly local bands, and the park also has a playground, puppet shows and other children's events.

FREE Nagy Imre Memorial House
Nagy Imre Emlékház
II.Orsó utca 43 (392 5011, www.nagyimreemlekhaz.hu). Bus 5. **Open** 10am-4pm Mon-Thur. **Admission** free. **Map** p58 C1 ㉓
Set in the villa where Imre Nagy and his wife lived from 1949 to 1956, the Memorial House tells the life of the fated hero of the anti-Soviet Uprising. The house itself is a fine example of 1930s Bauhaus, built by Lajos Kozma, while the exhibition was created by architect László Rajk, an anti-Communist activist and son of the former Interior Minister executed after a show trial in 1949.

FREE Tomb of Gül Baba
Gül Baba türbéje
II.Mecset utca 14 (237 4400 ext 1738). Tram 4, 6. **Open** 10am-6pm Mon-Sat. **Admission** free. **Map** p58 B2 ㉙

Restaurants

★ Arany Kaviár
I.Ostrom utca 19 (201 6737, 225 7370, 06 30 685 6000 mobile, www.aranykaviar.hu). M2 Széll Kálmán tér, or tram 4, 6. **Open** noon-3pm, 6pm-midnight Tue-Sun. **Main courses** Lunch Ft5,900-Ft7,900. Dinner Ft5,600-Ft18,900. **Map** p58 C1 ㉚ **Russian**
Opened by Attila Molnár and chef Sasha Nyíri in 1990, the lavish Arany Kaviár displays all the decorative and culinary touches of Imperial Russia. Lunch is the most affordable way to sample the steak stroganoff or catch of the day – the three-course 'Russian bistro' menu at Ft3,900 is a bargain. The caviar dishes, though, are for high-rollers only, with the varieties of Kamchatka Keta, Siberian Royal Black, Osetra and Russian beluga running up to Ft69,000. Beluga is also one of the finer types of vodka, along with Standart, Kauffman and Stolichnaya Elit.

Fuji
II.Csatárka út 54 (325 7111, www.fujirestaurant.hu). Bus 29. **Open** noon-11pm daily. **Main courses** Ft1,900-Ft16,900. **Map** p58 A1 ㉛ **Japanese**
Up affluent Rózsadomb, this spot is popular with locals and Japanese visitors. Though you won't find more authentic or fresher sushi in Budapest, it comes at a price. The sushi and sashimi menus cover every combination imaginable, such as the entry-level set for Ft11,900 per person. Specialities include deep-fried oysters and soya-cooked eel.
▶ You'll find a hub of Japanese restaurants closer to the river around Kolosy tér in Óbuda. Sushi Sei (III.Bécsi út 38-44, 240 4065, www.sushisei.hu) is one example.

Náncsi Néni
II.Ördögárok utca 80 (398 7127, www.nancsineni.hu). Tram 61 then bus 63, 157. **Open** noon-11pm daily. **Main courses** Ft2,650-Ft3,470. **Map** p58 C1 ㉜ **Hungarian**
Beloved by its many regulars, this spacious garden spot offers classic Hungarian dishes, immaculately done: Balaton catfish with garlic-sauce potatoes; duck breast with ginger, honey and orange sauce;

and goose liver with steamed grapes. Don't skimp on the starters, such as the goose crackling and the duck liver in its own fat. The garden, swing and children's playground make for a perfect family Sunday.

Remíz

II.Budakeszi út 5 (275 1396, www.remiz.hu). *Tram 61, or bus 22.* **Open** noon-11pm daily. **Main courses** Ft1,800-Ft4,380. **Map** p58 C1 ❸ **Hungarian**
Originally opened as a cake shop in 1992, the Remíz ('Tram Depot') soon branched out to become a full-blown and rather splendid restaurant in the capable hands of the Meződi family. The desserts here are excellent, while a diminutive mains menu includes enticing dishes such as crunchy catfish with truffles, and honey-chilli spare ribs. Other meaty favourites are prepared on a lava-stone grill. Two lovely rooms and a leafy garden provide the setting.
▶ *The Meződi family also runs Kisbuda Gyöngye at Kenyeres utca 34 (203 5509), another classic Hungarian restaurant in Óbuda.*

Cafés & Bars

Café Gusto

II.Frankel Leó út 12 (316 3970). Tram 4, 6. **Open** 8am-11pm Mon-Sat. **No credit cards.** **Map** p58 B2 ❸
Café Gusto is a cosy haunt in winter and a sunny spot in summer. In nicer weather, tables are at a premium on the terrace, but don't forget to pop your head in and have a look at the distinctive local caricatures by Marcus Goldson. Tasty pastas and cakes provide lunch or a mid-afternoon treat.

Oscar American Bar

II.Ostrom utca 14 (06 20 214 2525 mobile, www.oscarbar.hu). M2 Széll Kálmán tér, or tram 4, 6. **Open** 5pm-2am Mon-Wed; 5pm-4am Thur-Sat. **No credit cards. Map** p58 C1 ❸

Buda's young professionals mingle enthusiastically in the dark, cinematically themed Oscar American Bar. For all the stills and star portraits from Hungary and Hollywood, the most attractive features are the irresistibly long bar counter and the decent cocktails. The 40-page drinks menu is as comprehensive as any in Budapest.

Shops

Fény Street Market

Fény utcai piac II.Széll utca & Fény utca (345 4112, www.feny utcaipiac.hu). M2 Széll Kálmán tér, or tram 4, 6. **Open** 6am-6pm Mon-Fri; 6am-2pm Sat. **No credit cards. Map** p58 C1 ❸ **Market**
Set between Széll Kálmán tér and the Mammut mall, this much-loved market features organic and sought-after produce. Fény Street Market has stalls inside and out, and though by Budapest standards it's not cheap, it has a loyal and regular clientele.

Mammut

II.Lövőház utca 2-6 (345 8020, www.mammut.hu). M2 Széll Kálmán tér, or tram 4, 6. **Open** 10am-9pm Mon-Sat; 10am-6pm Sun. **Map** p58 C1 ❸ **Mall**
Two massive wings make up the Mammut mall, the newer one filled with the likes of Benetton and Mango, the older with dozens of smaller shops. There's a huge supermarket in the basement and a 13-screen multiplex cinema upstairs (*see p145*).

Ökopiac

XII.Csörsz utca 18 (06 30 435 5680, www. biokultura.org). Tram 59, or bus 110, 112, 212. **Open** 6.30am-1pm Sat. **No credit cards. Map** p59 F1 ❸ **Market**
Spread out on the grounds of the MOM Kulturális Központ since 2011, this organic market is the shop window for controlled, certified farms to sell a wide range of fruit and vegetables, goat's cheese and meat.

EXPLORE

Oscar American Bar.

Óbuda

Located on the west bank just north of Buda, Óbuda ('Old Buda') was its own entity until the unification of Budapest in 1873. Then it was a sleepy Danubian village of one-storey houses and cottages, populated by Serb, German and Magyar fishermen and artisans, today Óbuda can still feel like a bygone era. Traffic trundles past occasional Roman remains and low roofs atop 18th- and 19th-century façades. You could be on a film set. Attractive rates and proximity to town – the fast HÉV train links with Batthyány tér on the M2 metro line – have encouraged new businesses; a significant number of bars, shops and restaurants now cater to local employees. On weekdays, the hub of Kolosy tér appears workmanlike, its covered produce market a hive of activity. This is perhaps the busiest Óbuda has been since the Romans set up camp nearby 2,000 years ago – they called the site Aquincum, a bastardisation of 'Ak-Ink', the name used by the Celtic tribes who lived here before.

Vasarely Museum.

Don't Miss

1 Vasarely Museum Major overview of the op art master (p72).

2 Római part Lazy riverbank lined with bars and eateries (p70).

3 Aquincum Museum Roman Budapest beautifully displayed (p70).

4 Kassák Museum Discover the work of Hungary's avant-garde literary rebel (p72).

5 Kiscelli Museum Great Magyar modern art in bucolic surroundings (p72).

EXPLORE

FŐ TÉR & AROUND

The heart of Óbuda is the pretty cobbled main square around Zichy Castle, **Fő tér**, built in the 1750s. It's flanked by the transport hub of Szentlélek tér, with its own station on the HÉV suburban train line and a row of bus stops. Árpád Bridge runs alongside, carrying the main trams 1 and 1A (the line is currently being renovated). All is backdropped by grey, Communist-era housing blocks that line the main road to Szentendre.

Around the square, Varósháza (Town Hall) and surrounding buildings have been restored. The castle, set slightly back from the square, is ranged around a pretty, grassy courtyard. In this old aristocratic home, you'll find the modest **Kassák Museum** dedicated to the early 20th-century avant-garde writer and artist Lajos Kassák; the **Óbuda Museum** of local artefacts; the **Térszínház** theatre (388 4310, www.terszinhaz. hu); **Kobuci kert** (06 70 205 7282, www.kobuci. hu), a summer-only live music spot; and, most notably of all, the **Vasarely Museum**, dedicated to the father of op art. In another corner of the square, Imre Varga's playful 1986 statue group *People Waiting* consists of a charming clutch of life-sized bronze figures holding umbrellas.

Across Fő tér stands the **Zsigmond Kun Folk Art Collection** (III.Fő tér 4, 368 1138), a modest display of Hungarian and Moravian ceramics.

ROMAN ÓBUDA

Peaceful surroundings, with an ample supply of water, drew the Romans here around AD 50. By AD 90, there was a garrison of some 6,000 soldiers. This was the north-eastern outpost of Pannonia, a large region that encompassed much of modern-day Croatia, Slovenia and north-east Italy.

By AD 200, Aquincum was a city of some 40,000 inhabitants, with a public baths and two amphitheatres. As well as the main garrison – around today's excellent **Aquincum Museum** – visible pockets of historic Pannonia are dotted all around Óbuda. The **Roman Baths Museum** (Flórián tér 3-5) is a modest but free attraction located in an underpass. A few scattered relics also dot grassy Flórián tér above. Far more impressive, though, are the sections of a former military amphitheatre, found where Pacsirtamező utca meets Nagyszombat utca.

The main site of Aquincum is around the HÉV stop of the same name, either side of main road No.11 towards Szentendre. In the middle of the road, near the junction with Záhony utca, stands what's left of a Roman aqueduct. Set back between the road and the riverbank, the impressive **Aquincum Museum** is essential viewing for anyone interested in Roman Budapest – but it's not the only attraction. Alongside the museum, open to the public for six months of the year from April, the *romkert* ('ruin garden') comprises the remains of the civil community

here. The foundations of a forum, basilica and public baths can all be made out – though the single standing pillar of Jupiter is a copy, the original now in the Aquincum Museum.

BUCOLIC ÓBUDA

For most locals, 'Rómaifürdő' ('Roman Baths') doesn't just mean the stop on the HÉV line one up from Aquincum – it's a family-friendly lido (*see p142*) a short walk away down Rozgonyi Piroska utca. Opposite the campsite of the same name, this is an extensive park with several pools – the only noise you'll hear in this leafy retreat are the shrieks of delight elicited by the long waterslides. From here, it's a short walk down to the **Római part**, the long embankment lined with open-air riverside bars and eateries. Most operate year-round, but in summer there's a real holiday atmosphere of cheap communal entertainment. Local families devour the staple hake (*hekk*) and chips, kids throw stones into the river, and at some point a tune will break out on a Casio keyboard. There's organised recreation too, with teams of rowers making gentle waves on the Danube.

There's more discerning music at the **Fellini Római Kultúrbisztró**, a bar-cum-faux-gypsy caravan set up near where Losonc utca meets the riverbank. Sitting by the makeshift stage, you should be able to make out Megyeri Bridge at Budapest's city limits. In the opposite direction, less than a kilometre south, lies Óbuda Island. Generally empty most of the year, it packs out for a week in August when the southern tip, known as Hajógyári Sziget (Boat Factory Island), hosts the vast **Sziget festival** (www.szigetfestival.com). Separated from the mainland by a footbridge, a short walk from the Filatorigát HÉV stop, this stretch is dotted with old factories and boatyards, colonised by nightlife venues and movie studios.

Szentlélek tér HÉV stop and Óbuda's main square are close to here. Lining the south side of expansive, leafy Flórián tér, Kiscelli utca runs to the museum of the same name. Set in a former monastic complex, the **Kiscelli Museum** is one of Óbuda's most attractive and eclectic finds, displaying a century of Hungarian art and all kinds of historic curiosities.

Sights & Museums

★ Aquincum Museum

III.Szentendrei út 135 (250 1650, www.aquincum. hu). HÉV Aquincum. **Open** *Museum* Mid-end Apr & Oct 10am-5pm Tue-Sun. May-Sept 10am-6pm Tue-Sun. Nov-mid Apr 10am-4pm Tue-Sun. *Ruins* Mid-end Apr & Oct 9am-5pm Tue-Sun. May-Sept 9am-6pm Tue-Sun. **Admission** *Museum* Apr-Oct Ft1,600; Ft1,000 reductions. Nov-Mar Ft1,000; Ft800 reductions. *Ruins* Ft1,000; Ft500 reductions. **No credit cards.** **Map** p71 C2 ❶
See p73 **Hadrian's Hall.**

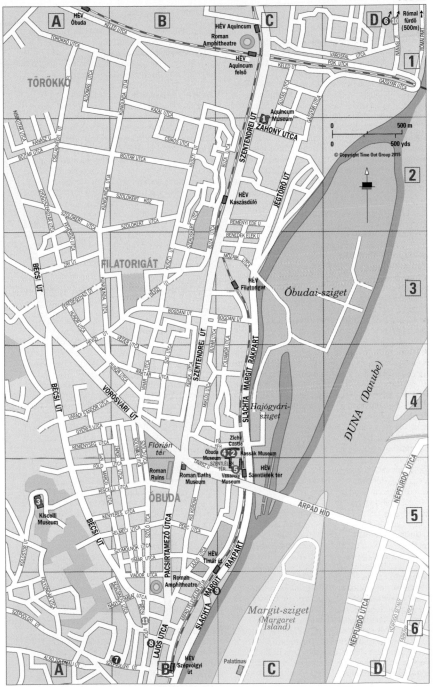

EXPLORE

EXPLORE

Kassák Museum

III.Fő tér 1 (368 7021, www.kassakmuzeum.hu).
HÉV Szentlélek tér, or tram 1, 1A. **Open** 10am-5pm
Wed-Sun. **Admission** Ft600; Ft300 reductions.
No credit cards. Map p71 C4 **❷**
The Kassák Museum covers the life and works
of the self-taught 20th-century poet, painter and
writer, who was involved in the fields of Futurism,
expressionism and Dadaism. A contributor to influential literary magazine *Nyugat* between the wars,
staunch socialist Kassák was briefly ostracised
from the cultural organs of Communist Hungary
before chairing the Writers' Association. Óbuda
was his last residence; he died in 1967. The Petőfi
Literary Museum (*see p81*) holds some 4,000 of
Kassák's books and periodicals, 1,700 works of fine
art and 3,000 photographs. What you see on display
here is only a small selection, but it should provide a
fair picture of the man considered to be the father of
Hungarian literary avant-garde.

★ Kiscelli Museum

III.Kiscelli utca 108 (388 7817, www.btmfk.iif.hu).
Tram 17, or bus 165. **Open** 10am-6pm Tue-Sun.
Admission Ft1,000; Ft500 reductions. *Temporary*
exhibitions Ft1,400; Ft700 reductions. **No credit**
cards. Map p71 A5 **❸**
This museum complex houses an important collection of Hungarian art from about 1880 to 1990.
The works displayed include fin-de-siècle masters
and paintings influenced by the Impressionists,
Pre-Raphaelites, cubists and surrealists. Among
them are Rippl-Rónai's *My Parents After 40 Years*
of Marriage, János Kmetty's cubist *City Park*, and
works by Alajos Strobl, Károly Ferenczy and Margit
Anna. Officially a branch of the Hungarian History
Museum, the Kiscelli has winding corridors filled
with cultural oddities that include a spooky sculpture
hall, a collection of dusty old printing presses, and
a complete antique pharmacy shipped here intact.
Look out, too, for the wonderful old shop signage. The
most atmospheric part of the complex is the ruined
church, its bare brick walls left intact after Allied
bombing and since transformed into the dim, ghostly
Municipal Picture Gallery. These days, it's used to
stage operas, fashion shows and other performances.

Óbuda Museum

III.Fő tér 1 (250 1020, www.obudaimuzeum.hu).
HÉV Szentlélek tér, or tram 1, 1A. **Open** 10am-6pm
Tue-Sun. **Admission** Ft800; Ft400 reductions.
No credit cards. Map p71 C4 **❹**
The history of Óbuda is told here in three clear divisions: medieval; from agriculture to industry; and
the modern age. Newsreel films of the time show
how Óbuda was transformed from village-like backwater to brave new world of communal housing
blocks and busy main roads. Household items from
the Flórián department store, the first in Budapest,
are also on display. The permanent collection consists of some 16,000 items.

► *The Óbuda Museum also oversees the Goldberger*
Textile Factory Collection (III.Lajos utca 136-138,
250 1020, www.textilmuzeum.hu), a new permanent
exhibition of looms, sewing machines and patterned
materials from the late 18th century onwards.

Vasarely Museum

III.Szentlélek tér 6 (388 7551, www.vasarely.hu).
HÉV Szentlélek tér, or tram 1, 1A. **Open** 10am-
5.30pm Tue-Sun. **Admission** Ft800; Ft400
reductions. **No credit cards. Map** p71 C5 **❺**
Viktor Vasarely is the Pécs-born modern artist
credited with starting the op-art movement in the
1960s. Vasarely's patterns create optical illusions
and 3D figures, some of which you've probably seen
before, even if you didn't know the name. This collection, held in the two-storey wing of the old aristocratic home of the Zichy family, contains some 400
of Vasarely's works. The exhibition starts with a
self-portrait and striking examples from the start of
his career – working in advertising design in France.

Restaurants

Csónakház Mulató

III.Római part 30 (06 70 380 5571, www.
csonakhaz.hu). Bus 34, or HÉV Római fürdő.
Open 4pm-11pm daily. **Main courses** Ft1,490-
Ft2,590. **Map** p71 D1 **❻ Fish/Hungarian**
The 'Boathouse Nightspot' on the Római embankment was built in 1920 – as a boathouse. Converted
into a restaurant, it now offers a simple menu of fish
and grilled meats. Just as you're getting used to the
Danube view, the likes of pike-perch, salmon or pork
chop arrive neatly presented with jasmine rice, spicy
potatoes or grilled vegetables. The choice doesn't
break any culinary boundaries – but that's not why
you're here. For a first date, anniversary, or work
get-togethers, the evening-only Boathouse is an ideal
choice, and one that won't break the bank.

Oceans 21

III.Szépvölgyi út 21 (06 30 940 3335, www.oceans
21.hu). Tram 17, or bus 29, 65. **Open** 11am-
11pm Mon-Thur; 11am-midnight Fri-Sun. **Main**
courses Ft2,000-Ft8,000. **Map** p71 B6 **❼ Fish**
With a giant shark sticking out from its entrance,
it's hard to miss this Hungarian-Italian seafood restaurant. So far, so tacky – and an interior done out
like an aquarium doesn't help either. But Alessandro
Manfredini and team cook up a storm, with dishes
such as mixed fish grill and vegetables, or a choice of
pasta options. Alternatively, have a gander at what's
on ice in the large display cabinet, all delivered from
north-east Italy. There's a huge wine list too.

Régi Sipos Halászkert

III.Lajos utca 46 (247 6392, www.regisipos.hu).
Tram 17, or bus 86. **Open** noon-10pm Mon-Thur,
Sun; noon-11pm Fri; noon-midnight Sat. **Main**
courses Ft1,190-Ft4,590. **Map** p71 B6 **❽ Fish**

This is one of Budapest's most venerable fish restaurants, with a pleasant back courtyard and old-school service. There are house soups of catfish, carp and carp innards, and the Sipos fish platter for two (Ft5,800) would sink a battleship.

Rozmaring Kertvendéglő

III.Árpád fejedelem útja 125 (367 1301, www. rozmaringkertvendeglo.hu). HÉV Tímár utca. **Open** noon-11pm Mon-Thur; noon-midnight Fri, Sat; noon-9pm Sun. **Main courses** Ft2,000-Ft8,000. **Map** p71 B6 **⑨ Fish**
With window tables overlooking Margaret Island, this is a great spot for a romantic dinner. Fish options include catfish fillet in breadcrumbs, plus trout, pike-perch or carp. There's plenty of meat on the menu too: crispy goose leg, Mangalica pork loin and grilled goose liver. Portions are predictably huge, the service as old-school as the surroundings.

Cafés & Bars

★ Fellini Római Kultúrbisztró

III.Kossuth Lajos udülőpart 5 (no phone, www. felliniromai.hu). Bus 34, or HÉV Római fürdő.
Open 2-11pm Tue-Fri; 10am-midnight Sat, Sun. **No credit cards. Map** p71 D1 **⑩**
From the Római fürdő HÉV stop, head down Emőd utca, then take Losonc utca to the river, where the lights and low-key communal hubbub draw you to a gypsy caravan: the Fellini Római Kultúrbisztró. But this incongruously bohemian spot is best accessed by bike, as the row of cycles testifies. The bar operates right on the riverbank, with deckchairs and small tables. A folk singer and/or violinist might offer convivial sounds from the modest stage, while the laid-back, thirtysomething clientele take in the watery view. Take mosquito spray.

Puskás Pancho Sport Pub

III.Bécsi út 56 (333 5656, www.symbolbudapest.hu/ Puskas). Tram 17, or bus 86. **Open** 7.30am-midnight Mon-Fri; 11.30am-midnight Sat, Sun. **Map** p71 B6 **⑪**
Themed after the famous footballer who gained the nickname 'Pancho' while playing in Spain, the PPSP is a simple but attractive sports bar. Note the signed copy of *Népsport* the day after Hungary's 6-3 victory over the English at Wembley. Hungarian and Spanish dishes complement beers and TV football on several screens, including one on the summer terrace.

HADRIAN'S HALL

Roman treasures in a whole new light.

Little was known of Roman Budapest until archaeologists dug up remains at the end of the 19th century. What can be seen today is mainly found at the **Aquincum Museum** (*see p70*). The renovated home for Budapest's Roman treasures allows the visitor to see them as they were laid out 2,000 years ago.

Legionnaire base and later capital of Lower Pannonia from AD 106, Aquincum was home to 40,000 citizens, the Proconsul's Palace – and, from 1894, one of the city's oldest and most overlooked museums. Today, having moved from cramped surroundings to the adjoining former electrical works, the two-storey Aquincum Museum allows the ancient artefacts plenty of space. The well-lit main hall shows painstakingly restored mosaics, frescoes, coins and statuary to the paying public for the first time. One end contains an illustration of the Proconsul's Palace, showing where these elements would have fitted.

At the back stands the sarcophagus of Aquincum resident Aelia Sabina ('remarkable organist'), whose inscription relates to the other great treasure on display. Now in its own space, the third-century Roman organ was found here in 400 pieces and later reconstructed. Thought in some quarters to have been powered by water, the organ was big news when it was discovered 75 years ago. Historians still hold open debates about it – another of the museum's public functions.

Downstairs, two spaces house the rest of the permanent collection. First is a room of local finds from the Neolithic and Bronze Ages, through to the Celts, the Romans and, lastly, the Avars. Highlights include a legionnaire's helmet and Celtic jewellery. Documentation, as upstairs, is given in English. An adjoining room features a huge panoramic colour photograph of today's Budapest, sliced into five panels, with names and arrows showing who lived where 2,000 years ago.

EXPLORE

Belváros

Belváros is the centre of town. Making up the lower half of central District V, it nestles snugly inside the Kiskörút, the little ring road that follows the line of Pest's former medieval walls. The shortest of the city's three concentric rings, the Kiskörút runs from Szabadság Bridge to the transport hub of Deák tér, a walkable journey of four tram stops. On one side of the Kiskörút are the edges of Districts VII, VIII and IX that fan out south and east from here – on the other lies Belváros, tucked in by the Danube.

Stroll along the busy shop-lined streets on and off focal Váci utca, without crossing over (or, rather, under) busy Szabad Sajtó út, to get an authentic feel of pre 20th-century Pest. Dotted with churches, seats of learning and obscure museums, it strikes a contrast with today's somewhat featureless Vörösmarty tér and Korzó, the main square and riverside embankment adjoining and closely parallel to Váci utca.

EXPLORE

Sziget Eye.

Don't Miss

1 Sziget Eye Check out Budapest from on high (p76).

2 Onyx Michelin-starred restaurant right on the main square (p78).

3 Petőfi Literary Museum The life and as yet unsolved death of Hungary's national poet (p81).

4 WonderLab Discover Budapest's top young designers in person (p85).

5 Gerlóczy Kávéház Prime café terrace for writing your novel (p82).

Pesti Vigadó.

VÖRÖSMARTY TÉR & AROUND

At the centre of Belváros – the centre of Budapest, in fact – is Vörösmarty tér. This pedestrianised square, at the terminus of the M1 metro line and a five-minute walk from the riverfront, has as its centrepiece a statue of patriotic poet and Shakespeare scholar Mihály Vörösmarty. Now ringed on three sides by showy but uninteresting stores and restaurants, including a branch of the Hard Rock Café, the square is redeemed by the grand **Gerbeaud** coffeehouse. A temple to the art of gooey cakes, the café's apron of terrace tables oozes continental class. Upstairs, the Michelin-starred **Onyx** restaurant overlooks part of the square and the Danube beyond. During December, the entire Gerbeaud façade becomes one enormous advent calendar and Budapest's main Christmas market fills the square.

For the rest of the year, portrait painters and lace pedlars hustle for business, their easels and stalls stretching into adjoining, pedestrianised Váci utca, traditionally the city's showcase commercial drag. This is strictly tourist central and every other store seems to be selling tack. As a counterbalance, Stylewalker was created to revive the artisanal traditions of the historic centre. Held every few months, Stylewalker is an open-door night for boutiques and workshops, when shoppers can stroll around, meet designers and see them in action.

Running along the south of the square, Deák Ferenc utca – 'Fashion Street' – sports high-end international chains, a couple of Hungarian-run boutiques and two five-star hotels. These hotels, the **Kempinski** and **Le Méridien** (for both, *see p212*), have front entrances overlooking Erzsébet tér. Once the site of the city's main smog-clogged bus station, the square has been revamped and relandscaped. International bus services have moved out to Népliget, while the station building

itself has become Design Terminal; so far there's just a restaurant, **Terminal**, but there are plans to harbour the creative industries. The welcome greenery alongside is the domain of skateboaders and, for the summer months, the **Sziget Eye** panoramic big wheel.

The other side of the square, half-filled by an attractive water feature surrounded by decking, contains the below-ground **Akvárium Klub** (*see p160*), a music venue and terrace bar/restaurant.

On the other side of Vörösmarty tér, parallel to Váci utca, the riverside promenade called the Korzó is almost as busy with pedestrians as Váci. Architecturally uninspiring, thanks to the international chain hotels lining the riverbank, the Korzó has sprouted several terrace cafés, all with the stunning backdrop of the Danube – and with equally startling prices.

At nearby Vigadó tér, the bustle usually includes zither-playing buskers, stalls selling folkloric souvenirs and the **Pesti Vigadó** concert hall (*see p168*). Across the other side of the tram tracks stands the Mahart terminal, offering sightseeing tours around Pest, as well as boats to Szentendre, then up the Danube Bend to Visegrád and Esztergom.

Sights & Museums

★ Sziget Eye

V.Erzsébet tér (no phone, www.sziget.hu). M1, M2, M3 Deák tér. **Open** *Late May-early Jan* 1-10pm Mon; 10am-10pm Tue-Thur, Sun; 10am-midnight Fri, Sat. Closed early Jan-late May. **Admission** Ft2,400; Ft1,500 reductions. **No credit cards. Map** p77 B2 ❶

Originally set up for the week-long Sziget Festival in August, in 2014 the Sziget Eye ran from late spring until after the New Year celebrations in 2015. Modelled on the London attraction that gave it its English name, the Sziget Eye stands 65m (215ft) tall and allows its 300-plus passengers a ten- to 15-minute

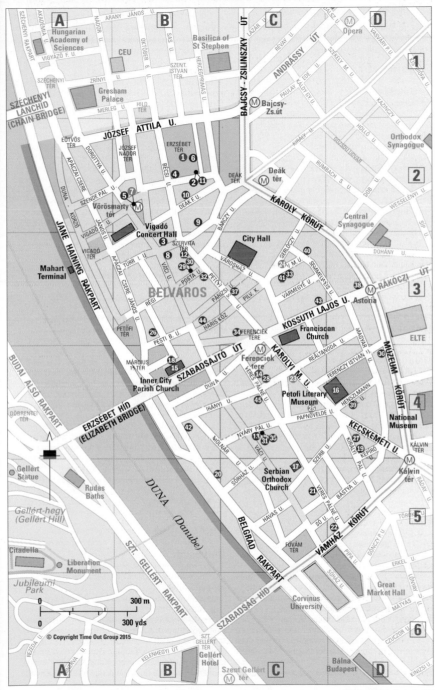

EXPLORE

gawp at Budapest. For the sum of Ft30,000, four of you can hire a VIP cabin, with champagne, for a 30-minute circuit in style.

Restaurants

Le Bourbon
Le Méridien Budapest, V.Erzsébet tér 9-10 (429 5770, www.lebourbonrestaurant.com). M1, M2, M3 Deák tér. **Open** noon-10.30pm daily. **Main courses** Ft2,400-Ft9,800. **Map** p77 B2 ❷ **Hungarian/international**
Enjoy Magyar and international cuisine in the bright, expansive, colonial-style dining room of Le Méridien Budapest. Executive chef Zsolt Endrédi oversees a seasonally changing menu that always lists local classics such as goulash, stuffed cabbage and Hungarian pancakes alongside international standards such as steaks, pasta and upmarket burgers. Barbary duck breast with an array of trimmings is typical of more complex dishes. By Budapest standards, it doesn't come cheap, though there's a two-course lunch deal (Ft2,900, served Monday to Saturday). The Sunday brunch here is renowned, as are the desserts, notably the Ocoa Royal chocolate cake and eight types of éclair. Service is as you'd expect at a five-star hotel.

Cyrano
V.Kristóf tér 7 (266 4747, www.cyrano.hu). M1, M2, M3 Deák tér. **Open** 8am-midnight daily. **Main courses** Ft4,490-Ft6,800. **Map** p77 B3 ❸ **Hungarian/international**
A good choice in tourist central – Cyrano and its two shaded terraces are just off Váci utca. The menu ranges far and wide: snails provençal still feature as a popular starter, but these days you'll also find the likes of Pacific-style Australian rack of lamb and Spanish red mullet among the global mains. There are Hungarian classics, too, such as gypsy-style paprika potatoes and goulash. Prices, considering the prime location, are more than fair and the service is refreshingly human in a part of town where few customers are regulars.

Nobu
Kempinski Hotel Corvinus, V.Erzsébet tér 7-8 (429 4242, www.noburestaurants.com). M1, M2, M3 Deák tér. **Open** noon-3.30pm, 6-11.45pm daily. **Main courses** Ft5,600-Ft12,100. **Map** p77 B2 ❹ **Japanese/Peruvian**
Co-founder Robert De Niro came to town in 2010 for the opening of this branch of the upscale sushi restaurant. Tables were booked for months, and reservations are still recommended, though it's almost as much fun to find a spot in the 56-seat lounge bar and select from the smaller menu. In the main dining room, diners with deep pockets look no further than Alaskan black cod with miso or wagyu rib-eye steak with Japanese mushrooms. Sushi and sashimi come in snow crab, freshwater eel and Japanese snapper

varieties and, given the quality of what's on offer, the Ft5,000 weekday business lunch of miso soup, sushi and a scoop of ice-cream is worth a try.

★ Onyx
V.Vörösmarty tér 7-8 (06 30 508 0622, www.onyx restaurant.hu). M1 Vörösmarty tér, or tram 2. **Open** noon-2.30pm, 6.30-11pm Tue-Fri; 6.30-11pm Sat. **Main courses** Ft8,500-Ft12,500. **Map** p77 B2 ❺ **Hungarian**
Budapest's second restaurant to gain a Michelin star, Onyx is a lavish, marble-clad dining room above the famous Gerbeaud coffeehouse (*see below*) on the city's showroom square. If you're in town for one night only, this might be the place to sample. It certainly couldn't be more central – or more cleverly conceived. Executive chef Szabina Szulló and sous chef Tamás Széll artfully reinvent Hungarian classics in nouvelle cuisine-sized portions while striking a perfect balance of flavours. Look out for the weekly-changing lunch menus – three courses for under Ft8,000. Service is formal and attentive.

Terminal Restaurant & Bar
V.Erzsébet tér 11 (06 30 419 5040, www. terminalrestaurant.hu). M1, M2, M3 Deák tér. **Open** 11am-midnight Mon-Wed, Sun; 11am-3am Thur-Sat. **Main courses** Ft2,790-Ft7,490. **Map** p77 B2 ❻ **Hungarian/international**
The prime minister's daughter is one of the owners of this well-run restaurant and bar. It's on the ground floor of a beautifully restored Bauhaus building, previously the city-centre bus terminal. The stylish lettering etched on to the full-length windows lends an air of glamour. A modern bistro-style menu runs from simple but tasty risotto and pasta dishes through to steaks and saddle of venison. The lunch menu (Ft1,990 for two dishes, Ft2,490 for three) changes weekly; gluten-free and vegetarian diners are catered for. Staff are young and courteous. As it's in a small park, the terrace is lovely, but be sure to have a look at the stunning interior.
▶ *In summer, adjoining Fröccsterasz (V.Erzsébet tér 13, 06 30 651 3170) comes into its own – it also opens for the evenings on winter weekends. Spritzers, cocktails and mixed drinks are the order of the day.*

Cafés & Bars

Gerbeaud
V.Vörösmarty tér 7-8 (429 9000, www.gerbeaud. hu). M1 Vörösmarty tér. **Open** 9am-9pm daily. **Map** p77 B2 ❼
This elegant institution was founded in 1870 and still radiates fin-de-siècle opulence. As soon as the weather is anywhere near clement, Gerbeaud fills a big chunk of the square with umbrella-shaded tables. December is another wonderful time to visit, when the whole façade is transformed into a giant advent calendar, overlooking the city's main Christmas market. Prices, aimed at tourist pockets,

are higher than elsewhere, but the cakes are of superior pedigree – founder Émil Gerbeaud invented the cherry cognac one here.

▶ *If you're after something more substantial than sticky cake, then upstairs restaurant Onyx (see p78) provides fine dining, Magyar-style.*

Shops & Services

Hampel Katalin
V. Váci utca 8 (318 9741, www.hampelkati.com). M1 Vörösmarty tér, or tram 2. **Open** 10am-6pm Mon-Fri; 10am-1pm Sat. **Map** p77 B3 ❽ **Fashion**
Katalin Hampel adapts historical Hungarian wear to today's standards and comfort.

Heaven Store
V. Fehérhajó utca 12-14 (266 3336, www. heavenstore.hu). M1, M2, M3 Deák tér. **Open** 10am-8pm Mon-Fri; 10am-6pm Sat. **Map** p77 B2 ❾ **Fashion**
Stella McCartney, Balenciaga, Marc Jacobs – all the big-hitters are stocked here, not five minutes' walk from Deak tér. You'll find womenswear, menswear and a whole bunch of accessories.

★ Nanushka
V. Deák Ferenc utca 17 (202 1050, www.nanushka. hu). M1, M2, M3 Deák tér. **Open** 10am-8pm Mon-Sat; 10am-6pm Sun. **Map** p77 B2 ❿ **Fashion**

Gerbeaud.

The queen of comfortable, cool cotton since 2005, Szandra Sándor sells worldwide, but this prime location is a showcase for her womenswear.

Le Parfum Croisette
V. Deák Ferenc utca 16-18 (06 30 405 0668, www.leparfum.hu). M1, M2, M3 Deák tér. **Open** 10am-7pm Mon-Fri; 10am-5pm Sat, Sun. **Map** p77 B2 ⓫ **Accessories**
Hungary's only *parfumier*, Zsolt Zólyomi, stocks niche fragrances and creates personalised perfumes.

Rózsavölgyi Zeneműbolt
V. Szervita tér 5 (318 3500, www.rozsavolgyi.hu). M1, M2, M3 Deák tér. **Open** 10am-7pm Mon-Fri; 10am-5pm Sat. **Map** p77 B3 ⓬ **Books & music**
An institution in the heart of town, with a fine selection of classical, ballet and opera recordings, as well as sheet music. There's folk and pop downstairs, and a café upstairs.

Valéria Fazekas
V. Váci utca 50 (337 5320, www.valeriafazekas. com). M3 Ferenciek tere. **Open** 10am-6pm Mon-Fri; 10am-4pm Sat. **Map** p77 C4 ⓭ **Accessories**
Hats of avant-garde style, in shapes and fabrics that stretch the imagination.

HISTORIC BELVÁROS

The Korzó ends where Petőfi tér, with its statue of Hungary's national poet, converges with Március 15 tér, with its stubby Roman ruins, in the shadow of the Elizabeth Bridge. The sunken remains of Emperor Diocletian's outpost, Contra Aquincum, are complemented by an accompanying display.

This quieter part of the Pest embankment has been renamed Jane Haining rakpart, after the Scottish missionary who was sent to Auschwitz from Budapest in 1944 (*see p80* **In the Know**). Overlooking this pleasant green space, the **Inner City Parish Church** is Pest's oldest building. Alongside stands one of two facing fin-de-siècle confections – the twin Klotild Palaces were built by Kálmán Giergl and Flóris Korb, both understudies of the great Alajos Hauszmann. Mirror-symmetrical, they provided the perfect frame for the original Elizabeth Bridge – and the perfect surroundings for the Belvárosi coffeehouse that once stood in the southern palace, where writer Gyula Krúdy was a regular.

Vacant for many years, the palace has recently been taken over by the five-star **Buddha-Bar Hotel** (*see p212*). On this same elegant stretch, Henrik Schmahl's elaborate Párizsi udvar was completed in 1913. The **Parisian Arcade** began life as the Inner City Savings Bank: bees (symbols of thrift) can be found throughout, a theme continued in the detail of the interior, and in Miksa Róth's arched glass ceiling. Neglected after 1989, in 2014 it was taken over by the same

EXPLORE

Mellow Mood Group behind the Buddha-Bar Hotel. In February 2015, they announced plans for a five-star hotel on this site as well, with a completion date in early 2017.

Szabad Sajtó út, the main road that serves Elizabeth Bridge, does more than just cut Váci utca in two. It creates two distinct halves of Belváros: one shiny and bustling, the other shabbier and more sedate. Váci utca itself feels more like a market than a high street, with antiques shops, terrace cafés and the odd church. Just behind is the real heart of historic Pest, the various branches of the Eötvös Loránd University (ELTE), founded in 1635, and scattered erudite and ecclesiastical attractions.

Tucked behind Váci utca, the **Serbian Orthodox Church** dates back to the 1730s – though local Serbs originally built a church here in the 1690s, immediately after the Turkish withdrawal from Buda. Attached to the main Petőfi Literary Museum in the nearby Károlyi Palace, the **Endre Ady Memorial Museum** on Veres Pálné utca is set in the last residence of Hungary's most noted poet of the early 20th century. Belonging to the same aristocratic family who owned the Károlyi Palace, Károlyi kert alongside is a pretty pocket park. The summer-only **Csendes Társ** wine bar (V.Magyar utca 18, www.kiscsendes.hu) provides alfresco tables around the northern gate. Partner bar **Csendes** (*see p153*), round the corner, is a key city hangout day and night, with DJs and live acts after dark.

Sights & Museums

Endre Ady Memorial Museum
V.Veres Pálné utca 4-6 (337 8563, www.pim.hu). M3 Ferenciek tere, or bus 5, 7, 8, 15. **Open**

10am-5pm Wed-Sun. **Admission** Ft500; Ft250 reductions. **No credit cards**. **Map** p77 C4 ㉔
Many walk past this modest but worthwhile attraction without even knowing it's there. Signified by his bust outside, the Endre Ady Memorial Museum is set in the poet's final residence. Inside are books, letters, photographs – and the deathbed where the writer suffered his last from the syphilis that was ravaging his body. The balcony is almost equally poignant – you can well imagine Ady shuffling out here to take his last look at Budapest in the chaos at the disastrous end of World War I. He died in January 1919.

Inner City Parish Church
Belvárosi Plébániatemplom
V.Március 15 tér 2 (318 3108, www.belvarosi plebania.hu). M3 Ferenciek tere, or tram 2, or bus 7, 15. **Open** from Jan 2016; call for details. **Map** p77 B4 ㉕

Károlyi kert.

Founded in 1046 on the burial site of the martyred St Gellért, this is Pest's oldest building, though little of its original structure remains. It's an extraordinary mixture of styles – Gothic, Islamic, Baroque and neo-classical – testifying to the city's turbulent history. The beauty of its interior is in the light and shadow of the Gothic vaulting, and most of the older detail is in the sanctuary, around the altar. Behind the high altar you'll find Gothic sedilia and a Turkish prayer alcove, still surprisingly intact from when the church was used as a mosque. At the time of writing the church is closed, but should reopen in January 2016.

Petőfi Literary Museum

Petőfi Irodalmi Múzeum
V.Károlyi Mihály utca 16 (317 3611, www.pim.hu).
M3 Ferenciek tere, or bus 5, 7, 8, 15. **Open** 10am-6pm Tue-Sun. **Admission** Ft600; Ft300 reductions. *Temporary exhibitions* Ft800; Ft400 reductions. **No credit cards. Map** p77 D4 ⑯
Set in the Károlyi Palace, this underrated attraction is dedicated to the life and works of Hungary's national poet, Sándor Petőfi, with further displays linked to other giants of Magyar literature. Three rooms, each with a timeline in English and Hungarian, chart the poet's progress from rural childhood to doomed hero of the War of Independence. Between, Petőfi became the first Hungarian poet to make his living by the pen and kick-started the 1848 uprising against the Habsburgs. Here, you'll find his last portrait and the chair on which he sat to pose for it, translations of his most poignant works, and documentation of his disappearance during a military retreat.

FREE Serbian Orthodox Church

Szerb templom
V.Szerb utca 4 (no phone, www.hramsvgeorgija budimpesta.rs). M3, M4 Kálvin tér, or bus 15. **Open** 9am-6pm Mon-Fri. *Mass* 8am Mon-Fri; 10pm Sun. **Admission** free. **Map** p77 C5 ⑰
The pretty Serbian Orthodox Church is enclosed in a garden courtyard that features old Orthodox gravestones embedded in the wall. A Serbian plaque in Cyrillic, with a pointing finger, shows the height of 1838 floodwaters. Originally constructed in the 1690s by Serbs after the defeat of Turkish forces here in Budapest, it was remodelled to its present state in the 1730s. The church remains a hub for the local Serb community. Inside the tall, narrow structure hides a treasure: a towering neo-Renaissance iconostasis at the altar, covered in a gallery of oil portraits, depicting major Orthodox saints.

Restaurants

Bábel Budapest Étterem

V.Piarista köz 2 (06 70 600 0800, www.babel-budapest.hu). M3 Ferenciek tere, or tram 2, or bus 5, 7, 8. **Open** 6pm-midnight Tue-Sat. **Main courses** Ft5,500-Ft8,900. **Map** p77 B4 ⑱ **Austro-Hungarian**

Inner City Parish Church.

Better than ever after moving to this new location in June 2014, the Bábel now focuses on inspired fine dining. Still heading the kitchen after a sojourn in Austria, György Lőrincz describes the menu as Austro-Hungarian – though the bulk of the ingredients are sourced locally. As well as a concise à la carte menu, with its stand-out scallops, crispy pork ear and potato gratin main, there are tasting menus (Ft23,000-Ft35,000). The mainly Hungarian wine selection runs to well over 100 bottles; sommelier Péter Blazsovszky will guide you through the maze. A neat, bare-brick decor leaves the focus on the food.
▶ *Next door to Bábel, Kiosk (V.Március 15 tér 4, 06 70 311 1969, www.kiosk-budapest.hu) is a lively, post-work bar/restaurant; the riverside location is matched by the quality (and range) of its burgers.*

Borssó

V.Királyi Pál utca 14 (785 9182, www.borsso.hu). M3, M4 Kálvin tér. **Open** 6-11pm Tue; noon-3pm, 6-11pm Wed-Sun. **Main courses** Ft2,900-Ft6,700. **Map** p77 D4 ⑲ **French/Hungarian**
This charming spot in the historic heart of Pest seamlessly combines French bistro cuisine with modern reworkings of Hungarian classics. Chef Norbert Kovács can whip up a lobster ravioli with garlic spinach starter as adeptly as he can prepare a main of rib-eye steak with fragrant chanterelle mushrooms and duck liver. Borssó also specialises in wine-tasting dinners (around Ft10,000 a head). The wines are mainly Hungarian, headed by the house Borssó Cuvée in both colours.

★ Gepárd és Űrhajó

V.Belgrád rakpart 18 (06 70 329 7815, www. gepardesurhajo.com). Tram 2. **Open** noon-midnight daily. **Main courses** Ft2,250-Ft4,950. **Map** p77 B5 ⑳ **Hungarian**

'Cheetah & Spaceship' is a funky wine bistro on the Pest embankment. The name and, in fact, the wines, come from renowned producer János Bolyki, also known for his imaginative labels. Chef Attila Mógor is another reason to take this establishment seriously: his pedigree includes Csalogány 26. Whether substantial, as in the venison goulash with red wine and potato cake, or light, as in the Dorozsmai-style catfish, Mógor and his team deliver the goods. Prices are very reasonable, not least the two-course weekday lunches at under Ft1,000 – with a Danube view thrown in.

► *János Bolyki also has a downtown wine store, Borszertár (V.Irányi utca 12, 06 70 381 8666, open 1-7pm Mon-Fri, noon-3pm Sat).*

Halkakas Halbisztró

V.Veres Pálné utca 33 (06 30 226 0638, www. halkakas.hu). M3, M4 Kálvin tér, or M4 Fővám tér. **Open** noon-10pm Mon-Sat. **Main courses** Ft1,300-Ft1,950. **Map** p77 C5 ㉑ **Fish**
This bright, cheery space run by a creative young crew makes the most out of indigenous freshwater fish. They come straight from an artificial lake in a remote spot between Balaton and the Danube – Rétimajor, where there's a fish farm run by the father of owner Zsuzsanna Lévai. The carp tastes cleaner than most, and the catfish has a juicy, heavy but flavourful meat. Chef Krisztina Kóbor uses catfish in her signature fish and chips, and it also shows up in the house kebab: chunks of it, strongly seasoned, then grilled. A variety of accompanying sauces – rémoulade, tsatsiki, and parsley and beetroot – help things along nicely.

Pampas Argentin Steakhouse

V.Vámház körút 6 (411 1750, www.steak.hu). M3, M4 Kálvin tér, or tram 47, 49. **Open** noon-midnight daily. **Main courses** Ft2,790-Ft19,800. **Map** p77 D5 ㉒ **Argentinian**
With only a handful of dedicated steakhouses in town, this one, serving aged Argentinian Angus, is arguably the best. Wagyu, USDA and Kobe beef now also feature – you can sample a wagyu burger without breaking the bank – as well as New Zealand deer and lamb. Top-quality cuts of meat are prepared by a kitchen that understands 'rare' means red. There's a real Spanish touch to the starters these days too, with Iberian hams and cheese platters.

Cafés & Bars

Centrál Kávéház

V.Károlyi Mihály utca 9 (266 2110, www.central kavehaz.hu). M3 Ferenciek tere, or bus 15. **Open** 8am-11pm daily. **Map** p77 C4 ㉓
The oldest of the classic coffeehouses, the Centrál opened in 1887, and operated until 1949. During that time, three influential literary periodicals were founded beneath its high ceilings – *A Hét, Nyugat* and *Újhold* – and leading literary names Móricz

Zsigmond, Gyula Krúdy and Frigyes Karinthy all met here, served by legendary waiter Guszti. Inside the historic threshold is a framed acknowledgement to long-term owner Győző Mészáros, who allowed writers leeway on their bar bills. During its 50-year hibernation, the Centrál served as headquarters for Hungary's national paprika industry, a gaming hall and a music club. Acquired by millionaire Dr Imre Somody in 1997, the Centrál got a billion-forint overhaul and reopened in 2000. Faithful to the past in its bottle-green and dark-wood decor, the Centrál also caters to contemporary tastes with breakfasts of smoked salmon and Mangalica ham, Cuban cocktails and the option of decaffeinated coffee. The house coffee comes with apricot brandy.

Gerlóczy Kávéház

V.Gerlóczy utca 1 (501 4000, www.gerloczy.hu). M2 Astoria, or tram 47, 49, or bus 7. **Open** 7am-11pm Mon-Fri; 8am-11pm Sat, Sun. **Map** p77 C3 ㉔
Some of the best breakfasts and lunches in town can be found at this exquisitely restored traditional coffeeshop on a leafy downtown square. More substantial meals are also available – boeuf bourguignon, stuffed cabbage and guinea fowl – but most regulars enjoy a long, late, leisurely breakfast on the terrace overlooking Kamermayer Károly tér. The interior is equally beautiful, its big mirror reflecting the snappy but unhurried bustle of the smart waiters. Some two dozen quality local wines are stocked – a handful are available by the glass – along with a couple of French vintages. This is Budapest at its best, combining the style of the early 1900s with the benefits of 21st-century European integration.

► *Check the 'Rooms de Lux' link on the website for details of 15 boutique rooms upstairs.*

Táskarádió

V.Papnövelde utca 8 (266 0413, www.taska radioeszpresszo.hu). M3, M4 Kálvin tér. **Open** 9am-midnight daily. **No credit cards.** **Map** p77 C4 ㉕
The 'Pocket Transistor' takes retro to the nth degree, dressing staff in Pioneer uniforms (dig those red neckerchiefs!) and lining its shelves with Sputnik-era TVs, toys and prams. The menu is also retro-themed (a Harvey Wallbanger is a Party Secretary, Progress! is spinach purée). This being the student quarter, prices are reasonable. There are so many teas, coffees and hot drinks (note the orange macchiato with Cointreau) that there's even a 'Coffee-Tea Responsible' to oversee them – unless that's another retro touch.

Shops & Services

Anda Emilia

V.Galamb utca 4 (06 30 933 9746, www. andaemi.com). M3 Ferenciek tere, or bus 5, 7. **Open** 11am-6pm Mon-Fri; 11am-2pm Sat. **Map** p77 B3 ㉖ **Fashion**

EXPLORE

Gerlóczy Kávéház.

One of the most revered and inventive couturiers in the industry, Anda designs soft, cerebral and structural women's collections, plus accessories.

★ Balaton Ízlelő
V.Királyi Pál utca 10 (951 5160, www.balaton izlelo.hu). M3, M4 Kálvin tér. **Open** *Summer* 10am-8pm Mon-Fri; 10am-2pm Sat. *Winter* noon-10pm Mon-Fri; 10am-2pm Sat. **Map** p77 D4 ㉗ **Food & drink**
Ham, wine and honey: the tastes and flavours of Lake Balaton have been brought to downtown Budapest by Annamária Kulcsár and her team. It's a great idea, and one brought to life with a real love of the territory. Lakeside producers – beekeepers, brewers, herb growers – are showcased with seasonal promotions.

Black Box Concept Store
V.Irányi utca 18 (06 30 414 8979). M3 Ferenciek tere. **Open** 11am-5pm Mon-Fri; noon-6pm Sat. **Map** p77 C4 ㉘ **Fashion/accessories**
This space showcases the works of key Hungarian designers in regular rotation, such as the stylish bags of Anh Tuan, the leather goods of Agneskovacs and the dark shaded womenswear of Noár Line.

Bomo Art Budapest
V.Régi posta utca 14 (318 7280, www. bomoart.hu). M3 Ferenciek tere. **Open**

10am-6.30pm Mon-Fri; 10am-6pm Sat. **Map** p77 B3 ㉙ **Gifts & souvenirs**
Károly Boldizsár's lovely little business has branched out from postcards and diaries to customised vintage maps and posters from the city's Golden Age, teleidoscopes and kaleidoscopes, CD holders, binders and photo albums. All are beautifully handcrafted, employing age-old book-binding skills, paper scents, and goat- and lamb-skin coverings.

Ékes Kesztyű
V.Régi posta utca 14 (266 0986). M3 Ferenciek tere. **Open** 10am-6pm Mon-Fri; 10am-1pm Sat. **Map** p77 B3 ㉚ **Accessories**
A family-run artisan store, open since 1883, Ékes makes gloves in various leathers, including boarskin, by hand.

Eventuell
V.Nyáry Pál utca 7 (318 6926, www.eventuell.hu). M3 Ferenciek tere. **Open** 11am-6pm Mon-Fri; 10.30am-2pm Sat. **Map** p77 C4 ㉛ **Accessories**
Contemporary Hungarian artisan textiles for the home and person: felt-silk mix stoles, limited-series throw rugs, knitted pillows and jewellery.

Frey Wille
V.Régi posta utca 19 (318 7665, www.frey-wille. com). M1, M2, M3 Deák tér, or M3 Ferenciek tere, or bus 15. **Open** 10am-6pm Mon-Fri; 10am-4pm Sat. **Map** p77 B3 ㉜ **Accessories**
Gustav Klimt and ancient Egypt are the inspirations behind this Austrian collection of fine jewellery and accessories in enamelled gold.
Other locations *VI.Andrássy út 43 (413 0174); Liszt Ferenc Airport, Terminal 2, Sky Court (296 5422).*

Garden Studio
V.Vitkovics Mihály utca 5-7 (06 30 259 3511, www.thegardenstudio.hu). M2 Astoria, or M3 Ferenciek tere. **Open** 10am-7pm Mon-Sat. **Map** p77 C3 ㉝ **Fashion**
Created by fashionista Dóri Tomcsányi and designer Bálint Sikó, this boutique in a quiet street brings to life their popular webstore. Among the clothes and accessories by some ten designers are Tomcsányi's own brightly patterned silk summerwear for women and pendant necklaces. The selection is not limited to Hungarian designers – keep your eyes peeled for the sassy knitted jumpers and beanie hats by Wood Wood from Copenhagen.

Je Suis Belle
V.Ferenciek tere 11, 4th floor (951 1353, www. jesuisbelle.hu). M3 Ferenciek tere. **Open** 2-7pm Thur, Fri. **Map** p77 C3 ㉞ **Fashion**
Consistently inventive, Dalma Dévényi and Tibor Kiss present chic, prêt-à-porter togs for women. Note that the showroom may move given the upcoming structural changes of the Párizsi udvar.

EXPLORE

Kamchatka Design
V.Nyáry Pál utca 7 (266 1720, www.kamchatka design.com). M3 Ferenciek tere, or tram 2. **Open** noon-6pm Mon-Fri; 10am-2pm Sat. **Map** p77 C4 ⑤ **Fashion**
Limited edition, casual womenswear, locally designed and made by Márta Schulteisz, as well as accessories and gorgeous textiles.

Központi Antikvárium
V.Múzeum körút 13-15 (317 3514, www. kozpontiantikvarium.hu). M2 Astoria, or tram 47, 49. **Open** 10am-6pm Mon-Fri; 10am-2pm Sat. **Map** p77 D4 ⑥ **Books & music**
Központi Antikvárium is a spacious collectors' shop, especially good for sourcing maps, engravings and wonderful (but pricey) local publicity posters from either side of World War II. It also carries a decent range of second-hand books in various obscure foreign languages.

▶ *This store, opposite the National Museum, is in a row of half-a-dozen second-hand bookshops, allowing for a fine afternoon's browsing.*

Magma
V.Petőfi Sándor utca 11 (235 0277, www. magma.hu). M3 Ferenciek tere. **Open** 10am-7pm Mon-Fri; 10am-3pm Sat. **Map** p77 C3 ⑦ **Accessories/homewares**
Anikó Vásárhelyi shows and sells local handiwork by a collective of talented artisans. Look out for ceramics, woodwork, silver and plastic jewellery, handmade and embroidered pillows, and funky bags.

Mono
V.Kossuth Lajos utca 20 (06 70 607 4906, www. monofashion.hu). M2 Astoria. **Open** 11am-8pm Mon-Fri; 10am-6pm Sat. **Map** p77 D3 ⑧ **Fashion**
This multi-brand shop stocks small-series creations by harder-to-find Hungarian designers, as well as

PIG IN CLOVER
Hungary can thank Spain for the revival of Mangalica, its ham of quality.

Not that these almost sheep-like pigs know much about it, but the indigenous breed of Mangalica is the great modern-day success story of Hungarian gastronomy.

Dishes featuring the meat appear on the menus of the better restaurants in Budapest – the salami is a particular delicacy and is sold in shops such as **Szalámibolt** (see *p85*). Mangalica pigs produce the meat of the moment. This hairy hog of the Carpathian Basin and the Balkans was crossed with the ethnic Serbian Sumadija in 1833 to produce a popular and easy-to-keep breed that dominated the market for more than a century. From the 1950s onwards, its numbers began to dwindle and the species all but died out in Hungary – in 1991 only an estimated 200 remained.

In spring of that year, Juán Vicente Olmos Llorente of the Spanish company Segovia Hams – having heard of a rare breed of pig that produced high-quality meat – made contact with Hungarian agrarian Péter Tóth. Mangalica pigs were duly bred in Hungary for their meat to be exported to Spain, where a century of experience in curing ham was put to good use. Mangalica sales took off, and

the demand saw a revival back in the homeland. Budapest's annual **Mangalica Festival** (www.mangalicafesztival.hu) provided the small number of producers with a showcase for their top-quality commodity, and it slowly began to feature on menus at high-end restaurants in Budapest.

Shopping for Mangalica was a different matter. Butchers, if they stocked it at all, would barely promote it, and consumers tended to stick to what they knew. One of the men behind the Mangalica Festival, Attila Végh opened his own outlet, one where you could both buy the meat and enjoy it in sandwiches, grilled dishes and cold platters: the **Húspatika** in south Buda. Since then, the business has moved to District VII, where it operates as a grill van in Budapest's bar vortex (VII.Kazinczy utca 18; open 11.30am-10pm Mon, Tue, Sun, 11.30am-11pm Wed, 11.30am-midnight Thur-Sat).

The festival has also moved, to prestigious Szabadság tér in downtown District V; it's a free event staged every February (see *p33*). In fact, there are Mangalica festivals across Hungary, in Debrecen, Székesfehérvár and Szeged. The mighty Mangalica has never had it so good... or so bad.

carrying its own line, NUBU, for women, men and kids. There's a featured designer every month, and a sassy shop window.

Pazicski
V. Henszlmann Imre utca 3 (411 0631, www. pazicski.hu). M3 Ferenciek tere, or M3, M4 Kálvin tér, or bus 15. **Open** 10am-6pm Tue-Fri; 10am-5pm Sat. **Map** p77 D4 ❸ **Fashion**
Stunning womenswear from the hands of Miklós Pazicski, in a perfect fusion of architectural structure and fluid femininity. Hungary's own Réka Vágó created the shoes that also grace the shelves.

Rododendron Art & Design
V. Semmelweis utca 19 (06 70 419 5329, www. rododendronart.com). M2 Astoria, or bus 7, or tram 47, 49. **Open** 10am-7pm Mon-Fri; 10am-5pm Sat; 11am-3pm Sun. **Map** p77 C3 ❹ **Gifts & souvenirs/accessories**
Imaginative jewellery, small pieces of artwork and wearable accessories created by some 30 Hungarian designers are ranged around this attractive white space. You'll also find notebooks, Lomography cameras, earrings, phone cases and purses, lovely children's books, necklaces and coat-hangers in the shape of a rhinoceros head.

SALE
WonderLab

Szalámibolt
V. Vitkovics Mihály utca 3-5 (337 1195, www. szalamibolt.hu). M2 Astoria, M3 Ferenciek tere. **Open** *Winter* 9am-7pm Mon-Fri; 10am-6pm Sat. *Summer* 9am-7pm Mon-Fri; 10am-6pm Sat, Sun. **Map** p77 C3 ❹ **Food & drink**
After 30 years in the hotel trade, Attila Lukács opened this temple to salami in 2010. During that time, indigenous Mangalica pork has become extremely successful on the domestic and international markets – though Lukács also purveys venison, game and goose varieties in salami form. Hams, cheeses and pálinka fruit grappas are also available. *See also* p84 **Pig in Clover**.

Tipton Eyewear at Orange Optika
V. Belgrád rakpart 26 (06 70 511 1203, www. tiptonbudapest.com). Tram 2. **Open** 11am-6pm Mon-Fri. **Map** p77 B4 ❹ **Accessories**
Zachary Tipton's Cinematique collection boasts salvaged Italian cellulose acetate frame fronts, customised with 16mm film – classics, Soviet space missions, Communist news, and black-and-white cartoons. The Vinylize collection is made of records.

Vadjutka
V. Kossuth Lajos utca 14-16 (no phone, www. vadjutka.hu). M2 Astoria, M3 Ferenciek tere. **Open** 11am-7pm Mon-Fri; 10am-3pm Sat. **Map** p77 C3 ❹ **Accessories**
Styling herself 'Judit Wild', former *HVG* journalist Jutka Vad has branched out to create her own funky jewellery, on show in this studio on the edge of the

Belváros. Falling leaves, cocktail glasses and cups of hot coffee, everything is fair game for Vad to feature on sassy rings, earrings and necklaces.

Vass Cipő
V. Haris köz 2 (780 7418, www.vass-cipo.hu). M3 Ferenciek tere, or bus 7. **Open** 10am-6pm Mon-Fri; 10am-2pm. **Map** p77 B3 ❹ **Accessories**
Craftsman László Vass makes fine men's shoes in excellent quality leather; shoes can be made to order.

★ WonderLab
V. Veres Pálné utca 3 (06 20 314 2058). M3 Ferenciek tere, or bus 15. **Open** noon-8pm Tue-Sat. **Map** p77 C4 ❹ **Fashion**
Labelling itself a 'concept store and creative workshop', WonderLab brings together some 30 Hungarian designers – literally. Customers are not only encouraged to browse the bags, items of womenswear, shoes, jewellery, sunglasses and seemingly countless accessories produced by the likes of Geomood, INQ Concept and Bori Bianka – but meet the designers themselves as they drop by and hang out with their peers.

EXPLORE

Lipótváros & Újlipótváros

Budapest gets down to business in Lipótváros. Blocky, late 19th-century streets and austere neoclassical architecture provide a contrast to the smaller, twisty thoroughfares and Baroque or Secessionist whimsy that mark much of downtown Budapest. The neighbourhood maintains the grid pattern that was imposed on it by the Új Épület, the massive Habsburg barracks that once stood at what is now Szabadság tér. The barracks, where leaders of the nascent Hungarian nation were imprisoned and executed in 1849, were the base for Vienna's control over the city. Today, this is still the centre for business and bureaucracy – this is where you'll find Parliament. From here, it's a short walk north to the Nagykörút and Újlipótváros, built as a stylish residential overflow of Lipótváros between the wars. Considered central despite a XIII District postcode, 'Újlipi' is highly prized real estate.

EXPLORE

Gresham Palace.

Don't Miss

1 Parliament This building defines the city (p93).

2 Borkonyha Wine and food in perfect harmony (p88).

3 Gresham Palace Art nouveau wonder, now a sumptuous hotel (p88).

4 Basilica of St Stephen Where the nation's great are honoured (p88).

5 Vígszínház Comedy Theatre Drama aplenty at Budapest's Baroque landmark (p96).

Basilica of St Stephen.

THE BASILICA & BUSINESS QUARTER

Looking across focal Erzsébet tér from Belváros, the skyline is dominated by Budapest's largest church, the **Basilica of St Stephen**. The square that opens out behind it, also named after Hungary's patron saint, is lined with touristy restaurants. From adjoining Sas utca down to the river, the need to feed the business crowd takes priority and some of Budapest's best restaurants are here, including **Mák Bisztró**, **Tigris** and **Borkonyha**. Several offer attractive weekday lunchtime deals, and reflect a growing trend for upscale wine bars (*see p90* **Cork and Fork**). It gets quieter in the evening, but top-notch wines and cocktails are on offer at places such as Borkonyha and **KNRDY**.

Pretty, pedestrianised Zrinyi utca leads down to the river, past the Central European University, one of several post-Communist institutions founded by Hungarian billionaire philanthropist George Soros. Zrinyi utca opens out on to Széchenyi tér, until recently known as Roosevelt tér. This attractive, grassy square is surrounded by classic Budapest landmarks. On the far side is the Chain Bridge, while the Hungarian Academy of Sciences and the **Sofitel Hotel** (*see p212*) face each other north and south. Overlooking it all, and the Danube beyond, stands the stunning **Four Seasons Gresham Palace** hotel (*see p217*). This is revamped Budapest at its five-star finest. The former headquarters of the London Gresham Life Assurance Company, this art nouveau masterpiece from the early 1900s was transformed into a luxury hotel a century later. Some of Zsigmond Quittner's original detail remains, and much was painstakingly restored according to his plans. It's worth popping in for a coffee or an evening drink in the exquisite cocktail bar just to admire the sumptuous lobby area.

Sights & Museums

Basilica of St Stephen
Szent István Bazilika
V. Szent István tér 1 (311 0839, www.bazilika. biz). M3 Arany János utca. **Open** 9am-5pm Mon-Fri; 9am-1pm Sat; 1-5pm Sun. **Admission** Recommended donation Ft200. *Towers* Ft500. *Museum* Ft500. **No credit cards. Map** p89 C6 ❶

The Basilica, designed in 1845 by József Hild, was finally consecrated in 1905. Construction was so disrupted by wars and the deaths of its two major architects that one wonders if God wanted it built at all. The original dome collapsed during an 1868 storm. Miklós Ybl, the new architect, had the entire building demolished, and rebuilt the original neoclassical edifice in the heavy neo-Renaissance style favoured by the Viennese court. Ybl died in 1891, before the Hungarian millennial celebrations of 1896, for which the Basilica had been set at a height of 96m (315ft). Some 50 years later, the Basilica was devastated by Allied bombing, and it was only fully restored in the 1980s. Today, the main attractions are the colourful frescoes of the saints around the bright ceiling and the mummified right hand of St Stephen, known as the 'Sacred Right', housed in its own side chapel. On 20 August, St Stephen's Day (*see p31*), the hand is marched around the square in a religious procession. Large bells occupy the Basilica's two towers, accessed by lift or stairs for fine views across the city.

Restaurants

★ Borkonyha
V. Sas utca 3 (266 0835, www.borkonyha.com). M1 Bajcsy-Zsilinszky út. **Open** noon-4pm, 6pm-midnight Mon-Sat. **Main courses** Ft3,850-Ft6,550. **Map** p89 B6 ❷ **Wine bar** *See p90* **Cork and Fork**.

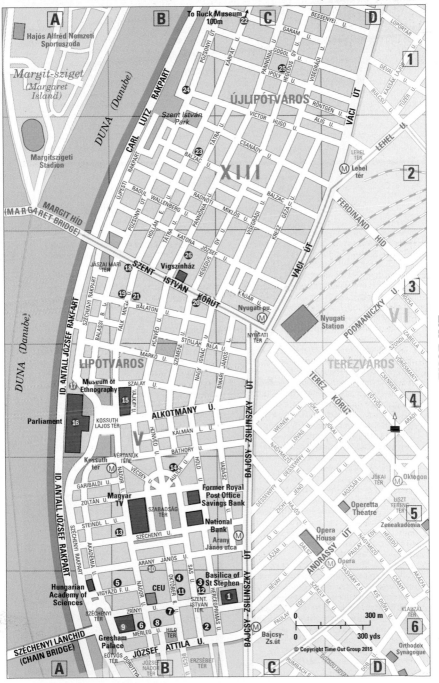

Café Kör

V.Sas utca 17 (311 0053, www.cafekor.com).
M1 Bajcsy-Zsilinszky út, or M3 Arany János utca.
Open 10am-10pm Mon-Sat. **Main courses**
Ft2,090-Ft4,690. **No credit cards.** Map p89 B6
❸ **Hungarian/Modern European**
Café Kör applies a creative gourmet touch to
Hungarian classics in a comfortable, bistro-like
atmosphere. There's a bar with a fine selection of
local wines and some small café tables, as well as a more
formal dining space. The refreshingly simple menu
is complemented by daily specials, and all dishes
generally range from good to memorable. Service can
be slow, but is usually friendly – repeat custom has
kept this place busy for well over a decade.

KNRDY

V.Október 6 utca 15 (788 1685, www.knrdy.com).
M1 Bajcsy-Zsilinszky út, or bus 15. **Open** 11.30am-
1am Mon-Sat; 11am-1am Sun. **Main courses**
Ft4,800-Ft14,900. **Map** p89 B6 ❹ **Steakhouse**
If you want to tuck into top-quality meat and you're
happy to spend big, KNRDY is the place to come.
Zoltán Konrády's restaurant deals in USDA prime

CORK AND FORK

Sip your way around Budapest's finest foodie wine bars.

When Tamás Horváth and sommelier Zoltán
Kalocsai were awarded a Michelin star in
2014 for **Borkonyha** (see *p88*), it was more
than an affirmation of their expertise as
restaurateurs. Borkonyha, 'Wine Kitchen',
is the latest in a new breed of Budapest
restaurants that put the grape on at least
equal footing with upscale gastronomy. At
Borkonyha, diners are treated to the Magyar
and Mediterranean delights cooked by Ákos
Sárközi, at the same time as having a choice
of 200 Hungarian wines by the glass, kept
at cellar temperature in a large display case
behind the bar. Having worked for seven years
at leading wine merchant **Bortársaság** (see
p64), Kalocsai has excellent connections –
a finer selection would be hard to find.

A pioneer in the revival of the now thriving
Hungarian wine industry, Bortársaság
spawned a whole new genre of foodie wine
bars when it opened **Klassz** (see *p104*),
still based at its prime spot on Andrássy út.
These include **Borbíróság** (www.borbirosag.
com) near the Great Market Hall, **Drop Shop**
(www.dropshop.hu) near Margaret Bridge
and the **Kadárka Bár** (www.facebook.com/
kadarkabar) on Király utca. Nearby **Doblo**
(see *p120*), meanwhile, mixes live music
and a savvy Hungarian-only wine selection
– without short-changing on the quality of
its home-cooked dishes.

Naturally, this trend has also seen wine
producers move into the restaurant industry.
Very early on, renowned winemaker József
Bock opened up his now equally renowned
Bock Bisztró (see *p125*) under the roof of the
five-star Corinthia Hotel on the Nagykörút.
More recently, winemaker Attila Gere, of
Villány, created a showcase for his heavenly
reds and other hand-picked labels by
Hungarian producers at **Tigris** (see *p91*).

Set behind the Basilica in a former luxury
hotel, Gere's establishment serves superb
goose liver and Mangalica dishes, and a
wonderful selection of wines.

Following in Gere's footsteps, **Di Vino**
(www.divinoborbar.hu) was set up in 2011
by Junibor, a local association of young wine
producers. Its members are aged between
23 and 37 – Hungary's next generation of
winemakers, including the children of the
most famous names in the business. Sent to
learn their trade in France and California, the
sons and daughters of Gere, Gál and Dúzsi
have since taken the ball and run with it, also
opening a Di Vino in the happening Gozsdu
udvar (see *p118* **Holding Court**). There, as
here, bottles come from around 30 young
producers, complemented by superb food.

Finally, in what is becoming Budapest's
quartier du vin behind the Basilica, **Innio**
(www.innio.hu) operates under the motto of
Innio, ennio, élnio – 'To drink, to eat, to live',
in bastardised Magyar-Latin – and stocks
some 300 wines from around the world.

Borkonyha.

black angus, Omaha black angus and Australian wagyu, dry-aged and ready to be sizzled as you wish. Accompaniments include duck-fat sautéed potatoes or olive-oil mashed potatoes, grilled onions and sauces such as pork-and-stilton. There are lighter choices too: seared Scottish salmon, perhaps.

MÁK Bisztró

V.Vigyázó Ferenc utca 4 (06 30 723 9383, www. mak.hu). Tram 2, or bus 15. **Open** noon-3pm, 6pm-midnight Tue-Sat. **Main courses** Ft3,500-Ft8,000. **Map** p89 B6 ❺ **Modern European**
With the recent departure of chef Krisztián Huszár, MÁK has had to rethink its concept. Out are the Basque influences Huszár brought to the table from his time serving under Michelin-starred chefs in Spain. In, though, are more affordable lunches. Hungarian Mangalica pork, bream and flounder all feature, expertly matched with fennel, marinated pearl onions or kohlrabi, and beautifully presented.

Salaam Bombay

V.Mérleg utca 6 (411 1252, www.salaam bombay.hu). Tram 2, or bus 15. **Open** noon-3pm, 6-11pm daily. **Main courses** Ft950-Ft3,900. **Map** p89 B6 ❻ **Indian**
Salaam Bombay's perky pink-and-blue dining room features a huge photo-mural of Mumbai harbour and a well-stocked cocktail bar. This slick restaurant promises 'Indian food redefined' and, although it doesn't really do that, it does offer excellent Goan seafood dishes and a selection of sizzlers.

TG Italiano

V.Október 6 utca 8 (266 3525, www.tomgeorge.hu). M1 Bajcsy-Zsilinszky út, or bus 15. **Open** noon-midnight Mon-Thur, Sun; noon-1am Fri, Sat. **Main courses** Ft1,650-Ft9,800. **Map** p89 B6 ❼ **Italian**
TG stands for Tom George, whose restaurant has been a mainstay of the business quarter for well over a decade. Chef Sergio Viti is still creating his excellent own-made pasta dishes, succulent meaty mains and fresh fish dishes, available as part of the two-course weekday lunch (a bargain at Ft2,200), as well as seasonal market specials. The wine list is vast.

Tigris

V.Mérleg utca 10 (317 3715, www.tigris restaurant.hu). Tram 2, or bus 15. **Open** noon-midnight Mon-Sat. **Main courses** Ft3,900-Ft6,800. **Map** p89 B6 ❽ **Wine bar**
See p90 **Cork and Fork.**

Cafés & Bars

See also p90 **Cork and Fork.**

Bar & Lobby Lounge

Four Seasons Gresham Palace, V.Széchenyi tér 5-6 (268 5100, www.fourseasons.com). Tram 2, or bus 16. **Open** 11am-1am daily. **Map** p89 B6 ❾

Some of the best (and priciest) cocktails in town are served with style at the Gresham Palace, either in a high-ceilinged area off the grand lobby or in an intimate, low-lit room. Both are within earshot of the gently tinkling piano. Just as you're feasting on the range of cocktails and frowning at the prices, you're presented with bowls of marinated olives, salted nuts and puff pastries. At this point it seems churlish to baulk at the bill for a coolly mixed cosmopolitan (with Absolut or Blavod) or champagne cocktail zinging with Louis Roederer. Malaysian satay, crab cakes and foie gras provide greater sustenance.

★ Espresso Embassy

V.Arany János utca 15 (06 30 964 9530, www. espressoembassy.hu). M3 Arany János utca. **Open** 7.30am-7pm Mon-Fri; 9am-5pm Sat, Sun. **Map** p89 B5 ❿
Co-owner Tibor Várady learned his trade at the café of trendy boutique-cum-workshop Printa (*see p121*). He then opened this coffee shop in a business district already swamped with coffee shops – and has cleaned up. Brews are made with arabica beans and beautifully presented, while the tasty cookies, muffins and cakes all have gluten-free alternatives. There's fast Wi-Fi, but a lack of space discourages a long session at the laptop.

Shops & Services

Bestsellers

V.Október 6 utca 11 (312 1295, www.bestsellers. hu). M1 Bajcsy Zsilinszky út, or M3 Arany János utca. **Open** 9am-6.30pm Mon-Fri; 10am-5pm Sat; 10am-4pm Sun. **Map** p89 B6 ⓫ **Books & music**
Tony Lang certainly knows his stock: this is expat Budapest's favourite bookshop, offering the city's finest selection of foreign literature.

USE Unused

V.Sas utca 15 (06 30 549 0868, www.use.co.hu). M1 Bajcsy-Zsilinszky út, or M3 Arany János utca. **Open** 10am-6pm Mon-Wed, Sat, Sun; 10am-7pm Thur; 10am-4.30pm Fri. **Map** p89 B6 ⓬ **Fashion**
Now with a new flagship store behind the Basilica, the successful designer trio of Eszter Füzes, Attila Godena-Juhász and András Tóth produce chic womenswear that mixes classic mid 20th-century style with contemporary design. Limited menswear and accessories are available too.

SZABADSÁG TÉR & AROUND

Further art nouveau architectural treasures await around Szabadság tér (*see p94* **Walk**), which was laid out during Hungary's brief flirtation with imperialism and conceived as the hub of the Habsburg era economy. 'Freedom Square' was originally created from the demolition of the Habsburg garrison that stood here until 1897, which also housed the prison

EXPLORE

EXPLORE

where prime minister Lajos Batthyány was incarcerated and executed in 1849 after the 1848 uprising. Suitably, it features a number of memorials to historic liberations, successful or otherwise. In front of the former Stock Exchange, a grand neoclassical pile designed by Ignác Alpár in 1905, is a memorial to Hungarians who suffered a grim fate at the hands of the Austrians here. Across the square stands a large white obelisk built by the Soviets to honour their troops who fell during the Liberation of Budapest in 1945 – placed on the very site that commemorated Hungary's losses as a result of the 1920 Treaty of Trianon (*see p195* **The Shape of Things to Come**). Debate has long raged whether this monument to the USSR shouldn't go the way of the Stalin-era statues at Memento Park (*see p57*) on the edge of town.

In July 2014, another controversial statue, the **Memorial to the Victims of German Occupation**, went up opposite the obelisk. Fenced off to stop vandalism, it's meant to symbolise the fact that the Nazis (represented by a flying eagle) coerced Hungary (the archangel Gabriel) into participating in the Holocaust.

Outside the American Embassy, on the eastern side of the square, stands a statue to Harry Hill Bandholtz. In 1919, the Michigan-born major general intervened to prevent the Romanian Army from liberating Hungarian treasures in the National Museum. He locked the doors with the only official-looking items he could find to hand: US censorship seals. On seeing the American eagle, the Romanians backed off.

The embassy stands alongside the Hungarian National Bank, which was created by Ignác Alpár to complement its contemporary, the former Stock Exchange, opposite. The Stock Exchange later became the headquarters of Hungarian State Television (Magyar Televízió), the so-called

MTV Building, before being bought by the Canadian Tippin Corporation in 2010. Some 35,000 square metres of prime office and retail space are set to open in 2017.

The brightest spot in this sombre, officious quarter is Ödön Lechner's startlingly ornate and colourful former Royal Post Office Savings Bank, now the Hungarian National Treasury (V.Hold utca 4, entrance from Szabadság tér 8; *see p94* **Walk**). It's closed to the public, but you can get a feel for Lechner's finest work by peeking into the lobby. As a final reminder of Austrian retribution for 1849, an 'eternal flame' diagonally behind the Soviet Army Memorial, on the corner of Báthory utca and Hold utca, commemorates the executed Count Batthyány.

Restaurants

Momotaro Ramen
V.Széchenyi utca 16 (269 3802, www.momotaro ramen.com). M2 Kossuth Lajos tér, or tram 2. **Open** 11am-10.30pm Tue-Sun. **Main courses** Ft950-Ft5,800. **No credit cards. Map** p89 B5 ⑬ Japanese/Chinese
The ramen noodle soups are just one reason to come to this superb low-key restaurant near Szabadság tér. Another reason is the dumplings, fried or prepared in a bamboo steamer, which are probably the best in Budapest. Momotaro also offers dim sum and great sesame chicken toasts. For a veggie ramen, ask for it to be cooked without a meat broth. You may have to share a long table during the busy lunch hour.

Shops & Services

Metropolitan
V.Aulich utca 4-6 (302 5243, www.metropolitan budapest.hu). M2 Kossuth Lajos tér. **Open** 10am-6pm Mon-Fri; 10am-2pm Sat. **Map** p89 B5 ㉔ Health & beauty

Szabadság tér.

Three floors of big-name brands, including Moschino Cheap & Chic, Philosophy di Alberta Ferretti and Pollini, plus Clarins facials and full-body massages.

PARLIAMENT & AROUND

On Vértanúk tere, between Szabadság tér and Kossuth Lajos tér, stands Tamás Varga's statue of Imre Nagy, tragic hero of the 1956 Uprising. It's positioned symbolically at the crest of a small bridge, looking towards Parliament and away from the Soviet obelisk. Another memorial to 1956 was unveiled in 2014 on Kossuth tér, specifically dedicated to the victims of the 25 October massacre during a protest outside Parliament. It is one of several new features – including pedestrianised areas and statues of Hungarian heroes – introduced as part of a relandscaping of the square.

With fewer cars on the road, **Parliament** seems to dominate Kossuth Lajos tér more than ever. Built, like the rest of Lipótváros, at a time when Hungary was getting a taste of empire, it was the largest parliament building in the world when it opened in 1902. Opposite, the **Museum of Ethnography** occupies a huge, echoing edifice conceived as the Ministry of Justice by architect Alajos Hauszmann.

The brooding statue of stick-thin poet Attila József, which once sat on a mound beside Parliament, has now been moved nearer the river in line with his poem, 'At the Danube'. Attila's life of poverty was ended by a train at Balatonszárszó in 1937, leaving behind inevitable talk of suicide.

A few steps along the river, towards the junction with Zoltán utca, a row of random shoes lining the embankment honour the victims who were shot and thrown into the Danube by right-wing Arrow Cross thugs in 1944 and 1945. Cast in iron and styled according to the fashions of the time, the shoes were created by sculptor Gyula Pauer in 2005.

The 2 tram runs along the embankment, from the Chain Bridge up towards Margaret Bridge, veering round Parliament as it does so, before following the Danube up Balassi Bálint utca to its terminus at Jászai Mari tér. Running parallel from Kossuth Lajos tér, Falk Miksa utca is lined with galleries and antiques shops, and contains the bulk of the city's auction houses.

Sights & Museums

Museum of Ethnography
Néprajzi Múzeum
V.Kossuth Lajos tér 12 (473 2400, www.neprajz. hu). M2 Kossuth Lajos tér, or tram 2. **Open** 10am-6pm Tue-Sun. **Admission** *All exhibitions* Ft1,400; Ft700 reductions. *Permanent exhibition only* Ft1,000; Ft500 reductions. **No credit cards**. **Map** p89 B4 ⑮

Conceived by Alajos Hauszmann of New York Palace fame to serve as the Supreme Court, this monumental, gilt-columned edifice with ceiling frescoes by Károly Lotz feels anything but folky. The permanent exhibition, up the grand staircase, details Hungarian village and farm life, folk art and customs, from the end of the 18th century to World War I. Aspects such as work, trade and marriage are illustrated by means of models and costumes, with ample English documentation. Note the map from 1891 outlining the peoples and languages of the Carpathian Basin. Negotiate the echoing corridors for temporary exhibitions on the ground and upper floors.

★ Parliament
Országház
V.Kossuth Lajos tér 103 (441 4415, www. parlament.hu). M2 Kossuth Lajos tér, or tram 2. **Open** *Visitor Centre* Apr-Oct 8am-6pm Mon-Fri; 8am-4pm Sat, Sun. Nov-Mar 8am-4pm daily. *English-language tours* 10am, noon, 1pm, 2pm & 3pm. **Admission** *EU citizens* Ft2,000; Ft1,000 reductions. *Non-EU citizens* Ft5,200; Ft2,600 reductions. **Map** p89 A4 ⑯

Still one of the largest parliamentary buildings in the world, the Országház comprises 691 rooms that have never been fully utilised – governing Hungary today takes up just 12% of the space. Designed by Imre Steindl and beautifully positioned on a curve of the Danube, the building defines the city and exploits the elegance of the river's sweep. The interior, though, is an exercise in establishment kitsch. Guided tours pass the numbered cigar holders outside the Upper House, where members would leave their Havanas during debates. The Sacred Crown in the Cupola Hall was a gift from the Pope to St Stephen in AD 1000 to mark Hungary's formation as a Christian state. It was moved here from the National Museum a few years ago, despite protests about the symbolic fusing of church and state. Only a limited number of visitor tickets are available on the day – so it's best to book online (EU citizens should bring their passport as proof of eligibility). There are no tours on national holidays (*see p29*).
▶ *Tickets can be purchased online (Ft200 fee) at www.jegymester.hu/parlament.*

Cafés & Bars

Café Smúz
V.Kossuth Lajos tér 18 (06 30 922 0850, www. viragneked.hu). M2 Kossuth Lajos tér, or tram 2. **Open** 9am-8pm Mon-Fri; 10am-8pm Sat, Sun. **Map** p89 A4 ⑰
Part of the Virág Neked ('Flowers for You') florist, Café Smúz is a destination coffee shop in its own right with a prime spot across from Parliament. Coffee comes from a La Marzocco machine, using beans from El Salvador. Café Smúz also serves booze: Hungarian artisanal beers, Horizont Flemish Porter, Indian Pale Ale and Japanese wheat beer complement a strong

EXPLORE

WALK STROLLING THE SECESSION

Budapest's exotic take on art nouveau.

Gutenberg-otthon

Much of the cultural dynamism of newly independent fin-de-siècle Budapest was born out of a rejection of the staid Habsburg status quo and a search for Hungarian roots. Architecturally, this meant Secessionism, a loose label influenced by the organic curves of French and Belgian art nouveau, and geometric and abstract lines of the Viennese Secession. Here, it also involved the bright motifs from mainly Transylvanian folk art, coloured ceramics and sinuous curves. In many ways, the movement was the product of the eccentric mind of Ödön Lechner (1845-1914). Neglected throughout the 20th century, he now enjoys recognition as a peculiar genius, a kind of Budapest version of Barcelona's Antonio Gaudí.

This pleasant walk starts in Lipótváros and takes you past several fine examples of Secessionist architecture. Allow two hours. Start at the landmark **Four Seasons Gresham Palace** hotel ❶ (see p217), facing the Chain Bridge. Built in 1906 for the London-based Gresham Life Assurance Company, it was splendidly restored as a luxury hotel just before its 100th birthday. Original architect Zsigmond Quittner used the best artisans of the day, who decorated the exterior with statues and gilt, and the sumptuous lobby with peacock gates, bright Zsolnay tiles and a glass atrium. The hotel's bar, restaurant and café give a flavour of the architectural style.

Stroll through Szabadság tér to Vidor Emil's whimsically asymmetrical **Bedő ház** ❷ (1903) at V.Honvéd utca 3. The organic curving lines and flowery façade mirror the art nouveau style of Vidor's Belgian counterparts. Two streets away, Ödön Lechner's groundbreaking former **Royal Post Office Savings Bank** ❸ (1899-1901; see p92), his crowning achievement, is uniquely Hungarian. The exterior's orderly form is disguised by a brightly coloured façade of glazed brick and

a freewheeling riot of line and pattern on the roof. These decorative elements are derived from Hungarian folklore and mythology. Told that these were difficult to view from the street, Lechner answered: 'The birds will see them.' The function of the building is acknowledged by beehives – symbols of thrift – at the corners, with bees crawling towards them. Today, it houses the Hungarian National Treasury and is closed to the public, but you can peek through the front door and catch a glimpse of the luscious lobby.

Lechner's visionary student Béla Lajta (1873-1920) probably did most to point Hungarian architecture towards its post-war future. Lajta's masterwork, a watershed in Hungarian architecture, is visible from Andrássy, opposite the Opera House. Gold-decked angels atop the **Új Színház** ❹ (1908-09; VI.Paulay Ede utca 35) peer down Dalszínház utca from their perch on Paulay Ede utca. Get close to see the bright blue tile sign and monkeys guarding ornate doors. The Új Színház ('New Theatre') combines the playfulness of fin-de-siècle architecture, the lean aesthetic of modernism and elements typical of art deco, a style that didn't catch on until the 1920s.

For further Secessionist treasures, you need to head to Districts VII and VIII, the first a ten-minute stroll from the Új Színház. Walking down Székely Mihály utca and over Király to Kazinczy utca, you'll come to Béla and Sándor Löeffler's clean-lined, off-kilter **Orthodox Synagogue** ❺ (1913), bending with the street. Across Rákóczi út, at Vas utca 11, Lajta again predicts art deco in his wonderful **Trade School** ❻, with a sheer exterior featuring six second-floor owls and ornate folk-art doors. Slip discreetly inside during school hours and check the beautiful interior.

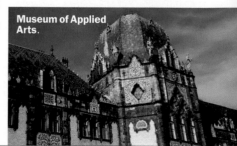
Museum of Applied Arts.

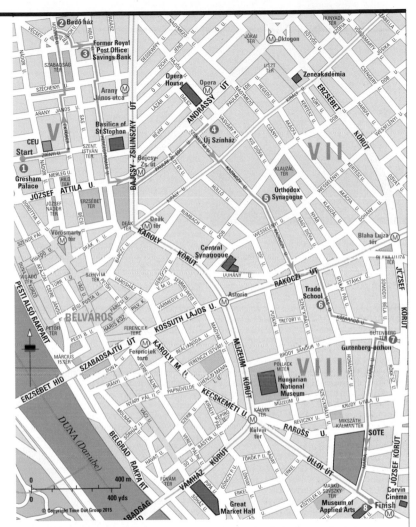

Head for nearby Gutenberg tér 4, home to László and József Vágo's luxury **Gutenberg-otthon** ❼ (1905-1907), with its wavy façade, bold sign and colourful details. Lechner was among its luminary tenants. Walk a few blocks south along József körút to the corner of Üllői út, where you can't miss Lechner's first major Secessionist work, the eye-catching **Museum of Applied Arts** ❽ (1893-96; see p136). Lechner deployed an array of Moorish and Indian designs – along with patterns from Hungarian folk culture. The explosion of

colour at the tiled entrance attests to Lechner's links with the Zsolnay ceramics factory in Pécs. Inside, floral motifs, some of which were whitewashed in the 1970s, can still be seen in the archways and arcades. Past the lobby, you'll see a multi-storey interior courtyard, capped by a stunning stained-glass skylight. The abundant natural light owes its freedom to another daring architectural move, the decision to erect the building on a steel frame. At that time, no other museum in Europe had been designed in such a way.

Budapest Poster Gallery.

wine list from Eger, Szekszárd, Villány, Balaton and Etyek. There are cocktails, too, though early-evening closing means Smúz is a post-work stop-off.

Shops & Services

BÁV
V. Szent István körút 3 (473 0666, www.bav.hu).
Tram 4, 6. **Open** 10am-7pm Mon-Fri; 10am-2pm Sat. **Map** p89 B3 ⓭ **Antiques/homewares**
BÁV, a chain of state-run pawn shops, is recognisable by its *Venus de Milo* sign. This one at the gateway to Falk Miksa utca – Budapest's main street for antiques – specialises in furniture, paintings and carpets. BÁV stores hold regular auctions; dates are given on the website.
Other locations V.Bécsi utca 1-3 (429 3020); V.Ferenciek tere 10 (318 3733).

Budapest Poster Gallery
V. Falk Miksa utca 28, Flat 61 (06 30 662 7274, www.budapestposter.com). Tram 2, 4, 6. **Open** 11am-1pm, 2-6pm Mon-Fri. **No credit cards.**
Map p89 B3 ⓭ **Gifts & souvenirs**
Set up by Ádám Várkonyi in 2010, this sixth-floor outlet deals in vintage Hungarian posters from 1890 onwards, as well as commercial graphic-design items. Travel, film and propaganda posters from either side of World War II, they're all here. First-class reproductions can be arranged and there's an online store too.

Katti Zoób
V. Szent István körút 17 (06 30 657 5794, www.kattizoob.hu). M3 Nyugati pu, or tram 4, 6.
Open by appt. **Map** p89 B3 ⓴ **Fashion**
Zoób's luxurious couture collections reference ancient Hungarian semiotics and art deco. She has also collaborated with Zsolnay Porcelain to create a contemporary jewellery collection, some of which is stocked at London's Harrods.

Wladis Galéria & Műterem
V. Falk Miksa utca 13 (354 0834, www.wladis galeria.hu). Tram 2. **Open** 10am-6pm Mon-Fri; 10am-2pm Sat. **Map** p89 B3 ㉑ **Accessories**
Hungarian designer Vladimir Péter, a professor at the Applied Arts University, opened this workshop in 1993. He mixes traditional and modern metalwork to create stunningly simple jewellery pieces.

ÚJLIPÓTVÁROS

The section of the Nagykörút dividing Lipótváros from Újlipótváros is busy Szent István körút, the only section of the ring road not named after a Habsburg. The centrepiece of the last stretch is the Baroque **Comedy Theatre** (*see p168*). Built in 1896 and renovated in 1995, it has staged performances by many of the country's top 20th-century musical dramatists, including Albert Szirmay, who worked with Gershwin in New York.

North of the Nagykörút, Újlipótváros was built in the first half of the 20th century and has a sleeker feel than the stately grandeur of Lipótváros. Moneyed young professionals have moved in, and a growing number of bakeries, cafés and restaurants have opened to cater to them. Set off the main street of Pozsonyi út, Szent István Park pleasantly opens out on to the river, surrounded by modernist residential blocks. The **Dunapark Kávéház**, built in 1937 and reopened as a restaurant in 2006, echoes the pre-war era.

Originally named Lipótvárosi Park, Újlipótváros was known as the International Ghetto during the darkest days of World War II. As an affluent, middle-class Jewish neighbourhood, the other side of Pest from the Jewish Ghetto of District VII, it provided Raoul Wallenberg and other diplomats with safe houses for Jewish citizens to prevent their deportation to the camps. Wallenberg was the brave young Secretary of the Swedish Legation to Budapest who, from his arrival here in July 1944, personally saved thousands of Jews from a terrible fate. In January 1945, during the worst of the fighting between the Nazis and Soviets, Wallenberg disappeared. To this day, his exact fate is not known – only that he was taken by the Russians to Moscow, where he died, most likely in 1947.

While parts of Wallenberg's story slowly came to light, a memorial to this selfless hero would have embarrassed the Communist authorities. He was acknowledged with nothing more than a street name, halfway between Szent István Park and the Nagykörút, where a plaque now stands at no.11. After 1989, a statue was at last erected in his honour in Szent István Park – another had already been unveiled in Buda, on Szilágyi Erzsébet fasor, shortly before the regime change. Újlipótváros is an area of Pest served by red trolleybuses. Introduced in 1949 in honour of

Rock Museum.

Stalin's 70th birthday, they began with line 70 – as they still do today. The 75 trolleybus runs through Újlipótváros, past Szent István Park, to Hösök tere and the national football stadium. Two stops up from Szent István Park, by Vág utca, is the RaM Colosseum events and concert venue, where the weekend-only **Rock Museum** is a niche but worthwhile attraction.

Sights & Museums

★ Rock Museum
Rockmúzeum
RaM Colosseum, XIII.Kárpát utca 23 (398 6290, www.rockcsarnok.hu). M3 Dózsa György út, or trolleybus 75. **Open** 10am-6pm Sat, Sun. **Admission** Ft500. *Photos* Ft1,000. **No credit cards. Map** p89 C1 ㉒
Founded by two enthusiasts, László B Tóth and György András Kelemen, this is a Hungarian rock hall of fame, a testament to a long-lost era of antiquated equipment and illegal radio broadcasts from the West. Exhibits include a primitive dry-ice machine and elegant Jolana guitars from Czechoslovakia. Note also the police truncheon used to keep rowdy fans in order for a Spencer Davis Group gig at the Kisstadion in 1967. Pride of place goes to the original studio used by Radio Free Europe DJ László Cseke for his legendary 'Teenager Party' shows, plus a huge map of pre-1989 Budapest with little buttons showing long-lost venues, plus biographies of the bands who played there.

Restaurants

Balzac 35
XIII.Balzac utca 35 (789 8915, www.balzac35.hu). Trolleybus 75, 76. **Open** 8am-10pm Mon-Fri; noon-10pm Sat, Sun. **Main courses** Ft1,950-Ft3,600. **Map** p89 B2 ㉓ **Hungarian**

Formerly Budapest's leading Belgian restaurant, Balzac 35 now promotes itself as a 'restaurant and culture café', offering stage space to Hungary's rapidly swelling fraternity of stand-up comedians on Thursday evenings. As a restaurant, it offers updated takes on age-old Hungarian favourites – Kolozsvár stuffed cabbage, crispy duck leg with classic garnish, catfish stew – in pleasant surroundings. It's hardly blazing a new culinary trail, but Balzac 35 is popular with an interesting crowd of savvy locals.

Dunapark Kávéház
XIII.Pozsonyi út 38 (786 1009, www.dunapark kavehaz.com). Trolleybus 75, 76. **Open** 8am-11pm Mon-Fri; 10am-11pm Sat; 10am-10pm Sun. **Main courses** Ft2,800-Ft4,500. **Map** p89 B1 ㉔ **Hungarian/Modern European**
Reopened in 2006, Dunapark is a faithful reconstruction of the original coffee house created by Béla Hoffstatter and Ference Dománý in 1937, when Újlipótváros was the place to be for creatives and intellectuals. While there's nothing much wrong with the Dunapark burger or crunchy duck leg, the kitchen isn't the main focus here – people come to sip coffee, scoff cake, admire the smooth lines of the exquisite interior and gaze at the Danube.

★ Laci! Konyha!
XIII.Hegedűs Gyula utca 56 (06 70 370 7475, www.lacikonyha.com). M3 Lehel tér, or bus 15, or trolleybus 75. **Open** noon-3pm, 6-11pm Mon-Fri. **Set menu** *Lunch* Ft2,200 or Ft3,100. *Dinner* Ft9,000. **Map** p89 C1 ㉕ **Hungarian**
The golden boy of Hungarian gastronomy has done it again. After working wonders at LouLou, Csalogány 26 and Aranyszarvas, Gábor Mogyorósi opened this unpromising basement in Újlipótváros in 2011 – and has had discerning diners and food critics beating a path to its door ever since. Open weekdays only, Laci! Konyha! organises its dishes around set lunches and dinners. With treats such as meat soup with duck breast, pork cheek with young radish, and blood sausage with apple mustard, this is contemporary Hungarian cuisine at something close to its very best.
► *Mogyorósi has also opened a venue downtown, Laci Pecsenye (V.Sas utca 11, 06 70 370 7474, www.lacipecsenye.eu).*

Shops & Services

Édés Élet Cukrászda
XIII.Pannónia utca 3 (06 20 448 6149). Tram 4, 6, or bus 9, 26. **Open** 10am-8pm daily. **No credit cards. Map** p89 B3 ㉖ **Food & drink**
Catering to the new Újlipi crowd, the 'Sweet Life' pastry shop produces some of the finest cakes and tarts in Budapest, many of them gluten-, sugar- and lactose-free. Customers can sit down with a fork and plate, but you're better off getting your treats wrapped and heading over to Margaret Island.

EXPLORE

District VI & Városliget

Bordered by District XIII on one side and District VII on the other, District VI is both a nightlife hub and a showcase of elegant boulevards and cultural landmarks. The most elegant boulevard of all, Andrássy út, runs the length of the district, from the junction with Bajcsy-Zsilinszky út downtown, past the Opera House, theatre-lined Nagymező utca and the transport hub of Oktogon, to Heroes' Square. Across from the square, Városliget (City Park) is an expansive green space with a boating lake, an ice rink and the ornate Széchenyi Baths. Alongside stand the Circus, the Zoo and the most prestigious restaurant in town, Gundel. Running below ground, continental Europe's oldest metro line follows Andrássy út up to Városliget and beyond. Above ground, District VI fans out north as far as Király utca, taking in clusters of bars and clubs on the south side of the Nagykörút.

EXPLORE

Opera House.

Don't Miss

1 Opera House Neo-Renaissance landmark from the Golden Age (p100).

2 Széchenyi Baths Wallow in ornate surroundings (p112).

3 House of Terror Grim but fascinating original torture centre (p109).

4 Heroes' Square 1,000 years of history in one plaza (p111).

5 Zoo Where the buildings are as fascinating as the animals (p112).

FROM ERZSÉBET TÉR
TO LISZT FERENC TÉR

District VI begins in the city centre, opposite the focal Erzsébet tér. From here, two main roads run parallel to each other: **Király utca**, one side of which is officially in District VII; and the city's grand avenue of **Andrássy út**. Narrow and always busy with pedestrians, rapidly gentrifying Király utca is integral to Budapest's bar vortex, as well as being home to stylish boutiques and a better category of restaurant. Running off it into the depths of District VII, the Gozsdu udvar courtyard (*see p118* **Holding Court**) and Kazinczy utca are crowded with drinkers every weekend and all summer long, a phenomenon that has helped change the character of previously down-at-heel Király utca. Not so long ago, 'King Street' was worth a stroll for second-hand Communist-era uniforms – now, young professionals browse for Indonesian lampshades or a loft to rent.

Even narrower, forgotten streets connect Király utca with quiet **Paulay Ede utca**, and then on to prestigious Andrássy út. Extending for 2.5 kilometres (1.5 miles) from Bajcsy-Zsilinszky út to Heroes' Square, Andrássy út is to Budapest what the Champs-Elysées is to Paris. It even ends with its own version of the Arc de Triomphe: the colonnade on Heroes' Square, right in front of **Városliget** (City Park; *see p111*).

The development of the boulevard from 1872 to 1885, and of many of the monuments along it, was part of the build-up for Hungary's 1896 millennial celebrations. Soon after its completion, prosaic Sugár út ('Avenue') was renamed in honour of the great statesman and leading light behind its creation: Count Gyula Andrássy.

The first half of Andrássy, between Bajcsy-Zsilinszky út and Oktogon (*see p107*), is narrower than the second half and lined with tall trees, making this stretch pleasantly shady. It's also far livelier, with busy terraced cafés and restaurants. Armani, Gucci and Zegna: all want their shop windows here. In 2013, an overblown attempt was made to gather numerous major fashion houses under one roof in the shape of five-storey **Il Bacio di Stile** (www.ilbaciodistile.com), topped with a panoramic restaurant and cocktail bar. However, Il Bacio has closed part of its operation and its future is uncertain.

But Andrássy út hasn't lost its glamour. One block further up, the **Opera House** (*see p166*) set the tone for the city's grand boulevard – both were opened within a year of each other. Miklós Ybl's neo-Renaissance masterpiece was another grandiose project created to reflect imperial splendour as the millennium of the Magyar conquest approached. Its cultural importance has always been linked to Magyar national identity. Ybl supervised every detail, including the Masonic allusions of the smiling sphinxes. The interior features seven kilograms of gold and 260 bulbs in an enormous chandelier.

Opposite the opera is the former Dreschler Palace, co-designed by Ödön Lechner as an apartment block in 1883, before he got heavily into Secessionist style. The ground-floor coffeehouse, with its arcaded terrace, was somewhere to be seen during the Golden Age. Later occupied by the

Capa Centre.

IN THE KNOW PICTURE THIS

Robert Capa, born in Budapest as Endre Friedmann, made his name in the Spanish Civil War and became a legend on D-Day. The only photographer to wade off the first carrier with US troops, on 6 June 1944, Capa shot four rolls of film while under German fire, returning to England that same day for the exclusive of the century. In the haste to process them for *Life* magazine in the lab back in London, three complete rolls and most of the fourth were ruined. All that remained were 11 grainy images – but their power and immediacy made Capa famous. He died ten years later after stepping on a landmine during the French war in Indochina.

Ballet Institute, the building is now being turned into a luxury hotel, due to open at the end of 2017. Round the corner, on Dalszínház utca, is one of the most striking examples of the work of one of Lechner's protégés, Béla Lajta. His extraordinary 1910 Parisiana nightclub, now the **Új Színház**, was restored to its full art nouveau splendour in 1998 (*see p94* Walk).

Heading up towards Oktogon, Nagymező utca is known as Budapest's Broadway. Between the wars, in the heyday of the Arizona nightclub, this was the place to be. Theatres such as the **Thália** (*see p168*) and the **Operett Színház** (*see p165*) are complemented by pre-show spots such as the **Komédiás Kávéház** (*see p105*), where veteran pianist Tibor Sóos plays the Broadway hits of yesteryear.

Reflecting another aspect of a long and proud tradition in visual culture, the **Mai Manó** gallery hosts exhibitions of work by renowned Hungarian photographers; it's named after a royal court photographer, who lived and worked in the building in the 1890s. It also has an excellent café.

Further south on Nagymező utca, in the former Ernst Museum, the recently opened **Capa Központ** gallery and cultural institute is named after the famous Hungarian war photographer Robert Capa. It's worth a look for the building alone, an art nouveau beauty.

Actors, artists and photographers mingled in this elegant quarter in the early 1900s, many later fleeing to Vienna or Paris, then New York or Hollywood, as the political climate grew colder. Others met at the nearby Café Japan, now the **Írók Boltja** (Writers' Bookshop), still a centre for literary events and a decent spot in which to find photographic histories of Budapest.

This stylish store stands on the corner of one of Budapest's most prominent squares: pedestrianised **Liszt Ferenc tér**. Named after the Hungarian composer who founded the

Zeneakadémia (Music Academy; *see p167*) at the southern end of the long, thin square, this bustling place has one of the heaviest concentrations of bars and restaurants in town. Most have terraces, creating a real Mediterranean atmosphere on summer evenings. The venues themselves lack much individuality, with the honourable exception of **Menza**, still retro and still fresh after more than ten years.

Standing with his back to the bar scene is a statue of Endre Ady, the poet's doleful eyes glaring at fellow writer Mór Jókai, whose statue presides over his namesake square opposite.

Sights & Museums

Capa Centre
Capa Központ
VI.Nagymező utca 8 (413 1310, www.capacenter. hu). M1 Oktogon or Opera. **Open** 11am-7pm Mon-Thur, Sat, Sun; 11am-9pm Fri. **Admission** Ft2,000; Ft1,200 reductions. **Map** p102 C5 ❶
Opened in 2013, on the centenary of his birth, this gallery honours the great Hungarian war photographer Robert Capa (*see left* In the Know). It occupies the former Ernst Museum, an art nouveau marvel designed in 1912 by Ödön Lechner and other major artistic figures as an exhibition hall and cinema. As well as staging exhibitions, the institute has founded a new photography award, part of its mission to promote young exponents of the genre. There's a scattering of original articles and books about Capa in the ornate lobby.

Mai Manó House
Mai Manó Ház
VI.Nagymező utca 20 (473 2666, www.maimano. hu). M1 Oktogon or Opera. **Open** 2-7pm Mon-Fri; 11am-7pm Sat, Sun. **Admission** Ft1,500; Ft700 reductions. **No credit cards. Map** p102 C5 ❷
This multi-level gallery occupies the former studio of court photographer Manó Mai (1855-1917), an appropriately photogenic fin-de-siècle architectural gem. It presents a reliably eclectic mix of Hungarian and international photographic art. The café is a destination in its own right.

Restaurants

Big Fish
VI.Andrássy út 44 (269 0693, www.thebig fish.hu). M1 Oktogon, or tram 4, 6. **Open** noon-10pm daily. **Main courses** Ft2,500-Ft6,000. **Map** p102 C5 ❸ Fish
Big Fish offers decent prices on wonderful preparations of fresh fish and shellfish. Go up to the counter and look your fish right in the eye, or choose shrimp, squid, oysters or even lobster – whatever's fresh. Tell them how you want it cooked and a waiter will bring it to the table. The interior is industrial minimalist, with outdoor seating on a bustling section of Andrássy.

EXPLORE

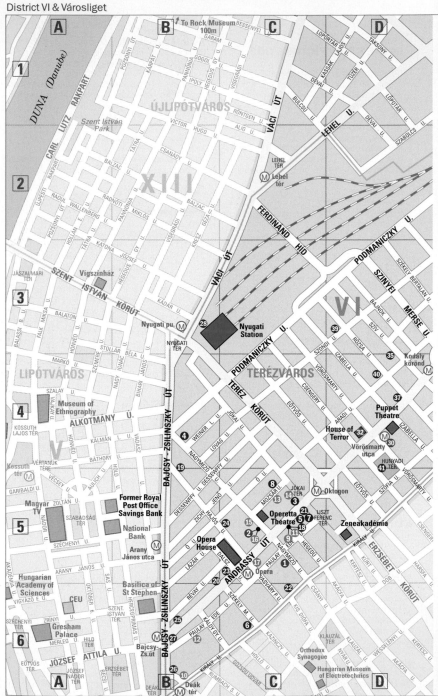

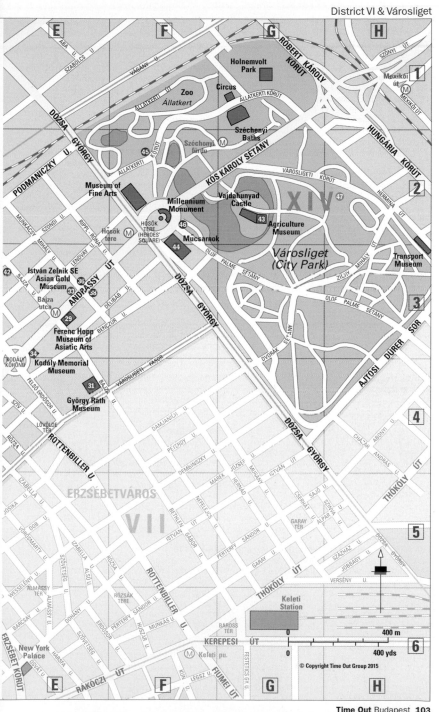

EXPLORE

Dang Muoi Pho Bistro
*VI.Nagymező utca 51 (06 30 955 2548,
www.vietnamietterem.hu). M1 Oktogon or
Opera.* **Open** 10am-10pm Mon-Sat; 11am-
10pm Sun. **Main courses** Ft1,390-Ft2,690.
Map p102 B4 **❹ Vietnamese**
A simple Vietnamese food stall at the Chinese
Market used to draw crowds to the further reaches of
District VIII on a quest for Budapest's best pho soup.
When the owners opened this restaurant (with basic
decor and low prices) in the theatre district, it was
an instant hit. Vietnamese-style mains are served,
and they've even expanded into sushi delivery, but
the main reason to visit is for the pho. The branch
at the Chinese Market lives on, along with two other
branches in Buda and deeper in south Pest.
Other locations I.Attila út 125 (06 30 992 4555);
Chinese Market, VIII.Kőbányai út 23 (no phone);
IX.Ernő utca 30 (06 30 945 0299).

★ **Klassz**
*VI.Andrássy út 41 (no phone, www.klasszetterem.
hu). M1 Oktogon, or tram 4, 6.* **Open** 11.30am-
11pm daily. **Main courses** Ft1,890-Ft5,490.
Map p102 C5 **❺ Wine bar**
This bright wine bar doesn't take bookings or even
have a phone number, but it's always packed. It's
owned by Bortársaság (Hungary's pioneering chain
of wine shops) and the courteous, savvy servers will
guide you through the frequently changing wine
list, with 35 local labels by the glass. Food includes
both continental and Hungarian dishes. *See also p90*
Cork and Fork.

LouLou
*VI.Székely Mihály utca 2 (877 6202, 06 70 333
5289, www.lou-lou.hu). M1 Opera.* **Open** noon-
3pm, 6.30-11pm Mon-Fri; 6.30-11pm Sat. **Main
courses** Ft2,400-Ft5,700. **Map** p102 C6 **❻ French**
Once upon a time, long before Budapest discovered contemporary gastronomy, Károly Rudits'
downtown restaurant LouLou was a culinary
trailblazer. Now he's back, with a classy space just
off Király utca, five minutes' walk from the Opera
House. Chef Attila Nagy, who's worked at Michelin-
starred Costes and under Gordon Ramsay, creates
some memorable dishes, such as pan-seared quail
with duck foie gras, and pressed wild boar shoulder
with polenta and red wine jus. Go for the set lunch
(Ft4,350 three courses, Ft5,550 for four), the à la carte
or the tasting menu (Ft18,900) – but do go.

Menza
*VI.Liszt Ferenc tér 2 (413 1482, www.
menzaetterem.hu). M1 Oktogon, or tram 4, 6.*
Open 10am-midnight daily. **Main courses**
Ft1,490-Ft3,990. **Map** p102 C5 **❼ Hungarian**
Still the locals' favourite bar-restaurant on Liszt
Ferenc tér, this retro spot done up to resemble a
1970s cafeteria pays homage to classic Hungarian
cookery. A change of chef has beefed up the meaty

offerings, but there are also non-Magyar dishes.
Prices are competitive, and the cocktail and wine list
is extensive. Watch out for daily two-course specials
(Ft1,090) and seasonal fruity drinks in summer.
▶ *For more Hungarian retro, head to the pre-1989
heaven of the Táskarádió bar; see p82.*

Ristorante Krizia
*VI.Mozsár utca 12 (331 8711, www.ristorante
krizia.hu). M1 Oktogon, or tram 4, 6.* **Open** noon-
3pm, 6.30pm-midnight Mon-Sat. **Main courses**
Ft1,850-Ft8,800. **Map** p102 C5 **❽ Italian**
There's nothing flash about Ristorante Krizia. But
over the years, this attractively lit cellar has been
doing its bit to raise the standard of Italian restaurants in Budapest. Chef-owner Graziano Cattaneo
is usually around, happy to recommend something
off-menu; otherwise, try the paper-thin prosciutto,
or a comforting main such as house-made lasa-
gnette with bolognese ragoût and asiago cheese. The
waiters radiate Mediterranean warmth. The three-
course lunch deal for Ft1,500 is a bargain.

Cafés & Bars

360 Bar
*Párisi Nagyáruház, VI.Andrássy út 39 (06 70 259
5153, www.360bar.hu). M1 Opera, or bus 105.*
Open *Summer* 2pm-midnight Mon-Wed; 2pm-
3am Thur-Sat; 10am-midnight Sun. **Map** p102 C5 **❾**
Cocktail in hand, gaze across the rooftops of
Budapest to the green hills beyond while a DJ pumps
out vibey tunes at this outdoor bar atop the historic
Párisi Nagyáruház (*see p106* **Lotz in Store**). Note
that's it's open only in summer.

Bar Budapest
*VI.Anker köz 3 (06 30 254 5704, www.thebar
budapest.com). M1, M2, M3 Deák tér.* **Open**
7pm-3am Mon-Sat. **Map** p102 B6 **❿**
The former Bar Domby remains a slick spot. The
bartenders look the part, and can conjure plenty of
superior cocktails. The low-lit room glitters with
golden surfaces. The crowd usually includes foreigners happy to pay an average Ft2,000 for a proper
cocktail, and a smattering of B-level local celebrities.

Book Café
*Párisi Nagyárúház, VI.Andrássy út 39 (461
5835, www.parisi.hu). M1 Opera, or bus 105.*
Open 10am-10pm daily. **Map** p102 C5 ⓫
A stunning coffeehouse occupying the Lotz Hall
on the first floor of the lovingly renovated Párisi
Nagyárúház – once a department store, now a book
emporium (*see p106* **Lotz in Store**).

Boutiq' Bar
*VI.Paulay Ede utca 5 (06 30 554 2323,
www.boutiqbar.hu). M1, M2, M3 Deák tér,
or M1 Bajcsy-Zsilinszky út.* **Open** 6pm-2am
Tue-Sat. **Map** p102 B6 ⓬

EXPLORE

A dedicated team opened this tidy little spot on a quiet side street just as the credit crunch hit. Were punters prepared to pay up to Ft2,000 for a Bohemian Swizzle (with Becherovka), a HausSpritzer (with Martini Rosato) or a Zwack & Soda (with Unicum Szilva)? The answer is a life-affirming *igen*, a thumbs-up for the brave Boutiq'ers who conceived a drinks menu outside the comfort zone of many potential tipplers. A bar for cocktail connoisseurs.

★ Caledonia
*VI.Mozsár utca 9 (311 7611, www.kaledonia.hu).
M1 Oktogon, or tram 4, 6.* **Open** 2pm-midnight Mon-Thur; 2pm-1am Fri; noon-1am Sat, Sun.
Map p102 C5 ⑬
Easily the most palatable of Budapest's expat pubs, this Scottish-themed hostelry attracts Brit and Magyar alike for TV football, all-day breakfasts and Belhaven brews from Dunbar. Some 100 Scottish single malts complement affordable Dreher and Kozel on tap, but, most of all, it doesn't feel like a forint flytrap for footie-focused foreigners. Patrick and Zsuzsa, who run the place, make a real effort. Live music on Saturdays, a monthly pub quiz and outdoor seating in summer are recent introductions.

Kiadó Kocsma
VI.Jókai tér 3 (331 1955). M1 Oktogon, or tram 4, 6. **Open** 10am-1am Mon-Fri; 11am-1am Sat, Sun. **Map** p102 C5 ⑭
This is really two bars in one. The street-level bar (including an intricately carved wooden loft showing art exhibitions) works better for mingling with strangers, while the cellar is where you bring a table's worth of friends. Accessed by a separate door outside, it has a couple of cosy rooms under vaulted

ceilings, with walled-off booths in the rear. Staff are efficient, easy-going bohemian types, and there's decent and affordable Hungarian bar food.

Komédiás Kávéház
VI.Nagymező utca 26 (302 0901, www.komedias kavehaz.hu). M1 Oktogon or Opera. **Open** 8am-midnight Mon-Fri; 1pm-midnight Sat, Sun.
Map p102 C5 ⑮
This elegant café in the heart of Budapest's Broadway harks back to the cabaret era. Every evening, a pianist in the open frontage tinkles tunes to customers inside and out, as theatregoers pass by with a smile. Catch the legendary Tibor Soós mid-week and he'll regale you with tales of his days with Leonard Bernstein in Vienna. The place has a French feel (it's also known as Café le Comédien), offering coffee varieties such as Café Cointreau, Café Can Can (with Advocaat) and Café le Comédien (with Baileys).

Mai Manó Kávézó
VI.Nagymező utca 20 (269 5642). M1 Opera or Oktogon. **Open** 8am-1am daily. **Map** p102 C5 ⑯
Attached to the photo gallery of the same name (*see p101*), the Mai Manó is suitably arty. Red banquettes line walls dotted with smoky photos and touches of faux Klimt. Good wine, quality liquors, and Arany Fácán and Soproni on tap complement excellent croissants and sandwiches, although most of the gossipy twentysomethings prefer nicotine. Breakfast and brunch include plenty of vegetarian options.

Művész
VI.Andrássy út 29 (343 3544, www.muvesz kavehaz.hu). M1 Opera. **Open** 9am-10pm Mon-Sat; 10am-10pm Sun. **Map** p102 C5 ⑰

Boutiq' Bar

EXPLORE

LOTZ IN STORE

The Párisi Nagyáruház is now revived – Lotz Hall and all.

Lotz Hall.

Of all the elegant commercial buildings along Andrássy út, no.39 is the most impressive. Built as the Terézvárosi Kaszinó in 1882, the building was transformed after Samuel Goldberger took it over in 1909. Goldberger envisaged a luxury department store similar to those in Paris – such as the one that he had already built on Rákóczi út, near Blaha Lujza tér, only for it to burn down in 1903.

Having purchased a building in the most glamorous location in town, Goldberger hired architect Zsigmond Sziklai to convert it from a place of prosaic recreation – with a beer hall, restaurant, and billiards and games rooms – into the finest shopping palace east of Vienna. Sziklai created an atrium, glass-walled lifts and a glass-roofed courtyard, with a panoramic walkway. One entrance, art nouveau in design, gave on to Andrássy út; the other, with neo-Renaissance touches, faced Paulay Ede utca. Thus was born the **Párisi Nagyáruház** ('Paris Department Store').

The upper part of the building was largely the work of porcelain manufacturer Vilmos Zsolnay, whose famous family firm was also responsible for the roof on top of Matthias Church and the **Museum of Applied Arts** (*see p136*). On these upper floors, the Paris Salon Art Gallery showcased antiques, furniture and the contemporary art of the day, as well as Zsolnay ceramics. Gorgeous murals by Károly Lotz decorated the auction house where the artworks were sold; the room, the Lotz Hall, had been the ballroom of the original Terézvárosi Kaszinó.

The Párisi Nagyáruház survived World War II, but not the 1950s. It became first a book warehouse, then the Divatcsarnok, a Communist-era clothes store, and by the 1990s had fallen into disrepair. The building lay empty and negelected for years until it was rebuilt in 2009, almost exactly a century after it opened as an art nouveau gem.

Today, the renovated emporium houses the flagship branch of the **Alexandra** bookshop chain (*see p107*). It's grand enough, but not a patch on the real jewel in the crown: one floor up, the beautifully restored Lotz Hall has been turned into the **Book Café** (*see p104*), where music recitals and book signings are held. And right at the top, the summer-only **360 Bar** (*see p104*) is the highest rooftop bar in the city – the perfect place for chilling with a cocktail while gazing out across the city.

One of the most prominent of the city's old-style coffeehouses (founded 1898), located diagonally across from the Opera House. The interior exudes antique elegance, while the small enclosed terrace is fantastic for people-watching. The coffees and cakes reflect Austro-Hungarian tradition, but there are cocktails and snack platters too. Tourists and Hungarian ladies of a certain age fill the place day and night, gazed upon by Budapest's stars of yesteryear in black-and-white portrait form.

Shops & Services

Alexandra Könyvesház
Párisi Nagyárúház, VI.Andrássy út 39 (484 8000, www.alexandra.hu). M1 Opera, or bus 105. **Open** 10am-10pm daily. **Map** p102 C5 ⑱ **Books & music**
This huge bookstore, showcase branch of Hungary's most prominent chain, shares the impressively restored Párisi Nagyárúház (*see p106* **Lotz in Store**) with the Book Café in the stunning Lotz Hall.
Other locations throughout the city.

Cydonia Vintage
VI.Hajós utca 43 (06 70 381 4849). M3 Arany János utca, or bus 9, or trolleybus 72, 73. **Open** noon-7pm Mon-Fri. **Map** p102 B5 ⑲ **Fashion**
Classic dresses, tops, jewellery and sundry accessories fill this vintage shop. All the items on display seem to have been worn for some impossibly glamorous social occasion.

Herend Porcelain
VI.Andrássy út 16 (374 0006, www.herend.com). M1 Opera. **Open** 10am-6pm Mon-Fri; 10am-2pm Sat. **Map** p102 B5 ⑳ **Homewares**
Herend has been producing Hungary's finest hand-painted porcelain since 1826; Queen Victoria picked her own delicate bird and butterfly pattern. This so-called Belvedere Brand Shop is the flagship of the fleet; there are other stores in and around Budapest and a demonstration workshop and major outlet at the Herend factory north of Balaton.
Other locations throughout the city.

★ Írók Boltja
VI.Andrássy út 45 (322 1645, www.irok boltja.hu). M1 Oktogon, or tram 4, 6. **Open** 10am-7pm Mon-Fri; 11am-7pm Sat. **Map** p102 C5 ㉑ **Books & music**
Once the seminal Café Japan, this shop has long been the domain of intellectuals. Hungarian books in English translation are available here, with a fine photo album selection.

Lab Shop
VI.Király utca 48 (321 3250, www.thelabshop. eu). M1 Opera, or tram 4, 6. **Open** 10am-8pm Mon-Fri; 10am-6pm Sat; 11am-6pm Sun. **Map** p102 C6 ㉒ **Fashion**

The Lab Shop sells urban sportswear and street gear for the active and actively brand-conscious. Expect footwear, eyewear, skate gear and accessories from the likes of Etnies, Oakley and Eastpak.

Manier Boutique
VI.Andrássy út 18 (483 1140, www.manier.hu). M1 Opera. **Open** 11am-7pm Mon-Sat. **Map** p102 C5 ㉓ **Fashion**
Luxury prêt-à-porter and designer streetwear by eccentric and experimental 'couturist' Anikó Németh.

Náray Tamás
VI.Hajós utca 17 (266 2473, www.naraytamas.hu). M1 Opera. **Open** 11.30am-6pm Mon-Fri. **Map** p102 C5 ㉔ **Fashion**
Costume designer for films, operas and TV talent shows, Tamás Náray can be trusted to come up with a stunning outfit for your special occasion (weddings included). His 'couture-à-porter' collections are highlights of the Hungarian fashion calendar.

Omorovicza Boutique & Spa
VI.Andrássy út 2 (302 4604, www.omorovicza.eu) M1 Bajcsy-Zsilinszky út. **Open** 10am-6pm Mon-Sat. **Map** p102 B6 ㉕ **Health & beauty**
Having built the Rácz Baths in Buda in the 1800s, the noble Omorovicza family rode the waves of European history before Stephen de Heinrich de Omorovicza met an American diplomat and introduced her to the wonders of Budapest's healing waters. Romance blossomed, and the Omorovicza brand was born. Harnessing the mineral powers of local thermal waters, Omorovicza creates upmarket beauty treatments – also available at the Four Seasons Gresham Palace (*see p217*), at Liberty, Harrods and the Park Lane Hotel in London, and at exclusive hotels across the US.

★ Retrock Deluxe
VI.Anker köz 2 (06 30 472 3636, www.retrock. com). M1, M2, M3 Deák tér. **Open** 11am-9pm Mon-Fri; 11am-8pm Sat, Sun. **Map** p102 B6 ㉖ **Fashion**
With a reputation for spotting new trends, Retrock is the place for all kinds of fashion and accessories, from lingerie to cycle clothing. Up-and-coming Hungarian designers include Dora Abodi and Doridea.

Vista
VI.Andrássy út 1 (429 9999, www.vista.hu). M1 Bajcsy-Zsilinszky út, or M1, M2, M3 Deák tér. **Open** 9.30am-6pm Mon-Fri; 10am-2.30pm Sat. **Map** p102 B6 ㉗ **Travel agency**
The largest private travel agency in town.
Other locations throughout the city.

OKTOGON & TERÉZ KÖRÚT

Oktogon, where the Nagykörút crosses Andrássy út, is a major intersection and, of course, octagonal. But the shape didn't always

EXPLORE

dictate the name: in Communist days, this was 7 November Square; before then, under Horthy, it was named after Mussolini. The fabulous neon signs that once characterised this crossing point have long been taken down, some of them to be on illuminated display on Museum Night, 21 June, at the **Museum of Electrotechnics** (*see p119*).

This section of the city's main tram-lined ring road is called **Teréz körút**, just as the historic name of District VI is Terézváros, in honour of Habsburg Empress Maria Theresa's visit in 1751. With the glamorous exception of a luxury hotel or two, the Nagykörút between Oktogon and Petőfi Bridge is almost uniformly grubby, with few venues worthy of mention. Between Oktogon and Nyugati Station, however, it takes on more of the character of the district around it.

First, there's the most popular arthouse cinema in town, the **Művész** (*see p145*). Three blocks towards Nyugati, the **Radisson Blu Béke Hotel, Budapest** (*see p218*) enjoys a century-old history. Opened as a classic railway hotel, the Britannia, in 1913, it became the home of a famed coffeehouse during the Silver Age between the wars. Renamed Béke ('Peace') after the war, it later hosted a renowned cabaret club, a genre known in Budapest as an *orfeum*. Hungary's best-loved comedians and singers of the 1960s and '70s performed here. The hotel group Radisson took it over in 1988, its first European venture – and first behind the Iron Curtain.

Teréz körút finishes at its most magnificent landmark: **Nyugati station**. Built by the Eiffel company of Paris in 1877, it's a pale-blue palace of iron and glass. The panes in front allow you to see inside the station, making the arriving and departing trains part of the streetlife. Built into one side of the station is the first Hungarian branch of America's most famous hamburger chain, its design an attempt to match the station's steam-age glamour. The echoing ticket hall hasn't changed much over the decades. (The international ticket office behind it is rarely busy – handy to know when Budapest's other major station, Keleti, is crowded with backpackers all summer long.)

On 15 July 1846, the first train journey in Hungary started from here, carrying notable dignitaries 33 kilometres (21 miles) to Vác in just under an hour. On board was Sándor Petőfi, invited to write one of the world's first poems about train travel. Within two years, another Petőfi poem had helped instigate war with Austria, and the poet would soon be dead.

Today, Nyugati is flanked by modern commerce. On one side, the pedestrianised plaza of **Nyugati tér** has a backdrop of gleaming shops and businesses; directly behind, the sprawling **Westend City Center** shopping mall is one of the biggest in the region, connected to the station via passageways lined with hawkers.

Views of Nyugati from the boulevard are spoilt by the unsightly road bridge carrying traffic over Nyugati tér towards the restored Lehel tér produce market. Below, the ever-busy 4 and 6 trams head one stop along the Nagykörút to Margaret Bridge – or one stop to Oktogon in the opposite direction.

Shops & Services

Westend City Center
VI. Váci út 1-3 (238 7777, www.westend.hu).
M3 Nyugati pu, or tram 4, 6. **Open** 8am-10pm daily. *Shops* 10am-8pm Mon-Sat; 10am-6pm Sun.
Map p102 B3 ❷❸ **Mall**
This huge mall is the city's busiest and most comprehensive – pretending to be a city within a city, with streets and squares, it can drive you to road rage. With 400 outlets across three storeys, pretty much all the key names in retail and services are here.

TOWARDS HEROES' SQUARE

Arrow-straight north from Oktogon, Andrássy út boulevard gets broader and brighter, as the tall, shady trees are replaced by younger, smaller ones. From here you can spy the archangel Gabriel on his Heroes' Square column.

Such a sight would have been a dreadful one to anyone being dragged up here by men in overcoats in the early 1950s, for at no.60 was the headquarters of the ÁVO, the secret police. In the very same building, the **House of Terror** museum opened in 2002, providing a sobering walk through prison cells and torture chambers.

Around the corner, on Vörösmarty utca, is the **Franz Liszt Museum**, set in the composer's former residence – the original home of the Music Academy he founded in 1875 (which is now on Liszt Ferenc tér, the other side of Oktogon). At Andrássy út 69 is the neo-Renaissance College of Fine Arts; once an exhibition hall, today it houses the **Budapest Puppet Theatre** (*see p143*), as indicated by a large neon sign of a child's outline drawing of a doll.

Kodály körönd roundabout was clearly once very splendid. Renovation has begun on the palatial townhouses here. The composer Zoltán Kodály used to live in a flat in turreted nos.87-89, now home to the **Kodály Memorial Museum & Archive**.

The final stretch of Andrássy út feels wider than the rest of the street, with villas set back from the road. It's a suitable setting for Budapest's de facto embassy quarter, marked by shiny plaques, bright flags and imposing gates. Diplomats have a decent choice of nearby terrace restaurants, such as the **Kogart**, which is also a large private gallery specialising in Hungarian contemporary art.

The neighbourhood also has a trio of museums of exotic collections accrued by intrepid global

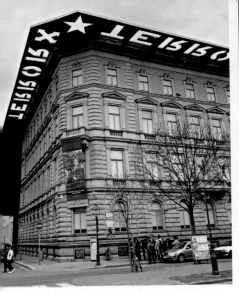

House of Terror.

travellers. There's the **György Ráth Museum** of mainly Japanese, Chinese and Indian artefacts, though it's overshadowed by the impressive **Ferenc Hopp Museum of Eastern Asiatic Arts.** These two institutions were joined in 2011 by another in similar vein, the **István Zelnik South-East Asian Gold Museum.**

The Ráth Museum is on Városligeti fasor, the northern section of Király utca past Lövölde tér. Quiet and shady, Városligeti fasor is lined with Secessionist buildings – for example, at nos.42, 44 and 47. The parallel road of Benczúr utca (back towards Andrássy út) is worth a look for the whimsical villas at nos.23, 24, 33 and 45, all designed between 1902 and 1911 by Emil Vidor.

Sights & Museums

★ Ferenc Hopp Museum of Eastern Asiatic Arts

Hopp Ferenc Kelet-ázsiai Művészeti Múzeum
VI.Andrássy út 103 (322 8476, www.hopp museum.hu). M1 Bajza utca. **Open** 10am-6pm Tue-Sun. **Admission** Ft1,000; Ft500 reductions. **No credit cards. Map** p103 E3 ㉙
In five trips around the world, wealthy optician Ferenc Hopp (1833-1919) amassed more than 4,000 pieces of Asian art, including Lamaist scroll paintings, old Indian art influenced by ancient Greece, and artefacts from Mongolia. After he died in this villa in 1919, it was converted into a museum, as his will intended. New displays from his massive collection were added in 2015, and the garden was renovated.

Franz Liszt Museum

Liszt Ferenc Múzeum
VI. Vörösmarty utca 35 (413 0440, www. lisztmuseum.hu). M1 Vörösmarty utca. **Open** 10am-6pm Mon-Fri; 9am-5pm Sat. **Admission** Ft1,300; Ft600 reductions. **Audio guide** Ft700. **No credit cards. Map** p102 D4 ㉚
A modest collection of memorabilia, including the composer's two Chickering pianos, furnishes the apartment where Liszt lived for five years until 1886. There's also a small concert hall with a regular programme of events.

György Ráth Museum

Ráth György Múzeum
VI. Városligeti fasor 12 (456 5100). M1 Bajza utca. **Open** 10am-6pm Tue-Sun. **Admission** Ft600; Ft300 reductions. **No credit cards. Map** p103 E4 ㉛
György Ráth (1828-1905) was an Asian art historian who collected scrolls, snuff bottles, miniature shrines, samurai armour and a carved lobster on a lacquer comb from Japan. The museum's permanent collection (enhanced by detailed English texts) is complemented by temporary exhibitions.

★ House of Terror

Terror Háza
VI.Andrássy út 60 (374 2600, www.terrorhaza.hu). M1 Vörösmarty utca. **Open** 10am-6pm Tue-Sun. **Admission** Ft2,000; Ft1,000 reductions. **Audio guide** Ft1,500. **Map** p102 D4 ㉜
This former villa belonging to the Perlmutter family was used by the fascist Arrow Cross Party as a place in which to torture Jews and political opponents before and during World War II; after the war, Hungary's version of the KGB, the ÁVO, simply took it over. It's now an award-winning museum revealing the inhumanities of the mid 20th century, and a memorial to those who were interrogated, tortured or killed in the building. There's little doubt as to the nature of the museum as soon as you walk in.

EXPLORE

Symbols of the Communist and Arrow Cross parties lie straight ahead, while in the ticket queue a video shows a tearful eyewitness to the atrocities of 1956. A tall column of victims' portraits stands by the lift that takes you to the second floor, where the exhibition starts with the Nazi era. Videos, uniforms and original radio broadcasts (transmitted via an ominously heavy old telephone) tell of Holocaust and war; a listening post, Zil car and walls of pigfat bricks tell of communist oppression here and in the countryside. On a video screen, a deadpan Jenő Somogyi, who cleaned up after torture victims here, describes tearing up their last letters to loved ones. Grim basement cells complete your visit, made slightly cheerier by a room of postcards sent from the West by 1956 emigrés to the soundtrack of 'Memories Are Made of This' in Hungarian.

István Zelnik South-East Asian Gold Museum

Zelnik István Délkelet-ázsiai Arany Múzeum
VI.Andrássy út 110 (482 3190, www.thegold museum.eu). M1 Bajza utca. **Open** 11am-5pm Tue-Thur, Sun; 11am-7pm Fri, Sat. **Admission** Ft3,400; Ft1,700 reductions. **Map** p103 E3 ㉓
Another trove of oriental cultural treasures, this museum differs from its two near neighbours – the György Ráth and the Ferenc Hopp – in that its creator, much-travelled former diplomat István Zelnik, is still alive. Ritual and sacred objects, religious art and jewellery are neatly divided by culture and civilisation over two floors of the former Rausch Villa; there's also a tearoom and a library.

Kodály Memorial Museum & Archive

Kodály Emlékmúzeum és Archívum
VI.Andrássy út 87-89 (352 7106, www.kodaly. hu). M1 Kodály körönd. **Open** (by appt only) 10am-noon, 2-4.30pm Wed-Fri. **Admission** Ft230. **Map** p103 E3 ㉔
A modest collection of musical and folksy artefacts are ranged around the rather modest abode of composer and musicologist Zoltán Kodály, who lived here for most of his adult life, until his death in 1967. There's also an archive of manuscripts and documents. Kodály's methods of music tuition are still in use today. If you want to visit, contact the museum two days before your intended visit.

Restaurants

Chez Daniel

VI.Szív utca 32 (302 4039, www.chezdaniel.hu). M1 Kodály körönd. **Open** noon-3pm, 7-11pm daily. **Main courses** Ft2,200-Ft4,400. **Map** p102 D4 ㉟ **French**
On a good day, this restaurant run by chef-patron Daniel Labrosse serves the best French meal in town. On an off-day, service can be shambolic. Having worked around France before meeting his Hungarian wife, Daniel appreciates the importance

of good ingredients: he's sniffed out his own truffle supplier and makes some of the best goose liver terrine in town. He's recently added some North African dishes to the menu. The wine list focuses on whites from Alsace and Beaujolais, best sipped in the lovely hidden courtyard. Book ahead in summer.

Kogart

VI.Andrássy út 112 (354 3830, www.kogarthaz. hu). M1 Bajza utca. **Open** 10am-6pm Mon-Fri. **Main courses** Ft2,100-Ft4,200. **Map** p103 E3 ㊲ **Hungarian/Mediterranean**
The ground floor of an art gallery in a restored villa provides a grand setting for this restaurant offering Mediterranean and Magyar cuisine. The lavishly decorated, wood-panelled dining room is attractive, though the quiet terrace off Andrássy is probably the superior place to sit. A grill appears on the terrace in summer, expanding the menu. Pasta and fish dishes are dependable, but chef István Kiripolszki also caters to meat-eaters, with veal, duck and wild boar. The menu has been scaled down – though it includes a daily changing two-course lunch (Ft1,900) – while opening hours are now restricted to daytime weekdays only.

Millennium Da Pippo

VI.Andrássy út 76 (374 0880, www.millennium dapippo.hu). M1 Kodály körönd. **Open** noon-midnight daily. **Main courses** Ft2,100-Ft5,350. **Map** p102 D4 ㊲ **Italian**
A lovely little corner local with a rustic atmosphere and great food at neighbourly prices. The kitchen, run by a friendly gent from Syracuse, make its own pasta; the thin-crusted pizzas are superb; and the steaks and fish are dependable. A whole section of the menu is named after Italy's World Cup-winning side of 2006 – this is a major spot for *calcio*, as testified by the Juve shirts and Serie A screened on Sunday afternoons. Service is slick and friendly. Pavement tables are at a premium in summer.

La Perle Noire

VI.Andrássy út 111 (462 2189, 555 1545, www. laperlenoire.hu). M1 Bajza utca. **Open** noon-midnight daily. **Main courses** Ft3,200-Ft5,900. **Map** p103 E3 ㊳ **Hungarian/international**
This upscale villa-and-terrace eaterie in the diplomatic quarter is very impressive. The seasonal menu does a bit of globetrotting, calling in on Argentina, France and Italy, but is perhaps most at home in Hungary. The stuffed cabbage roll with Mangalica pork and veal is a stand-out, as is hunter's-style rabbit leg with mango and dumpling with truffle jus. Also, don't miss the goulash with beef neck.

Taj Mahal

VI.Szondi utca 40 (301 0447, www.tajmahal.hu). M1 Kodály körönd, or M3 Nyugati pu. **Open** noon-11pm Tue-Sun. **Main courses** Ft1,560-Ft4,380. **Map** p102 D3 ㊴ **Indian**

Located on a quiet corner behind Nyugati Station, this is one of the few places in town to offer south Indian dishes. In fact, the menu spans all Indian regions, including spicy Goan, though the dominant cooking style is north Indian; the clay tandoor oven turns out exquisitely cooked meats and fresh naans. The lofty interior, featuring chandeliers and colourful textile paintings, is staffed by polite young women in saris. The Taj Mahal also offers delivery – unusual for good restaurants in Budapest.

Shops & Services

Anh Tuan
VI.Rózsa utca 74 (06 30 983 3499, www.anh-tuan.com). M1 Kodály körönd. **Open** by appt.
Map p102 D4 ⓸ **Fashion**
One of Budapest's most interesting designers, Anh Tuan returned from a stint at the London College of Fashion to launch his own womenswear line. Of Vietnamese origin, Tuan revels in luxurious colours, combining old and new techniques to produce sassy handbags and mini rucksacks as part of his biannual collections. This is his showroom – his designs are also available at the recently opened multi-brand boutique Treasure (V.Aulich utca 5, 06 70 775 0804).

★ Culinaris
VI.Hunyadi tér 3 (341 7001, www.culinaris.hu). M1 Vörösmarty utca. **Open** 9am-7pm Mon-Fri; 8am-7pm Sat. **Map** p102 D5 ⓵ **Food & drink**
This grocer brings global delights (including fresh veg, spices and preserves) to landlocked Hungary; it's also next door to one of the city's better produce markets. The branch on Balassi Bálint utca is open on Sundays and does sit-down meals.
Other locations III.Perc utca 8 (345 0780), V.Balassi Bálint utca 7 (373 0028).

Maison Marquise
VI.Bajza utca 56 (06 70 674 1073, www.maison marquise.com). M1 Bajza utca. **Open** by appt.
Map p103 E3 ⓶ **Fashion**
Maison Marquise is the luxury brand launched in 2012 by designer Bori Tóth, after nearly a decade of building up her ready-to-wear line Tothbori. Own-designed printed silks and classic feminine lines are the hallmarks of MM's outfits, which have recently shown influences from the Far East.

HEROES' SQUARE & VÁROSLIGET

A proud symbol of confident 19th-century nationalism, **Heroes' Square** (Hősök tere) is a monumental celebration of mythic Magyardom. Completed for the 1896 Magyar millennium, which celebrated the anniversary of Hungarian tribes arriving in the Carpathian Basin, the square is focused on the **archangel Gabriel**,

staring down Andrássy út from his perch on top of a 36-metre (118-foot) column. Posed around the two curving colonnades at the column's base are statues of Hungarian kings and national heroes, from St Stephen to Lajos Kossuth. Now often crowded with teenage skateboarders, Heroes' Square has witnessed key events in modern Hungarian history – most significantly, the ceremony for the reburial of Imre Nagy in June 1989. This marked the communal call for democracy in Hungary.

While the Hungarian National Gallery (*see p50*) is the nation's most prestigious venue for local artists, Hungary's major European collection is in the stately **Museum of Fine Arts** (Szépművészeti Múzeum, 469 7100, www.szepmuveszeti.hu) on the north side of Heroes' Square. Currently undergoing a major overhaul until spring 2018, it has a magnificent collection of Spanish Masters, an excellent trove of Venetians, a Dürer, several Brueghels, a beautiful work attributed to Raphael and some Leonardos. Facing it across the square is the **Műcsarnok**, which hosts contemporary art exhibitions and the occasional live band or DJ party.

Beside the Műcsarnok, in a cobblestone lot called **Felvonulasi tér** (Parade Square), is a conspicuous modern memorial, set up where the Communist leadership used to wave to passing citizens on May Day. A group of rusting steel girders gradually merge to solidify into a big metal triangle – to mark the 1956 Uprising. The memorial was unveiled on 23 October 2006, the 50th anniversary of the start of the Uprising, in the place where a statue of Stalin was torn down during the 1956 riots. Near the '56 memorial is a symbolic disc-cum-hourglass, whose sands run out over the course of the year as 1 May approaches.

Heroes' Square is essentially the front gate to the **Városliget** (City Park), Budapest's main area for leisure. A cycle path runs round its 125 hectares – most bars, restaurants and beer gardens here have places to lock your bike. Laid out by French designer Nebbion, its public amenities start with a lake and renovated (winter-only) ice rink. Dotted around are facilities for various types of communal recreation: basketball courts, five-a-side football pitches, table-tennis tables, large chessboards. There are also courts for the local sport of *labtengó*, short for *labtenisz*, a kind of volleyball for footballers.

There's a nostalgic feel to the Városliget – of simpler, communal pleasures that were first enjoyed here long before malls and laser zones came along. Indeed, many of its attractions date back a century or more. It was here that the millennial celebrations of 1896 left ceremonial formalities behind: locals danced, dined and even tried out ballooning. Erected for the occasion, the faux-historic **Vajdahunyad Castle** still stands;

EXPLORE

EXPLORE

incorporating copies of elements from famous Hungarian castles throughout history, it's a jumble of architectural styles – the Baroque wing contains the large **Hungarian Museum of Agriculture**. Open-air concerts take place here in summer, which is also when the tranquil boating lake is open.

The castle also has one of Budapest's most bizarre statues: a seated faceless figure in a spooky hooded cape. This is *Anonymous*, a reference to the unknown medieval scribes who wrote the original histories of Hungary, an idea conceived during the 1896 millennial celebrations. Elsewhere in the park are statues of George Washington, Winston Churchill and Ronald Reagan.

Towards the park's northern edge along Hermina út stands the **Petőfi Csarnok** concert hall. The 'PeCsa' has hosted gigs by the likes of Björk and Nick Cave, plus numerous Hungarian bands, but in 2014 it was announced that it would be torn down and a new Museum Quarter established here – as yet of indeterminate purpose and description. The fate of the popular adjoining weekend flea market is also not known. The nearby **Transport Museum** (Közlekedési Múzeum; www.mmkm.hu) is closed until 2018 for a complete overhaul. One of the first of its kind to open in Europe, this venerable attraction has such gems as vintage railway carriages, early aeroplanes and an exact replica of the space capsule flown by Hungary's only astronaut, Bertalan Farkas, in 1980.

The far side of City Park, however, is the area where the heavyweight attractions are located. Behind the M1 metro station of the same name, the **Széchenyi Baths** (*see p205*) are one of Budapest's key sights. Europe's largest thermal baths originated when hot springs were discovered in Heroes' Square in the 1870s. They provided the public with a place for fun, ad hoc recreation for years, until a bathhouse was built. And not just any bathhouse, but a sumptuous pile created in neo-Baroque and neoclassical style by Győző Czigler. Expert geothermal engineer Vilmos Zsigmondy, whose statue stands in the main entrance to the baths today, had the natural waters piped through. Outdoor pools were added in 1927. Now with a whirlpool feature, and renovated to its former glory, the 'Szecska' is open 16 hours a day – and busy for most of them.

Opposite, just over Állatkerti körút, is a row of three family-friendly attractions. Closed down to much dismay in 2013, the old-school Amusement Park (Vidám Park) reopened six months later as the **Holnemvolt Park** ('Once Upon a Time' Park; *see p140*). Before the closure, families queued around the block for a last chance to go on the vintage rides, some of which have been renovated and kept for the new park. Created in tandem with

the nearby Zoo, it has a farmyard and petting zoo and is open from spring until November.

In between Holnemvolt Park and the Zoo, Budapest's **Capital Circus** (*see p143*) offers further old-school entertainment. From Wednesday through Sunday, acrobats, clowns and, yes, lion tamers, provide a circus show of the classic variety, drawing on Hungary's long tradition in the genre and inviting the best talent from Europe and the Far East.

Budapest's **Zoo** (*see p140*) is one of the world's oldest, celebrating its 150th anniversary in 2016. As well as its four-legged, finned or winged residents, the zoo is renowned for the ornate structures that house them. This was the result

Heroes' Square.
See p111.

of a complete rebuild from 1909-12, when art nouveau was all the rage. Kornél Neuschloss designed the main entrance and the exotic Elephant House, while Károly Kós and Dezső Zrumeczky added elements of Transylvanian folk art (an essential underlying element of the architectural vernacular of the day) to their various pavilions. Progressive management at the zoo has seen an impressive number of newborns in recent years – a baby giraffe, zebra and Indian antelope in January 2015 alone.

Alongside the zoo is the city's most prestigious dining establishment, **Gundel**. Opened in 1894 as the Wampetics, it was taken over in 1910 by top chef Károly Gundel, who transformed local cuisine by bringing in French influences. The prices may have changed, but the menu and appearance both echo the Golden Age, and the 1896 celebrations that created so much of the City Park and District VI stretching back towards town.

Sights & Museums

Hungarian Museum of Agriculture

Magyar Mezőgazdasi Múzeum
XIV. Vajdahunyad Castle (422 0765, www. mezogazdasagimuzeum.hu). M1 Hősök tere. **Open** *Mid Feb-early Nov* 10am-5pm Tue-Sun. *Early Nov-mid Feb* 10am-4pm Tue-Fri; 10am-5pm Sat, Sun. **Admission** Ft1,100; Ft550 reductions. **No credit cards. Map** p103 G2 ❸
In a stunning Baroque wing of Vajdahunyad Castle, this large museum is dedicated to rural Hungary. The capacious halls examine hunting, farming, fishing, agriculture, forestry and winemaking. Though a little dry, there are some treasures, such as the skeleton of Hungary's pride and joy of yesteryear, racehorse Kincsem. Clamber up the imposing stone staircase to the Hall of Hunting, a great room of vaulted ceilings and stained glass, crammed full of hunting trophies, antlers, horns, hooves and fur.

Palace of Arts

Műcsarnok
XIV. Dózsa György út 37 (460 7000, www. mucsarnok.hu). M1 Hősök tere or Széchenyi fürdő. **Open** 10am-6pm Tue, Wed, Fri-Sun; noon-8pm Thur. **Admission** Ft1,800; Ft900 reductions. **Map** p103 F3 ❹
This gallery of contemporary Hungarian art is in a permanent face-off with the more traditional Museum of Fine Arts across Heroes' Square. With huge banners draped over its neoclassical columns, it tempts the crowds away from Rembrandt with an engaging programme of provocative exhibitions, cultural events and, every autumn, the Budapest Art Fair. Since it has no permanent collection to fall back on, the Műcsarnok always has to reinvent itself – an exercise that will be easier while the Fine Arts undergoes major renovation until 2018.

Restaurants

Gundel

XIV. Gundel Károly út 4 (889 8910, 06 30 603 2480, www.gundel.hu). M1 Hősök tere or Széchenyi fürdő. **Open** noon-midnight daily. **Main courses** Ft4,900-Ft25,000. **Map** p103 F2 ❸ **Hungarian**
So revered it occupies a street renamed after it, the city's most famous restaurant opened in 1894. It was here that chef Károly Gundel helped create modern Hungarian cuisine by incorporating French influences; he invented many now-standard dishes, such as Gundel pancakes. The menu is a bit old-fashioned. Starters and desserts almost outshine the main courses, which include fine versions of Hungarian standards and Magyar takes on international dishes. The Sunday brunch (11.30am-3pm, Ft7,900) is a more relaxed and affordable way to enjoy this institution.
▶ *Breakfasts, goose liver, steak sandwiches and cakes are available at the restaurant's Latinovits Bar. Next door, the Bagolyvár restaurant (www.bagolyvar.com), opened by Károly Gundel in 1913, offers quality fare at affordable prices and has a terrace to boot.*

★ Városliget Café & Restaurant

XIV. Olof Palme setany 5 (06 30 869 1426, www. varosligetcafe.hu). M1 Hősök tere or Széchenyi fürdő. **Open** noon-10pm daily. **Main courses** Ft2,490-Ft9,900. **Map** p103 F2 ❸ **Hungarian**
In the grand building overlooking the ice rink, chef István Szántó honours traditional Habsburg cuisine. The key dish here – though you can also find T-bone steaks and roast lamb – is the untranslatable *tányérhús*. Simply put, this is boiled beef in broth, a favourite of Franz Josef's, involving beef marrow bone, Hungarian grey cattle and beef tongue, assorted root vegetables, ground paprika – and half-a-day's preparation. The meat is also available in sandwich form in the 'anytime' menu of salads and pastas. It's a café too, the coffee presented as you might find it in the better places of Vienna.

Cafés & Bars

★ Pántlika

XIV. Városliget, across from Hermina út 47 (06 70 376 9910, www.pantlika.hu). M1 Széchenyi fürdő, or trolleybus 70, 72, 74. **Open** *Apr-Oct* noon-midnight Mon-Thur, Sun; noon-1am Fri, Sat. Closed *Nov-Mar.* **No credit cards. Map** p103 H2 ❼
Run by Viktor Papp, a fan of socialist-realist architecture and design, this funky little retro bar is built into what was meant to be an information booth for a doomed Expo in the 1960s. It's now a DJ spot and terrace getaway in summer, with cheap drinks and hearty food. The affable Papp is also an aficionado of *pálinka*, and stocks more varieties of Hungarian grappa than almost any other place in town.
▶ *On the other side of Városliget, near the ice rink, Kertem is an outdoor venue with live music and DJs; see p154.*

EXPLORE

District VII

District VII, Erzsébetváros, is Budapest's Jewish quarter – and also its most happening neighbourhood. Guarding its threshold is the huge Dohány utca Synagogue; in 1944-45 it stood at one of the entrances to the Jewish Ghetto. Behind it today is a whole bunch of bars, which have sprung up as part of a local phenomenon known as the *romkocsma*, or ruin bar. Pretty much specific, but not exclusive, to District VII, these bars occupy neglected courtyards in communal residential houses. Streets such as Király utca and Dob utca are occupied in this way most weekends and all summer, while the more mainstream Gozsdu udvar has recently become swept up in the action too. Further up on the Nagykörút – here known as Erzsébet körút – stand two of the city's finest hotels, the Boscolo and the Corinthia. Beyond them, District VII seems a long way from gentrifying: the streets, patrolled by red trolleybuses, have changed little in decades.

EXPLORE

Gozsdu udvar.

Don't Miss

1 Dohány utca Synagogue One of the world's largest – and finest (p116).

2 New York Café Legendary coffeehouse, now part of a fancy five-star hotel (p125).

3 Gozsdu udvar See what a little popularity can do to a fin-de-siècle courtyard (p118).

4 Szimpla kert The prince of 'ruin bars' (p116).

5 Telep Funky gallery, bar, boutique and event space, all in one (p116).

SYNAGOGUE TO KAZINCZY UTCA

At the historic gateway to District VII – dominating the western end of Dohány utca and this busy section of the Kiskörút – the **Synagogue** was opened in 1859, nearly a decade before Jews in Hungary were granted emancipation as part of the Compromise with Vienna of 1867. For the next few decades, Jewish traders and entrepreneurs moved to Hungary from less welcoming parts of eastern Europe, most notably Russia. The area behind the Synagogue, Erzsébetváros (District VII), filled with mainly poorer Jewish families – those unable to afford larger properties in Terézváros (District VI) or beyond. Streets such as Király utca were thronged with small shops and businesses.

Until very recent gentrification, the streets of District VII behind the Synagogue – Dob utca, Síp utca, Kazinczy utca – were dark, tatty and full of odd detail. In some ways they still are, despite the creative businesses, nightclubs and bars that have now permeated these once neglected neighbourhoods. It's not as picturesque as Prague's Jewish quarter, but although 700,000 Hungarian Jews died in the Holocaust, enough survived to mean that District VII was still a living community.

That community then survived both the exodus of younger, wealthier Jews into less noisy and congested districts, and post-war attempts by the Communist government to homogenise the area: flats emptied by the Holocaust were given to workers brought into Budapest to rebuild the city after the war. Back in the 1990s, before scores of bars, shops and restaurants sprang up, you could hear Yiddish on Kazinczy utca or eat a kosher pastry at the **Fröhlich Cukrászda** (VII. Dob utca 22, www.frohlich.hu).

On Rumbach Sebestyén utca stands another synagogue (no.11, 343 0420, www.rumbachutca izsinagoga.hu), inactive for many years but worth a look for its Moorish Revival appearance. The street ends at what has become another bar/restaurant hub, the pedestrianised zone running from Károly körút to the Gozsdu udvar. Start at the well proportioned square of Madách Imre, full of busy terrace tables; down the road of the same name is **Telep** (VII. Madách Imre út 8, 06 30 633 3608), part-gallery, part-eaterie, part-club, part-shop and part-performance space.

Head left at the end of Madách Imre út and you'll enter the bar-lined offshoot of Kazinczy utca, where you'll find **Félix Hélix** and **400**. Straight ahead is the **Gozsdu udvar** (see p118 **Holding Court**). If anything typifies District VII's transformation from forgotten community to foreigner-friendly fun zone, it's this long passageway-cum-courtyard that links Király utca with Dob utca.

Kazinczy utca itself is a somewhat twisting, narrow street containing various attractions, interspersed with Jewish eateries. The **Museum of Electrotechnics** is a charming curiosity. Motors, machines and sundry household items from the radio era are displayed in a converted, pre-war, Bauhaus-style transformer station. A few doors further along stands an Orthodox synagogue, which was built in 1911-13 by the Löffler brothers, Sándor and Béla. Its façade displays the beautiful stained-glass work by the master of the genre, Miksa Róth – this is a lesser-known example of local art nouveau. *See also p94* **Walk**.

Most of all, though, Kazinczy utca is the home of *the* 'ruin bar'. Or, rather, the home of *the* ruin bar, **Szimpla kert** (*see p158*), the one that started it all off. Today, these venues are such an integral part of the city fabric that there are ruin-bar mugs sold in tourist shops.

Sights & Museums

Dohány utca Synagogue & Jewish Museum

Dohány utcai Zsinagóga és Zsidó Múzeum
VII. Dohány utca 2 (462 0477, www.dohanyutcai zsinagoga.hu). M2 Astoria, or tram 47, 49.
Open *Mar-Oct* 10am-6pm Mon-Thur, Sun.
Nov-Feb 10am-5pm Mon-Thur, Sun; 10am-3pm Fri. **Admission** Ft2,500; Ft1,400 reductions.
No credit cards. Map p117 D2 ❶

The Dohány utca (or Great) Synagogue seats 3,000 worshippers in separate men's and women's galleries. Built in Moorish Revival style by Austrian Lajos Förster, and opened in 1859, its signature exotic twin onion domes rise 43m (141ft) over the complex that later developed around it. Today, bright brickwork glows in blue, yellow and red, the heraldic colours of Budapest. Interlaced eight-pointed stars in the brick detailing, continued in the stained glass and mosaic flooring inside, are a symbol of regeneration. The divisions of its central space are based on the cabalistic Tree of Life, giving it a similar floor plan to a Gothic cathedral; the ceiling entwines Stars of David outlined in gold leaf.

A small Jewish Museum in one wing displays a collection of ritual objects and a moving depiction of the Hungarian Holocaust. The objects are arranged in three rooms according to function – Sabbath, holidays and life-cycle ceremonies – and are well documented in English. Behind is the small Heroes' Temple, built in 1931 for Jewish soldiers killed in World War I. Also unusually for a synagogue, there's a cemetery, a mass grave for Jews massacred by fellow Hungarians in 1945, with a collection of retrieved Jewish headstones. In the garden of remembrance, now named the Raoul Wallenberg Memorial Park, sculptor Imre Varga's poignant weeping willow features the family names of the victims delicately inscribed on its leaves.

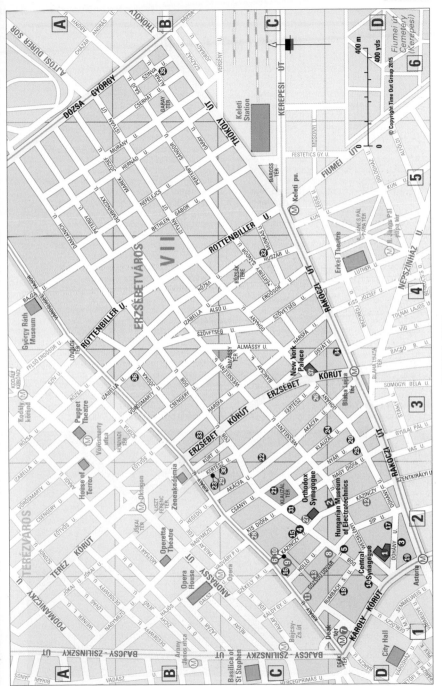

EXPLORE

HOLDING COURT

Gozsdu udvar courtyard is now a brilliant bar hub.

Unprepossessing doorways mark each entrance to **Gozsdu udvar**, a courtyard with six interlinked sections that connects Király utca 13 to Dob utca 16. Were it not for the people coming and going through the doorways, you might not even notice it. In fact, ten years ago, you wouldn't have done.

Gozsdu udvar was the legacy of Hungaro-Romanian politician and lawyer Manó Gozsdu. In 1854, he bought the land, first building a row of warehouses on it. After his death in 1869, Gozsdu's will declared that his assets should pass to the 'Romanian nation in Hungary and Transylvania' via his foundation. As well as sponsoring two generations of Romanian students in Budapest, the foundation commissioned noted architect Győző Czigler to create a series of courtyards here in 1901.

For decades, its post-war fate was entangled in cross-border bureaucracy. Nationalised in 1952, Gozsdu udvar was claimed by the Romanian state in 1990 – a claim rejected by Hungary. Abandoned, it passed into private hands in 1999. It took another decade for the place to come alive again, filling with bars, shops and nightspots.

It was a slow start. First there was little more than one decent bar-restaurant, **Vian** (www.cafevian.com), and a branch of the gym and spa chain Holmes Place. A couple of apartment lodgings opened. Then came a few more hostelries, most notably busy, large-scale, all-in-one **Spíler** (see p121).

Then came **GOUBA**. Its five letters standing for Gozsdu Bazaar, GOUBA (www.gouba.hu; Apr-July, Sept-Oct 10am-5pm Sun) is a weekly artisanal market set up the length of Gozsdu udvar. More than 100 Hungarian designers, craftsmen, artists, ceramicists and antiques dealers offer their wares amid the bar-lined buildings. Jewellery, clothes, homewares, objets d'art and assorted gifts are on display, while street performers and musicians provide impromptu entertainment. Snacks, cakes, jams and fresh juices are available, as well as local wines and spirits.

The result was to give Gozsdu udvar a real sense of community – this wasn't just another showcase for foreigners. Even when GOUBA takes a break, over the winter and height of summer, you'll still stroll past various stalls selling artisanal jewellery and knick-knacks most nights of the week.

And night-time is when the place really buzzes. Today Gozsdu udvar is arguably the busiest bar hub in Budapest. The **GMK** music venue (see p161), the Spíler beer garden and the **Sörcsata** (www.sorcsata.hu), with its vintage vehicles in its inner courtyard – these are the kind of places that keep people barhopping within Gozsdu udvar.

Spinoza.

Museum of Electrotechnics
Elektrotechnikai Múzeum
*VII.Kazinczy utca 21 (342 5750, www.
elektromuzeum.hu). M1, M2, M3 Deák tér.* **Open**
10am-2pm Thur-Sat. **Admission** Ft800; Ft400
reductions. **No credit cards. Map** p117 D2 **2**
Ideally located in a 1930s Bauhaus transformer
station, this museum focuses on the history of
the electrical-power industry and heavy-current
electrical engineering. Sounds dauntingly technical? Fortunately, men in white coats use archaic
demonstrations to help bring the displays down to
a layman's level. The early household equipment
is fascinating. The museum courtyard features
an impressive collection of neon signs, salvaged
from the city streets, brought to life once a year for
Museum Night on 21 June.

Restaurants

Fausto's
*VII.Dohány utca 3 (06 30 589 1813, www.
fausto.hu). M2 Astoria, or tram 47, 49.*
Open noon-3pm, 7-11pm Mon-Fri; 6-11pm
Sat. **Main courses** Ft7,800-Ft8,500. **Map**
p117 D2 **3 Italian**
Ever since it opened in 1994, Fausto's has been
one of the best restaurants in the city. Owner Fausto
Di Vora remains dedicated; most evenings, he's here
ensuring everything is running smoothly. Mains
might feature fillet of sole with confit of artichoke,
and sea bass with chickpeas and fruits de mer – fish
has always been a strong point here – while the
pasta dishes are a cut above the opposition. There's
a three-course lunch available for Ft5,000, but most
diners are here to flash a fair bit of cash. Numerous
efficient staff ensure good service. The wine list is

massive and, like all else here, expensive. The decor
is tasteful and modern.
▶ *Next door, Fausto's Osteria (VII.Dohány utca 5,
269 6806) offers a more concise, less expensive
menu in intimate surroundings.*

Macesz Huszár
*VII.Dob utca 26 (787 6164, 06 30 499 5585,
www.maceszhuszar.hu). M1, M2, M3 Deák
tér, or trolleybus 74.* **Open** noon-11pm Mon-
Wed, Sun; noon-midnight Thur-Sat. **Main
courses** Ft2,290-Ft5,990. **Map** p117 C2
4 Jewish/Hungarian
Don't expect a kosher kitchen, even though it's
billed as a Jewish bistro, and located in the heart of
the Jewish quarter. This food is typical Hungarian-
Jewish cuisine, which means the local version of the
bean and goose *cholent* (called *sólet* here), other goose
dishes, a veal schnitzel and, of course, matzo-ball
soup. The T-bone steak and saddle of venison might
not be what your *yiddishe momme* would make, but
are fine dishes nonetheless. If you want authen-
ticity, order *flódni* for dessert: a delicious Jewish-
Hungarian pastry made of layers of apple, walnut
and poppyseed. A good selection of local wines and
a short list of house cocktails round things off.

★ Spinoza
*VII.Dob utca 15 (413 7488, www.spinoza
cafe.hu). M2 Astoria, or M1, M2, M3 Deák tér,
or trolleybus 74.* **Open** 8am-midnight daily.
Main courses Ft1,950-Ft4,350. **Map** p117 D2
5 Jewish/Hungarian
Restaurant, piano bar and cabaret venue, Spinoza
echoes the *cafés chantants* of the Belle Époque.
Founder Anna Sándor has also explored rich Jewish
culinary traditions – the menu here is particularly

EXPLORE

Printa Akadémia.

strong on goose dishes and eastern Mediterranean salads. Evergreen pianist Tibor Sóos plays in the main dining room (all dark wood and framed art), while klezmer acts perform on Fridays in a small adjoining concert room.

Cafés & Bars

400

VII.Kazinczy utca 52B (06 20 776 0765, www. 400bar.hu). M1, M2, M3 Deák tér. **Open** 11am-3am Mon-Wed; 11am-5am Thur-Sat. **Map** p117 C2 ⑥
The 400 is a safe bet for a serious night out – and has engendered a separate scene all of its own down this pedestrianised spur linking Kazinczy to the Gozsdu udvar. Partygoers mob the four-sided island bar most evenings, as well as the terrace in summer. A projection screen comes into play for major football matches, and there are often DJs. Nenad, a well established chef in these parts, ensures that quality Serbian grilled meats fly out of the kitchen at an impressive rate. The name is a reference to the size in square metres of the main room.

Castro Bistro

VII.Madách Imre tér 3 (06 20 214 6466). M1, M2, M3 Deák tér. **Open** 11am-midnight Mon-Thur, Sun; 11am-1am Fri, Sat. **Map** p117 D1 ⑦
A key spot at the tip of District VII, Castro is not only a popular afternoon hangout but also a prime spot for affordable drinks and grub in the evening. The menu of Mediterranean favourites is served by friendly staff. A couple of doors down is a handy overflow, which shares the same address, kitchen and decor of funky artwork and brocade tablecloths.

Doblo

VII.Dob utca 20 (06 20 398 8863, www.budapest wine.com). M1, M2, M3 Deák tér. **Open** 2pm-2am Mon-Fri; 5pm-3am Sat; 5pm-1am Sun. **Map** p117 D2 ⑧

The first wine bar on the block opened back in 2009 and is still lively. *See also p90* **Cork and Fork.**

★ Félix Hélix

VII.Kazinczy utca 52B (06 30 416 6959, www. felixhelix.hu). M1, M2, M3 Deák tér. **Open** 9am-3pm, 6pm-1am Mon-Fri; 3pm-1am Sat, Sun. **Map** p117 C2 ⑨
Successful restaurateur/bar-owner Oran MacCuirc's latest venture is Félix Hélix. The food is good, but as the evening runs its course attention switches from the dinner plate to a well chosen selection of music – occasionally live (ethno-Balkan outfit Taraf de Akácfa are welcome regulars). A long terrace, side-by-side with those of its neighbours, creates an alfresco vibe for most of the year.

Pirítós Pub

VII.Kazinczy utca 52C (631 5268, www.piritos pub.hu). M1, M2, M3 Deák tér. **Open** 3pm-midnight Mon-Wed; 3pm-3am Thur-Sat; 3pm-11pm Sun. **Map** p117 C2 ⑩
In an area crammed with bars, somewhere called the 'Toast Pub' shouldn't do as well as it does. But Pirítós doesn't have a nice buzz around its small bar area because of grilled bread alone. People come for the beer. Slovak Kaltenecker, brewed in Košice, comes in all kinds of fruit flavours, as well as chilli or ginger. Equally, the toasties aren't just ham and cheese – try the steak tartare version.

Pop Bisztró

VII.Király utca 11 (299 5940). M1, M2, M3 Deák tér. **Open** 6pm-1am Mon; 4pm-1am Tue, Wed; 4pm-4am Thur-Sat. **Map** p117 C1 ⑪
The first bar on Király utca as you stroll from the transport hub of Deák tér, wantonly retro Pop Bisztró is also a DJ haunt. Backdropped by gilded Barbie dolls in rude poses, glam-era music cuttings and a shrine to the cassette tape, a with-it bar staff from Veszprém brings considerable vim

to proceedings. They also mix up some excellent Fény vodka cocktails.

El Rapido
VII.Kazinczy utca 10 (783 4627, www.elrapido.hu). **M2** *Astoria, or bus 7.* **Open** 10.30am-3am Mon-Thur; 10.30am-4am Fri; noon-4am Sat; noon-1am Sun. **Map** p117 D2 ⓬
This intimate Mexican diner, with a long, unfussy menu of fajitas, quesadillas and burritos, is frequented, even revered, as a ruin bar. It's not just the skip-found furniture and generally scruffy vibe – it's more that everyone here, on the night, wants to party. The 40 types of tequila certainly help the process.

Spíler
Gozsdu udvar, VII.Király utca 13 (878 1320, www.spilerbp.hu). **M1, M2, M3** *Deák tér.* **Open** 8am-2am daily. **Map** p117 C1 ⓭
Located in the middle of the elongated, buzzing courtyard of Gozsdu udvar, Spíler currently consists of a huge pub (styled as a gastropub) and, opposite, an Asian-themed party spot, Shanghai Spíler. In warmer months, there's a beer garden too. *See p118* **Holding Court.**

Shops & Services

Bejuska
VII.Dob utca 2 (344 8444, www.bejuska.hu). **M1, M2, M3** *Deák tér.* **Open** 11am-6pm Mon-Wed; noon-7pm Thur; 11am-7pm Fri; noon-4.30pm Sat. **Map** p117 D1 ⓮ **Accessories**
Local, handmade bags by Zsuzsi, made of various materials, plus other Hungarian and international accessories, including Denmark's Pilgrim jewellery.

Café Analog/Lomography Embassy
VII.Kazinczy utca 35 (445 2560, www.lomography. hu). **M1, M2, M3** *Deák tér.* **Open** 9am-7pm Mon-Fri; 10am-6pm Sat. **Map** p117 C2 ⓯
Electronics & photography
'The Future is Analogue' is the motto of this flagship store for Lomographic cameras and photo accessories. There's also a café and photo laboratory.

Goa Home
VII.Király utca 19 (352 8442, www.goaworld.hu). **M1, M2, M3** *Deák tér.* **Open** 10am-7pm Mon-Fri; 10am-2pm Sat. **Map** p117 C2 ⓰ **Homewares**
A trove of chairs, tables, kitchenware and jewellery from around India, Indonesia and elsewhere is complemented by an adjoining in-house café.

Látomás
VII.Dohány utca 16-18 (06 70 930 0303, www.latomas.hu). **M2** *Astoria, or tram 47, 49.* **Open** 11am-7.30pm Mon-Fri; 11am-6pm Sat. **Map** p117 D2 ⓱ **Fashion**
Julie Szontagh's three shops sell imported prêt-à-porter at good prices. Stock changes every few weeks.

Other locations *VI.Király utca 39 (womenswear, 786 6659); Ultra, VII.Akácfa utca 27-29 (womenswear, 792 8902); VII.Kertész utca 20 (menswear, 06 70 930 0393).*

Printa Akadémia
VII.Rumbach Sebestyén utca 10 (06 30 292 0329, www.printa.hu). **M1, M2, M3** *Deák ter.* **Open** 11am-7pm Mon-Fri; noon-6pm Sat. **Map** p117 D1 ⓲ **Fashion/accessories**
A gallery, workshop and café as well as a shop, selling everything from clothes to gifts by talented Hungarian designers. Must-have Budapest sweatshirts, T-shirts and bags come in fabulous contemporary designs by Zita Majoros – note the decorative use of a District VII street plan.

Tisza Cipő
VII.Károly körút 1 (266 3055, www.tisza cipo.hu). **M2** *Astoria, or tram 47, 49, or bus 7.* **Open** 10am-7pm Mon-Fri; 10am-4pm Sat. **Map** p117 D2 ⓳ **Accessories**
The Communist answer to Adidas, newly hip after being revived. The shoes come in funky colours, and there is an accessories range.
Other location *Westend City Center, VI.Váci út 1-3 (238 7505).*

KLAUZÁL TÉR & AROUND

The heart of the Jewish quarter is Klauzál tér, which has a playground and a park where old men play chess and cards in summer. Gone are the days, though, when then Budapest resident Bobby Fischer would appear, barely disguised behind his beard, only to vanish again. Fresh food stalls spill out on to the square from the main covered market on Saturdays. Next to it, the cheap lunchtime **Kádár Étkezde** serves hearty, home-style Magyar cuisine.

This part of District VII has a more communal feel – you're as likely to brush past a local on the street as a tourist, which isn't the case closer to the Gozsdu udvar. Focal point Király utca assumes more of a workaday character.

This neighbourhood, either side of the Nagykörút but specifically within District VII, was the haunt of composer Rezső Seress. He wrote the heart-breaking ballad 'Gloomy Sunday' (covered by Billie Holiday and Sarah Vaughan, among others), but never saw the royalties that were rightfully his. A pianist at the Kispipa restaurant on Akácfa utca, Seress stayed in District VII until he was sent to a concentration camp. He survived, but committed suicide in 1968. A plaque marks his home at Dob utca 46B.

The **Kispipa** (VII.Akacfa utca 38, 342 2587, www.kispipa.hu) is still going, though it's pretty sorry now – it might be worth a look-in or a coffee. There are plenty of dining options – the big-hitter of 2014, **Mazel Tov**, is down the street at no.47.

EXPLORE

Restaurants

Araz
VII.Dohány utca 42-44 (815 1100, www.araz.hu).
M2 Blaha Lujza tér, or tram 4, 6, or bus 7, or
trolleybus 74. **Open** 7am-11pm daily. **Main**
courses Ft2,850-Ft5,650. **Map** p117 D3 ⊘
French/Hungarian
The signature restaurant of the Continental Hotel
Budapest (formerly the Zara) has two menus: one
French, one Hungarian. Head chef Áron Barka is
responsible for dishes such as spicy Dijon-crusted
sirloin with sweet potato soufflé and roast spinach, and Kárpáti-style pike-perch with a skewer of
parsley potatoes. There are a few Jewish favourites,
such as goose-leg confit on *cholent*, matzo-ball soup
and *flódni* pastry. Sunday brunch is recommended.
You may find better French in town – just – and you
may find better Hungarian, but this is a fine effort
all round. The building was a spa in the 1820s, and a
wonderful art nouveau hotel a century later.

Kádár Étkezde
VII.Klauzál tér 9 (321 3622). Tram 4, 6.
Open 11.30am-3.30pm Tue-Sat. **Main**
courses Ft900-Ft1,600. **No credit cards.**
Map p117 C2 ⊘ **Hungarian**
This charming no-frills restaurant opened in 1957
and offers Hungarian home-style cooking in the
heart of the old Jewish quarter. Autographed photographs and caricatures of Hungarian showbiz stars
adorn the walls, and each table has its own (dangerously high-powered) soda siphon. Share a table
with a stranger and check for daily specials, such as
libacomb (goose leg) with red cabbage and mashed
potato, or the fabulous Jewish dish *sólet*, made of
smoked goose breast and baked beans. This is also
a place for *főzelék*, puréed vegetables with a fried egg
on top. In short, the most authentic Hungarian food
you can muster without having a Magyar mother.

★ Mazel Tov
VII.Akácfa utca 47 (06 70 626 4280). Tram 4, 6,
or trolleybus 74. **Open** 6pm-4am Tue-Fri; noon-
4am Sat, Sun. **Main courses** Ft790-Ft2,190.
Map p117 C3 ⊘ **Jewish/Mediterranean**
Expertly prepared Jewish/eastern Mediterranean
street food is matched here with the vibe, structure and surroundings of a ruin bar. Mazel Tov
('Congratulations') can party with the best of them
while still being able to bring a damn tasty *pargit* or
shakshouka with feta to your table. Most dishes are
under Ft2,000, and the idea is to spread them over
your large wooden dining table and share. After
11pm, by which time some kind of entertainment
– often live music – is unfolding, pittas (falafel, sha-
warma or Jerusalem mix) are served. Mazel Tov also
keeps ruin-bar hours, so a relaxed early evening
amid the tasteful bare brick and light wood of its
neat interior can easily turn into a long night, as
people gravitate to the back garden.

▶ *Some of the people behind Mazel Tov also*
run Dafke (VII.Madách Imre út 3, 06 30 896
5748, www.dafkedeli.com), an excellent Jewish
café and delicatessen.

M Restaurant
VII.Kertész utca 48 (before 5pm 06 70 633 3460,
after 5pm 322 3108, metterem.hu). Tram 4, 6.
Open 6pm-midnight Tue-Sun. **Main courses**
Ft2,100-Ft3,200. **No credit cards. Map** p117 B2
⊘ **French/Hungarian**
Bars, ruin bars and faux ruin bars have come
and gone but this spot has managed to survive all
the changes – in fact, it has raised the bar as far as
cuisine goes. The menu changes daily but if you hap-
pen across prime rib steak or beef in red wine with
thyme polenta, you're in luck. For true fine dining,
head over to District VI, but for a memorable *soirée*
à deux in slightly quirky surroundings, you could
do far worse.

Repülő Puli
VII.Klauzál utca 13 (06 30 258 0965). M2
Blaha Lujza tér, or tram 4, 6. **Open** 4pm-
midnight Tue, Wed; 4pm-2am Thur-Sat.
Main courses Ft890-Ft2,100. **Map** p117 D3
⊘ **Hungarian/international**
The popular Repülő Puli – part café, part restau-
rant, complete with terrace to boot – lures a younger
crowd over from Kazinczy and Király to Klauzál
utca. The menu has something for everyone – classic
French and Hungarian dishes, burgers and superior

Mazel Tov.

sandwiches, late-breakfasts, and even fondues – and the place is very dog-friendly. A rough translation of Repülő Puli is 'Flying Poodle', though a *puli* is not quite a poodle; it's a domestic breed resembling a moving mass of pipe cleaners.

Il Terzo Cerchio

VII.Dohány utca 40 (354 0788, www.ilterzo cerchio.hu). M2 Blaha Lujza tér, or tram 4, 6, or bus 7, or trolleybus 74. **Open** 11.30am-11.30pm daily. **Main courses** Ft2,150-Ft4,900. **Map** p117 D3 ㉕ **Italian**
The pizzas, hot from the brick oven in the middle of the back room, are flavourful, thin-crust winners – reason enough to dine here. Toss in fish and meat grilled on a wood stove, and fine own-made pasta and you've got a real crowd-pleaser. There are 40-plus wines on offer, all of Italian or Hungarian provenance.

Cafés & Bars

Aznap

VII.Dohány utca 68 (06 30 418 2048). M2 Blaha Lujza tér, or tram 4, 6. **Open** 5pm-2am Mon-Wed; 5pm-4am Thur-Sat. **No credit cards**. **Map** p117 C3 ㉖
Opened in 2014 (in what was Dauer bar), Aznap is more bar than nightspot but keeps late hours and stages live music. It's a savvy, bare-brick venue, with decent drinks (well-chosen Hungarian wines and craft beers) and superior bar snacks. Sport plays on TV, and the place attacts a crowd of regulars.

Fekete Kutya

VII.Dob utca 31 (06 20 580 3151). M1, M2, M3 Deák tér. **Open** 5pm-2am Mon-Sat; 5pm-midnight Sun. **Map** p117 C2 ㉗
'Black Dog' is one of the busier new openings on the block, partly thanks to the range of Czech beers on draught, partly thanks to occasional eclectic music acts, but mainly thanks to its buzzy atmosphere. People are here because the kind of people they like to mingle with – funky, young, reasonably discerning – like to be here too. The arcaded corridor immediately outside offers the many smokers an attractive space to commune.

Kandalló Kézműves Pub

VII.Király utca 33 (788 3568, www.kandallopub. hu). Tram 4, 6. **Open** 4pm-midnight Mon-Thur; 4pm-3am Fri; noon-3am Sat; noon-midnight Sun. **Map** p117 C2 ㉘
Firmly at the forefront of the new trend for craft beers, the 'Fireplace Artisanal Pub' varies its half-dozen strong draught options, but usually has bottles of Bigfoot 2222, Hammurapi or Fóti Zwickl chilling in its well-stocked fridge. To find out what's on tap, check the board. Kandalló also goes big on burgers, with a goat's cheese version for vegetarians. When occasion demands, sports play on the TV.
▶ *Another newbie with a focus on artisanal ales is the Léhűtő Kézműves Söröző (Lehűtő Craft Beer Bar). It's at the Gozsdu udvar (VII.Holló utca 12-14, 06 731 0430).*

EXPLORE

Szimpla Kávézó/Berlin Craft Beer Bar

VII.Kertész utca 48 (06 20 210 9167, www.szimpla. hu/kavezo). Tram 4, 6. **Open** 10am-2am daily. **No credit cards.** **Map** p117 B2 ㉙
Old favourite Szimpla/Dupla has re-emerged as Szimpla Kávézó, now driving the trend for craft beers. As well as introducing Meckatzer, Andechs and other German goodies (also served at two sister establishments in Berlin), the Szimpla team has also brought in Brewdog from Aberdeen, Crate from London, and so on. Throw in a buzzy ambience, a little out-there art on the walls, and you're looking at another smash from the Szimpla hit factory.

Shops & Services

Laci Bácsi Lemezboltja

VII.Kertész utca 42 (332 1325, www.hangle mezek.hu). Tram 4, 6. **Open** noon-7pm Mon-Fri; 9am-1pm Sat. **No credit cards.** **Map** p117 C2 ㉚ **Books & music**
Vinyl enthusiast László Molnár has turned his massive collection into the basis for this decent second-hand shop. You'll find a solid selection of retro gems, as well as some more recent releases.

Laoni

VII.Klauzál tér 1 (322 7481, www.laoni.hu). Tram 4, 6. **Open** 10am-7pm Mon-Fri. **Map** p117 C2 ㉛ **Accessories**
Ilona Ács's quality leather wallets, handbags and accessories, all handmade on the premises, fill this quiet corner shop.

ERZSÉBET KÖRÚT & BEYOND

This section of the Nagykörút, Erzsébet Körút, was named after Empress Elisabeth in 1879, an early indication of the reverence in which Hungarians held – and still hold – the wife of Franz Josef I. Distant from her husband, the beloved 'Sissi' was close to Count Gyula Andrássy and was said to be influential in making sure Hungary's voice was heard at court in Vienna. She may have been the one to have persuaded Franz Josef to accept the Compromise of 1867, the same year that their coronation took place in Budapest.

By the time Sissi was assassinated, stabbed by an Italian anarchist on the shores of Lake Geneva in 1898, the ring road named after her was as prestigious as adjoining Teréz körút. Two years before, Swiss-born architect Reszó Ray and the Glück brothers had built the Royal, the grand hotel created for the Hungarian millennial celebrations of 1896. They had to buy three plots of land here – this was then not the Nagykörút ('Great Ring Road') but Külsőkörút ('Outer Ring Road'), the fringes of urbanised Pest. This 'outer' area was all called Terézváros, until this section was renamed after the fated empress.

New York Café.

Opened with a grand ball in 1896, the Royal was the finest (and largest) hotel in Hungary. Of its 350 rooms, 100 had their own bathroom. Lifts, electric lighting and a telephone exchange provided infrastructure; palm trees and a hairdressing salon provided style; and a coffeehouse attracted the many great writers of the day, their portraits now lining the restored grand ballroom.

The third city after Paris and London to invite the Lumière Brothers to show their moving pictures, Budapest was a pioneer in the early film industry, and the Royal was a prime mover in this phenomenon. In 1915, the ballroom was converted into the city's first permanent cinema, the Apollo – World War I had stopped the dances. Women would come here to look for any sign of their husbands, sons and lovers on matinée newsreels from the war. The Apollo continued to operate as a cinema and concert hall – Josephine Baker performed here in the 1920s. It outlived the Royal, which closed as a hotel in the 1940s. All were restored when Maltese group Corinthia bought the property and reopened it as a luxury hotel (**Corinthia Grand Hotel Royal**; *see p221*), with ballroom, in 2003. An extra floor had to be added so that the Corinthia could be granted the term 'Grand'. Today, it also contains the **Bock Bisztró**, one of the city's finer restaurants.

The literary set and film fraternity, and later Hollywood movie moguls, also gathered at the splendid **New York Café**, further down Erzsébet körút towards Blaha Lujza tér. Built in 1894 by Alajos Hauszmann, this handsome venue was

EXPLORE

the meeting place for writers, artists, directors and potential starlets. Its post-war demise was reversed with a modern-day hotel conversion that returned it to its original splendour: today's Boscolo Budapest (*see p219*).

Blaha Lujza tér, officially in District VIII on the other side of Rákóczi út, was named after the actress and singer, Lujza Blaha. Known as the 'National Nightingale', Blaha performed at the National Theatre that stood here until it was demolished to make way for the second metro line, the red M2, in the early 1960s. The theatre moved to a more prosaic building on Hevesi Sándor tér on the other side of the *körút*, hidden away and unloved until 2002 when the millennial arts complex in south Pest superceded it.

This swathe of District VII, before Városliget, is still a run-down neighbourhood of cheap bars and repair shops. Curiosities include the former Kulacs restaurant at Osvát utca 11, now closed, where a plaque marks the writing of the song 'Gloomy Sunday' by former regular Rezső Seress. It's worth a quick detour into this neighbourhood to see the sumptuous façade of Armin Hegedűs's 1906 primary school at VII.Dob utca 85.

Restaurants

Ba Bar Bisztró

VII.Huszár utca 7 (06 20 919 7979, www.babar. hu). M2, M4 Keleti pu, or bus 5, 7, 8. **Open** noon-11pm Mon-Sat. **Main courses** Ft1,650-Ft4,390 **Map** p117 C4 ❷ **Hungarian/international**
Once a chic lounge bar isolated on the fringes of the seedy streets around Keleti Station, Ba Bar is now reaping the benefits of the arrival of metro line 4. Very superior bar food features the likes of chicken breast with paprika, wiener schnitzel, and Ba Bar burger with chips, plus there's a lively, party vibe.

★ Bock Bisztró

Corinthia Grand Hotel Royal, VII.Erzsébet körút 43-49 (321 0340, www.bockbisztropest.hu). Tram 4, 6. **Open** noon-midnight Mon-Sat. **Main courses** Ft3,700-Ft7,700. **Map** p117 B3 ❸ **Hungarian**
Winemaker József Bock has enjoyed considerable success with his three restaurants, of which this is the flagship (there's also one in Buda, and one at Balaton). Classic Magyar dishes such as sausage lecsó and Hortobágyi-style catfish, are reinterpreted with contemporary touches. There are 25 Bock wines, and more than 100 others. Staff are on the ball. Booking is advisable. *See p90* **Cork and Fork**.
Other location *Vendéglő a KisBíróhoz, XII.Szarvas Gábor út 8D (376 6044, www.vendegloakisbirohoz.hu).*

Montenegrói Gurman

VII.Rákóczi út 54 (06 70 434 9898, www. blaha.mnggurman.com). M2 Blaha Lujza tér, or tram 4, 6, or bus 7. **Open** 24hrs daily. **Main**

courses Ft1,290-Ft3,690. **No credit cards**. **Map** p117 D3 ❹ **Montenegrin**
Not to be confused with the string of kebab joints on and off the Nagykörút, this is a genuine Balkan grill, with prime meat ground to create the classic *pljeskavica* and *ćevapčići* dishes you'll find all over former Yugoslavia, here made with quality veal, and accompanied by flat *lepény* bread baked on the premises. It's also worth investigating the less widespread *uštipci*, veal meatballs with spicy paprika, cheese, bacon and garlic. Prices are low; the giant mixed-meat platter, *kevért hústál*, costs Ft4,490. This branch offers free home delivery.
Other location *VIII.Práter utca 54 (06 70 434 9898, prater.mnggurman.com).*

Olimpia

VII.Alpár utca 5 (321 0680, www.alparutca5.hu). M2, M4 Keleti pu, or bus 7, or trolleybus 76, 79. **Open** noon-3pm, 7-10pm Tue-Fri; 7-10pm Sat. **Main course** *Lunch* from Ft1,800. **Set dinner** Ft6,700-Ft9,200. **Map** p117 B6 ❺ **Hungarian**
Each night, Olimpia's kitchen serves a superb seven-course meal to a lively crowd of foodies, who keep the place booked solid. The starting point is classic Hungarian cuisine, but the kitchen ranges well beyond tradition. Dinner lasts about three hours; it's no-choice (tell them in advance if there's something you can't eat). A good list of Hungarian wines is fairly priced. Reservations are essential.

★ Zeller Bistro

VI.Izabella utca 36-38 (06 30 651 0880). M1 Vörösmarty utca. **Open** noon-3pm, 6-11pm daily. **Main courses** Ft1,500-Ft4,800. **Map** p117 B3 ❻ **Hungarian/continental**
The hottest table in town is a friendly cellar restaurant with a family atmosphere and personable staff who clearly love their food. Dishes such as roasted goose liver sit next to truffle soup, rosé duck breast and perfectly cooked lamb or steak. Desserts also hit the spot. Booking is essential; you can wait weeks for a table at dinner, so go for lunch instead.

Cafés & Bars

New York Café

Boscolo Budapest, VII.Erzsébet körút 9-11 (886 6117, www.newyorkcafe.hu). M2 Blaha Lujza tér, or tram 4, 6. **Open** 9am-midnight daily. **Map** p117 C3 ❼
Steeped in legend, the New York Café was renovated in 2006 as part of a five-star hotel (Boscolo Budapest; *see p219*). The original building, which housed the offices of the New York Life Insurance Company, also contained a café on the ground floor. Unveiled on 23 October 1894, it quickly became the hangout for Budapest's literati. Playwright Ferenc Molnár is said to have stolen the keys and thrown them into the Danube to make sure that the café would always stay open. The post-war era saw the venue decline, but it's back on track with its new incarnation.

EXPLORE

Districts VIII, IX & Beyond

EXPLORE

The stately Hungarian National Museum stands at the gateway to District VIII on the Kiskörut, the inner ring road. From nearby Astoria, Rákóczi út divides District VIII from District VII as it runs up towards Keleti station. Beyond this veritable steam palace is the national football stadium, currently being rebuilt for Budapest's prestigious co-hosting of Euro 2020. On the other side of the National Museum is Kálvin tér and District IX; this newly pedestrianised zone around an equally new metro station is a busy crossing point. The three main thoroughfares of Baross utca, Üllői út and Ráday utca fan out from Kálvin tér – Baross heads past a bar hub around Mikszáth Kálmán tér; Ráday is rammed with restaurants; and Üllői út leads to another landmark sight, the Museum of Applied Arts. Beyond the museum, Üllői út carries on past the new Ferencváros stadium towards the airport.

Great Market Hall.

Don't Miss

1 Hungarian National Museum Stately setting for the history of Hungary (p128).

2 Museum of Applied Arts Secessionist star with decorative furniture from the Golden Age (p136).

3 Ecseri piac Legendary flea market (p137).

4 Great Market Hall For that string of red paprika to take home (p137).

5 Costes Michelin-starred magic (p136).

EXPLORE

DISTRICT VIII NORTH & ZUGLÓ

Busy Rákóczi út divides District VII from its grimier southern neighbour, District VIII. Bounded by Üllői út and Rákóczi, the urban pie-slice of Józsefváros (the Habsburg name for District VIII) has as its focal point the **Hungarian National Museum** on the Kiskörút. This southern half of the inner ring road follows the line of the old city walls – within is Belváros. Múzeum körút is named after the National Museum, as is, on the next corner, the century-old **Múzeum** restaurant. It was opened soon after the museum it was named after. Alongside, the Múzeum Cukrászda serves cake, coffee and harder stuff to busy tables. Over the road are the Központi Antikvárium (*see p84*) and a whole row of other second-hand booksellers. Múzeum körút ends at **Astoria** (*see p215*), where the grand but faded 1912 hotel dominates the intersection to which it has lent its name. Rákóczi út runs up to Blaha Lujza tér, a major crossing point with the Nagykörút. The square lies just within District VIII, scruffy and rubbish-strewn, the location for the afternoon soup kitchen for the significant number of homeless who hang around here. Gypsy violinists entertain for coins in the metro underpass. Above ground, the former Socialist-era Corvin department store is topped by one of the city's best nightspots, **Corvintető** (*see p153*).

District VIII beyond the Nagykörút is vast and unpredictable. On and around Népszinház utca there are many fine buildings, such as Béla Lajta's 1912 Harsányi House at no.19, and Emil Vidor's 1906 Dreher apartment block with its huge mosaic. Népszinház utca ('People's Theatre Street') leads to the newly renamed II. János Pál pápa tér (formerly Köztársaság tér), containing the newly renovated **Erkel Theatre** (*see p165*). First unveiled in 1911 as the Népopera, the People's Opera, the theatre underwent several changes before it came under the collective umbrella of the Opera House.

As well as a reopened theatre, the square also contains a new metro station on line 4. Népszinház utca continues to **Fiumei út Cemetery**, known by all as Kerepesi, the resting place of Hungary's great and good. The graves of politicians, artists and industrialists give a comprehensive overview of Hungarian society of the last century or more. Over Kerepesi's wall stands the main railway station, Keleti. Built as part of the great rail expansion of the 1800s, Keleti was the hub of an imperial network that kept its minorities dependent: all lines went via Pest. There's still no direct link from Zagreb to Vienna. Although parts of this imposing station look all the better for an impressive renovation, other parts remain dark and gloomy. Outside, a new concourse links with the terminus of metro line 4.

Beyond the industrial clutter and tangle of rails behind the station, past the **Arena Plaza** mall (*see p145*) with its IMAX cinema, the national stadium is being completely rebuilt to co-host Euro 2020 (*see p129* **2020 Vision**). For Hungary, bidding to stage the Olympics four years thereafter, this will be the biggest global event the country has ever hosted.

The stadium complex, which also includes the Papp László Sportaréna, a major concert hall, sits just inside District XIV, Zugló. Also including Városliget, the **City Park** (*see p111*), most of District XIV lies past the furthest of the city's three ring roads, Hungária körút.

Sights & Museums

FREE Fiumei út Cemetery

Fiumei úti Sírkert
VIII.Fiumei út 16 (323 5203, www.nemzeti sirkert.hu). M2, M4 Keleti pu, or tram 23, 24, 28. **Open** 7am-dusk daily. **Admission** free. **Map** p130 C6 ❶

Now officially named after its location but still known by all as Kerepesi, the national cemetery is laid out on a monumental scale. It's a fine place for a stroll amid grand memorials. Wide, leafy avenues lead you to key mausoleums: those of novelist Mór Jókai, arch-compromiser Ferenc Deák, bourgeois revolutionary Lajos Kossuth and Count Lajos Batthyány. Nearby, music-hall chanteuse Lujza Blaha is tucked up in a four-poster bed, serenaded by adoring cherubs. Poet Attila József, thrown out of the Communist Party but rehabilitated in the 1950s, was buried here 20 years after his suspected suicide.

Hungarian National Museum

Magyar Nemzeti Múzeum
VIII.Múzeum körút 14-16 (327 7773, www. hnm.hu). M3, M4 Kálvin tér, or M2 Astoria, or tram 47, 49. **Open** 10am-6pm Tue-Sun. **Admission** *Permanent exhibition* Ft1,100; Ft550 reductions. *All exhibitions* Ft1,400; Ft700 reductions. **No credit cards. Map** p130 D1 ❷

If you're going to visit just one museum in Pest, this would be a good choice. Built to Mihály Pollack's neoclassical design, the building was where poet Sándor Petőfi read his 'National Song' on 15 March 1848, the start of the revolt against Habsburg domination. The permanent exhibition covers Hungary from its foundation to 1990, in two separate sections demarcated by the Turkish withdrawal of 1686. With general documentation of each era in English, the HNM is particularly strong on the 18th and 19th centuries. There are rooms dedicated to the 12 demands of 1848, industrial development, and the Golden Age: 'From the happy times of peace to the collapse of the monarchy, 1900-1919'. Coffeehouses, groundbreaking periodicals and imaginative advertising mark Hungary at its height. Also of note are the Bauhaus designs, cinema, and souvenirs of

2020 VISION

A new national football stadium for Hungary after 60 years of hurt.

The Puskás-era Népstadion.

When Budapest was chosen in September 2014 to co-host Euro 2020, football's most prestigious event after the World Cup, it brought the Hungarian game back into the international spotlight for the first time in 60 years. Hosting four matches for this Europe-wide tournament will mean a complete rebuilding of the national stadium – the Népstadion – an iconic structure visible from the train window as you pull into or out of nearby Keleti Station.

Since losing the World Cup final in 1954, soccer-loving Hungary has been a bit player in the global game. The national team hasn't even appeared at a major finals since 1986. Shortly before that fateful final, the great Hungarian team of the day beat England 7-1 at the recently opened national stadium, the heaviest defeat ever suffered by football's former masters. It came almost exactly six months after Hungary had beaten England 6-3 at Wembley, arguably the most famous single match in the history of the game. Yet six weeks after the 7-1 whitewash, hot favourites Hungary inexplicably lost the World Cup final 3-2 to West Germany.

In the six decades since, the Népstadion hasn't had cause to celebrate as it did for the 7-1 match – or for its opening the previous 20 August, Hungary's national day, in 1953. The Népstadion, the People's Stadium, was built for the people by the people – and by the players. Star man Ferenc Puskás and team-mates pitched in with fellow citizens to lug bricks and cart cement.

The Socialist-Realist design was conceived by Károly Dávid junior, an architect with experience at Le Corbusier's office in Paris, who had also created the superb (and currently redundant) Terminal 1 at Budapest's airport. Behind the stadium stood a cluster of Socialist statuary in heroic poses: sportsmen and soldiers frozen in time.

Ten thousand doves were released, 12,000 gymnasts performed in synch and more than 2,000 sportsmen took part in the grand opening in 1953. These included Puskás and team, who beat Spartak Moscow 3-2 in an exhibition game. Gazing on in admiration was Stalinist dictator Mátyás Rákosi, who had relegated the then president of the International Olympic Committee, Detroit-born Avery Brundage, to the press box – a representative of imperialist America had no right to a seat in the VIP section.

The original Népstadion was built at a then cost of Ft160 million, without factoring in the significant free communal labour. Initial estimates for version 2020, scheduled for completion in 2018, are Ft90-Ft100 billion.

The stadium was renamed after Ferenc Puskás while the great old star lay incapacitated from Alzheimer's disease. In January 2015, the last member of the great side, Jenő Buzánszky, died, and the final living link to 1953-54 was lost. But such is the reverence for the Népstadion and its ghosts that the new arena will be built inside it. With original plans for a new venue alongside now scrapped, the 68,000-capacity ground will feature sloping, three-tier stands within the original structure. The running track will be removed and a panoramic one placed outside. Other new features include an indoor arena, a hotel, a conference centre, a gym and a sports museum.

Also central to Budapest's bid to host the Olympics in 2024, the new arena forms part of football-mad Hungarian Prime Minister Viktor Orbán's massive investment in the sport he loves. New stadiums at Ferencváros, Debrecen and the little village of Felcsút, where Orbán grew up, all opened within a short time of each other in 2014. Now all they have to do is fill them…

EXPLORE

EXPLORE

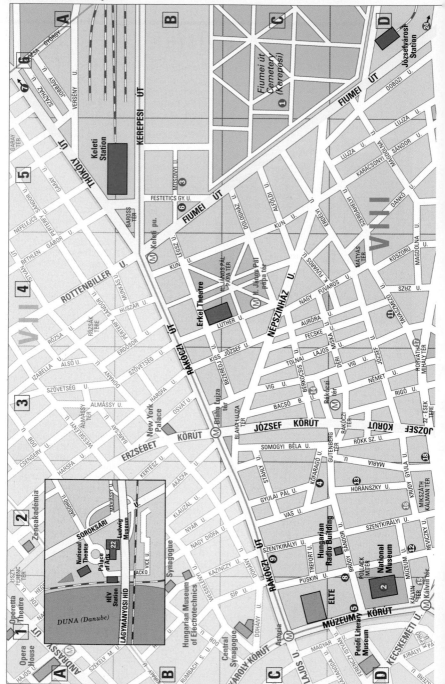

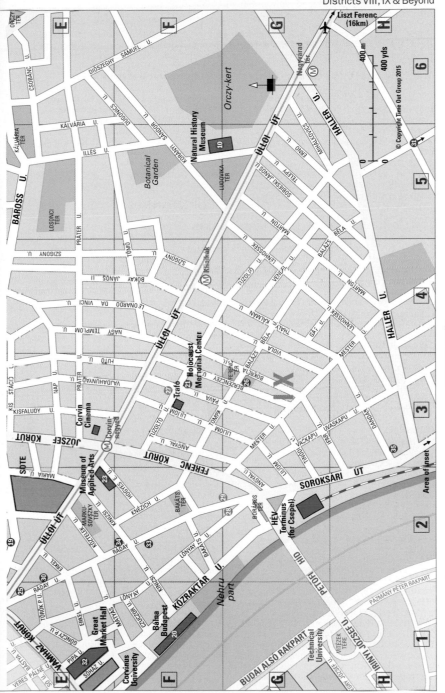

EXPLORE

EXPLORE

Admiral Horthy depicting the inter-war period. There's also a lapidarium with Roman and medieval remains, and regular temporary exhibitions.

FREE Museum of Crime & Police History

Rendőrség-történeti Múzeum
VIII.Mosonyi utca 5 (477 2183, www.police historymus.com). Tram 24. **Open** 9am-5pm Tue-Sat. Closed every 2nd Sat. **Admission** free. **Map** p130 B5 ❸
Not for the faint-hearted, this gruesome museum leaves little to the imagination with its photos of grizzly murders and mysterious crime scenes. Despite a lack of English text, the exhibits are brought to life by a charming ex-cop tour guide with unwavering enthusiasm. Treats in store include Hungary's very own version of Lassie – stuffed, as is the deer involved in a ruthless murder. Note also the detailed account of the infamous Whisky Robber, a serial thief and folk hero from the 1990s.

Restaurants

Fülemüle

VIII.Kőfaragó utca 5 (266 7947, www.fulemule.hu). Tram 4, 6. **Open** noon-10pm Mon-Thur, Sun; noon-11pm Fri, Sat. **Main courses** Ft1,450-Ft5,600. **No credit cards. Map** p130 C2 ❹ **Jewish/Hungarian**
Always a favourite for home-style cooking, 'the Nightingale' has received an overhaul at the hands of owner András Singer. There's now a separate section of the menu categorised as 'Jewish Hungarian' (crispy duck leg, goose liver). Don't miss the house speciality of *sólet*, a kosher bean stew with smoked goose. Fülemüle comes into its own for the traditional Hungarian goose feast in November.

Múzeum

VIII.Múzeum körút 12 (267 0375, www.muzeum kavehaz.hu). M3, M4 Kálvin tér, or M2 Astoria, or tram 47, 49. **Open** 6pm-midnight Mon-Sat. **Main courses** Ft3,600-Ft7,200. **Map** p130 D1 ❺ **Hungarian**
Opened in 1885, Múzeum retains its fin-de-siècle charm: the tall arched windows, ornate tiles, frescoes and dark wood trim are augmented by the tinkling of the resident pianist. The food also harks back to Hungary's heady heyday atop a dual empire. Tradition forges on in the likes of goose liver, stuffed cabbage, catfish and veal paprika. The formal and unobtrusive service suits the atmosphere.

Rosenstein

VIII.Mosonyi utca 3 (333 3492, www.rosenstein. hu). M2, M4 Keleti pu, or tram 24. **Open** noon-11pm Mon-Sat. **Main courses** Ft1,800-Ft8,400. **Map** p130 B5 ❻ **Jewish/Hungarian**
This wonderfully old-school Jewish-Hungarian restaurant is found in an unlikely setting down a side street near Keleti Station. Under the watchful eye of chef-owner Tibor Rosenstein, pork-stuffed cabbage,

catfish soup, *sólet* and roast duck are prepared in the style of the Golden Age. One of the dishes is usually included in the daily Ft2,200 lunch-special menu.

★ Wang Mester Konyhája

XIV.Gizella utca 46A (251 2959, www.kinai konyha.hu). Tram 1, 1A. **Open** 11.30am-11pm Mon-Fri; noon-11pm Sat, Sun. **Main courses** Ft2,490-Ft9,900. **Map** p130 A6 ❼ **Chinese**
Budapest's most celebrated creator of authentic Chinese cuisine, TV star Wang Qiang (aka Wang Mester) runs a smart operation in Zugló. The menu ranges widely, from a whole peking duck (order 24hrs in advance) to turbot with ginger and onion. There are lots of vegetarian options too.

Shops & Services

Artista

VIII.Puskin utca 19 (328 0290, www.artista fashion.com). M2 Astoria. **Open** by appt only. **No credit cards. Map** p130 D2 ❽ **Fashion**
Artista was established in 1993 by three Hungarian designers – Katalin Imre, Nóra Rácz and Katalin Stampf. The main showroom is in Vienna, but there's a by-appointment shop here and an outlet at nearby Mono (*see p84*). The look is classic yet indulgent, with recent special editions working Gustav Klimt and Egon Schiele influences.

Magyar Pálinka Háza

VIII.Rákóczi út 17 (06 30 421 5463, www.magyar palinkahaza.hu). M2 Blaha Lujza tér, or bus 7. **Open** 9am-7pm Mon-Sat. **Map** p130 C2 ❾ **Food & drink**
Excellent selection of top-class Hungarian fruit brandies in a bewildering variety of flavours, all tastefully wrapped to make the perfect gifts.

DISTRICT VIII SOUTH

Behind the National Museum, former mansions rub shoulders with the Socialist-style Magyar Rádió headquarters, which was the scene of bloodletting during the 1956 Uprising. This neighbourhood is known as Palotanegyed – the Palace Quarter – where nobles had their villas close to central Pest. Though the neighbourhood is only now slowly receiving a much-needed clean-up, you can still sense its former grandeur – perhaps with a summer evening meal in the grounds of the **Épitész Pince** restaurant.

Bars from bustling Kálvin tér to the enclosed Mikszáth Kálmán tér are busy year-round, thanks to a strong student presence. The building that houses the **Zappa Café** and **Trafik** music venue (*see p162*) was once home to seminal underground music venue Tilos az Á. It closed down in 1994 and now broadcasts as a radio station (www.tilos.hu). Nearby, Krúdy Gyula utca runs up to the Nagykörút.

Slow gentrification has also begun north of here, with twee new street lights lining pedestrianised sections of Baross utca. The most insalubrious patch used to be Rákóczi tér, which still retains its decorative old food-market hall and now has a new metro station. The popular **Csiga Café** bar has helped to breathe new life into the area.

The heart of Józsefváros is the poor area south of Népszinház utca, centred on Mátyás tér. Courtyards buzz with ragged life, and the nearby **Roma Parliament** and cultural centre is still going despite the withdrawal of government funding. As well as a Roma neighbourhood, District VIII is home to a Chinese community and there are plenty of decent Chinese restaurants in the area. The focus of this de facto Chinatown used to be Józsefvárosi piac, a sprawling, cheap market that was closed down during a major police raid in June 2014. Stalls were quickly set up in a former factory complex opposite – now the Négy Tigris, the Four Tigers market. From here, District VIII stretches out towards a complex containing the Botanical Gardens, Orczy kert park and the **Natural History Museum**

Sights & Museums

Natural History Museum

Magyar Természettudományi Múzeum
VIII.Ludovika tér 2-6 (210 1085, www.nhmus.hu). M3 Klinikák or Nagyvárad tér. **Open** 10am-6pm Mon, Wed-Sun. **Admission** Ft1,600; Ft800 reductions. **No credit cards. Map** p131 G5 ⑩
This mish-mash of a museum comprises of two main elements: stuffed animals brought back by Hungarian explorer Iván Halász from his travels in Africa, and models of past and current wildlife of the Carpathian Basin. The latter is by far the most interesting aspect, also displaying skulls of the Nordic, Mediterranean and Magyar peoples who occupied the basin at the time that Árpád and chums were conquering it for Hungary. Before Árpád, there were cave bears – even lions – in the region. Rocks and minerals are also displayed.

Roma Parliament

VIII.Tavaszmező utca 6 (06 39 474 1325). Tram 4, 6. **Open** varies. **Admission** varies.
Map p130 D4 ⑪
This mid 19th-century mansion is the headquarters for political activism on behalf of the Roma people, plus there's an arts centre with plays in the Romany language and exhibitions by Roma artists. Government funding was cut in 2010 but, so far, this important institution has managed to keep going.

Restaurants

Épitész Pince

VIII.Ötpacsirta utca 2 (266 4799). M3, M4 Kálvin tér. **Open** 11am-10pm Mon-Thur; 11am-midnight

Fri, Sat. **Main courses** Ft1,690-Ft3,790.
Map p130 D2 ⑫ **Hungarian**
Occupying a century-old villa and atmospheric courtyard garden, the 'Architect's Cellar' provides delightful food and an equally delightful setting. The Épitész Pince is modern, both in terms of its arty interior and its menu, with the likes of Dutch spinach soup or camembert- and plum-stuffed chicken breast vying with traditional dishes such as goulash or roast goose and apple-steamed cabbage. Occasional soirées with live jazz or readings appeal to the cultured crowd.

Padron

VIII.Horánszky utca 10 (06 30 900 1204). M3, M4 Kálvin tér. **Open** 5-11pm Mon-Sat. **Tapas** Ft490-Ft1,190. **Map** p130 D2 ⑬ **Spanish**
The Hungarian Beck family fell in love with the cuisine of Andalucia and set up this superior tapas joint in the Palace Quarter. The menu features great renditions of classic tapas dishes – garlic prawns and ox-tripe stew are among the many stand-outs, and vegetarians can make a feast of tapas-sized servings. A good wine list includes lots of Spanish vintages. Evenings only.

Cafés & Bars

★ Csiga Café

VIII.Vásár utca 2 (06 30 613 2046). M4 Rákóczi tér, or tram 4, 6. **Open** 9am-midnight Mon-Sat; 10am-midnight Sun. **Map** p130 C3 ⑭
This durable mainstay for the alternative crowd has recently worked out that providing quality, affordable food is perhaps more attractive, and certainly more lucrative, than providing cheap drinks to bohos, and so the focus now is more on the kitchen. New earlier opening hours for breakfast, and regular lunchtime and early-evening crowds of diners testify to its success. Whether bar, café or bistro, the Csiga stands out for its relaxed atmosphere, lovable staff and mix of easygoing regulars. Its signature arty interior has long been copied elsewhere.
▶ *The driving force behind the Csiga, Oran MacCuirc, now runs convivial terrace spot Félix-Hélix (see p120) on Kazinczy utca.*

Fecske Presszó

VIII.Baross utca 10 (293 1980, www.fecskepresszo. com). M3, M4 Kálvin tér. **Open** 10am-midnight Mon-Fri; noon-midnight Sat; 2pm-midnight Sun.
Map p130 D1 ⑮
Close to universities and a main library, Fecske packs in the students who hang around the bar-starred Palotanegyed area. The cellar bar features quirky decor and old black-and-white photos. Fun-loving staff keep the buzz going. The well-priced tap beer doesn't hurt either: Kozel is Ft520 for 500ml, Pilsner Urquell Ft660. There's also HB wheat beer on draught at Ft720. The kitchen serves breakfast until noon and cheap Hungarian classics the rest of the time.

EXPLORE

Mei Kawa.

Lumen
VIII.Mikszáth Kálmán tér 2 (no phone, www.
photolumen.hu). M3, M4 Kálvin tér, or tram
4, 6. **Open** 9am-7pm Mon-Fri; 11am-4pm Sat.
No credit cards. Map p130 D2 ⑯
The modest enclosed square of Mikszáth Kálmán tér
was once the centre of the known universe, housing
legendary alternative music club Tilos az Á. Where
the Tilos had its side bar, the László brothers, Péter
and Gergely, have set up a photo gallery and installed
an intimate, stylish café, both called Lumen. It runs
daytime only, beginning with breakfast. Bacon and
eggs, soft-boiled eggs or cheese-and-salami croissants accompany strong Illy coffee. Lunchtime soup
may be followed by a slice of Armenian poppyseed
cake made by a friend of the family. More familial
communality comes with the Saturday brunch for
relatives, friends and fellow travellers.

Zsiga
VIII.Horváth Mihály tér 2 (06 70 333 3478).
M4 Rákóczi tér, or tram 4, 6, or bus 9. **Open**
10am-9pm Mon-Thur; 10am-11.30pm Fri, Sat.
No credit cards. Map p130 D4 ⑰
While backpackers and stag-weekenders swamp
the ruin bars of the Jewish Quarter, discerning local
barflies have abandoned District VII to descend on
District VIII – specifically, the Zsiga. Retro Magyar
pop tunes and occasional films are complemented
by a quality kitchen, but most come for the bar
buzz, created by an ever-growing circle of bohemian regulars. A back garden comes into its own in
the summer months.

Shops & Services

Fakopáncs Fajátékbolt
VIII.Baross utca 46 (06 20 379 8189, www.
fakopancs.hu). Tram 4, 6. **Open** 10am-6pm
Mon-Fri; 9am-1pm Sat. **Map** p130 D3 ⑱ **Children**

A paradise for non-electronic goodies, with fantasti-
cally priced dollies, finger puppets, wooden toys and
cognitive games.

Mei Kawa
VIII.Baross utca 3 (06 30 627 8790, www.meikawa.
com). M3, M4 Kálvin tér, or tram 47, 49. **Open**
1-8pm Mon-Fri. **Map** p131 E2 ⑲ **Fashion**
Emese Kasza's limited-edition pieces for men and
women mix straight-cut tailoring with a relaxed,
easy-to-wear feel. Meika is for women, Kawa for
men. The store is part of a collective atelier at this
property known as Flatlab, right by Kálvin tér.

DISTRICT IX & BEYOND

District IX's northern part is bordered on
three sides by the Kiskörút, Üllői út and the
Danube. Like District VIII, the busiest point is
at Kálvin tér, from where Vámház körút runs
down to the river and the former customs house
it's named after.

For decades, the embankment here was
dominated by the university (today the high-
ranking Corvinus) and the **Great Market Hall**
(Nagyvásárcsarnok). The university was once
the main customs office, and an underground
canal used to run from the river, taking barges
through the customs house and into the market
hall. Opened in 1897, the three-storey hall was
a spectacular shopping mall in its day, but fell
apart under Communism. It was restored and
reopened in 1994, with a new Zsolnay tile roof.

In November 2013, a new building was
unveiled near the university: the glass-fronted
Bálna Budapest complex (*see p137* **In the**
Know). Its shops still lack the custom enjoyed
year-round by the Great Market Hall, which is
firmly on the tourist trail, but its little-known
river-facing cafés provide respite from the

throng nearby. A few months later, a new metro station was opened at Fővám tér, right outside the Great Market Hall.

Running parallel to the river, fanning out from Kálvin tér, are Üllői út (the major road that runs out to the airport) and the pedestrianised stretch of tourist-friendly eateries along Ráday utca. Among its somewhat bland venues, Ráday is home to Michelin-starred **Costes** and, at its far end nearer the Nagykörút, the excellent **Jedermann** café. Traffic constantly roars down Üllői út, blackening the otherwise impressive façade of the landmark **Museum of Applied Arts**. If you're going to admire any example of Secessionist architecture in Budapest, it should be this, the masterwork by the master of the genre, Ödön Lechner.

On its way out to the airport, Üllői út passes the gleaming new stadium of **Ferencváros** (www.fradi.hu), Hungary's most popular football club and a symbol of District IX. The €40 million Groupama Aréna was opened with a friendly match against Chelsea in August 2014, one of several new stadiums built around Hungary by football-mad Hungarian Prime Minister Viktor Orbán.

The intersection of Üllői út and the Nagykörút is also the site of the old Kilián barracks, and next to that, on the other side of Üllői út, is the **Corvin**, now a multi-screen cinema (see p145) and mall. Standing here is a statue of a boy with a rifle, in honour of the rebels, many of them children, who died here in the 1956 Uprising. Soldiers in the nearby Kilián barracks were among the first to join the insurgents. Rebels took over the Corvin for tactical reasons: the semi-enclosed theatre offered a protected location from which to attack tanks advancing down the Nagykörút.

Beyond the Nagykörút, this once shabby district has undergone a transformation, its quiet streets interspersed with grassy spaces such as Ferenc tér, home to pram-pushing young professionals. The contrast with adjoining District VIII is palpable. The main thoroughfares of Mester utca, Balázs Béla utca and Tűzoltó utca are pleasant places to stroll, and have the family-friendly facilities of Haller Park at their southern end. Just off Tűzoltó utca, the **Trafó** (see p169) is a multi-tasking arts venue in an old transformer building, with dance, theatre and music, plus occasional exhibitions.

The **Holocaust Memorial Center** on Tűzoltó utca is one of only a few such institutions built with state money, and it's an essential stop on any tour of Jewish Budapest. Heading towards the river, **Dandár utca** contains the lesser-known Turkish baths of the same name, with the same mineral content as the water in the fancier Gellért in Buda. A couple of doors down, the **Zwack Museum** (IX.Dandár utca 1, 476 2383, www.zwack.hu, open 10am-5pm Mon-Sat) offers

a history of the dark liqueur. Admission (Ft1,800) includes an audio guide and a sample at the end. Alongside stands the plant where this national drink is produced.

Nearby rises the riverside arts complex built for the millennium. It comprises the **National Theatre** (see p168) and the **Palace of Arts** (see p168), known locally by its acronym, MÜPA. The latter contains the Bartók National Concert Hall, the **Ludwig Museum** and the Festival Theatre. Slowly developing around the arts complex is the Millennium City Center, a commercial and residential development along a 1.5-kilometre (one-mile) stretch of the Danube. This burgeoning area is linked to Buda by Rákóczi Bridge, until recently known as Lágymanyosi, another hangover of the nixed World Expo project from the 1990s. The whole site enjoys fine views of this previously unsung stretch of the Danube. It's also overlooked by the transit hub of Boráros tér, from where HÉV suburban trains run on to the rusty industrial zone of Csepel island, which is ripe for redevelopment.

East of District IX are the grey expanses of District X and District XIX, most notable for the vast **Új Köztemető Cemetery** and the sprawling flea market of **Ecseri piac**.

Sights & Museums

FREE Bálna

IX.Fővám tér 11-12 (210 1085, www.balna budapest.hu). M3 Corvin-negyed or Klinikák. **Open** 10am-8pm daily. **Map** p131 F1 **20**
Opened in 2013, Bálna is part mall, part arts centre. It has yet to find its feet, but offers pleasant riverside cafés. *See also p137* **In the Know**. *Photo p136.*

Holocaust Memorial Center

Holokauszt Emlékközpont
IX.Páva utca 39 (455 3333, www.hdke.hu). *M3 Ferenc körút or Klinikák.* **Open** 10am-6pm Tue-Sun. **Admission** Ft1,400; Ft700 reductions. **Map** p131 F3 **21**
This fascinating museum may not have the profile (or location) of the main Synagogue but is certainly worth the trip to southern Pest. The exhibition starts with an explanation of what the Holocaust is, and then leads you – via dark corridors and pinpoint lines of white light, against an aural background of soldiers' boots crunching on gravel – through the horrors that occurred here during the last century. 'From the Deprivation of Rights to Genocide' takes in Hungary's loss of territory in 1920, subsequent attempts to regain it, and repressive moves against Jews before the deportations of 1944. Individual family histories personalise this dark era, while the many videos include a time-lapse one of a particular day in May 1944, at Auschwitz-Birkenau. Roma victims are not forgotten either. The walk culminates with a visit to the synagogue.

EXPLORE

★ Ludwig Museum

Ludwig Múzeum
*Palace of Arts, IX.Komor Marcell utca 1 (555
3444, www.ludwigmuseum.hu). Tram 1, 2, 24.*
Open 10am-8pm Tue-Sun. **Admission** Ft1,900.
Map p130 inset ㉒

The city's main showcase for modern and contemporary art, the Ludwig was founded in the momentous
year of 1989 and first occupied the site of the defunct
Museum of the Working Class, before moving to
custom-built premises by the Danube within the
Palace of Arts. The LuMu is the first port of call for
an up-to-date overview of central European art since
the 1960s, thanks to a frequently updated permanent
display, and it's also home to the broadest collection
of international art in Hungary today.

★ Museum of Applied Arts

Iparművészeti Múzeum
*IX.Üllői út 33-37 (456 5107, www.imm.hu).
M3 Corvin-negyed, or tram 4, 6.* **Open** 10am-6pm
Tue-Sun. **Admission** Ft3,500; Ft1,750 reductions.
No credit cards. Map p131 E2 ㉓

A statue of its architect, Ödön Lechner, sits outside
this magnificent building, a masterful example
of his efforts to create a Hungarian style (*see p94*
Walk). As the compact, first-floor exhibition shows,
the building was created to showcase objets d'art
and furnishings, the first of its kind outside London
and Vienna. Experts such as its first director,
György Ráth, gathered works from world's fairs and
major shows by way of a significant fund set up by
the Hungarian National Assembly. We have Ráth's
successor, Jenő Radisics, to thank for the noteworthy art nouveau and Zsolnay items, the beautiful
book-binding and glassware. Among the otherwise
less impressive later acquisitions is Miksa Róth's
stained-glass telephone box from Budapest's famed
Café Japan, now the Írók Boltja (*see p107*). Upstairs
is Ferenc Batári's collection of Ottoman carpets.
There are detailed explanations in English.

FREE Új Köztemető Cemetery

X.Kozma utca 8-10 (433 7300). Tram 28, 37.
Open 7.30am-5pm daily. **Admission** free.
Map p130 D6 ㉔

One of the largest cemeteries in the city contains
the well-signposted final resting place of Imre Nagy,
the prime minister who defied the Soviets in 1956. He's
in Plot 301, with 260 others executed for the Uprising,
in the farthest corner to the right of the entrance.
▶ *Nearby is the large Jewish Cemetery, with
mausoleums and headstones in Secessionist style.*

Restaurants

★ Costes

*IX.Ráday utca 4 (219 0696, www.costes.hu).
M3, M4 Kálvin tér, or tram 47, 49.* **Open**
6.30pm-midnight Wed-Sun. **Main courses**
€15-€38. **Map** p131 E1 ㉕ **Haute cuisine**

Still one of the most talked-about places in town after
earning Budapest's first Michelin star in 2010, Costes
presents the fabulous cuisine of Miguel Vieira Rocha,
who has brought new levels of quality and contemporary verve to the city's dining scene. Opt for one
of the four- to seven-course menus (€75-€110, with
wine €110-€170) – bite-sized portions of seasonally
led textures and flavours allow you to enjoy the full
range of Vieira Rocha's handiwork. A concise à la
carte menu features mains such as pigeon two ways
with beetroot and coffee. Prices are set in euros, but
payment can be made in forints as well.

Petrus

*IX.Ferenc tér 2-3 (951 2597, www.petrus
restaurant.hu). Tram 4, 6, 51.* **Open** noon-
3.30pm, 6.30-11pm Mon-Sat. **Main courses**
Ft2,990-Ft5,690. **Map** p131 G3 ㉖ **Bistro**

Deep in yuppie central at Ferenc tér, owner-chef
Zoltán Feke has recently been earning huge praise
for this simple, affordable restaurant. 'Old-school
bistro' would be one description – fish of the day,
beef bourguignon, blood sausage with puy lentils –
but you'll also find the likes of Mangalica pork chop
sous vide. Highly recommended.

Cafés & Bars

Élesztő

*IX.Tüzöltö utca 22 (06 70 233 5052, www.
elesztohaz.hu). Tram 4, 6.* **Open** 3pm-3am daily.
Map p131 F3 ㉗

Bálna. *See p135.*

IN THE KNOW SAVE THE WHALE

Bálna ('Whale'; see p135), designed by Kas Oosterhuis, is a humpbacked, metal-glass shell laid over a Habsburg-era complex of warehouses. From 2013, it has hosted artisanal boutiques, the New Budapest Gallery (www.budapestgaleria.hu), and craft-beer house Jónás Kézmüves Sörház. What Bálna doesn't contain, though, is people. While the Great Market Hall (see right), five minutes' walk away, is packed, the Bálna allows you to browse displays of Ajka glassware without the crush. Good news for visitors, bad news for traders. As of March 2015, a Sunday fair offers antiques and pieces of contemporary design. But whether the Whale ends up stranded will depend on what other cards it has up its sleeve.

Budapest's new-found passion for craft beers is characterised by this excellent microbrew pub, which opened in 2013. There's a grill kitchen from 6pm until midnight, and the bar stays open until 3am daily. 'Yeast' even offers brewing courses, plus a regular programme of entertainment. The 21 craft beers change frequently – bar staff are happy to advise.

Hat-három (6-3) Borozó

IX.Lónyay utca 62 (06 20 934 1302). Tram 2, 4, 6. **Open** 7am-10pm Mon-Thur; 7am-midnight Fri, Sat; 9am-7pm Sun. **No credit cards. Map** p131 G2 ㉘
This intimate wine bar is a temple to the greatest victory in the history of Hungarian football, the 6-3 (*hat-három*) trouncing of former masters England at Wembley Stadium in 1953. Key to the victory was the deep-lying centre-forward Nándor Hidegkuti, who used to own this bar. Framed sepia photographs decorate the walls, the best one showing a gaggle of celebrating Magyars running away laughing from a recently filled English net. You can order the usual array of wines, beers and spirits to celebrate the victory – and watch the TV for a display by modern-day counterparts of the sorry local game.

Jedermann

IX.Ráday utca 58 (06 30 406 3617, www.jedermann.hu). Tram 4, 6. **Open** 8am-1am daily. **Map** p131 G2 ㉙
Situated on the ground floor of the Goethe Institute, the popular Jedermann is run by local bar guru Hans van Vliet, a jazz man through and through. Some of Hungary's finest exponents of the genre perform on the modest stage on Mondays, Wednesdays and Saturdays – the rest of the week, Jedermann is a buzzy, likeable café. Food is also served, and the daily Ft890 menu sees tables full in the main space most lunchtimes. There's also a pleasant back garden open from spring onwards.

Shops & Services

Babaház

IX.Ráday utca 14 (213 8295, www.dollhouse. uw.hu). M3, M4 Kálvin tér. **Open** 10am-6pm Mon-Sat. **No credit cards. Map** p131 E2 ㉚ **Children**
Pretty dolls from a pre-Barbie era fill this workshop and store where Ilona Kovács creates her masterpieces from the 19th century. Be careful, though: the limbs are real porcelain and the manes are real hair.

★ Ecseri piac

XIX.Nagykörösi út 156 (06 20 924 7279, www.ecseripiac-budapest.hu). Bus 54, 55. **Open** 8am-4pm Mon-Fri; 8am-2pm Sat; 8am-1pm Sun. **No credit cards. Map** p131 H5 ㉛ **Market**
The mother of all flea markets includes a warren of antiques dealers' shacks serving big buyers from the West. At weekends, the area is filled with vendors spreading their wares on blankets and card tables.

Great Market Hall

Nagyvásárcsarnok
IX Vámház körút 1-3 (366 3300, www.piaconlinehu). M4 Fővám tér, or tram 2, 47, 49. **Open** 6:30am-5pm Mon; 6.30am-6pm Tue-Fri; 6.30am-3pm Sat. **No credit cards. Map** p131 E1 ㉜ **Market**
Renovated to its original turn-of-the-century glory, this large, tourist-friendly indoor market is lined with strings of garlic and bright paprika, salamis and preserves, along with fresh produce. Upstairs are snack and drink stalls and souvenir shops.

Jutkavirág

IX.Ráday utca 37 (217 6872, www.jutkavirag.hu). M3 Corvin-negyed, or bus 15. **Open** 9am-6pm Mon-Sat; 9am-1pm Sun. **No credit cards. Map** p131 F2 ㉝ **Florist**
Beautiful bouquets made to order. Having worked here since 1973, Jutka took over the family business from her godmother, who opened the store in 1956.

Ráday Gémklub Játékbolt

IX.Ráday utca 30B (06 20 263 3534, www.gemklub. hu). M3, M4 Kálvin tér. **Open** 10am-8pm Mon-Tue, Thur; 10am-midnight Wed; 10am-10pm Fri; 10am-1pm Sat. **Map** p131 F2 ㉞ **Children**
Ráday stocks all sorts of games that require skill and brainpower. Rubik's inventions other than the Cube, chess games, puzzles and wooden building blocks grace the shelves.

Zwack Shop

IX.Dandár utca 1 (456 5247, www.zwack.hu). Tram 2. **Open** 9am-6pm Mon-Fri; 10am-6pm Sat. **Map** p131 H3 ㉟ **Food & drink**
Zwack produces Unicum, Hungary's national drink in the Jägermeister mould. Its flagship store stocks all Zwack products, from fine wines to *pálinka* – with Unicum the dark and bitter core. There's a museum in the same complex (see p135).

EXPLORE

Arts & Entertainment

Children

Budapest is very child-friendly with plenty of affordable leisure activities, many of which take place outdoors. Lidos open all summer long, with regular baths such as the Széchenyi doubling up as great places to take the family for a day messing about in the water. It's located in the City Park (Városliget), Budapest's main area for recreation, which is also home to a decent zoo, an old-school circus and an equally old-school amusement park. In fact, much in Budapest is pleasingly old-school: adults jump up to offer their seat for a young child on a tram, old ladies make a fuss of babies in shops, and there's a general communal awareness that kids should be taken care of and celebrated. As a result, it's no surprise that children are most definitely welcome in the city's cafés and restaurants.

MUSEUMS & ATTRACTIONS

Budapest has few suitable museums for children. The Transport Museum on the edge of the City Park is currently closed for a complete overhaul and isn't due to reopen until 2018. The **Natural History Museum** (*see p133*) is pretty stuffy, but occasionally hosts interesting temporary exhibitions. The old-school **Museum of Electrotechnics** (*see p119*) can also be fun.

Budakeszi Vadaspark

Budakeszi, Szanatórium utca (06 23 451 783, www.vadaspark-budakeszi.hu). Bus 22, 22A to Szanatórium utca, then follow the signs through the woods. **Open** 9am-4pm Mon-Fri; 9am-5pm Sat, Sun. *Petting Zoo I* 10am-noon Tue-Sun. *Petting Zoo II* 12.30-3pm Tue-Sun. **Admission** Ft1,200; Ft600-Ft800 reductions; free under-2s. **No credit cards.**
A less crowded out-of-town alternative to Budapest Zoo, with the chance to get up close and personal with water buffalo, mouflon and brown bears.

★ Budapest Zoo

Állatkert Budapest Szivében
XIV.Állatkerti körút 6-12 (273 4900, www.zoo budapest.com). M1 Széchenyi fürdő. **Open** *Summer*

9am-6pm Mon-Thur; 9am-7pm Fri-Sun. *Winter* 9am-4pm daily. **Admission** Ft2,500; Ft1,800-Ft2,200 reductions; free under-2s. **Map** p247 J1.
Due to celebrate its 150th anniversary in 2016, Budapest Zoo is welcoming new residents all the time – January 2015 saw the arrival of a baby giraffe, zebra and Indian antelope. Since Australia House was opened in 2010, koalas have become another popular attraction. You'll need an afternoon to see it all, including the animal shows, feeding times and petting corner. Residents' names are written in English and Hungarian, with a full explanation about habitat. Grown-ups might appreciate the art nouveau architecture of the Palm House and Elephant House.
▶ *The Állatkert Játszóház (www.jatekmester.hu, Ft1,200-Ft1,500/hr, Ft900/hr with zoo ticket) is a separate play area within the zoo featuring games, a climbing frame and water feature.*

Holnemvolt Park

XIV.Állatkerti körút 14-16 (363 8310, www. zoobudapest.com/pannonpark). M1 Széchenyi fürdő. **Open** *Mid Mar-Oct* 11am-7pm Mon-Fri; 10am-8pm Sat, Sun. Closed Nov-mid Mar. **Admission** Ft500. **Map** p247 J1.
When the much-loved Vidám Park closed down, the adjoining Zoo took it over and reopened it as Holnemvolt ('Once Upon a Time'), a cross between a

petting zoo and an amusement park. The antiquated cave train and merry-go-round (a heritage attraction) remain, and are now joined by pony rides, a bungee trampoline and resident camels and flamingos. You pay extra for the puppet shows – everything else runs on tokens (Ft200 each).

Margaret Island Little Zoo
Margitszigeti Kisallatkert
XIII.Margitsziget (273 4900). M3 Nyugati pu or tram 4, 6, then bus 26, 26A. **Open** *15 Apr-23 Oct* 10am-6pm daily. Closed 24 Oct-14 Apr. **Admission** Ft500. **No credit cards.**
Close to the city centre, Margaret Island is home to plenty of green space and a small petting zoo housing deer, rabbits and ponies. There are also lots of waterfowl, mandarin ducks and white-cheeked pintails, as well as sundry birds of prey. Other animals come and go – since this former run-down deer park was taken over by Budapest Zoo, improvements have been considerable.

★ Palace of Wonders
Csodák Palotája
XXII.Nagyteténvi út 37-43 (814 8050, www.csopa. hu). Bus 33, 114, 133, 150. **Open** 9am-7pm Mon-Fri; 10am-8pm Sat, Sun. **Admission** Ft2,200; Ft1,700 reductions. **Map** p245 A3.
Moved from the Millenáris Park to the Campona complex in 2012, the Palace of Wonders is the most modern and interactive of Budapest's kid-friendly attractions. Current features include a giant piano, an air cannon, a waterfall illusion and a velvet harp.

Planetarium
Népliget (263 1811, www.planetarium.hu). M3 Népliget. **Shows** (five times daily) 9.30am-4pm Tue-Sun. **Admission** Ft1,500; Ft1,300 reductions. *English-language show* Ft1,500. **No credit cards.**
The Planetarium combines temporary exhibits and educational children's shows in Hungarian, plus occasional English-language shows such as 'Hubble Universe' and 'Wonders of the Sky'.

★ Tropicarium
XXII.Nagytetényi út 37-43 (424 3053, www. tropicarium.hu). Bus 33, 114, 133, 150. **Open** 10am-8pm daily. **Admission** Ft2,500; Ft1,800-Ft2,100 reductions; free under-4s. **Map** p245 A3.
Referring to itself as a 'shark zoo', the Tropicarium contains a petting tank full of rays, plus alligators, free-flying birds and, of course, sharks – six of the giant variety glide around an observation tunnel. Feeding takes place at 3pm on Thursdays.

ACTIVITIES

Budapest's many baths and lidos (*strand*) offer plenty of summer entertainment, but note that bigger ones such as **Széchenyi** (*see p205*)

don't offer discounted admission for children – a day out there with two kids is an expensive proposition. The two listed here, **Római Beach** and **Palatinus Beach**, are child-friendly and affordable. Towels are available for hire.

Aqua Park
Aquaworld Hotel, IV.Íves út 16 (231 3600, www.aquaworldresort.hu). M3 Újpest-központ then bus 14E, or free shuttle bus from Heroes' Square (9.30am, 1.30pm, 5.30pm, 7.30pm daily). **Open** 6am-10pm daily. **Admission** Ft2,950-Ft5,690; Ft1,350-Ft3,990 reductions; free under-3s.
Located on the northern outskirts of town, this is Budapest's best waterpark. There are 11 slides, including the Kamikaze, the Tornado and the Flying Carpet, plus pools of the wave, lido and outdoor-adventure variety. There's plenty laid on for toddlers too. A free shuttle bus runs from Heroes' Square.

City Park Ice Rink
Városligeti Műjégpálya
Városliget, XIV.Olof Palme sétány 5 (363 2673, www.mujegpalya.hu). M1 Hősök tere. **Open** (winter only) 9am-1pm, 5-9pm daily. **Admission** Ft1,000-Ft2,000; Ft800-Ft1,500 reductions; free under-5s. **Map** p247 J2.

Budapest Zoo.

Római Baths.

The city's main ice rink is located just behind Heroes' Square, looking pristine in its Habsburg finery after a major renovation in 2011. First opened in 1870, the ice rink gained its neo-Baroque building two decades later, in time to host the European Figure Skating Championships in 1895. Still one of the biggest open-air rinks in Europe, the Városligeti Műjégpálya now also sports a decent restaurant (see p113).

Görzenál

III.Árpád fejedelem útja 125 (250 4799, www. gorzenal.hu). Bus 86. **Open** *Mid Mar-mid Nov 2pm-dusk Mon-Fri; 9.30am-dusk Sat, Sun. Closed mid Nov-mid Mar.* **Admission** Ft900. Skate hire Ft500/3hrs.

This extensive and inclusive skate park in Óbuda caters to both novice and experienced skaters, with tuition offered at Ft2,000/hr plus the admission fee. BMX riders and streetball teams are also welcome.

Kids' Park

Kölyökpark
Mammut II, II.Lövőház utca 1-5 (345 8512, www. gyerekpark.hu). M2 Széll Kálmán tér, or tram 4, 6. **Open** *10am-9pm Mon-Fri; 9am-9pm Sat; 9am-8pm Sun.* **Admission** Ft880/30mins. **No credit cards. Map** p245 A3.
Indoor playground with the usual range of monkey bars, slides, towers and tunnels.
Other locations throughout the city.

Millenáris Park

II.Kis Rókus utca 16-20 (336 4000, www. millenaris.hu). M2 Széll Kálmán tér, or tram 4, 6. **Open** varies. **Admission** varies. **Map** p245 A3.
This custom-built venue hosts craft workshops, puppet shows, children's theatre and playgroups.

Opening times and admission vary according to the attraction – the Millipop Playhouse for toddlers is open from 10am to 8pm daily.

Palatinus Baths

Palatinus Strandfürdő
XIII.Margitsziget (340 4505, www.palatinus strand.hu). M3 Nyugati pu, then bus 26. **Open** *22 June-20 Aug* 9am-8pm daily. *21 Aug-14 Sept* 9am-7pm daily. Closed 15 Sept-21 June. **Admission** Ft2,600-Ft3,000; Ft1,900 reductions.
The city's best-loved lido lies halfway up Margaret Island and is busy all summer long. Popular since opening before World War II, the Palatinus comprises a swimming pool, a lido and an adventure pool with neck showers and whirlpool corridors.

Római Baths

Római Strandfürdő
III.Rozgonyi Piroska utca (388 9740, www.romai strand.hu). HÉV Római fürdő, or bus 34, 106. **Open** *25 May-1 Sept* 9am-8pm daily. Closed 2 Sept-24 May. **Admission** Ft1,700-Ft2,600; Ft1,700-Ft1,800 reductions.
Up in Óbuda, a short walk from the HÉV stop, these baths are arguably the most child-friendly in town, and certainly the most affordable. Extensive grassy areas surround the main pool with a flume and large slide, plus there's a separate toddlers' pool and a lane pool for serious swimmers. The outdoor snack bar provides cheap treats, or bring a picnic.

PERFORMING ARTS

Budapest Fesztivál Zenekar

Office: III.Polgár utca 8-10 (489 4330, www.bfz. hu). HÉV Szentlélek tér, or bus 86. **Shows** vary. **Admission** varies.

In the home country of Bartók and Kodály, you're bound to find classical music performances adapted for children. Their nickname is *kakaókoncertek*, because kids are rewarded for their patience with a hot chocolate at the end. The most popular are given by the Budapest Fesztivál Zenekar.

Budapest Puppet Theatre
Budapest Bábszínház
VI.Andrássy út 69 (342 2702, www.budapest-babszinhaz.hu). M1 Vörösmarty utca. **Shows** *Sept-June* daily. Closed July, Aug. **Open** *Box office* 9am-6pm daily. **Admission** varies. **Map** p246 G3.
International fairy tales and Hungarian folk stories make up the repertoire of this established puppet theatre (look out for the beautiful neon sign on Andrássy út). The language barrier is usually not a problem and the shows are always highly original. The website indicates the suitable age group for each performance.

Capital Circus
Fővárosi Nagycirkusz
XIV.Állatkerti körút 12A (343 8300, www.fnc.hu). M1 Széchenyi fürdő. **Shows** 3pm Wed-Fri; 11am, 3pm, 7pm Sat; 11am, 3pm Sun. **Open** *Box office* 10am-6pm Mon-Fri; 9am-7.30pm Sat; 9am-6pm Sun. **Admission** Ft1,900-Ft4,500; Ft1,500-Ft3,100 reductions; free under-4s. **Map** p247 J1.
Established at the end of the 19th century, the city's circus remains charmingly old-fashioned. Its permanent building opposite the Széchenyi Baths stages shows all year round, featuring acrobats, magicians, jugglers, clowns and animals.

Municipal Cultural House
TEMI Fővárosi Művelődési Háza (FMH)
XI.Fehérvári út 47 (203 3868, www.fmhnet.hu). M4 Újbuda-központ, or tram 47, 49. **Shows** vary. **Admission** varies. **No credit cards**.
Activities include children's theatre shows, a folk-dance club for children with music provided by the renowned local Muzsikás ensemble, playgroups for three- to six-year-olds, and dance, gymnastics and aerobics courses for little ones.

PARKS & PLAYGROUNDS

Budapest's two main parks, **Városliget** (City Park; *see p111*) and **Margitsziget** (Margaret Island; *see p45*), provide a great family day out. Városliget has outdoor courts for basketball, five-a-side football and foot-tennis, as well as a fenced-in playground in the south corner. Both parks have cycle paths, and Margitsziget also has pedalos for hire.
Several squares around urban Pest contain playgrounds and courts for ball games. These include **Honvéd tér** near Nyugati Station,

downtown **Hild tér** and **Szabadság tér**, and **Klauzál tér** in the Jewish Quarter. Pick of the bunch is **Károlyi kert**, a pretty pocket park near Astoria. Up in Buda, **Vuk játszótér** (I.Bérc utca, at the corner of Szirtes utca) is a charming playground themed around the cartoon fox, Vuk.

QUIRKY TRANSPORT

Budapest offers plenty of unusual, family-friendly rides, some of which accept standard public-transport tickets (Ft350). The **Cog-wheel Railway** (*see p65*) that snakes up into the Buda Hills from Városmajor is part of the public-transport network. The start of the railway is just a short hop from Széll Kálmán tér on tram 61, which carries on to Hűvösvölgy and the **Children's Railway**. Alternatively, from Városmajor, you can catch the 102 bus and head up to the **Chairlift** (Libegő; *see p65*).
Back in the city centre, the **Sziget Eye** (*see p76*) panoramic wheel now runs for most of the year. For a **boat** down the Danube, you can either take one of several sightseeing tours from the Vigadó tér terminus on the Pest embankment – or, on the city transport network, waterborne line 11 runs several times a day from Haller utca to Árpád út in Újpest, via Petőfi, Szabadság, Margaret and Árpád bridges. The whole journey lasts 90 minutes.

Children's Railway
Gyermekvasút
II.Hűvösvölgy (397 5392, www.gyermekvasut.hu). Tram 61. **Departures** (hourly) 9am-5pm Tue-Sun. **Tickets** Ft700; Ft350 reductions. **No credit cards**.
One of Budapest's most enduring and endearing kiddie-centric attractions, the Children's Railway was a Soviet concept introduced here in 1948. Still the longest of its kind, this 11.2km (seven-mile) narrow-gauge railway chugs through pleasant greenery from Hűvösvölgy to Széchenyi-hegy. Children, though no longer referred to as 'Pioneers', still staff the train service, leaving the driving to an adult. The whole journey takes 45 minutes – at Széchenyi-hegy, a ten-minute walk down Golfpálya út allows you to connect with the Cog-wheel Railway (*see p65*) and make an afternoon of it.

Nostalgia Train
Nosztalgiavonat
Information & tickets: Next to Platform 10, Nyugati station, VI.Nyugati tér (269 5242, www.mavnosztalgia.hu). M3 Nyugati pu, or tram 4, 6. **Tickets** vary. **Map** p246 F3.
Hungarian Railways operates this steam-engine service with old-fashioned carriages, which sets off from Nyugati Station to several destinations throughout the year. Balaton and the Danube Bend are the most popular destinations.

Film

Looking at Budapest's film listings for any given day, the domination of malls over independent cinemas quickly becomes clear. The cinemagoer can choose from a dozen multiplexes across town, leaving just a handful of independents to struggle for custom. The staunchly arthouse Odeon Lloyd closed in 2012, followed by the Vörösmarty in 2014 (which originally opened as the Savoy in 1935). But others do survive, including the cherished Művész and Cirko-gejzir ('Films as Nowhere Else, Somewhere Else'), and these leftfield venues have begun to play up their unconventional credentials. The Cirko-gejzir has recently started to offer individual visitors and companies the chance to customise their own seats, including the sofas in the front row, while the Buda Bed Cinema in Óbuda has gone one better and filled its screening room with nothing but... beds.

CINEMA IN BUDAPEST

More and more full-length features are being made at home, from mainstream comedies to edgy dramas, and many of them are shown at the revived **Hungarian Film Week** in October. Of particular note in 2014 was Kornél Mundruczó's *Fehér isten* ('White God'), made with a €1.6 million grant from the Hungarian Film Fund. This gripping tale of a girl in a dog-run society won the Un Certain Regard prize for innovative and daring new works at the Cannes Film Festival 2014. It was also selected as Hungary's entry for Best Foreign-Language Film at the 2015 Oscars.

Other notable Hungarian directors include György Pálfi, whose 2014 feature *Szabadesés* ('Free Fall') gave 'Magyar film buffs reason to be proud,' according to *Variety*.

Grants have also been handed out for the renovation of cinemas themselves – the restored, century-old **Uránia Nemzeti Filmsínház** is an architectural treasure, while the **Puskin** is now approaching its 90th (nearly continuous) year of screening movies. Though no glittering beauty, the **Toldi** is a destination in its own right thanks to its trendy in-house bar, busy whatever is being screened.

Going to the pictures is cheap entertainment. Two tickets for a multiplex or independent still cost around €10-€12, with free parking at many mall cinemas if you ask at the cash desk. Each cinema has listings on its website – the multi-multiplex group **Cinema City** provides English-language times and online ticket sales at www.cinemacity.hu/en. Its Aréna cinema contains the largest IMAX in the region. The three-venue independent umbrella **Artmozi** has Hungarian-only information at www.artmozi.hu for the Müvész, Puskin and Toldi.

★ Buda Bed Cinema
III.Bécsi út 38-44 (437 8362, www.budaeg. com). Bus 9, 17, 86, or HÉV Szépvölgyi út.
Admission per bed Ft5,555.
Opened in autumn 2014 and an immediate hit as an '...and finally' item on news broadcasts across Europe, the BBC creates an entirely new genre of venue for filmgoers: the *ágymozi* or bed cinema. Naturally, as in every bedroom, there are rules – no shoes, no snoring and no pillow fights. Sex is also a no-no. Films, mainly but not exclusively Hungarian-language mainstream hits, are screened every day from late morning or early afternoon, with the last feature at midnight. There are kid-friendly movies,

too, and each ticket is valid for a couple, or couple with up to two children under ten.

Cinema City Aréna

Aréna Plaza, VII.Kerepesi út 9 (06 40 600 600, www.cinemacity.hu). M2, M4 Keleti pu, or tram 24. **Admission** Ft1,670-Ft2,120; Ft1,420-Ft1,840 reductions (free parking with ticket). **Map** p247 K5. The largest IMAX screen in the region, showing a wide range of documentaries and 3D blockbusters. There are also no less than 17 conventional screens.

Cirko-gejzir

V.Balassi Bálint utca 15-17 (269 1915, www. cirkofilm.hu). Tram 2, 4, 6. **Admission** Ft950-Ft1,490. **No credit cards. Map** p246 D2. This small cinema showcases obscure independent movies from around the world. All films are screened in their original language with Hungarian subtitles. You can park your bike in the lobby.

Corvin Mozi

VIII.Corvin köz 1 (459 5050, www.corvinmozi.hu). M3 Corvin-negyed, or tram 4, 6. **Admission** Ft1,050-Ft1,890 (free parking with ticket). **Map** p250 G7. Budapest's most attractive multiplex, set within an elegant Secession/Bauhaus-style building, has the latest projection and sound equipment, and a café. The surrounding area, a Resistance stronghold in the 1956 Uprising, is now a pleasant pedestrianised zone.

Kino

XIII.Szent István körút 16 (950 6846, www.akino. hu). M3 Nyugati pu, or tram 4, 6. **Admission** Ft700-Ft1,300. **No credit cards. Map** p246 E2.

This two-screen arthouse cinema is often the best place to catch contemporary Hungarian releases with English subtitles. The smaller screen is accessible for wheelchair users, and the trendy café serves all-day breakfast and runs from 8am to midnight.

Művész

VI.Teréz körút 30 (332 6726, 459 5050, www. muveszmozi.hu). M1 Oktogon, or tram 4, 6. **Admission** Ft1,100-Ft1,400; Ft900-Ft1,000 reductions. **Map** p246 F3. This five-screen arthouse gem offers a good selection of new independent releases you're not likely to find elsewhere. Soundtrack CDs, art books and jewellery are sold in the lobby. There's guarded bike parking during shows.

Örökmozgó Filmmúzeum

VII.Erzsébet körút 39 (342 2167, www.film archive.hu). Tram 4, 6. **Admission** Ft800-Ft1,200. **No credit cards. Map** p246 G4. Known for its eclectic schedule featuring everything from silents to documentaries, the Örökmozgó was converted into a cinema from a film museum in 1991. It still contains a library of 20,000 books, including rare items from the early days of film. Modern-day offerings include foreign-language films played with their original soundtrack and simultaneous Hungarian translation via headsets. Newer films often have English subtitles.

Palace Mammut

Mammut mall, II.Lövőház utca 2-6 (06 40 600 600, www.cinemacity.hu). M2 Széll Kálmán tér, or tram 4, 6. **Admission** Ft1,670-Ft2,520; Ft1,670-Ft2,100 reductions (free parking with ticket). **Map** p245 A3.

ARTS & ENTERTAINMENT

'Buda Bed Cinema.

One of seven multiplexes in the Cinema City chain, the 13-screen Mammut near Buda's busiest transport hub mostly features Hollywood blockbusters and new Hungarian releases.

★ Puskin
V.Kossuth Lajos utca 18 (429 6080, www.puskin mozi.hu). M2 Astoria, or tram 47, 49, or bus 7. **Admission** Ft1,100-Ft1,400; Ft900-Ft1,000 reductions. **Map** p249 F6.
The venerable Puskin (as in the Russian writer) looks pretty much as it did when it started showing movies back in 1926 – at the time it was one of the biggest screens in Europe. It was originally called the Fórum, and before that it was the Magyar Világ coffeehouse. The 420-seat main hall still has classic 1920s design touches, now coupled with 21st-century acoustics and visuals. There are two other screens, too, and a schedule of Hollywood releases, plus a handful of foreign and Hungarian features.

Tabán Kinotéka
I.Krisztina körút 87-89 (459 5050, 06 30 731 4975, www.tabankinoteka.hu). Tram 18. **Admission** Ft1,000-1,200; Ft900 reductions. **Map** p245 A3.
Closed in 2013 and reopened (and slightly renamed) in 2014, the much-loved Tabán now features a renovated interior, two screening rooms (Kubrick and Fellini), modern acoustics and digital projection. To its credit, the management hasn't just gone for a safe, mainstream schedule – the Tabán regularly screens European features well worthy of investigation. There's a videotheque too – a DVD rental library that opens 30 minutes before the start of the first feature.

Toldi
V.Bajcsy-Zsilinszky út 36-38 (472 0397, 459 5050, www.toldimozi.hu). M3 Arany János utca. **Admission** Ft1,400; Ft900-Ft1,000 reductions. **Map** p246 C3.
The landmark Toldi, though modern in style after a 2008 revamp, still features touches of its black-and-white heritage – its name is displayed with a stylish flourish over the façade, for example. This spacious venue shows modern indie releases and Hungarian films old and new. It's also a popular festival venue. The bustling in-house bar is an added bonus.

★ Uránia Nemzeti Filmszínház
VIII.Rákóczi út 21 (486 3400, www.uranianf.hu). M2 Astoria or Blaha Lujza tér, or bus 7. **Admission** Ft800-Ft1,800; Ft800 reductions. **Map** p247 H5.
The grand dame of Budapest's dream palaces, the Uránia is one of the most elegant cinemas in Europe. Opened as a theatre in 1899, the Uránia began to screen films from 1900 onwards. Hungary's first independent feature was shot here a year later. The elegant Venetian/Moorish-style building has now been restored to its original glory – for a unique (and eminently affordable) cinematic experience, treat yourself to one of seven exclusive boxes. As Hungary's National Film Theatre, the Uránia features new local releases as well as international works, and is a mainstay of the festival circuit.

Uránia Nemzeti Filmszínház.

Hungarian Film Week.

FILM FESTIVALS

Anilogue Budapest International Animation Festival

Anilogue Budapesti Nemzetközi Animációs Fesztivál

Tickets & information: Uránia Nemzeti Filmszínház, VIII.Rákóczi út 21 (www.anilogue. com). **Date** Nov.

Anilogue is Hungary's largest festival devoted to animated film. Four days of shows, a competition for European animation and a daily after-party with non-stop screenings are staged at the venerable Uránia (*see p144*). The 2014 event was won by Danish director Esben Toft Jacobsen for *Beyond Beyond*, about a dissatisfied rabbit.

Busho Short Film Festival

Puskin (see p144), V.Kossuth Lajos utca 18. Tickets & information: 422 1083, www.busho.hu. **Date** early Sept.

Run by enthusiasts since 2004, Busho overcame the sad closure of its previous home, the Vörösmarty cinema, to stage a tenth anniversary event in 2014 at the Puskin and smaller venues nearby. Busho has always been a strong supporter of young filmmaking talent, both local and international. The festival features work from Europe, Asia and the Americas, in three categories: experimental, short drama and animation. Tickets are sold for the whole five days, for one day or for particular shows, with prices running from Ft500 to Ft4,000. The last day is given over to awards. Entries are limited to 30 minutes' running time and there's a nominal €10 entry fee.

Hungarian Film Week

Magyar Filmhét

Tickets & information: Cinema City MOM Park, XII.Alkotás út 53 (www.cinemacity.hu, www.filmhet.hu). **Date** mid Oct.

Following the demise of Magyar Filmszemle, Hungary's main cinematic event, Hungarian Film Week made a welcome return in 2014 with some 30 local works scheduled, in categories such as documentary, animation, full-length feature and short feature. Tickets cost an across-the-board Ft610.

Mediawave

Festival office in Győr (www.mediawave.hu). **Date** late Apr-May.

Based in Győr, halfway between Budapest and Vienna, this five-day event is Hungary's major international competitive festival for short, experimental and documentary films. Music, dance and theatre performances are equally important. The venue for the 25th anniversary in 2015 was Fort Monostor in Komárom, near the Slovak border.

Titanic International Film Festival

Titanic Nemzetközi Filmfesztivál

Tickets & information: Uránia Nemzeti Filmszínház, VIII.Rakóczi út 21 (www.titanicfilmfest.hu). **Date** mid Apr.

New arthouse and cult movies from Asia, Europe and North America are shown across nine days at three main venues in town: the Uránia, the Toldi and the Örökmozgó. In 2014, there were films from as far afield as the Philippines and Kazakhstan – though it was a Bulgarian feature, *Viktoria*, by Maya Vitkova, that took the €8,000 prize for best movie.

IN THE KNOW IN SHORT

On any given day, you should be able to find at least a handful of English-language films being screened across town, with Hungarian subtitles. If you're looking at a Hungarian-language listings resource, *mb* next to a particular film means *magyarul beszélö* (Hungarian-language only), *szin* means *szinkronizált* (dubbed) and *fel* or *f* means *feliratos* (subtitled). *Ang* is short for *angol* (English). Film lengths are usually given in *perc* (minutes).

ARTS & ENTERTAINMENT

Gay & Lesbian

Despite the conservative wave hitting social and political life in Hungary – these days the Pride Parade feels more like a protest rally than a carefree celebration – LGBT life in Budapest is flourishing as never before. The quiet, old-school hangouts and exclusively gay clubs still thrive, but they no longer dominate the local scene. Instead, the weekend fun has now been taken over by a multitude of party nights held at regular venues around the capital, creating a more mixed and open vibe. As there are more independent events than gay clubs, sometimes it's hard to keep up with what's going on where, even for locals. To help you through the maze, look out for free magazine *Humen* (www.humenmagazin.com) or visit www. qalendar.hu to plan your fun.

FESTIVALS & EVENTS

Pride Film Festival
www.budapestpride.com. **Date** Jan.
Run by the Budapest Pride organisation, the PFF involves a wide variety of features, short films and documentaries, along with special guests, workshops and side events.

LGBT History Month
www.lmbttortenetihonap.hu. **Date** Feb.
Hungary first became involved in this annual Europe-wide event in 2013. Held every February, it involves a series of artistic, cultural and social events focusing on the life, culture and history of the LGBT community.

Budapest Pride
www.budapestpride.com. **Date** July.
The most important event in the Hungarian gay calendar is summer's Pride festival, which marked its 20th edition in 2015. Along with the march itself, there are lots of parties, conferences, film screenings and exhibitions.

Magic Mirror @ Sziget Festival
www.sziget.hu. **Date** Aug.
Sziget Festival is the largest music and arts event in the region, held on an island north of Budapest every August. The most eclectic entertainment is invariably staged in the Magic Mirror tent: gay-oriented cabaret, music and performance culminating in a nightly disco.

TranszFeszt
www.transzfeszt.hu. **Date** Oct.
Hungary's first ever trans-themed festival started in October 2014 as a three-day free event celebrating trans artists and their work, with the aim of bringing the trans community together.
▶ *Trans events are also hosted by Transvanilla (www.transvanilla.hu), an organisation representing trans, intersex and genderqueer people in Hungary.*

LIFT
www.labrisz.hu. **Date** Nov.
The Lesbian Identities Festival, or LIFT, features three days of film screenings, workshops, literary readings, an exhibition and an after-party. Local lesbian organisation Labrisz has been behind the event since it was inaugurated in 2005.

WHERE TO STAY

Connection Guesthouse
VII.Király utca 41 (267 7104, www.connection guesthouse.com). M1, M2, M3 Deák tér. **Map** p246 F4.

This gay hotel has modest rooms for rent, some with showers. A late breakfast is served.

KM Saga
IX.Lónyay utca 17 (www.gaystay.net/KMSaga). *M3, M4 Kálvin tér, or M4 Fővám tér.* **No credit cards. Map** p249 F7.
Gay-owned guesthouse with five ornately decorated rooms. Online booking only.

RESTAURANTS

Club 93 Pizzeria
VIII. Vas utca 2 (06 30 630 7093). M2 Astoria or Blaha Lujza tér, or bus 7. **Open** noon-midnight daily. **No credit cards. Map** p249 G5.
This small pizzeria has been serving Italian faves, cocktails and desserts since 1993.

Kazán
VI.Ó utca 51 (326 0920, www.kazanklub.hu). *M1 Oktogon, or tram 4, 6.* **Open** 4pm-midnight Tue-Thur; 4pm-6am Fri, Sat. **Map** p246 F4.
This gay-friendly pub serves hot snacks such as *piadinas*, burgers and Hungarian speciality *lángos*.

BARS & CLUBS
Gay

Action Bar
V.Magyar utca 42 (266 9148, www.action. gay.hu). M3, M4 Kálvin tér, or night bus 909, 914, 914A, 916, 950, 950A, 979, 979A. **Open** 9pm-5am daily. **Admission** free (min spend Ft1,000). **No credit cards. Map** p249 F6.

Budapest Pride.

This popular cellar bar has the busiest darkroom in town and fancy new toilets with see-through walls. Highlights include live shows and striptease on Fridays, Oral Academy on Saturdays and a bear club every last Saturday of the month. Look for the letter 'A' on the decrepit door.

Alterbuzi
Various locations (www.facebook.com/alterbuzi). **Admission** varies.
One of the newest queer parties in town, this alternative event attracts different generations with a good mixture of indietronica, post-punk, alt rock and golden oldies.

Alterego
VI.Dessewffy utca 33 (06 70 345 4302, www. alteregoclub.hu). M1 Oktogon, or M3 Arany János utca, or tram 4, 6, or night bus 923, 979. **Open** 10pm-6am Fri, Sat. **Admission** Ft1,000-Ft1,500. **No credit cards. Map** p246 F4.
A stylish beacon in the dark night, Alterego attracts well dressed gay men and their friends. Drag shows are staged after midnight, accompanied by mainstream pop. Dress up to get past the door.

★ Brutkó Diszkó
Various locations (www.brutko.hu). **Admission** Ft1,000.
Budapest's original non-mainstream queer party is a rare phenomenon these days, but it's worth the wait. Popular among new wave, house and techno fans.

Budapest Bears
Various locations (www.budapestbears.hu). **Admission** varies.
This bear community organises gatherings, parties and the annual Mr Bear contest.

Capella
V.Belgrád rakpart 23 (06 30 913 2994, www.capella cafe.hu). M3 Ferenciek tere, or tram 2, or night bus 907, 908, 956, 973, 979, 990. **Open** 10pm-4am Wed, Thur; 10pm-6am Fri, Sat. **Admission** varies. **No credit cards. Map** p249 E7.
Capella is Budapest's most central and longest-running gay club. This multi-level venue brings a mixed crowd – including straights, especially at weekends. Drag shows take place after midnight.

★ Confetti
Various locations (06 30 388 0799, www.facebook. com/confettiparty). **Admission** Ft2,000.
This long-running party series attracts pretty people with pecs for themed soirées – expect dancing, drinks and entertainment acts. *Photos p150.*

Coxx
VII.Dohány utca 38 (344 4884, www.coxx.hu). *M2 Astoria, or tram 47, 49, or night bus 907, 908, 909, 914, 914A, 950, 950A, 956, 973, 979, 979A,*

ARTS & ENTERTAINMENT

ARTS & ENTERTAINMENT

Confetti. See p149.

990. **Open** 9pm-4am Mon-Thur, Sun; 9pm-5am Fri, Sat. **Admission** free (min spend Ft1,000). **No credit cards. Map** p249 G5.
Located below an internet café, you'll find this cruising labyrinth of desire, complete with cages, slings, glory holes, wet rooms, multiple bars and even a small sex shop. Party themes include gang-bang, bear, military and the like.

Funny Carrot
V. Szép utca 2 (06 30 871 9327, www.funnycarrot. hu). M2 Astoria, or tram 47, 49, or night bus 907, 908, 909, 914, 914A, 950, 950A, 956, 973, 979, 979A, 990. **Open** 7pm-6am daily. **Admission** varies. **No credit cards. Map** p249 F6.
This mellow hangout offers a laid-back vibe, perfect for chatting and chilling out to retro tunes, plus daily two-for-one drink deals. In the same building, you'll find the late-night Habroló bar (950 6644, www.habrolo.hu).

Garçons
Various locations (www.garconsbudapest.com). **Admission** Ft2,000.
Held once a month, this trendy night attracts fashionistas for electropop and nu-disco vibes.

Hello!
Toldi Mozi, V. Bajcsy-Zsilinszky út 36-38 (www. facebook.com/hellopartybp). M3 Arany János utca, or night bus 914, 914A, 931, 950, 950A. **Admission** Ft1,000-Ft1,500. **Map** p246 E4.
Fun, trashy pop night revolving around gay icons past and present. It's usually held at this spot, but do check in advance.

Jour
Ankert, VI. Paulay Ede utca 33 (06 30 360 3389, www.ankert.hu, www.facebook.com/jourparty). M1 Opera, or tram 4, 6, or night bus 923. **Admission** varies. **Map** p246 F4.
Nu-disco and deep house vibes alternate with guest DJs and themed nights in this eclectic party series. Check the website for details – the venue can change.

Madrid Bar
V. Semmelweis utca 17 (06 70 410 2185, www. madridcafebar.com). M2 Astoria, or tram 47, 49, or night bus 907, 908, 909, 914, 914A, 950A, 956, 959, 973, 979, 979A, 990. **Open** 6pm-5am. **Map** p249 F5.
Centrally located, quiet gay bar with a living room feel. Classic pop, karaoke and drag shows make up the entertainment.

Mystery Bar
V. Nagysándor József utca 3 (312 1436, www. mysterybar.hu). M3 Arany János utca, or night bus 914, 914A, 931, 950, 950A. **Open** 5pm-4am daily. **Map** p246 E4.
Formerly known as Le Café M, the Mystery Bar is located in the financial quarter and provides a cool rendezvous spot. Daily drink offers attract a mix of locals and tourists.

★!Szkafander
Ankert, VI. Paulay Ede utca 33 (06 30 360 3389, www.ankert.hu, www.szkafander.blog.hu). M1 Opera. **Map** p246 F4.
This veteran DJ crew is mostly famous for its weekly party !Tape. Deep house, dancefloor-filling pop and

a diverse crowd guarantee a fun vibe. It's usually held at this District VI spot.

Why Not Café
V.Belgrád rakpart 3-4 (780 4545, www.whynot cafe.hu). M4 Fővám tér, or night bus 979, 979A. **Open** 10am-4am daily. **Map** p249 E7.
Popular daytime and pre-club bar with a Danube view. Special-offer drinks might encourage you to grab the mic and let it all out at the Tuesday and Saturday karaoke parties.

Lesbian

Ösztrosokk
Various locations (www.osztrosokk.hu). **Admission** Ft1,000-Ft1,500.
Women-only groups hold court for the lesbian community with resident DJs and theme parties.

Szociális Helyiség
VII.Kazinczy utca 52C (06 20 974 0078, www.facebook.com/szocialishelyiseg). M1, M2, M3 Deák Ferenc tér, or night bus 909, 914, 914A, 916, 950, 950A, 979A. **Open** 5pm-2am daily. **Map** p246 F5.
Risen from the ashes of the Eklektika, this quirky bar in the Jewish Quarter is especially popular with lesbians. Food's good, too, with fine burgers and fries.

WOW – Women on Women
Various locations (www.facebook.com/ wmnonwmn). **Admission** Ft1,000.
Monthly, catchy pop-dance event with guest DJs. Despite the name, WOW attracts a diverse crowd.

SAUNAS

Magnum
VIII.Csepreghy utca 2 (06 30 844 6864, www. gaysaunabudapest.com). M3 Ferenc körút, or M3, M4 Kálvin tér, or night bus 909, 914, 914A, 979, 979A. **Open** 1pm-midnight Mon-Thur; 1pm-4am Fri; 1pm Sat-midnight Sun. **Admission** Ft3,500 (over-30s); Ft2,800 (18-30s). **Map** p249 G7.
Magnum is a labyrinth with a sauna, steam room, massage, showers for two, lounge area with TV, gym, darkroom and cabins. Fridays see black-out parties at 10pm, and the place is open non-stop from Saturday lunchtime to Sunday night. HIV testing is occasionally available.

Szauna 69
IX.Angyal utca 2 (210 1751, www.gaysauna.hu). Tram 4, 6. **Open** 1pm-1am Mon-Thur, Sun; 1pm-2am Fri; 1pm-4am Sat. **Admission** Ft2,100 (over-25s); Ft1,300 (under-25s). **Map** p249 G8.
Finnish sauna, infra sauna, steam room, jacuzzi, bar and private rooms attract a youngish crowd to this blue mosaic-clad lounge. Sunbeds and massages are also on offer.

CRUISING AREAS & BATHS

Néplïget, a park by the metro station of the same name, has cruising by day, and more by night near the Planetarium. North of town, the partly nudist **Omszki Lake** is recommended for swimming and cruising. Take the HÉV train to Budakalász – the lake is about a 20-minute walk. The **Palatinus Baths** (www.palatinus strand.hu) on Margaret Island have male and female nudist terraces, while the **Rudas Baths** (www.rudasfurdo.hu) by Elizabeth Bridge are men-only on Mondays, Wednesdays, Thursdays and Fridays, with Tuesdays reserved for women.

SPORT & ACTIVITIES

Atlasz
www.atlaszsport.hu.
Atlasz was created in 2004 to provide LGBT people with a safe and comfortable environment to train, keep fit and learn new sports among friends. From jogging to kayaking, badminton to karate, there are plenty of courses at affordable prices.

Tempelfit
www.tempelfit.hu.
Tempelfit is a new, expanding chain of gay-friendly gyms with state-of-the-art equipment, a sauna, personal trainers and a vitamin bar.

Vándormások
www.vandormasok.hu.
This queer hiking and cycling group has been organising several trips a year since 1991.

Nightlife

Many people come to Budapest for the nightlife alone. Every weekend, District VII fills with revellers, a significant number of them foreign visitors. Budapest's status as a party capital has been built on a unique concept: the *romkocsma*. Roughly translated as 'ruin bar', these are funky party spaces set up in run-down courtyards and residential buildings. The granddaddy of them all is Szimpla kert. Most provide DJs at weekends; some put on gigs too. In terms of dedicated concert venues, the A38 stands out amid a cornucopia of weird and wonderful spaces. Behind this maverick nightlife scene lie some lax licensing laws and grey areas of ownership. Meanwhile, cheap admission and drinks prices engender a keen crowd but discourage international acts from including Budapest as part of any European tour. If it's glitzier dance clubs you're after, a clutch has opened in District VI, around the Basilica.

Corvintető.

LATE-NIGHT BARS & CLUBS

Budapest is a summer-night city: garden bars, ruin bars and terrace bars all come into their own from June onwards, and many year-round venues set up temporary outdoor offshoots. During the rest of the year, long-established venues such as **Csendes** and **Instant** appeal to both late-night bar-hoppers and clubbers, with a regular line-up of DJs and live acts – in Budapest, the line between bar and club is blurred (for bars whose main trade is before midnight, see the 'Cafés & bars' sections of the Explore chapters).

Typically, admission to most venues will only be charged if there's a DJ or band performing, and then it's usually minimal (approx Ft500-Ft1,000). Only glitzier spots, such as **Hellobaby**, charge more, and even then it's Ft2,000 tops, with free entry for women. Credit-card payment is only common in flashier venues – anyone trying to pay with plastic for their Ft600 beer in some bohemian dive bar in deepest Pest will be laughed out of town.

Even venues such as **Szimpla kert** have bouncers on the door these days, and certainly at weekends – they're well versed in dealing with inebriated foreigners.

Anker Klub
VI.Anker köz 1-3 (06 70 621 0741, www.anker klub.hu). M1, M2, M3 Deák tér, or night bus 907, 909, 914, 916, 931, 950, 979. **Open** *9am-4am daily.* **Map** *p249 E5.*

This former bank gets its name from its address, on the periphery of Budapest's party district and close to its main transport hub. It doubles as a restaurant and late-night hangout with lounge DJs, but proximity to neighbours means that it's somewhat more subdued than other bars deeper in the district.

▶ *Nearby partner operation Ankert (VI.Paulay Ede utca 33, 06 30 360 3389, open 6pm-3am Wed-Sat) is one of the district's better garden bars, with two courtyards and underground DJs.*

Auróra
VIII.Auróra utca 11 (06 20 992 8484, www. facebook.com/auroraunofficial). M4 II János Pál pápa tér, or tram 4, 6, or night bus 907, 908, 923, 973, 979. **Open** *10am-midnight Mon-Wed, Sun; 10am-4am Thur-Sat.* **Map** *p250 H6.*

Opened in summer 2014 and set halfway along a down-at-heel street in District VIII, in-the-know Auróra requires visitors to press the right bell on a residential doorway, then head up past a few bohemian types posing on the staircase. After following the hubbub to the right door, you enter a space not unlike a community centre, with a bar in one corner and, at some point, a DJ in another. You might also catch some other type of performance, workshop or music session – the quirkier the better.

Corvintető
Above Corvin department store, VIII.Blaha Lujza tér 1-2 (06 20 772 2984, www.corvinteto.com). M2 Blaha Lujza tér, or tram 4, 6, or night bus 907, 908, 923, 973, 979. **Open** *9pm-6am Wed-Sat.* **Map** *p249 G5.*

When it comes to offering a drink with a view, this bar stands above the rest – by a few storeys. Several flights of stairs, or an old industrial lift manned by a guy in a suit flogging miniatures, take you to the top floor of the 1970s-style Corvin department store for all-night fun. In the enclosed top-floor disco, local and visiting DJs spin most nights, with the occasional live band. In warmer weather, the expansive rooftop terrace draws the crowds – stay long enough and you can catch the sunrise. This is probably the best choice if you only have one night in town.

▶ *Start the night in the same building with dinner at funky street-level eaterie Jelen Bisztró (www. mostjelen.hu/jelen).*

Csendes
V.Ferency István utca 5 (06 30 727 2100, www. facebook.com/csendesvintagebar). M2 Astoria, or night bus 907, 908, 923, 973, 979. **Open** *10am midnight Mon-Wed; 10am-2am Thur, Fri; 2pm-2am Sat; 2pm-midnight Sun.* **Map** *p249 F6.*

By the downtown pocket park of Károlyi kert, the old Fiume coffeehouse is now a fully-fledged bohemian bar close to the university quarter (trash art fills the walls). During the day, an affordable kitchen (Csendes Létterem) comes to the fore. By sundown, every table's usually full with drinkers. Entertainment is kept fresh: expect DJs and live music, with plenty of Hungarian retro.

Fogasház. *See p155.*

LET'S GET TRASHED

The ruin bar is the cornerstone of the city's nightlife scene.

Ruin bars are peculiar to Budapest. It's a concept mainly dreamed up in District VII, where venues were set up around the courtyard of run-down residential buildings, or in the disused yard alongside. Skip-found furniture, a trashy bohemian feel and fairy lights created the atmosphere – a cross between a squat party and an underground DJ event, with a free mini-festival thrown in. A drinks menu was chalked up behind the bar ('counter service only' was another innovation), the music was cranked up, often a movie or images of some kind were projected on to a brick wall, and the party went on until the first trams started running the next morning.

Referred to as *romkocsma* ('ruin bar') or *romkert* ('ruin garden'), they were mostly a summer phenomenon, and as fleeting as the season in which they flowered. Some lasted a couple of years – long enough, in the case of the Rácz-kert or West-Balkán, to help alter the character of urban nightlife forever. It was no longer enough to offer cheap drinks, served by sexy staff, with a mainstream party soundtrack. Prague had that, Kraków even.

At first, their shady legality and the slow machinations of Hungarian bureaucracy meant that a couple of business-minded bohemians could set up in almost any neglected urban space, throw up the fairy lights, open a bar, maybe install a table-football table, spread the word, and clean up from June to September. All bar-hoppers had to do was keep their ears to the ground.

A change of mayoral leadership (from liberal to stern right-wing), a tightening of licensing laws, the swift redevelopment of Districts VII and VIII, and sleepless neighbours gradually rained on many a *romkocsma* parade. But the genie was already out of the bottle – there was money, fistfuls of money, to be made from ruin bars. District VII, around Klauzál tér and Kazinczy utca, began to resemble a vast outdoor squat party as leading year-round venues desperately searched for (and found) an outdoor summer annexe.

In the case of the once thriving Ellátó, where Klauzál tér meets Kis Diófa utca, its nearby *kert* has superceded it. **Ellátó kert** (www.facebook.com/ellato.kert), on nearby Kazinczy utca, has long been one of the city's prime outdoor spots in summer, while the parent bar has since closed down. The Kazinczy location is no coincidence – it's also home to the hardiest *romkocsma* of all, **Szimpla kert** (*see p158*). Its parent bar, Szimpla, on Kertész utca, has long since folded, but the Szimpla kert remains a major hub. Its rough-and-ready surroundings, artfully contrived, attract throngs of drinkers year-round. The garden gets half-covered in winter, while the warren of rooms arranged around a covered courtyard are packed every weekend.

Nearby **Doboz** (*see p155*) maintains the weird art, bizarre installations and courtyard aspect of many a *romkocsma*, while also throwing in a more abstract conceit: that everyone should be dancing in a bloody big box ('*doboz*'). So partygoers can lose themselves in soundproofed, high-decibel madness, while neighbours can watch late-night re-runs of *Columbo* in peace. Meanwhile, the excellent **Kertem** (www.facebook.com/kertemfesztival), set up in the City Park, brought decent grilled food to the party, an idea that's been expanded upon at partner burger restaurant and party bar **Téli Kertem** (www.facebook.com/telikertem).

Szimpla kert.

Doboz.

Some ruin bars adopt the character of their surrounding district and don't feel 'ruin' at all. Glitzy **Hellobaby** (see right) occupies a historic villa on showpiece Andrássy út. More glam than grime, it encourages more moneyed visitors to party like pop stars without a care as to what gets spilled on the furniture. A short walk from the Basilica, **Ötkert** (see p157) was the first among the District V clubs to adopt trendy ruin-bar decor, albeit not as authentically as its District VII counterparts. But it does have a rooftop, open to the stars on summer nights.

Sadly, ruin-by-rote has also become the norm, with places such as **Rom kert** (see p158) taking the basic concept, sanitising it, and providing pricey drinks to go with mainstream party music.

Finally, a few canny operators have sought to take the concept and run with it. The team behind the admirable **Mazel Tov** (see p122) has combined great food with a *romkocsma* atmosphere, decent DJs and a cool District VII location.

▶ *Around the corner, summer-only sister venue Csendes Társ (V.Magyar utca 18, www.facebook. com/csendestars) is an intimate bar with a superb selection of wines and outdoor tables by the entrance to Károlyi kert.*

Doboz
VII.Klauzál utca 10 (06 20 449 4801, www. doboz.pm). M2 Blaha Lujza tér, tram 4, 6, or night bus 907, 908, 923, 973, 979. **Open** 3pm-3am Mon-Wed; 5pm-5am Thur-Sat. **Map** p249 G5. *See p154* **Let's Get Trashed**.

Fogasház
VII.Akácfa utca 51 (783 8820, www.fogashaz.hu). Tram 4, 6, or night bus 923. **Open** 6pm-4am Mon-Sat. *Garden* 4pm-4am daily. **Map** p246 G5.
This District VII spot started life as an underground venue and artists' space, cobbled together from the remains of a derelict apartment building. The façade is marked by an old sign depicting a set of teeth found during the club's renovation, hence the name 'House of Teeth'. Affordable drinks and a consistently busy dancefloor with top resident DJs make it one of the most popular bars in the district. The Fogaskert garden next door extends the funky feel and is where most of the action happens in warmer months. Above the main venue on the first floor, Lärm (*see p156*) is for serious late-night partyheads and a quality DJ destination in its own right. *Photo p153.*
▶ *In the same complex, bare-brick Liebling (06 70 638 5040) is a late-night bistro and wine bar.*

Hellobaby
VI.Andrássy út 52 (06 20 776 0767, www. hellobabybar.hu). M1 Oktogon, or tram 4, 6, or night bus 923, 979. **Open** 10pm-4am Fri, Sat. **Map** p246 F4.
See p154 **Let's Get Trashed**.

Instant
VI.Nagymező utca 38 (311 0704, www.instant. co.hu). M1 Opera or Oktogon, or tram 4, 6, or night bus 923, 979. **Open** 4pm-6am daily. **Map** p246 F4.
One of the largest and hippest late-night bars in District VI, Instant draws a young, savvy crowd of locals and out-of-towners. Its location in an abandoned apartment block in the heart of Budapest's Broadway lends it a quirky house-party vibe. DJs spin in the cellar and the two upstairs dancefloors, while the four bar counters keep the booze flowing. Funky decor includes an upside-down room with all the furnishings plastered to the ceiling, while a herd of rabbits hangs suspended above the main courtyard. *Photo p156.*

Iskola!
VI.Hegedű utca 3 (413 0093, www.iskola.org). M1 Oktogon, or tram 4, 6, or night bus 923, 979. **Open** noon-10pm Mon, Tue; noon-4am Wed-Sat. **Map** p246 F4.

ARTS & ENTERTAINMENT

Instant. *See p155.*

The former home of cult venue Tűzraktér is now considerably more mainstream, with a younger crowd – as befits its name, 'School'. Party music has replaced the wails of the underground, and a traditional Hungarian kitchen and daytime opening are a sea change from the bread-and-dripping and pre-dawn antics of old. It's all clean-cut fun, with a dollop of live music thrown in.

Jurányi Ház

II.Jurányi utca 1 (06 70 777 2533, www.juranyi haz.hu). Tram 4, 6, or night bus 916, 956, 960, 990. **Open** *Café 9.30am-midnight Mon-Thur; 9.30am-2am Fri; 10am-2am Sat; 10am-midnight Sun.* **Map** p246 F4.

This space, in an imposing former residential building tucked behind Margit körút, is mainly used for alternative theatre performances, but there's occasional live music too. The café is a late-night hangout popular with a student crowd.

Kolor

Gozsdu udvar, VII.Király utca 13 (06 20 415 1820, www.facebook.com/kolorprojekt). M1, M2, M3 Deák tér, or night bus 907, 909, 914, 916, 931, 950, 979. **Open** *noon-4am daily.* **Map** p246 F4.

Multitasking Kolor is located at the entrance to Gozsdu udvar. During the week, it provides a decent bar space and kitchen, plus club nights such as long-running Monday Sessions with resident DJs spinning hip hop. At weekends, parties here can be some of the best in town, with bumping house and other styles in the atmospheric cellar.

Kraft

V.Széchenyi István tér 7-8 (06 70 396 7892, www. dubkraft.hu). Tram 2, or bus 15, 16, 105, or night bus 916. **Open** *8pm-5am Thur-Sat.* **Map** p246 F4.

Set in the former digs of District V's Creol bar near the Gresham Palace, Kraft caters to a mainstream crowd of locals and passing tourists. Decked out with industrial features, Kraft offers three weekly nights of house, hip hop, R&B and nu disco. The cocktail list is extensive, the dress code smart-casual.

Lärm

VII.Akácfa utca 51 (06 30 940 4063, www.larm.hu). Tram 4, 6, or night bus 923. **Open** *11pm-6am Fri, Sat.* **Map** p246 G5.

The best local underground DJs spin to a crowd of serious dancefloor junkies in a cosy room above District VII staple Fogasház (*see p155*). The sophisticated Martin Audio sound system easily accommodates the heavy bass-thumping beats, and the minimalist decor is dark enough for dancing without distraction.

Mika Tivadar

VII.Kazinczy utca 47 (06 20 965 3007, www. mikativadarmulato.hu). M1, M2, M3 Deák tér, or night bus 907, 909, 914, 916, 931, 950, 979. **Open** *5pm-midnight Mon-Wed, Sun; 5pm-3am Thur; 5pm-5am Fri, Sat.* **Map** p249 F5.

Mika Tivadar is brought to you by the same folks behind the Kőleves restaurant and nearby Kőleves kert – this is their third outpost on Kazinczy utca. The swanky space in an equally swanky building features high ceilings and a large bar counter bedecked with a mosaic of spare change. Occasional DJ parties and concerts on the cellar stage keep the young regulars entertained.

Mono Bar

VII.Akácfa utca 12-14 (790 1861, www.mono bar.hu). Tram 4, 6, or night bus 923. **Open** *10am-1am Mon-Thur; 10am-3am Fri; noon-3am Sat; noon-midnight Sun.* **Map** p249 G5.

The Mono is one of scores of popular spots in the District VII bar vortex. What sets it apart are its half-dozen tap beers, HD TVs for footie and laptop DJs four nights a week. There's a large summer terrace, and just enough tapas, salads and sandwiches to remove the need to eat elsewhere before you come.

Morrison's 2

V.Szent István körút 11 (374 3329, www. morrisons.hu). Tram 4, 6, or night bus 923, 931, 934. **Open** *5pm-4am Mon-Sat.* **Map** *p246 D2.*
Budapest's largest venue is hard to miss – just join the heaving queue of youngsters outside. A massive heated courtyard leads to a labyrinth of rooms in the cellar. These subterranean dens cater to all tastes, from retro tunes to live concerts, house party music to karaoke. Each is equipped with its own bar (mind the house brew). The crowd is energetic and libidinous, and the enthusiasm is highly infectious.
▶ *Morrison's has two more locations: a glitzier one in the park just behind Népliget metro station (06 70 527 5272, www.ligetclub.hu, open 8pm-5am Fri, Sat), and another appealing to over-30s near the Opera House (VI.Révay utca 25, 269 4060, open 7pm-4am Thur-Sat).*

Nemdebár

II.Széll Kálmán tér 5 (06 20 519 8687, www. facebook.com/nemdebar). M2 Széll Kálmán tér, or tram 4, 6, or night bus 916, 956, 960, 990. **Open** *3pm-1am Mon, Tue; 3pm-2am Wed, Thur; 3pm-3am Fri; 4pm-3am Sat; 6pm-midnight Sun.* **Map** *p245 A3.*

This is the only late-opening alternative spot in Buda worth its salt, located at Széll Kálmán tér (which it still refers to, defiantly, as 'Moszkva tér'). The arty venue promises 'rude staff, catchpenny art and unbearable music'. Of course, it delivers nothing of the sort, but provides a welcoming space for top-notch DJs and radical filmmakers. *Photo p158.*
▶ *Partner venue Nemdepöti (II.Lövőház utca 24, same phone) has a terrace space but can only operate until 11pm – and not in the depths of winter.*

Nomuri

V.Sas utca 15 (06 30 849 8586, www.nomuri.co). M1 Bajcsy-Zsilinszky út, or M3 Arany János utca, or night bus 907, 909, 914, 916, 931, 950, 979. **Open** *10pm-5am Fri, Sat.* **Map** *p246 E4.*
Nomuri caters to chic partygoers in search of superb cocktails and house beats in a slick yet relaxed atmosphere. Free admission for women ensures a good mix. A 'lifestyle hotel' is being created by the Baldaszti Group in the same complex.

Ötkert

V.Zrínyi utca 4 (06 70 330 8652, www.facebook. com/otkert). Bus 15, 16, 105, or night bus 916. **Open** *11am-midnight Mon; 11am-2am Wed, 11am-5am Thur-Sat; 11am-11pm Sun.* **Map** *p246 D5. See p154* **Let's Get Trashed.**

PRLMNT

VI.Teréz körút 62 (911 0901). Tram 4, 6, or night bus 923, 931, 934. **Open** *10pm-5am Fri, Sat.* **Map** *p246 D2.*

Mika Tivadar.

ARTS & ENTERTAINMENT

Nemdebár. *See p157*.

A convenient stop on the way to anywhere in the Jewish quarter drinking zone, the Szóda is also a destination venue in itself – you could easily spend the entire evening here. Upstairs in the big bar area, there's comfortable low seating and manga art on the walls and ceiling. Downstairs is a dancefloor where DJs spin for uninhibited regulars. *Photo p160*.

Trafiq
V. Hercegprimás utca 18 (06 30 464 0646, www. trafiq.hu). M3 Arany János utca, or night bus 907, 909, 914, 916, 931, 950, 979. **Open** 8pm-4am Thur-Sat. **Map** p246 E4.
This downtown bar-club comprises a labyrinthine spread of rooms with a chandelier-bedecked dancefloor at the back, plus a retractable roof. Trafiq fills with a good mix of tourists and locals who tend to leave their inhibitions at the door.

Vittula
VII. Kertész utca 4 (no phone, www.vittula.hu). M2 Blaha Lujza tér, or tram 4, 6, or night bus 907, 908, 923, 973, 979. **Open** 6pm-2am Mon-Wed, Sun; 6pm-4am Thur-Sat. **Map** p249 G5.
Vittula is one of the best bars in town, a boisterous four-space cellar drenched in rockabilly and indie sounds until the early hours. Friendly staff serve pints of Arany Fácán to a loyal, edgy clientele. On its night, this is somewhere close to heaven. *Photos p161*.

ROCK, ROOTS & JAZZ

Budapest's global reputation for live music has been built on the quite incredible success of the week-long **Sziget** festival, started in 1993 and the biggest of its kind in the region (*see p30* **Island Life**). Recently, its sister event at Lake Balaton, **Balaton Sound** (*see p31*), has more than matched it in terms of its line-up, with electronic music the main focus. But these two stand-out events apart (and with the honourable exception of the unique **A38** boat), Budapest still suffers by comparison with Vienna or Zagreb as far as the range of live venues is concerned.

Clubs such as **Roham** and, most notably, **G3 Rendezvényközpont**, the hardy successor to the late-lamented Gödör Klub, should be applauded for keeping the music scene fresh and worthy of investigation. At the opposite end of the spectrum, big-name acts are struggling for choice now that the national Puskás Ferenc Stadion (*see p129* **2020 Vision**) is being rebuilt and the Petőfi Csarnok is being knocked down.

Rock & Pop

★ A38
XI. Pázmány Péter sétány (464 3940, www.a38.hu). Tram 4, 6, or night bus 906, 918. **Map** p249 F9.
Docked on the Buda side of Petőfi Bridge, this former Ukrainian cargo ship is the city's best and

PRLMNT is short for Parliament – presumably after the P-Funk group and not the namesake government building. DJs spin in the spacious main hall and lounge, VIPs are waited on in exclusive areas, and everyone goes 'ooooh!' when the roof retracts in summer and people spill out on to the balcony to gawp at the Nagykörút.

Rom kert
I. Döbrentei tér 9 (06 30 540 6991, www.rudas romkert.hu). Tram 18, 19, 41, or bus 5, 7, 8, 86, or night bus 907, 908, 956, 973, 990. **Open** noon-8pm Mon, Tue, Sun; noon-5am Wed-Sat. **Map** p248 D6.
See p154 **Let's Get Trashed**.

Szimpla kert
VII. Kazinczy utca 14 (06 20 261 8669, www. szimpla.hu). M2 Astoria, or bus 7, or night bus 907, 909, 914, 916, 931, 950, 973, 979, 990. **Open** noon-2am daily. **Map** p249 F5.
See p154 **Let's Get Trashed**.

Szóda
VII. Wesselényi utca 18 (461 0007, www.szoda. com). M2 Astoria, or bus 7, or night bus 907, 909, 914, 916, 931, 950, 973, 979, 990. **Open** 5pm-3am Mon-Thur; 5pm-5am Fri, Sat. **Map** p249 F5.

ESSENTIAL BUDAPEST ALBUMS

Sounds of the city.

BARTÓK AT THE PIANO
BÉLA BARTÓK (1994)

This six-volume set of original recordings features the great composer in person from 1920 to 1945. Six hours of music are divided between sessions in Hungary and America, where Bartók fled in 1940. The Washington concert brings in his lifelong friend, Budapest-born violinist Joseph Szigeti.

KALANDRA FEL!!
AE BIZOTTSÁG (1983)

Alt pioneers AE Bizottság somehow managed to have this first album released on state label Hungaroton. A mix of art punk and raw underground, it captures the short lifespan of this influential band. Members István ef Zámbó, László feLugossy and Andreas Wahorn are still active.

MAJD MEGSZOKOD
BËLGA (2002)

Arguably *the* groundbreaking Hungarian album of the noughties, the debut by Budapest's Bëlga is an inspired mix of rap, hip hop and pop, the lyrics snatches of everyday speech and situations. Creative force DJ Titusz went on to form the influential Carbonfools – both acts still perform regularly.

KARADY KATALIN
KARADY KATALIN (1979)

This compilation of gloomy evergreens by the tragic songstress, captured and tortured by the Gestapo in 1944, includes classics 'Jó éjt Budapest' ('Good Night Budapest') and 'Hamvadó Cigarettavég', describing a lovelorn cigarette smoulder. Its success revived interest in the exiled femme fatale.

ESZKIMÓ ASSZONY FÁZIK
TRABANT (1984)

This rare five-track, seven-inch single accompanied the groundbreaking film of the same name. The story of a tragic *ménage à trois* within an underground band – between a drunken classical pianist, a nihilist singer and a deaf and dumb zookeeper – it captures Budapest's alternative scene at the time.

A LEGSZEBB SZERELMES
DALOK TUDÓSOK (2013)

This is the latest, and most complete, album from these stalwarts of Budapest's underground scene, still gigging today. Funny as a box of frogs, firing off wild brushstrokes of jazz and punk, Tudósok are led by the charismatic drMáriás, a major artist in his own right. Check out their videos too.

generally busiest venue, with major local acts and good mid-range ones from abroad. Concerts take place on the lower deck, with a restaurant in the middle (reservations 464 3946) and dancing on the top deck in summer. *Photos p163.*

Akvárium Klub
V.Erzsébet tér 14 (06 30 860 3368, www. akvariumklub.hu). M1, M2, M3 Deák tér, or night bus 907, 909, 914, 916, 931, 950, 979. **Open** *Box office* 10am-8pm daily & before each show. **Map** p249 E5.
In a brilliant location below Erzsébet tér in the very centre of Budapest, the Gödör Klub that operated here was expropriated by the authorities and transformed into the somewhat sanitised Akvárium. Gödör was pushed out to hidden premises on nearby Király utca; Akvárium continues to run as one of the prime concert spots in town. Professional to a fault, including Martin Audio acoustics, Akvárium comprises a main hall, a smaller one, the Volt music bar – where local and international DJs spin towards the end of the week – the Aqua Bistro and a sprawling terrace that spills out from the extensive patio area to the steps and surrounding park.

Barba Negra
IX.Prielle Kornélia utca 4 (06 20 563 2254, www.musicclub.barbanegra.hu). Tram 18, 41, 47, 48, or night bus 973. **Open** *Box office* noon-8pm Mon-Sat.
Just off Fehérvári út, Barba Negra carries on the long, proud and loud tradition of south Buda rock barns. The tattooed and leather-clad gather in spacious beerhalls equipped with a stage given over to ear-splitting rock and metal two or three nights a week. A vague pirate theme barely gets noticed amid the cheery beer-chugging.
► *Further along Fehérvári út, even deeper into south Buda, Club 202 (see below) is in a similar vein.*

Budapest Park
IX.Soroksári út 60 (06 30 702 2919, www. budapestpark.hu). Tram 2, 24, or nightbus 901, 918, 923, 937, 979. **Open** *Box office* May-Sept 1-8pm Mon-Sat. *Shows* May-Sept Mon-Wed, Sun varies; 5pm-5am Thur-Sat. Closed Oct-Apr. **Map** p249 G8.
This 11,000sq m festival-style music and DJ venue operates from May to September at a remote location near the Palace of Arts. Taking over from the late and much-loved Zöld Pardon, the outdoor venue caters to a mainly student crowd, offering spectacular light shows and Hungarian bands of national renown.

Club 202
XI.Fehérvári út 202 (208 5569, www.club202.hu). **Open** varies. *Tram 18, 47, or night bus 973.*
This long-established spot is in distant south Buda, right by a tram stop. It's one of Budapest's larger stages for rock bands, offering weekly rock'n'roll parties and heavy-metal acts, plus three bars, a dancefloor and a games room. The overdone Wild West theme is a hangover from its days as the Wigwam club.

Dürer kert
XIV.Ajtosi Dürer sor 19-21 (789 4444, www. durerkert.com). Trolleybus 74, 75, or night bus 979. **Open** 4pm-5am daily. **Map** p247 K3.

Szóda. *See p158.*

Dürer combines good music and a friendly atmosphere in a large venue next to the City Park. Formerly a university campus, the medium sized concert halls host local and international bands. Come summer, the wonderfully isolated courtyard provides the real draw; a couple of busy bars, lots of well-spaced tables and atmospheric lighting. There's even an outdoor stage for live bands, which tends to get used before 10pm; afterwards, everything moves to the indoor halls. Music-wise, the focus here is on punk, metal and alt rock.

G3 Rendezvényközpont
Central Passage, VI.Király utca 8-10 (06 20 201 3868, www.facebook.com/g3rendezvenykozpont). M1, M2, M3 Deák tér, or night bus 907, 909, 914, 916, 931, 950, 979. **Open** 6pm-2am Mon-Sat. **Map** p246 F4.
Having been removed from its prominent premises at Erzsébet tér, the revered Gödör Klub found itself tucked into a commercial passageway a short walk down Király utca from Deák tér. In 2014, this became the G3 Rendezvényközpont, an events venue with a large, flexible interior performance space. Most nights of the week, part of this space is given over to either live music (mainly of the Hungarian alternative variety) or party DJs. Bands have to bring their own crowd (and atmosphere) as people don't really hang out here as a matter of course, but otherwise it's a well-run, central spot to catch some decent live acts.

Gozsdu Manó Klub (GMK)
Gozsdu udvar, VII.Király utca 13 (06 20 779 1183, www.facebook.com/gozsdumano). M1, M2, M3 Deák tér, or night bus 907, 909, 914, 916, 931, 950, 979. **Open** 4pm-2am Mon-Wed, Sun; 4pm-5am Thur-Sat. **Map** p246 F4.
This great little venue is located halfway along Gozsdu udvar, a stand-out spot in a row of blandness. As such, its funky, street-level bar attracts a fair amount of passing trade – if you're just popping in, do take a look at the gig schedule. Three or four times a week, there's post-punk, alt rock, rockabilly, hardcore or pure pop – all for a nominal cover fee. There's also a bar downstairs, at the back of the intimate concert space.

Kis Á
V.Irányi utca 25 (06 30 525 1161, www.facebook.com/kisaklub). Bus 15, 16 or 105, or night bus 916. **Open** noon-midnight Mon, Sun; noon-5am Tue-Sat. **Map** p249 E6.
Opened in 2015, the not-for-profit 'Little Á' is incongruously set amid a range of restaurants aimed at the business crowd and a new crop of glitzier nightspots. Taking its name and attitude from the original Tilos Az Á club, which headed the alternative scene in the early 1990s, Kis Á provides a basement for out-there live acts, a gallery on the top floor and a bar tucked in between.

Vittula. *See p158.*

► *The former Tilos Az Á, in Mikszáth Kálmán tér in District VIII, is now the Zappa Café, with another live venue, Trafik (see right), round the corner in its former cellar.*

Kobuci kert

III.Fő tér 1 (06 70 205 7282, www.kobuci.hu). HÉV Szentlélek tér, or tram 1, or night bus 923, 934. **Open** varies. **Map** p246 F4.
Located in the historic grounds of Zichy Castle, this summer-only outdoor space is the main concert venue in Óbuda. A mix of homegrown pop, folk and rock acts perform in the inner courtyard in a family-friendly atmosphere.

Kuplung

VI.Király utca 46 (06 30 755 3527). M1 Opera, or tram 4, 6, or night bus 923, 979. **Open** 3pm-2am Mon-Thur; 3pm-5am Fri; 4pm-5am Sat; 4pm-2am Sun. **Map** p246 F4.
This former ruin bar is now more a straightforward concert venue, with regular gigs in the main hall (and the open courtyard in summer) – expect pop, rock and the occasional alternative act. Kuplung also hosts workshops and exhibitions.

Papp László Budapest Sportaréna

XIV.Stefánia út 2 (422 2600, www.budapest arena.hu). M2 Puskás Ferenc Stadion, or night bus 901, 908, 918, 931, 937, 956, 990. **Open** *Box office* 9am-5pm Mon-Fri or until start of performance.
The former Budapest Sportcsarnok multipurpose stadium has 12,500 seats and six bars. Its flexible functionality (ice rink transformed into rock venue in 30 minutes) takes away any ambience it might offer – judging from the schedule for 2015, few international acts are tempted to take to its stage.

Roham

VII.Dohány utca 22 (no phone, www.facebook. com/roham.club). M2 Astoria, or bus 7, or night bus 907, 908, 973, 990. **Open** 4pm-midnight Mon-Thur, Sun; 4pm-4am Fri, Sat. **Map** p249 F5.
Once an even smaller spot just across Rákóczi út on Vas utca, Roham has reopened as an equally friendly live venue on the periphery of Budapest's bar central. Here you might find an Italian goth band or a giant of the Hungarian underground, such as Tudósok, on stage. It's also an exhibition space for alternative art.

Syma

XIV.Dozsa György út 1 (460 1100, www.syma.hu). M2 Puskás Ferenc Stadion, or night bus 901, 908, 918, 931, 937, 956, 990. **Open** *Box office* 9am-5pm Mon-Fri or until start of show.
Just north of Keleti station, this multipurpose venue usually hosts trade fairs and indoor sports, with the occasional evergreen home-grown music act.

Trafik

VIII.Mikszáth Kálmán tér 2, entrance on Szentkirályi utca (06 70 384 2717). M3, M4 Kálvin tér, or tram 4, 6, or night bus 909, 914, 979. **Open** 6pm-2am Mon-Sat. **Map** p250 H8.
Around the corner from the Zappa Café, Trafik is set in the intimate cellar of the revered Tilos Az Á club. While the somewhat tasteless Zappa Café does little to honour the memory of this legendary alternative haunt – or, indeed, Frank Zappa – Trafik tries to stay true to its subterranean heritage.

Trafó

IX.Liliom utca 41 (456 2040, www.trafo.hu). M3 Corvin-negyed, or tram 4, 6, or night bus 914, 923, 950, 979. **Open** *Box office* 4-8pm daily (4-10pm concert days). **Map** p250 H8.
As well as hosting theatre and dance performances, this long-established cultural complex also contains a cellar club for regular live acts.

Jazz

Unlike its pop acts, Hungary's jazz musicians have always been more appreciated abroad. From fusion to mainstream and ethno-jazz, from Dixieland to big band, there have been a number of outstanding musicians. Some still play in the handful of venues around Budapest – jazz fans should look out for inspired saxophonist Mihály Dresch, drummer Elemér Balázs and guitarist Ferenc Snétberger. Along with the two venues below, one bar in particular stages regular quality live jazz thanks to the expert whims of its Dutch manager (*see p137* **Jedermann**). On the same street, the **If Kávézó** (IX.Ráday utca 19, 299 0694, www.ifkavezo.hu) is a jazz café with live sounds most nights of the week.

Budapest Jazz Club

XIII.Hollán Ernő utca 7 (798 7289, www.bjc.hu). Tram 4, 6, or night bus 923, 934. **Open** 10am-10pm Mon-Sat. **Map** p249 D5.
One of the city's best-known jazz venues occupies an old arthouse cinema. Top Hungarian acts feature, along with a handful of international guests.

Budapest Music Centre

IX.Mátyás utca 8 (216 7894, www.bmc.hu). M4 Fővám tér, or tram 2, or night bus 979. **Open** *Box office* 9am-9pm Mon-Fri; 10am-9pm Sat, Sun & before each show. **Map** p246 F3.
Concerts take place most nights at the BMC, mostly jazz or jazz-based. Founded by trombone player László Gőz, it's also home to the local BMC record label, featuring some 3,000 jazz and classical artists.

Folk & World Music

Hungary's prominence in the music scene owes much to the rich traditions of Magyar folk music. This music is best enjoyed at a *táncház*,

A38. See p158.

a participatory folk dance where first-timers are shown the steps before the band swings into action. Lively *táncház* events take place at spots such as the stand-out **Fonó Budai Zeneház**, with acoustic and folk most nights. The **Kobuci kert** (*see p70*) in Óbuda also stages regular folk shows, as does the **Pótkulcs** (VI.Csengery utca 65B, 269 1050), which features the younger stars of the scene. It's more of a music session in a vaulted wine cellar than a classic *táncház*, but dancers find room as the evening gets late. For details on all folk events, see www.tanchaz.hu.

Aranytíz Kultúrház

VI.Arany János utca 10 (354 3400, www.aranytiz. hu). M3 Arany János utca, or night bus 914, 931, 950. **Open** *Shows* 8pm-late Sat. **Map** p246 E4.
The rebranded Aranytíz Kultúrház has long hosted a Saturday evening *táncház* in downtown Pest. There's family-friendly dance tuition from 5pm, then the main band gets going from 8pm.

★ Fonó Budai Zeneház

XI.Sztregova utca 3 (206 5300, www.fono.hu). Tram 41, 47, or night bus 973. **Open** noon-11.30pm Mon-Fri; 5-11.30pm Sat.
The Fonó Budai Zeneház is the focal point for folk music in Budapest, with all manner of workshops, various branches of folk culture, and a record label that has published the likes of Félix Lajkó, Besh o DroM and Csík Zenekar. In terms of concerts, Wednesdays feature traditional *táncház* bands, which are often brought in from the countryside. Fridays are the big night out and worth the trek to south Buda.

Marczibányi téri Művelődési Központ

II.Marczibányi tér 5A (212 2820, www. marczi.hu). Bus 11, 149. **Open** *Shows* 8.30pm-midnight Thur.
Among the regular theatre performances and dance shows here, Thursdays mean *csángó* dancing at the Guzsalyas Dance House.

Performing Arts

The city of Liszt, Bartók and Kodály is also where you'll find one of Europe's great opera houses and most famous concert venues, the magnificently renovated Music Academy, founded by Franz Liszt himself. Down in south Pest, the Palace of Arts is home to both the Bartók National Concert Hall and the National Philharmonic Orchestra. Alongside, the National Theatre is a long way from its original, revered home on Blaha Lujza tér – and from Budapest's theatreland of Nagymező utca, known as Broadway. Recent cuts in funding mean that English-language theatre is currently almost non-existent. Dance needs no translation, though, and anyone can enjoy the range of performances here. Local balletic traditions run deep, while troupes dedicated to the preservation of Hungarian folk dance are following the lead of classical composers Bartók and Kodály. A thriving contemporary dance scene also enjoys an enthusiastic following.

CLASSICAL MUSIC & OPERA

Hungarians are raised with a profound sense of their country's rich musical history. After the greatest Hungarian composers of the 20th century – Béla Bartók and Zoltán Kodály – had incorporated elements of traditional folk music into their work and teachings, Hungarian music freed itself from the influence of Germany and Vienna. The introduction of these melodic structures was as important to Hungary's new-found national identity as the works of any local writer, architect or politician.

Today, impressive performances by Budapest's eight symphony orchestras are enjoyed by a significant and knowledgeable, if rather conservative, concert-going public. Although the standard of performance is high – only a notch down from the world's best, in fact – musicians' salaries here are still well below those in the West. The stand-out **Budapest Festival Orchestra** (www.bfz.hu), winner of a Gramophone award for best orchestral recording, was founded in 1983 by its principal

conductor, Iván Fischer, and pianist Zoltán Kocsis. Since then, it has consistently been able to keep its standards and budget high, and is consequently able to invite big-name soloists and conductors from abroad. As well as orchestral concerts – most of which sell out – the players also give chamber-music concerts. In 2013, Fischer courted controversy with his opera *The Red Heifer*, about the rise of the right wing in contemporary Hungary.

The **National Philharmonic** (www.filharmonikusok.hu) is also a force to be reckoned with in Budapest. With its own stable of top-class local musicians and Hungarian conductor Zoltán Kocsis at the helm, its Bartók performances should not to be missed.

The **Hungarian State Opera** stages some 60 opera and ballet productions each year at two venues in town. The showpiece venue is the opulent **Opera House** on Andrássy út, where the bulk of the German repertoire and the most prestigious Italian productions are staged. Once the site of mainstream operas, the **Erkel Theatre** made a welcome return to the fold in 2013 after a long renovation.

164 Time Out Budapest

Tickets & Information

The season runs from September to June, with anything from two to ten or more concerts each night. Tickets are usually available and affordable unless a major international artist is involved. The most important classical music event is the **Budapest Spring Festival** (*see p29*), a two-week cultural extravaganza in March.

Koncert Kalendárium, an extensive listing in Hungarian and English of classical and opera events, is available online at www.muzsikalendarium.hu. The main online ticket agencies are **Eventim** (www.eventim.hu), **Jegy** (www.jegy.hu) and **Jegymester** (www.jegymester.hu). The main venues listed below have their own box offices – the **Palace of Arts** also has ticket outlets at Andrássy út 28 (10am-7pm Mon-Fri, 11am-7pm Sat), and at the Allee (*see p61*), Mammut (*see p67*) and MOM Park (*see p62*) malls.

Venues

Bartók Memorial House
Bartók Emlékház
II.Csalán út 29 (394 2100, www.bartokmuseum.hu).
Bus 5, 29. **Open** *Box office* 1hr before performance & during standard museum opening hours.
No credit cards.
Bartók's last Budapest residence, now a museum (*see p65*), hosts chamber music recitals. The low ceiling can be somewhat claustrophobic, but the chairs are eminently comfortable.

Budapest Congress Centre
Budapest Kongresszusi Központ
XII.Jagelló út 1-3 (372 5400, www.bcc.hu). M2
Déli pu, then tram 61. **Open** *Box office* 3-6pm Mon, Wed. **No credit cards. Map** p248 A7.
This ugly convention centre with poor acoustics is where many world-famous stars perform, thanks to its large seating capacity of 1,750. Don't bother with famous smaller ensembles unless you can secure seats at the front.

Budapest Operetta Theatre
Budapest Operett Színház
VI.Nagymező utca 17 (472 2030, tickets 312 4866, www.operett.hu). M1 Oktogon or Opera.
Open *Box office* 10am-7pm Mon-Fri; 1-7pm Sat, Sun. **Map** p246 F4.
The revered Budapest Operetta Theatre is of interest to non-Hungarian speakers as shows are often accompanied by English surtitles. Productions of classic Magyar light opera are its stock in trade, as well as Hungarian versions of popular Western musicals. The theatre itself is gorgeous, its 900-seater auditorium illuminated by a century-old chandelier.

Erkel Theatre
Erkel Színház
VIII.II János Pál pápa tér 30 (332 6150, www.opera.hu). M4 II János Pál pápa tér. **Open** *Box office* Concert days 11am-performance time Tue-Sat; 4pm-performance time Sun. Non-concert days 11am-1pm, 1.45-5pm daily. **Map** p250 H5.
Reopened in 2013 after a six-year revamp, the Erkel Theatre is the sister venue to the grand Opera House.

Budapest Festival Orchestra.

Hungarian State Opera House.

The stripped-down, modern building tucked away in District VIII houses Hungary's largest auditorium, capable of holding 1,819 spectators. It's named after Ferenc Erkel, who composed the Hungarian anthem and was the first music director of the Opera House. Opened in 1911, this establishment was designed to be the people's theatre and provide the general public with affordable opera. After World War II, it came under the overall umbrella of the Opera House.

Great Hall of the Hungarian Academy of Sciences
MTA Diszterme
V.Széchenyi István tér 9 (411 6100, www.mta.hu). Bus 16, 105, or tram 2. **Open** *Box office* 1hr before performance. **No credit cards. Map** p246 D5.
This ornate hall, situated close to the Chain Bridge, provides fine acoustics for chamber music and smaller orchestras. The seating is arranged on a first come, first served basis.

Hungarian Radio Marble Hall
Magyar Rádió Márványterme
VIII.Pollack Mihály tér 8 (328 8779). M3, M4 Kálvin tér, or tram 4, 6. **Open** *Box office* 1hr before performance. **No credit cards. Map** p249 F6.
In an intimate setting (just 120 seats), the Hungarian Radio Marble Hall hosts classical and jazz concerts.

Hungarian State Opera House
Magyar Állami Operaház
VI.Andrássy út 22 (353 0170, www.opera.hu). M1 Opera. **Open** *Box office* Concert days 11am-performance time Mon-Sat; 4pm-performance time Sun. Non-concert days 11am-5pm daily. Closed July. **Map** p246 F4.
Opened in 1884, the Opera House has a wonderfully rich history – Mahler and Otto Klemperer were among its musical directors. When it was renovated and reopened exactly a century later, the Opera House had everything but top-notch performers

and directors – weak finances and mismanagement had sent the best talent abroad. Then, in 2007, a new leadership team was appointed, including world-renowned conductor Ádám Fischer (he resigned in 2010 due to political differences). The Opera House remains the home of the Hungarian National Ballet.

▶ *The Opera House has another ticket outlet round the corner, at VI. Hajós utca 13-15 (332 7914, open 10am-5pm Mon-Fri).*

Margaret Island Open-Air Stage

Margitszigeti Szabadtéri Színpad
XIII. Margitsziget (301 0147, www.szabadter.hu).
Tram 4, 6, or bus 26, or night bus 923. **Open**
Box office noon-5pm Tue-Fri (summer only).
Musicals, classical favourites and crowd-pleasing opera are the focus of this summer-only venue on Margaret Island.

Matthias Church

Mátyás templom
I. Szentháromság tér 2 (355 5657, www.matyas-templom.hu). *Varbusz from M2 Széll Kálmán tér, or bus 16.* **Open** *Box office* 1hr before performance. **No credit cards. Map** p245 B4.
A top venue for organ recitals and concerts of sacred music all year round. Arrive early and get a seat close to the front to beat the cavernous acoustics.

Music Academy

Zeneakadémia
VI. Liszt Ferenc ter 8 (462 4600, tickets 321 0690, www.zeneakademia.hu). *M1 Oktogon, or tram 4, 6.*
Open *Box office* 10am-6pm daily & 1hr before performance. **Map** p246 G4.

This Secessionist gem reopened in 2013 after a €45-million revamp that took nearly two years to complete. It was Franz Liszt who founded its forebear, at his Budapest residence, in 1875. It later moved to Andrássy út; then, in 1907, to this gorgeous creation by Flóris Korb and Kálmán Giergi. As well as its 960-seat main hall – worth attending for the magnificence of its surroundings and acoustics alone – the Zeneakadémia also houses a music university and library, home to the Liszt Collection of books and manuscripts. Liszt himself sits outside (in statue form), recently joined by Sir Georg Solti, after whom an equally new chamber hall has been named.

Nádor Hall

Nádor terem
XIV. Ajtósi Dürer sor 39 (344 7072, www.vakisk.hu/nador-terem). *Trolleybus 72, 74, 75.* **Open**
Box office 1hr before performance. Closed July & Aug. **No credit cards.**
A gorgeous art nouveau concert hall in the Institute for the Blind, with excellent acoustics and a rich programme of singing recitals, chamber music and baroque ensembles.

Óbuda Social Circle

Óbudai Társaskör
III. Kiskorona utca 7 (250 0288, www.obudai tarsaskor.hu). *HÉV to Szentlélek tér, or tram 1, or bus 9, 86.* **Open** *Box office* 9am-7pm daily.
No credit cards.
This charming little building is one of the few survivors from early 19th-century Óbuda. Intimate and atmospheric, it hosts excellent recitals and chamber music concerts.

Palace of Arts. See p168.

Palace of Arts

Müvészetek Palotája
IX.Komor Marcell utca 1 (555 3300, www.mupa. hu). Tram 1, 2, 24, or bus 54, 103. **Open** *Box office* 10am-6pm daily or until performance. Closed July & Aug. **Map** p250 inset.

The acoustically sound Bartók National Concert Hall is the main venue within the overblown Palace of Arts, a state-funded millennial landmark in the riverside arts complex of south Pest. This is the home for the top-class National Philharmonic Orchestra, directed by renowned virtuoso Zoltán Kocsis – and it's a real treat when he occasionally sits down at the keyboard. The National Concert Hall has sufficient wherewithal and capacity (1,700 seats) to accommodate the most prestigious orchestras from abroad. *Photo p167.*

Pesti Vigadó

V. Vigadó tér 2 (328 3300, www.pestivigado.hu). M1 Vörösmarty tér, or tram 2. **Open** *Box office* 10am-6.30pm daily. **Map** p249 D5.

Reopened in 2014 after a ten-year revamp, the Pesti Vigadó has an enviable heritage. Johann Strauss the Younger and the Elder both performed here in the 1800s, while the Vigadó also staged the première of Mahler's *First Symphony*. In more modern times, with its riverside location, the Vigadó has mainly tailored its programme to tourists.

THEATRE

With the closure of the Merlin, and general political machinations and funding cuts, there's currently hardly any English-language theatre in Budapest. What little mainstream activity there is comes courtesy of the **Budapest English Theatre** (www.budapestenglishtheatre.com), which manages to find occasional space at the Spinoza (*see p119*), the Bródy Studios (*see p220* **The Brody Bunch**), and the little-known Művelődési Szint (aka Műszi; VIII.Blaha Lujza tér 1, entrance on Somogyi Béla utca) on the third floor of the Corvin department store.

At the other end of the scale is **Scallabouche** (www.scallabouche.com), founded by the well-travelled Alexis Latham. Defiantly improv, its company an international mix, Scallabouche works mainly but not exclusively in Hungarian, with occasional shows in English. The territory, though often blurred, usually has a British backdrop: a radical interpretation of Noël Coward, say. It's not for everyone but Scallabouche must be saluted for challenging what passes for the status quo in contemporary Hungary. Its main space, fittingly, is the **Jurányi** (*see p156*), an underground student hangout.

Though poorly financed, Hungarian-language theatre packs the city's half-dozen main venues most nights. English surtitles are still not the norm, but some productions do carry them – and if you're

learning Hungarian, there's plenty of opportunity to follow a familiar play from the classic repertoire that many houses stick to. More challenging, contemporary pieces are staged at the **Trafó House of Contemporary Arts** (*see p162*).

Tickets & Information

The Hungarian-language season runs from September to June. Curtains rise quite early, at 7pm or 7.30pm. Productions run in repertory and can continue for ages. Most major theatres have ticket outlets at shopping malls such as Allee (*see p61*), the Mammut (*see p67*) and MOM Park (*see p62*). Prices are in the Ft1,500-Ft4,000 range.

Venues

Comedy Theatre

Vígszínház
XIII. Szent István körút 14 (340 4650, tickets 329 2340, www.vigszinhaz.hu). M3 Nyugati pu, or tram 4, 6. **Open** *Box office* 11am-7pm daily. **Map** p246 E2.

The Comedy Theatre is the handsome fin-de-siècle setting for contemporary drama and popular musicals such as *Fiddler on the Roof*. Productions tend to be very visual – but Hungarian-language only.
► *The Vígszínház's second theatre, the Pesti Színház, is at Váci utca 9 (same website), with the same company and more intimate productions.*

National Theatre

Nemzeti Színház
IX. Bajor Gizi park 1 (476 6800, tickets 476 6868, www.nemzetiszinhaz.hu). Tram 1, 2, 24, or bus 54, 103. **Open** *Box office* 10am-6pm Mon-Fri; 2-6pm Sat, Sun. **Map** p250 inset.

The latest incarnation of the National Theatre opened in 2002 amid much controversy, first over its location, then over disputes between its architect and artistic director. Although the jury is still out regarding its aesthetic appeal, there's no denying that the riverside setting is superb. The acoustics have also

IN THE KNOW
BUDAPEST'S BROADWAY

There are few English-language shows on Nagymező utca, but it can be fun to visit this historic stretch, with footprints of Hungary's theatrical greats. Enjoy pre-show drinks at the **Komédiás Kávéház** (*see p105*), where theatrical types unwind by singing along with regular pianists. Venues include the high-brow **Radnóti** (no.11, www.radnotiszinhaz. hu) with its award-winning resident troupe, and the elegant **Thália** (nos.22-24, www. thalia.hu), not to mention the legendary **Budapest Operetta Theatre** (*see p165*).

National Theatre.

come in for criticism, but the technical capabilities of the stage are unparalleled. The stage can be raised or lowered at 72 points, the lifts offer a panoramic view of the city, and the façade of the old building lies half-submerged in a pool by the main entrance.

DANCE

The Budapest classical ballet scene draws heavily on Russian traditions, as well as local ones. The **Hungarian Dance Academy** (www.mtf.hu) has instilled the kind of discipline and excellence that's produced the likes of Iván Markó, who went contemporary and soloed with Maurice Béjart in Paris before founding the Győr Ballet and Hungarian Festival Ballet in the 1990s. The traditional scene is dominated by the **Hungarian National Ballet**, based at the Opera House (see p166). Focusing on superbly executed renditions of classical works, it also performs at the Erkel Theatre (see p165).

Films of the folk dances that inspired composer Béla Bartók are preserved in the video library of the state-funded **Hungarian Heritage House** (www.heritagehouse.hu). You can see them being performed by the in-house **Hungarian State Folk Ensemble**, which also travels the world presenting stylised tributes to traditional dances.

The **National Dance Theatre** in the Castle District often hosts more purist folk troupes, such as the athletic, professional **Honvéd Dance Ensemble** (www.honvedart.hu), choreographed with discipline and imagination by Zoltán Zsuráfszky. The **Csillagszeműek** ('Starry-Eyed'; www.csillagszemu.hu) consists of talented children and teens, schooled by octogenarian master Sándor Timár.

Contemporary dance is full of exciting local talent. The moves of dancer and choreographer **Éva Duda** (www.evaduda.net) catapulted her to worldwide recognition at a young age. **Yvette Bozsik** (www.yvettebozsik.com), perhaps

Hungary's most internationally recognised contemporary choreographer, has a striking style that leans towards grotesque comedy, and her productions – at the National Dance Theatre and **Trafó House of Contemporary Arts** – have often used actors. Hungarian-born **Pál Frenák** (www.frenak.hu) is a creative maverick who's been sending shockwaves through the Budapest dance scene for years. The **Szeged Contemporary Ballet** (www.szegedikortarsbalett.hu) is a large, exciting troupe that often performs in Budapest.

Venues

MU Színház

XI.Kőrösy József utca 17 (209 4014, www.mu.hu). M4 Újbuda-központ, or tram 4. **Open** *Box office* By phone 10am-6pm Mon-Fri. In person 1hr before performance. **Map** p249 D9.
This space with no resident company hosts alternative dance and theatre groups. A good place to see what's happening on the fringe.

National Dance Theatre

Nemzeti Táncház
I.Színház utca 1-3 (201 4407, www.nemzeti tancszinhaz.hu). Várbusz from M2 Széll Kálmán tér, or bus 16. **Open** *Box office* 10am-5pm Mon-Thur; 10am-3pm Fri. **Map** p245 B4.
The Culture Ministry set up this venue in the Castle District. Dance productions are of the highest quality.

Trafó House of Contemporary Arts

IX.Liliom utca 41 (215 1600, www.trafo.hu). M3 Corvin-negyed, or tram 4, 6. **Open** *Box office* 4-8pm daily (until 10pm on performance days). **Map** p250 H8.
The busiest contemporary dance venue in town, with performances by the best Hungarian companies, such as Mozgó Ház Társulás, Pál Frenák and Yvette Bozsik. Trafó has close links with foreign cultural institutes and often stages guest productions.

Escapes & Excursions

Escapes & Excursions

Exploring the rest of Hungary from Budapest is easy and affordable. The most popular getaways are Lake Balaton, the hub of Hungary's resort industry, and the Danube Bend. Budapest is almost ten times bigger than any other town, so city breaks tend to be modest, although Eger and Pécs contain enough of interest to fill a weekend – each has a visible Ottoman heritage and a thriving contemporary wine culture. Bus and train travel from the capital is relatively cheap, and no journey to the provinces should take more than four hours. Motorways are generally well maintained, but the standard of driving might leave a little to be desired when Budapest leaves en masse for Lake Balaton on summer weekends.

GETTING AROUND

Landlocked Hungary has plenty to offer, and what's on offer can usually be reached by car, train, bus or even boat within two or three hours from Budapest, which means there are plenty of options for day trips. From the city centre, the main motorways and destinations are reasonably well signposted. The four main Budapest train stations are all served by their own metro station on the four-line network, and are quick to reach from anywhere in the city centre. The city's main bus station at Népliget also has its own metro station.

Before leaving the city by car, drivers will need to purchase a motorway e-voucher, usually at a service station. Rail and bus passengers can buy tickets online (*see p223*) or at stations. To beat the queues at the two main rail terminals of Keleti and Nyugati, automatic ticket machines are positioned around the station buildings, with English-language options. Szentendre, Visegrád and Esztergom can all be accessed by boat from the terminal at Vigadó tér, on the Pest embankment.

By boat

One boat runs daily (Apr-Oct) up the Danube to Szentendre, Visegrád and Esztergom. In July and August, there's an extra afternoon service as far as Szentendre. Hydrofoils run at weekends to Visegrád and Esztergom, For full schedules, visit www.mahartpassnave.hu.

Vigadó tér terminal
V. Vigadó tér (484 4000, 484 4013). M1 Vörösmarty tér, or tram 2. **Map** p249 D5.

By bus

Bus travel from Budapest's Népliget station (M3 metro) is easy. There are also bus stations at Népstadion and Árpád Bridge. Volánbusz has nationwide coverage and links with Eurolines. You can find bargains online if you book ahead. Certain areas of Hungary (north or south of Lake Balaton, for example) are most easily reached by bus.

Volánbusz
382 0888, www.volanbusz.hu.

ESCAPES & EXCURSIONS

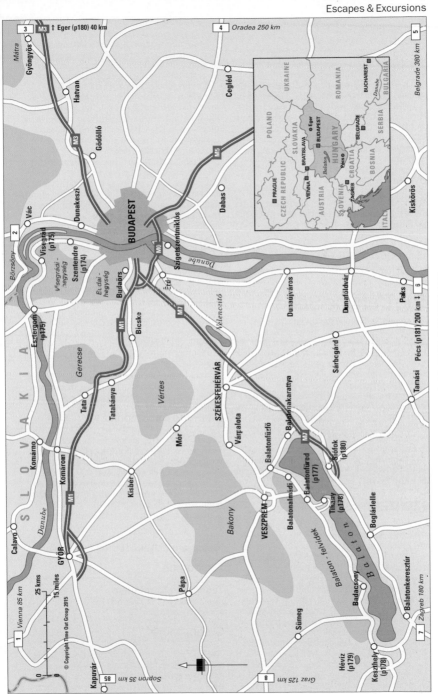

By car

Major routes are now easier to travel, but you have to pay a toll, which is registered to your number plate. This service is available at petrol stations. For further details, *see p225*. Getting out of Budapest is easy, with well-signposted routes. From Buda, follow the M7 for the Balaton region and the M6/E73 for Pécs. From Pest, follow the M3/E71 signs for Eger. From the Buda side of Árpád Bridge, take route 10 for Esztergom, and route 11 for Szentendre and Visegrád.

By train

Trains are cheap and reliable. The fastest, InterCity, require a seat reservation for a nominal fee. Timetables are posted at main stations.

MÁV
06 40 49 49 49, from abroad +36 1 444 4499, www.mavcsoport.hu.

The Danube Bend

The kink in the Danube about 40km (25 miles) north of Budapest is one of the most scenic stretches in the river's 2,860-kilometre (1,780-mile)course. Here, the Danube widens and turns sharply south into a valley between the tree-covered Börzsöny and Pilis Hills, before flowing on to Budapest.

The two main towns on the west bank of the Danube Bend, **Visegrád** and **Esztergom**, were both Hungarian medieval capitals – one with a hilltop citadel, the other a royal seat with the nation's biggest cathedral. They are easily accessible from Budapest by train, bus or boat.

Closer to town, **Szentendre** is a favourite day trip; it's an old Serbian village and artists' colony at the end of the HÉV line. A cycle path runs there too.

SZENTENDRE

Szentendre, a settlement of 20,000 people, is 20 kilometres (12 miles) north of the capital and offers shaded walks along the Danube, glimpses of Serbian history and a sizeable collection of art galleries. An old artists' haunt, it's now a tourist destination with odd museums (marzipan, wine), overpriced crafts and horse-drawn carriages. Ignore the tack – there's plenty to do.

Serb refugees reached Szentendre centuries before the souvenir-sellers. Their legacy is a small immigrant community and a handful of Orthodox churches, some still in operation. The Serbs came here in several waves, escaping war and persecution to enjoy religious freedom under Habsburg rule – and to prosper in the wine and leather trades. Although the exteriors are

Baroque, their churches preserve Orthodox traditions; all sanctuaries face east, irrespective of dimension or streetscape. The resulting layout gives the town a distinctly Balkan atmosphere.

The first church is **Požarevačka**, in Vuk Karadzics tér, open at weekends. Inside is the town's oldest iconostasis: iconic representations of saints that are joined together in a screen. In the main square, Fő tér, **Blagovestenska Church** provides a mix of deep music, incense and a glorious iconostasis. The most stunning place of worship is the **Belgrade Cathedral**, seat of the Serbian Orthodox bishop, with its entrance in Pátriáka utca. The entryway is decorated with oak wings in rococo style, the pulpit is carved and painted, and there's an ornate bishop's throne. In the same grounds is a Serbian church art museum, with trappings of gold and other precious metals.

After a series of floods and epidemics laid the town low, artists moved into Szentendre in the 1920s, to find a living museum of Serbian houses and churches. Later generations set up galleries, with varying degrees of merit. The first, **Vajda Lajos Stúdió** (Péter Pál utca 6A, 06 20 349 0080, www.vajdalajosstudio.hu), was named after the surrealist painter and key member of the famed Kassák circle. You can also see his works at the **Vajda Lajos Múzeum** (Hunyadi utca 1, 06 26 310 244) and the **Erdész Galéria** (Bercsényi utca 4, 06 26 302 736, www.galleryerdesz.hu). Look for colourful sculptures in town by ef Zámbó, once of seminal underground band **AE Bizottság** (*see p159*), now gigging with his Happy Dead Band.

Where to eat & drink

There are decent restaurants on the river and at Fő tér, where the **Kereskedőház Café** (no.2, 06 30 586 6422, www.kereskedohazcafe.hu) is a fine choice for coffee or lunch. At the Danube end of Görög utca, **Café Christine** (no.6, 06 20 369 7008, www.cafechristine.hu) and nearby **Görög Kancsó** (Duna korzó 9, 06 26 303 178, www. gorogkancsoetterem.hu) offer a wide choice of dishes. For something more traditional, **Korona** (Fő tér 18, 06 26 313 651, www.korona-etterem.hu) has been in operation for more than two centuries.

Resources

Tourinform Szentendre
Dumtsa Jenő utca 22 (06 26 317 965, www.iranyszentendre.hu).

Getting there

The HÉV train (every 15mins from Batthyány tér) reaches Szentendre in 40mins. Some trains terminate at Békásmegyer, the limit of the city BKV ticket – pay a *pótdíj* (supplement) or buy a

Visegrád Citadel.

ticket all the way to Szentendre. If you're partying in Szentendre, the first train back to Budapest is at 4.18am. In summer, a boat (Apr Sept, Ft2,000, Ft2,500 return) sets off from Vigadó tér at 10am and returns from Szentendre at 5pm Tue-Sun.

VISEGRÁD

The view from the **citadel** in Visegrád takes in a lovely stretch of the river, but the sleepy village below is only worth seeing for the palace ruins. The citadel and **Visegrád Palace** were built in the 13th and 14th centuries. The latter hosted the Visegrád Congress of 1335, when Magyar, Czech and Polish kings (and their courts) quaffed 10,000 litres of wine over trade talks. Representatives of the so-called 'Visegrád Group' of Hungary, Poland, the Czech Republic and Slovakia still meet here to discuss joint concerns. In the 15th century, King Mátyás overhauled the palace in Renaissance style. It fell into ruin and was buried under mudslides, to be rediscovered in 1934.

Today, restored rooms house displays about everyday life in medieval times. Original pieces uncovered in 1934 can be found at the **Mátyás Museum**, in the Salamon Tower, halfway up the hill. You can reach the citadel via a strenuous half-hour walk up the stony Path of Calvary, by thrice-daily bus, or by catching a taxi (06 26 314 314) up Panoráma út.

Where to eat, drink & stay

Have a bite on the terrace of the **Renaissance** restaurant by the boat landing (Fő utca 11, 06 26 398 081, www.renvisegrad.hu). For lunch, try the **Gulyás Csarda** (Nagy Lajos király utca 4, 06 26 398 329). The **Hotel Visegrád** (Rév utca 15, 06 26 397 034, www.hotelvisegrad.hu) is a centrally located spa lodging with 73 rooms,

some of which overlook the Danube. There's a heated pool in winter, an open-air pool in summer and a bowling alley.

Resources

Visegrád Tours
Rév utca 15 (06 26 398 160, www.visegradtours.hu).

Getting there

An hourly Volánbusz bus (Ft900) takes 1hr 15mins from Újpest Városkapu vasútállomás (XIII.Balzsam utca 1). In summer, a boat sets off from Vigadó tér at 10am and returns from Visegrád at 5.45pm Tue-Sun (Apr-Sept, Ft2,500, Ft3,000 return, 3hrs). A hydrofoil (May-Sept, Ft4,000, Ft6,000 return, 1hr) leaves Vigadó tér at 9.30am and returns from Visegrád at 5.30pm every weekend.

ESZTERGOM

Esztergom is Hungary's most sacred city, home of the archbishop and the nation's biggest church. Not all of its 30,000 inhabitants are pious; there's a string of bars and restaurants overlooking the river and Slovakia.

Esztergom was Hungary's first real capital. The nation's first Christian king, Szent István, was crowned here in 1000. He built a royal palace, parts of which can be seen in the **Castle Museum** south of the **Basilica**. Esztergom was the royal seat for nearly three centuries, until invasions by Mongols, then Turks, all but destroyed the city. The huge Basilica still dominates, though. When the Catholic Church moved its base back to Esztergom in 1820, Archbishop Sándor Rudnay wanted a monument built on the ruins of a church destroyed by the Turks; three architects created this bleak structure. A bright spot is the **Bakócz Chapel**, built in red marble by Florentine craftsmen, dismantled during the Ottoman occupation and reassembled in 1823.

Where to eat, drink & stay

The **Mediterraneo** (Helischer utca 2, Primás Sziget, 06 33 311 411, www.mediterraneo.hu), overlooking the river, offers decent game and fish dishes, as well as steaks from the grill. It also has B&B accommodation. Just below the Basilica, the **Prímás Pince** (Szent István tér 4, 06 33 541 965) creates mains such as roasted foie gras with gorgonzola and pear, and steamed pike-perch with roasted vegetables and chive sauce. The four-star **Hotel Bellevue** (Örtorony utca 49, 06 33 510 810, www.bellevuehotel.hu) is just out of town at Búbánatvölgy, but offers a superior spa break away from it all. Back in town, the **Schweidel Szálló** (Schweidel József utca 6, 06 20 291 7740, www.schweidelszallo.hu) is clean, comfortable and conveniently located close to the train station. Many local lodgings offer special packages that include discounted admission to **Aqua-Sziget** (www.aquasziget.hu), the largest water park in the region.

Resources

Tourist information
Széchenyi tér 1 (www.esztergom.hu).

IBUSZ
Kossuth Lajos utca 5 (06 33 520 920, www.ibusz.hu/irodak/esztergom).

Getting there

A regular train to Esztergom leaves from Nyugati station (Ft1,200, 1hr 30mins). The bus from Árpád-hid station (Ft840) is slightly quicker and cheaper. In summer, a boat (May-Aug, Ft,3000, Ft4,000 return, 4hrs 30mins) sets off from Vigadó tér at 9am and returns from Esztergom at 4.30pm Tue-Sun. A hydrofoil (May-Oct, Ft5,000, Ft7,500 return, 1hr 30mins) leaves Vigadó tér at 9.30am and returns from Esztergom at 5pm on weekends.

Lake Balaton

Budapest empties in August. Everyone leaves in droves for Lake Balaton, landlocked Hungary's prime summer destination. Discos and clubs set up, many at the party hub of **Siófok**, close to Zamárdi where **Balaton Sound** (*see p31*) brings in the festival masses for five days in July. Now almost as prominent as the renowned Sziget festival that spawned it, Balaton Sound attracts big international names in hip hop and electronic

Lake Balaton.

music. Balaton isn't all about hedonistic partying, though – the north shore is more about fine wines and tranquil relaxation.

Traffic willing, you can drive to Siófok from Budapest in an hour (the train takes two), so in theory Balaton can be done in a day – but the motorway can be choked on Sunday evenings and last trains back leave relatively early. If you're stuck around Balaton overnight, private rooms (look out for 'Zimmer Frei' signs) are affordable.

The Balaton is one of Europe's largest lakes, a huge area of water for such a small, landlocked country. Hungarians have flocked here for generations: even those on modest salaries have access to a weekend house on the shores.

As a foreigner, unless you get invited by a local, your trip here may be somewhat different: think high-rise hotels, concrete beaches, white plastic chairs, advertising umbrellas and a string of over-priced resorts. Although there are quieter parts, a trip to this lake is first and foremost an excursion into deepest naff – which doesn't mean to say that it can't also be a lot of fun.

Its allure goes way back, having attracted Celts, Romans, Huns and Slavs, whose word for swamp, *blatna*, probably gave the lake its name. The Magyars brought fishing and farming, and built a lot of churches, before the Mongols arrived in 1242. The Turks occupied the south shore and scuffled with Austrians on the other side in the 16th and 17th centuries. Once they were driven out, the Habsburgs came along and blew up any remaining Hungarian castles.

Most of the best sights, therefore, date from the 18th century, when viticulture flourished and Baroque was in vogue. Landmarks include the Abbey Church in **Tihany** and the huge Festetics Palace in **Keszthely**. Nearby is the world's second-largest thermal lake, **Hévíz**.

Although **Balatonfüred** was declared a spa in 1785, it wasn't until the 19th century that bathing and the therapeutic properties of the area's thermal springs began to draw the wealthy in large numbers. In 1836, Baron Miklós Wesselényi, a leading reformer of the era, was the first to swim from Tihany to Balatonfüred. Lajos Kossuth suggested steamships, and Count István Széchenyi rustled some up. Passenger **boat services** (www.balatonihajozas.hu) still link most of the major resorts and are an appealing way to get around, though the ferry from the southern tip of the Tihany peninsula to Szántód – a ten-minute journey spanning the lake's narrowest point – is the only one that takes cars.

The southern shore – now an 80-kilometre (50-mile) stretch of tacky resorts – was developed after the 1861 opening of the railway. The line along the hillier and marginally more tasteful north shore wasn't opened until 1910. But the Balaton mainly remained a playground for the well-to-do until the Communists rebuilt the area for mass recreation. Hungary was one of the few places to which East Germans could travel, and the Balaton became the place where West Germans would meet up with their poor relations. Tourism is still geared towards the needs of Germans, and in some shops and restaurants German is the first language.

The lake itself is unusual. A 77-kilometre-long (48-mile) rectangle, 14 kilometres (8.5 miles) at its widest, it covers an area of 600 square kilometres (232 square miles) but is shallow throughout – Lake Geneva contains 20 times as much water. At its deepest (the Tihany Well by the peninsula that almost chops the lake in half), Balaton reaches 12 metres (39 feet) down. At Siófok and other south-shore resorts, you can wade out 1,000 metres (half a mile) before the water comes up to your waist. It's safe for kids, if somewhat silty.

Motorboats are forbidden, but you can sail or windsurf. Fishing is popular too. Balaton is home to around 40 varieties of fish, many of which are served in local restaurants. The *fogas*, a pike-perch, is unique to the lake and goes well with the very drinkable local wines.

Although prices are high, there are plenty of affordable restaurants and hotels, plus private rooms found on spec or through tourist offices.

BALATONFÜRED

Standing at the top of Balatonfüred's cobbled main square of Gyógy tér, it's easy to imagine wealthy 18th-century spa tourists making this pretty old town Balaton's first resort. The square slopes down to a shaded park by the lakeside, where **Tagore sétány** is lined with trees. A long pier sticks out into the lake, inviting moonlight strollers to admire the twinkling lights of Siófok across the lake.

Visitors came to take the waters, sometimes staying at the Baroque-style State Hospital of Cardiology on Gyógy tér. These days, tourism on the north shore centres around boating, clubbing and the half-dozen beaches. The largest is **Kisfaludy Strand** (Aranyhid sétány, www.balatonfuredistrandok.hu). The pricier **Annagora Aquapark** (Fürdő utca 35, 06 87 581 430, www.annagora.com) has a wave pool, waterslides and other attractions. Balatonfüred's harbour has a busy marina and ferries to Tihany and Siófok.

Where to eat & drink

Near the end of the lakeside promenade, **Borcsa** (Tagore sétány, 06 87 580 070, www.borcsaetterem.hu) has a terrace, live music and a lot of local fish. Also close to the lake, the **Balaton Étterem** (Kisfaludy utca 5, 06 481 319, www.balatonetterem.hu) is as traditional as you can get, preparing its fish soup with catfish and roe, or providing two diners with a hulking fish platter of catfish, carp and zander, prepared both grilled and breaded.

On the inland edge of town, **SunCity** (Fürdő utca 35, www.suncity-balaton.hu), the former Sundance leisure complex, has several bars, as well as clubs such as Honey and Lipstick with resident DJs. Near the water, the **Helka Music Club** (Széchenyi utca 8, 06 30 639 1363, www.facebook.com/clubhelka) is another party spot, with international DJs, even out of season. Old-school standby the **Columbus Club** (Honvéd utca 3, 06 70 636 6707, www.facebook.com/columbusclub.hungary) operates hand-in-hand with SunCity.

Where to stay

On the main square, the truly grand four-star **Anna Grand** (Gyógy tér 1, 06 87 581 200, www.annagrandhotel.hu) has a luxurious spa centre – and a luxury price tag. In the same bracket is **Hotel Wellness Flamingo** (Széchenyi út 16, 06 87 581 060, www.flamingohotel.hu). **Korona Panzió** (Vörösmarty utca 4, 06 87 343 278, www.koronapanzio.hu) is much cheaper and does weekly deals.

Resources

Tourinform Balatonfüred
Blaha Lujza utca 5 (06 87 580 480, www.balatonfured.info.hu).

Getting there

By car, take the M7 from Budapest to exit 64 for the E66/route 8 towards Veszprém. Just past Veszprém, go left on route 73 towards Balatonfüred; at Csopak, turn right on the E71. The 138km (86-mile) trip takes about 2hrs. InterCity trains from Kelenföld (Ft2,700) take 2hrs 30mins. There are currently only three direct trains a day – most journeys require two or three changes while the line is being overhauled.

TIHANY

A national park containing an historic village, the Tihany peninsula offers one of Balaton's quieter getaways, and some gorgeous vistas. The 12-square-kilometre (4.5 square-mile) peninsula juts five kilometres (three miles) into the lake, almost cutting it in half. Tihany village lies near a small 'inner lake', separated from the Balaton by a steep hill. Atop the hill, the twin-spired **Abbey Church** opened in 1754 and is among Hungary's most important Baroque monuments. King Andrew I's 1055 deed of foundation for the church originally on this site was the first written document to contain any Hungarian (a few score place names in a mainly Latin text). The **Abbey Museum** in the former monastery next door documents the area's history. Best of all, though, is the view: the church is set on a sheer cliff.

Where to eat & drink

Csárdás (Kossuth Lajos utca 20, 06 87 438 067), near the church, does good country-style Hungarian food and Balaton fish dishes. **Kakas** (Batthyány utca 1, 06 87 448 541, www.kakascsarda.hu) is a rambling old restaurant, converted from a barn in 1984, with a pleasant terrace. Carnivores can devour T-bone steak, goose and veal, with plenty of fish on offer too. There's also a half-board room – the room is modest, the meal won't be.

For jumping bars or nightlife, leave Tihany. For spectacular views of the Balaton, drinks and good cakes, visit **Rege Kávézó** (Kossuth utca 22, 06 87 448 280, www.regecukrászda.hu).

Where to stay

Holiday Hotel Tihany (Batthyány utca 6, 06 20 910 7080, www.holidayhoteltihany.hu), the only hotel in the old village, has a pool and 14 doubles. Prices come down about 20 per cent between mid September and mid June. Overlooking the lake, the modern, all-suite **Echo Residence** (Felsőkopaszhegyi út 35, 06 87 448 043, www.echoresidence.hu) has serious spa facilities. The modest **Adler Hotel & Restaurant**

(Felsőkopaszhegyi utca 1A, 06 87 538 000, www.adlerhoteltihany.hu), with an outdoor pool, sauna and jacuzzi, offers attractive half-board deals, even in high season.

Resources

Tourinform Tihany
Kossuth utca 20 (06 87 448 804, www.tihany.hu).

Getting there

By car, head for Balatonfüred (*see p177*) and continue on the E71 for another 3.5km (2 miles). The 141km (88-mile) trip takes just over two hours. Arriving by train at Balatonfüred, catch a bus or taxi the remaining few kilometres.

KESZTHELY

Keszthely, a big town with a university, is the only settlement on Lake Balaton that's not completely dependent on tourism. But it still offers visitors two busy lidos and the region's most popular historical sight.

Festetics Palace, a 100-room Baroque pile in pleasant grounds north of the town centre, was created by the family who once owned this whole area. Enlightened aristocrat Count György Festetics (1755-1819) built the palace, made ships, hosted a salon of leading literary lights, and founded both the Helikon library – in the southern part of the mansion and containing more than 80,000 volumes – and the original agricultural college, these days the **Georgikon Museum** (Bercsényi utca 67). The Gothic parish church on Fő tér was built in the 1380s and fortified in 1550 in the face of the Ottoman advance. In 1747, it underwent a Baroque revamp.

Where to eat & drink

The main pedestrianised street of Kossuth Lajos utca is lined with bars and restaurants. Here, you'll find **John's Pub** (no.46, 06 30 237 9025, www.johnspubkeszthely.hu), which runs a full restaurant in tavern-like surroundings. **Halászcsárda** (Csárda utca 9, 06 83 310 036, www.halaszcsardakeszthely.hu, closed Nov-Mar) provides a more typical Hungarian experience.

Pike-perch is in safe hands at the restaurant of the **Hotel Bacchus** (*see p179*), along with many local wines. The weekend-only **512 Club** (Csík Ferenc sétány 2, 06 70 250 2950, www.512club.hu) offers live music to a student crowd.

Where to stay

Helikon (Balaton-part 5, 06 83 889 600, www.hotelhelikon.hu), on the lakeshore, offers tennis, horse riding and rooms including two meals and use of pool and gym. **Hotel Bacchus** (Erzsébet királyné útja 18, 06 83 510 450, www. bacchushotel.hu), a short walk from the lake, is similarly priced. The three-star **Kristály Hotel** (Lovassy Sándor utca 20, 06 83 318 999, www.kristalyhotel.hu) has 40 affordable rooms, plus a spa and sauna.

Resources

Tourinform Keszthely
Kossuth Lajos utca 30 (06 83 314 144, www.keszthely.hu).

Getting there

By car, take the M7 from Budapest past Siófok to exit 170 for route 68. Take route 68 to a roundabout, then switch to route 76. After 8km (5 miles), turn right on route 71. The 190km (118-mile) trip takes about 2hrs. From Kelenföld station, trains (Ft3,700) take 3hrs 30mins. While the line is being overhauled in 2015, there are few direct services. At least two changes are usually required, at Lepsény and Szántód. The fastest direct bus takes 2hrs 20mins from Népliget station, with services around every 1hr 30mins.

HÉVÍZ

A short distance from the western tip of Lake Balaton, Hévíz is a phenomenon all its own. Europe's largest thermal lake, attracting bathers since medieval times, was enhanced for tourism by aristocrat György Festetics. By the 1890s, Hévíz was a spa destination for the well-to-do.

Bathing takes place all year round. The deep blue, slightly radioactive warm water is full of Indian water lilies and middle-aged Germans floating around with rubber rings. Best of all, the pointed wooden bathhouse complex set on stilts stretches right out into the middle of the lake. The water's curative effects on rheumatic and locomotive disorders make Hévíz a health centre as well as a tourist resort.

Where to eat & drink

Magyar Csárda (Tavirózsa utca 2-4, 06 83 343 271, www.magyarcsarda.hu) serves well-priced, home-style meals on a large corner patio. **Papa's & Mama's** (Petőfi utca 16, 06 30 271 0200) has a huge menu and panoramic terrace. **Vadaskert Csárda** (Keszthely-Kertváros, Hévízi utca, 06 83 312 772, www.vadaskertcsarda.hu), just outside town, is a lovely garden and terrace with traditional food and live gypsy music.

Where to stay

Upmarket spa hotels offer treatments based around the curative waters. At the top end are the **Carbona** (Attila utca 1, 06 83 501 500, www.carbona.hu) and two Danubius hotels: **Hévíz** (Kossuth utca 9-11, 06 83 889 400, www. danubiushotels.com) and **Aqua** (Kossuth utca 13-15, 06 83 889 500, www.danubiushotels.com).

Resources

Tourinform Hévíz
Rákóczi utca 2 (06 83 540 131, www.west-balaton.hu/heviz).

Hévíz.

ESCAPES & EXCURSIONS

Getting there

By car, take the M7 from Budapest, past Siófok to exit 170 for route 68. Follow route 68 to a roundabout, then switch to route 76. After about 8km (5 miles), turn right on route 71. Just after Keszthely, turn left on Sümegi utca; 1.5km later, turn left on Ady Endre utca; Hévíz is 1km further on. The 193km (120-mile) trip takes about 2hrs. Hévíz is also a 15min bus journey from Keszthely station – or a short taxi ride.

SIÓFOK

The easiest hop from Budapest, Siófok is sin city: loud, brash and packed in high season. Although it's the lake's largest resort, there isn't much sightseeing on offer. Nightlife is another matter. The Petőfi sétány strip runs for two kilometres or just over a mile. Here, you'll find vast Communist-era hotels, bars with oompah bands, amusement arcades, topless bars, parked cars blasting out techno, and an endless procession of Hungarian, German and Austrian tourists.

Where to eat & drink

Diana Hotel (*see below*) has a fine restaurant serving excellent pike-perch. Sophisticated lakeside **Mala Garden** is also a hotel and restaurant (*see below*), with a menu that reflects its exotic decor – Thai soups, chicken breast grilled in Greek goat's milk yoghurt, and *zarzuela* are the order of the day here. **Roxy** (Szabadság tér 4, 06 84 506 573, www.roxyetterem.hu) is a decent brasserie with cheap daily specials.
The **Borsodi Beach Club** (Petőfi sétány 3, www.beach-club.eu) dominates the main drag with its man-made sandy beach, sky bar, DJs and bands playing day and night. **Flört** (Sió utca 4, 06 20 333 3303, www.flort.hu), one of Hungary's top nightclubs, brings in excellent DJs and has a fun space with a roof terrace. Its main rival is the slick **Palace** (Vécsey Károly utca 20 & Deák Ferenc sétány 2, 06 30 200 8888, www.palace.hu), outside town.

Where to stay

The **Diana Hotel & Restaurant** (Szent László utca 41-43, 06 84 315 296, www.dianahotel.hu) is a family-friendly three-star. The **Mala Garden** (Petőfi sétány 15A, 06 84 506 687, www.mala garden.hu) is a Bali-themed four-star with spa, pool, sauna and treatment facilities. The four-star **Janus Boutique** (Fő utca 93-95, 06 84 312 546, www.janushotel.hu) is part of the Best Western chain and offers rooms and apartments. On the strip itself, **Hotel Napfény** (Mártírok utca 8, 06 84 311 408, www.hotel-napfeny.com) is cheaper, with spacious rooms and balconies.

The **Hotel Yacht Club** (Vitorlás utca 14, 06 84 310 084, www. www.hotel-yacht-club.hu) has a newly upgraded spa and restaurant.

Resources

Tourinform Siófok
Fő tér 11 (06 84 310 117, www.siofokportal.com).

Getting there

By car, take the M7 from Budapest to exit 98; then take route 7 for 5km (3 miles). The 103km (64-mile) trip takes approx 1hr 10mins. With lines from Déli station currently being overhauled, most trains (Ft2,300) run from Kelenföld and involve a change at Lepsény. Journey time should be less than 2hrs, 1hr 30mins at best.

Eger

With a castle that was the scene of a historic victory, a quaint pedestrianised downtown area, and a rich tradition of making and drinking wine, Eger has plenty to offer visitors.
Located 128 kilometres (80 miles) north-east of Budapest, the town is at the foot of the low, rolling Bükk Hills, ideal for fishing, hunting and camping. The vines here produce the grapes that make wines such as Hungary's best-known – Egri Bikavér (Bull's Blood), a hearty, dry red blend of local wines – along with sweet, white Tokaj dessert wine. Nearby Tokaj, an hour's drive from Eger, is also lined with cellars.
Inside Hungary, Eger is best known as the place where a small, outnumbered group of Magyars held off 10,000 invading Ottomans during a month-long siege in 1552. The Turks came back and finished the job 44 years later, but the earlier siege of Eger has been fixed in the nation's imagination by Géza Gárdonyi's 1901 adventure novel *Egri csillagok* (*Eclipse of the Crescent Moon*). Gárdonyi's version, which has the brave women of Eger dumping hot soup on the Turks, is required school reading, and his fiction seems almost to have replaced the actual history. There's a statue of the author within the castle, and a **Panoptikum** featuring wax versions of his characters. Copies of the novel are on sale all over town, and there's a **Gárdonyi Géza Memorial Museum**.
The castle was blown up by the Habsburgs in 1702. What remains is big, but there's not too much to see. Still, it's a delightful place for a stroll and it affords a fine view over Eger's Baroque skyline. Tours, available in English, offer a recap of the battle's history and a chance to see the interior of the battlements. You can just walk around, visit the castle's various exhibits or try your hand at archery.

Eger Basilica.

25-minute walk from Dobó tér or a short cab ride. It can be difficult to find a taxi back – try calling **City Taxi** (06 36 555 555, www.citytaxieger.hu).

Where to eat & drink

The best place to eat in town is the restaurant of the **Senátor Ház Hotel** (*see below*), a mix of Hungarian and modern European with first-rate service. Book at weekends. Also on Dobó tér, **Forst-Ház** (no.1, 06 36 311 587, www.forsthaz. hu) is a standard restaurant and coffeehouse, with cheap deals on weekdays and a leafy terrace. Behind the main Gárdonyi Géza Theatre, **Fehérszarvas Vadásztanya** (Klapka György utca 8, 06 36 411 129, www.feherszarvasetterem. hu) specialises in game and wild boar, as can be seen from the trophies on the wall. The kitchen usually runs until midnight and there's live music.

As well as a handful of terrace cafés on and around Dobó tér, look out for **Bíboros** (Bajcsy-Zsilinszky utca 6, 06 70 428 4993, www.biboros. hu), a popular bar-café in a prominent location.

Where to stay

The three-star **Senátor Ház Hotel** at Dobó tér 11 (06 36 411 711, www.senatorhaz.hu) is comfortable and well situated. For a spa break, the **Hotel Eger & Park** (Szálloda utca 1-3, 06 36 522 200, www.hotelegerpark.hu) has saunas and a pool. The **Park Hotel Minaret** (Knézich Károly utca 2, 06 36 517 000, www.minarethoteleger.hu) stands beside its namesake landmark, offering 36 three-star rooms.

Resources

TDM – Tourinform Eger

Bajcsy-Zsilinszky utca 9 (06 36 517 715, www.eger.hu).

Getting there

By car from Budapest, take the M3, then turn off for Eger just after 100km (60 miles), at Kál. Passing Kápolna, take route 3, then route 25 after Kerecsend. The whole journey from downtown Budapest to Eger should take 2hrs 15mins, a journey of 135km (84 miles).

InterCity trains run every 2hrs from Keleti (Ft2,700) and take just under 2hrs to reach Eger.

Another place for a great view is atop the one minaret left from the Turkish occupation, though the ascent of the stairs inside is rather long and claustrophobic. Located at the corner of Knézich utca and Markó Ferenc utca, this is one of the northernmost minarets in Europe. The mosque that was once attached is gone.

Eger's Baroque buildings are splendid, most notably the 1771 **Minorite church**, centrepiece of Dobó tér. The **Basilica** on Eszterházy tér is a neoclassical monolith, crowned with crucifix-brandishing statues of Faith, Hope and Charity by Italian sculptor Marco Casagrande. Designed by József Hild, who also designed the one in Budapest, this cathedral has a similarly imposing façade that looks all the larger due to the long flight of steps from the square below. The statues of Hungarian kings and the apostles along these steps were also made by Casagrande. The **Lyceum** opposite, which is now a teachers' college, has a 19th-century camera obscura in its east tower observatory that projects a view of the entire town.

Although you can find commercial wine cellars downtown, the local vintages are most entertainingly sampled just out of town – at **Szépasszonyvölgy**, the Valley of Beautiful Women, a horseshoe-shaped area of dozens of wine cellars, with tables scattered outside. The offerings here – from small, private cellars – aren't necessarily Eger's best, but the wine is cheap. Gypsy fiddlers entertain drinkers, and parties come to eat, dance and make merry. Try to get there by the afternoon, as most places close by early evening. The valley bustles during a two-week harvest festival in September. It's a

Pécs

For a city break outside Budapest, Pécs is easily the best option. European Capital of Culture in 2010, 'the Gateway to the Balkans' has enough historic sites of interest, cultural firepower and nightlife to easily fill a weekend.

Not everything connected with ECC 2010 went according to plan, however. For the first few months, the city was a building site, with many of its regular museums still closed. On the plus side, in place today are the **Regional Library & Knowledge Centre**, the **Conference & Concert Centre** and, notably, part of the **Zsolnay Cultural Quarter** (*see p183* **All Fired Up**). Although a work in progress, this most ambitious element is built around the old factory complex where the Zsolnay firm created its famous glazed tiles, as seen on Budapest's Matthias Church and Museum of Applied Arts.

The attractive old town features a clutch of interesting sights and busy nightlife fuelled by a large student population. So close to Croatia that locals nip over the border for more favourable betting odds, Pécs seems far from Budapest.

Romans settled here and called it Sopianae. The town prospered on the trade route between Byzantium and Regensburg; King István established the Pécs diocese in 1009, and the first university in Hungary was founded here in 1367.

Then came the Turks in 1543, pushing the locals outside the walls that still define the city centre. Signs of the historic struggle between Magyars and Muslims are evident in the **Belvárosi Plébániatemplom** (Inner City Parish Church) that dominates the town's main square, Széchenyi tér. Under the Ottomans, an ancient Gothic church was torn down and the stones were used to make the **Mosque of Pasha Gazi Kassim**. Jesuits later converted the mosque to its present state, which is decidedly unchurchlike: the ogee windows, domed and facing Mecca, are at variance with the square's north–south orientation. The minaret was demolished in 1753, but inside the church, on the back wall, are recently uncovered Arabic texts. As if to counter this, the main interior features a grand mural depicting Hungarian battles with the Turks. In the square outside is an equestrian statue of János Hunyadi, the Hungarian leader who thwarted an earlier Turkish invasion.

The **Mosque of Pasha Hassan Jokovali** is at Rákóczi utca 2. The most intact Ottoman-era structure in Hungary, this was also converted into a church, but in the 1950s the original mosque was restored. Excerpts from the Koran on the mosque's plaster dome have been recovered, and next door is a museum of Turkish artefacts. Hungary's only active mosque, built more recently, is located about 30 kilometres (20 miles) south, in the small town of Siklós.

Overlooking Dóm tér stands the **Basilica of St Peter** (06 72 513 057), dating from the 11th century. Highlights include stunning frescoes, the red marble altar of the Corpus Christi Chapel and incredible wall carvings on the stairs to the crypt. Here also are the **Cella Septichora** (06 72 224 755, www.pecsorokseg.hu) ancient burial chambers.

Káptalan utca, a street running east off Dóm tér, is packed with museums and galleries. At no.2, the **Janus Pannonius Zsolnay Museum** (06 72 514 045, www.zsolnay.hu) is an essential stop for anyone interested in the history of this renowned brand. At No.3 is an annexe of the Janus Pannonius museum, dedicated to **Victor Vasarely** (06 30 934 6127, www.jpm.hu), in the house where the op-artist was born.

Where to eat & drink

From Széchenyi tér, pedestrianised Király utca is lined with restaurants: elegant **Enoteca Corso** (no.14, 06 72 630 1206) is an upscale bistro. For Balkan meats, the lovely old **Áfium** (Irgalmasok utcája 2, 06 72 511 434, www.afiumetterem.hu) is a must. To treat the one you love, book a table (and a taxi) for the **Hotel Kikelet** (*see below*) or the less exclusive but arguably more charming **Tettye** (Tettye tér 4, 06 72 532 788, www.tettye.hu), a family-run restaurant with a lovely garden.

Bars also line Király utca, though the best choice after dark for drink, food, live music and atmosphere is the **Pécsi Est Café** (Rákóczi út 46, 06 20 667 7559, www.pecsiestcafe.hu), ten minutes from the main square.

Where to stay

Hotel Palatinus (Király utca 5, 06 72 889 400, www.danubiushotels.com) was grand in its day, and has a lovely café and roof terrace – but rooms barely merit the three-star status. The 13-room **Főnix Art & Boutique Hotel** (Hunyadi út 2, 06 72 311 680, www.fonixhotel.com), north of Széchenyi tér, is more stylish than its two-star status might indicate. The sleek, four-star **Corso** (Koller utca 8, 06 72 421 900, www.corsohotel.hu) is hard to beat, especially given the standard of its restaurant. If you're willing to stay slightly out of town, then **Hotel Kikelet** (Málics Ottó út 1, 06 72 512 900, www.hotelkikelet.hu) is hands-down the best choice, with a pool, spa and smart restaurant.

Resources

Tourinform Pécs
Széchenyi tér 7 (06 72 213 315, www.iranypecs.hu).

Getting there

By car from Budapest, follow signs for the E71/ M7. After 16km (10 miles), take the E60/M0. At 24km (15 miles), take the exit for the E73/M6 towards Dunaújváros/M60 Pécs. At 151km (95 miles), take route 6 towards Pécs. The journey from central Budapest should take 2hrs 35mins.

InterCity trains run every 2hrs from Kelenföld or Keleti (Ft4,000) and take just under 3hrs to reach Pécs.

ALL FIRED UP

The Zsolnay Cultural Quarter champions the renowned local ceramics brand.

Designed to feature as the star attraction of the city's once-in-a-lifetime role as European Capital of Culture in 2010, the **Zsolnay Cultural Quarter** (37 Vilmos Zsolnay út, 06 72 500 350, www.zsolnaynegyed.hu) in Pécs is at last firing on all cylinders. Ranged around the original factory, this far-reaching attraction now draws a significant number of visitors from Budapest and, just over the border, Croatia.

The refashioning of the largest listed industrial complex in central Europe cost some Ft11 billion. Gradually opened from December 2011 onwards, the ZCQ has always kept the Zsolnay legacy as its spotlight. It was Vilmos Zsolnay, son of factory founder Miklós, who took this ceramics company to a whole new level in the second half of the 19th century. Gaining recognition and awards for his bright designs at the world's fairs in Vienna and Paris in the 1870s, Vilmos then perfected the process of eosin glazing, which allows for colours to sparkle.

Around the same time, he also experimented with pyrogranite, firing his ceramics at high temperatures to make them frost-resistant. Bright shades of greens and reds, coupled with a durable material, allowed the likes of Ödön Lechner and Samu Pecz to create decorative urban masterpieces around Budapest. The Museum of Applied Arts (see p136) and the Great Market Hall (see p137) showcased the unique Zsolnay brand and sealed its legend. Any further development was curtailed, first by World War I and its dire economic consequences, then by the destruction of World War II, then nationalisation under Communism.

Zsolnay regained its name, then its financial independence, during the final years of the Communist regime. Today, Zsolnay is still creating exquisite pieces for the global market – but the days of employing nearly 700 workers are long gone.

Its story is told and illustrated at the centrepiece to the ZCQ, the **Zsolnay Family & Factory History Exhibition** (Ft1,200, Ft600 reductions). Displaying gorgeous examples of vases, figurines, statuettes and other decorative artefacts, the exhibition has based much of its extensive documentation on the 2,500-page memoirs of Teréz Zsolnay, daughter of Vilmos and an avid collector herself. She was also sister-in-law of the company's most celebrated designer, Tádé Sikorski.

In another part of the complex, the **Golden Age of Zsolnay** (Ft1,400, Ft700 reductions) is set in the renovated villa where Tádé Sikorski and his wife Júlia lived and worked. Today, it houses the Gyugyi Collection. László Gyugyi was a US-based collector who amassed some 600 pieces over the course of four decades. Bought by the City of Pécs, the collection shows how Gyugyi used his expertise to highlight Zsolnay creations as an integral part of development in international style and to illustrate the history of this art form.

Another private collector, Barnabás Winkler, is responsible for the so-called **Pink Exhibition** (Ft1,200, Ft600 reductions) of 1,300 objects, all of similar shades but with radically different designs.

A complete ruin until its recent overhaul, the **Zsolnay Mausoleum** (Ft800, Ft400 reductions) was also designed by Sikorski. Clad with glazed tiles of dark green, it is said to be aligned in such a way that, at noon on the winter solstice, light bathes the interior and reveals the secret of the eosin process.

For the rest of the year, visitors can explore these techniques for themselves at the **Zsolnay Live Manufacture** (Ft500, Ft300 reductions). The basic materials and delicate nuances of the production process are on view as workers demonstrate their skill.

The ZCQ continues to add attractions to fulfil its remit as a cultural hub. Most recently, the **Planetarium** (Ft1,100, Ft700 reductions) has been unveiled, to complement the **LAB – Interactive House of Playful Sciences** (Ft450), both family-friendly distractions from the ceramics displays. Galleries, cafés, a puppet theatre and concert spaces make up the rest of the complex.

In Context

History

A tale of two cities.

TEXT: BOB COHEN & MATTHEW HIGGINSON

Budapest is two cities in one. The twin settlements of Buda and Pest developed separately on opposite sides of the Danube. Leafy, hilly Buda still seems like a quiet, provincial retreat from the dusty bustle of Pest across the river. Pest is the commercial, political and cultural hub of the Hungarian capital. Set on a vast plain, it seems open to all possibilities. The fault line is, in fact, tangible. Budapest sits on an ancient geological rift, a line of least resistance that drew the waters of the Danube south in their search for a resting place. It's too deep to disturb amalgamated Budapest today, but the fault line ensured that the hills stayed on one side and the level plain on the other. When the first humans arrived here, many thousands of years ago, those hills were seen as prime real estate, a defensible settlement with a fabulous view. Later still, the plain of Pest proved the ideal greenfield site for the extensive urban expansion that took place at record speed in the late 19th and early 20th centuries.

Roman remains at Aquincum

PREHISTORIC BEGINNINGS

The earliest evidence of human history in what is now Hungary consisted of agricultural communities around the River Tisza, where large Neolithic sites have been discovered. During the first millennium BC, Illyrian populations shared the plains with groups of Celtic peoples, known as the Eravisci. They settled by the natural springs of Buda; excavations have unearthed a Celtic site on Gellért Hill, and remains at Óbuda, an area conquered by the Romans in 35 BC.

The region entered written history when it was officially incorporated into the Roman Empire in 14 BC under the name Pannonia. Known to the Romans as Aquincum (see *p73* **Hadrian's Hall**), Buda was a modest trading town on the far edge of the empire. Today, this area is referred to as Óbuda ('Old Buda'), and is north of present-day Buda. It still contains much evidence of Roman life. (More Roman ruins can be seen by the Danube in Pest, at Március 15 tér.)

Meanwhile, political and cyclical climatic changes in Central Asia were inducing the first of a series of westward migrations in what is called either the 'Age of Barbarians' or the 'Age of Migrations'. In AD 430, the Huns, a Central Asian confederacy of Turkic-speaking nomads, burst into Europe. Under Attila, they defeated the Romans and vassals alike. Attila returned to Pannonia in 453 without sacking Rome, but died mysteriously on the night of his wedding to Princess Ildikó. Legend has it that he's buried near the River Tisza, in eastern Hungary.

The Huns then returned to their homelands. Next came the Avars, then the Bulgars, Turkic peoples from the Volga steppes. Meanwhile, the lands west of the Danube were being populated by more sedentary, agricultural Slavs, related to today's Slovenians.

WHERE DID THEY COME FROM?

The exact origin of the Hungarian people is unknown – and the subject of much debate. We know that Magyar is a branch of the Finno-Ugric language group, a sub-group of the Altaic language family of Finns, Turks, Mongolians and many Siberian peoples. The earliest Hungarian homeland was in dense forest between the Volga and the Urals.

These proto-Hungarians had moved south into the central Volga region around 500 BC. In the first centuries AD, the Hungarians came into contact with Turkic cultures pushing west but, historically speaking, the Magyars first made a name for themselves in the seventh and eighth centuries as vassals of the Turkic-speaking Khazar Empire between the Black and Caspian seas. By the 800s, the Hungarians were based in today's Ukraine and had begun raiding deep into Frankish Europe. St Cyril described the Magyars he met in 860 as *luporum more ululantes*, 'howling in the manner of wolves'. Faced with a gang from Asia pillaging the Holy Roman Empire, Western Christendom amended the Catholic mass with: 'Lord save us from sin and the Hungarians'.

While the main Magyar armies spent the spring of 895 raiding Europe, their villages were devastated by Bulgars and Pechenegs. The surviving tribes of Magyars, led by their king, Árpád, fled across the Verecke Pass in the northern Carpathians and on to the Hungarian plain. Meeting little resistance from the local Slavs, Goths and Avars, the

Hungarians pushed their competitors, the Bulgars, south of the Danube, and began raiding as far west as France, Germany and northern Spain. They continued to plunder until they were defeated by the German King Otto I at the Battle of Augsburg in 955.

Retiring to the Pannonian plain, the Hungarians realised that an alliance with a major power might be a good idea. This would mean having to deal with the Christian church.

THE BIRTH OF A NATION

Hungary was poised between the Byzantine Orthodox and Roman churches when King Géza, Árpád's grandson, requested missionaries be sent from Rome to convert the Magyars to the Western church – still trumpeted as a pivotal decision to be 'linked with the West'. Géza was baptised with his son, Vajk, who adopted the name István (Stephen) upon his accession to the Hungarian throne at Esztergom on Christmas Day in 1000.

King Stephen didn't have an easy time convincing his countrymen. Tribes loyal to the older, shamanic religion led a revolt in 1006. One consequence was the death of Venetian missionary St Gellért, put into a spiked barrel and rolled down Gellért Hill by miffed Magyar traditionalists. Stephen quickly crushed the revolt and set about destroying the power of the chieftains by appropriating their land and setting up a new class of nobles. He minted

Battle of Augsburg, 955.

coins, forged alliances, built castles and put Hungary on the road to a feudal society. He was canonised in 1083.

Stephen's son, Imre, died young, and the next 200 years saw many struggles for the throne of the House of Árpád, a preferred tactic being to blind potential rivals. Despite this, Stephen's successors consolidated and expanded the kingdom, conquering as far as Dalmatia. At home, tribal revolts were common.

The tensions between the landowning nobility and the office of the king were eventually settled by the signing of the 'Golden Bull' under King András in 1222. It recognised the nobility as the 'Hungarian Nation', granted them an exemption from taxation and laid the framework for an annual assembly of nobles, called the Diet. This was to be held in Rákos meadow in Pest; the annual gathering of the nation's high and mighty provided a push that helped Pest develop into a central market town.

In 1241, the invasion of the Mongol hordes devastated Hungary. Towns were sacked, crops burned and regions depopulated. The invaders chased King Béla IV as far south as Dalmatia, only to return east a year later in the wake of the death of the Great Khan.

Béla built a series of castles, including the one in Buda, which would gradually come to dominate the Magyar realm.

THE RISE AND FALL OF RENAISSANCE BUDA

When Béla's son, András III, died without leaving an heir, the House of Árpád came to its end. The Hungarian crown settled on the head of Charles Robert of Anjou in 1310, inaugurating 200 years of stability. Charles Robert and his son, Louis the Great, made Hungary into one of the great powers of medieval Europe, a position financed by gold and silver from mines in Slovakia and Transylvania. Their successor was Sigismund of Luxembourg, convenor of the Council of Constance and eventually the Holy Roman Emperor. The ruthless, wily, twice-married Sigismund died heirless in 1437.

Meanwhile, the threat lay to the south. The remorseless expansion of the Ottoman Empire in the Balkans was finally stemmed by János Hunyadi, the Transylvanian prince who regained control of Belgrade in 1456. Church bells rang all over Europe. Hunyadi's death then led to a bloody struggle for the Hungarian throne, until in 1458 one of his sons, Mátyás, found himself king by default at the age of 16.

With Mátyás, known to Western historians as Matthias Corvinus, Buda became the focus of Hungarian society. He undertook building within Buda Castle and constructed a palace at Visegrád. Among his achievements was the Royal Library, one of the world's largest. It is said that Mátyás roamed the countryside, disguised as a peasant, seeking out injustices in the feudal system. Even today, his name symbolises good governance. 'Mátyás is dead,' goes the saying, 'and justice died with him.' Further afield, Mátyás halted the Ottoman advance in Bosnia while expanding his empire to the north. His chief instrument of war – a highly efficient one – was the multi-ethnic Black Army of mercenaries. With his own standing army – a rarity for the time – Mátyás didn't have to depend on the nobles for recruits.

When Mátyás died heirless in 1490, his legacy of culture and order collapsed. The nobles resented him as a strong leader who could dispense with their services, and chose a weak successor. They appropriated land and taxes, sold his library and dismissed the Black Army. Hungary has never won a war since.

In 1514, the Pope ordered a crusade against the Turks. Hungary's peasantry under György Dózsa rallied near Pest and turned against the nobles. They were defeated. Dózsa was burned on a hot iron throne and his followers made to bite into his roasting flesh. The nobility voted in the Tripartum Law, reducing the peasantry to serfdom and forbidding them to bear arms. Their timing could not have been worse. When young Hungarian King Lajos II, with 10,000 armoured knights, met the Turkish cavalry on the swampy plains of Mohács on 29 August 1526, some 80,000 Ottoman *spahi* cavalrymen routed the Hungarians. Lajos drowned in a muddy stream, weighed down by heavy armour.

TURKISH AND HABSBURG RULE

The Turks continued north, sacking and burning Buda. They retreated briefly, but returned in 1541 to occupy the castle. Buda became the seat of power in Ottoman Hungary and the country was divided into three. A rump Hungary was ruled by the Habsburgs in the west and north. The Turks controlled the heartland, with Transylvania nominally independent as a principality largely under Turkish control. Buda developed into a provincial Ottoman town. Matthias Church was converted into a mosque, and the hot springs below it inspired the construction of Turkish baths. Pest was a village mostly populated by Magyars. Few Hungarians resided in Buda, since there were no churches there. As the Reformation made itself felt throughout the Hungarian region, anti-clericalism and the wariness of the Catholic Habsburgs among petty nobles made Hungary a rich recruiting ground for Protestant reform. The austere tenets of Calvinism found eager adherents across the Puszta.

Ottoman defeat at the Siege of Vienna in 1683 saw the beginning of the end of their threat to Christian Europe. In 1686, the Habsburgs attacked the Ottoman stronghold at Buda Castle and took the city after a brutal six-week siege. Buda was reduced to rubble, while Pest was depopulated. After a further decade of war, the Turks lost their Hungarian

Statue of King Árpád in Heroes' Square.
See p193.

Battle of Mohács, 1526.

began to look to Vienna as the centre of power. Meanwhile, the peasants were still impoverished serfs using medieval tools, and Hungary was still an agricultural backwater feeding an ever more industrialised Austria.

In Buda, a Baroque city of German-speaking officialdom emerged from the Ottoman occupation. Pest developed into a commercial centre for the grain and livestock produced on the Hungarian plains and shipped along the Danube. As immigrants arrived from other Habsburg domains, Jews began moving in from Bohemia and Galicia, settling in Pest, just beyond the dismantled city walls in what is today District VII. This neighbourhood became the centre of Hungarian Jewry, and is still the most complete Jewish quarter remaining in Eastern Europe.

'As the 19th century dawned, Hungarians eagerly embraced their own tongue as a revolutionary and literary language.'

realm, confirmed at the Peace of Karlowitz in 1699. This marked the end of the Ottomans in Hungary – and the rise of the Habsburgs.

Life under the Habsburgs was harsh. They suspended the constitution and put Hungary under military occupation. Severe Counter-Reformation measures included the sale of Protestant pastors as galley slaves in Naples.

In 1703, the Hungarians rebelled, led by the Transylvanian magnate Ferenc Rákóczi II. His rag-tag army kept up the fight for eight years before being overwhelmed by Habsburg might. Rákóczi died in Turkish exile. To prevent further rebellion, the Austrians blew up every castle in the country and ordered that the walls of each fortified town and church be dismantled. The Szatmár Accord of 1711 saw Hungary recognise Habsburg rule; the Habsburgs in turn recognised Hungary's constitution and feudal Diet. The privileges of the landed gentry, who ran the administration by elected committee, would remain in place until after World War I.

As peace took hold and reconstruction got under way, Buda and Pest began to acquire a Central European character. The reign of Maria Theresa (1740-80) marked the integration of Austria and Hungary. Hungary's nobility

THE AGE OF REFORM

Repercussions of the French Revolution were felt all across Europe, even in Hungary. A conspiracy of Hungarian Jacobins was nipped in the bud, and its leaders were executed near Déli station on land still known as the 'Field of Blood' (Vérmező).

Their ideas gained an audience through the Hungarian-language writings of Ferenc Kazinczy. As the 19th century dawned, Hungarians eagerly embraced their own tongue as a revolutionary and literary language, even if it was only spoken by peasants and by nobles in the Calvinist east. The Hungarian language now began to unite people as 'Hungarian' and not 'Habsburg'.

This period is known as the Age of Reform. Buda and Pest perked up under the Embellishment Act, an 1808 law that helped develop the city according to modern ideas. After the floods in 1838, Pest was redesigned along a pattern of concentric-ringed boulevards. The key figure was Count István Széchenyi, who sought to bring Hungary out of its semi-feudal state and into the world of industrialisation, credit finance and middle-class gentility. While he championed the ideal of development within the Habsburg Empire, other members of the Diet were not convinced. Lajos Kossuth, a minor noble of Slovak origin, was the eloquent voice of nationalist sentiment against Austrian rule. His popular appeal to the powerful middle gentry saw Széchenyi overshadowed.

Pressure on Habsburg affairs elsewhere led to a lessening of repression in 1839, and a reform-oriented Diet was convened, led by Ferenc Deák. Kossuth lambasted the Austrians. The debate grew until civil uprisings spread across Europe in 1848. On 3 March, Kossuth delivered a parliamentary speech demanding a Hungarian Ministry and an end to tax privileges for land-owning nobles.

On 15 March, Kossuth met with the cream of Hungarian dissident liberals in the Pilvax coffeehouse to develop a revolutionary strategy. Among the rebels was the poet Sándor Petőfi who, later that day, famously read his newly penned poem 'Nemzeti dal' ('National Song') on the steps of the National Museum – an event still commemorated every 15 March on Revolution Day.

A proposal for a liberalised constitution, giving Hungary far-reaching autonomy, was dispatched to Vienna that day and consented to by the frightened imperial government. On 7 April, the Emperor sanctioned a Hungarian Ministry headed by Count Lajos Batthyány, and including Kossuth, Széchenyi and Deák. Hungarian was made the language of state; freedoms of the press, assembly and religion were granted; noble privileges were curtailed; peasants were emancipated from serfdom.

This may have satisfied some, but Kossuth wanted a separate fiscal and army structure. The new Diet went against the emperor and voted in funding for the creation of a 200,000-man army. Kossuth's tactic was short-sighted. Hungary's minorities comprised over 50 per cent of the population, but they essentially lost all rights under the new constitution. This made it easy for Vienna to encourage a Croatian invasion of Hungary to induce a compromise, and soon the region was at war. Buda and Pest fell early to the Austrian army,

and the Hungarian government moved to Debrecen as fighting continued. By early 1849, however, Hungarian troops had the upper hand.

Emperor Franz Joseph appealed to the Tsar of Russia for help. With Russian troops, the rebellion was quickly, and brutally, crushed, and Kossuth fled to Turkey. Petőfi was killed on a battlefield in Transylvania. The Hungarian generals were executed, an event celebrated by Austrian officers clinking beer glasses – a custom that was socially taboo in Hungary until recently.

DUAL CAPITAL AND DEVELOPMENT

Following the crushing of the rebellion, Hungarian prisoners had to construct an Austrian military redoubt, the Citadella, on Gellért Hill. Its guns were intended to deter any future Hungarian attempts to dislodge Habsburg power.

The Austrians' military defeat in Italy in 1859, however, made accommodation with the Magyars a political necessity. In Pest, the remnants of the Liberal Party coalesced around Ferenc Deák, who published a basis for reconciliation with the Austrians in 1865. The Ausgleich, or Compromise, of 1867 made Hungary more like an equal partner in the Habsburg Empire. Austria-Hungary was to be a single entity with two governments and two parliaments, although ruled by Habsburg royalty, who would recognise the legitimacy of the crown of St Stephen. For the first time since 1526, Hungarians were again rulers of modern-day Slovakia, Transylvania, northern Serbia and northern Croatia as far as the Adriatic.

The year 1867 also saw a law guaranteeing civic and legal equality to Jews, whose status was unique in the region. Many arrived from Poland and Russia, their know-how driving industry and construction. This half-century until World War I is known as the Golden Age. Buda, Óbuda and Pest were officially united as Budapest in 1873. Pest boomed with urban development projects, the boulevards of Andrássy út and the Nagykörút linking once separate districts. Pest became the hub of a rail system bringing many in from the country. Even today, Hungarians refer to Budapest simply as 'Pest'.

Landowners deserted the countryside to man the vast bureaucracy needed to administer the state-run railway, schools, hospitals and postal service. The city's population rose from 280,000 in 1867 to almost a million in 1914; by 1900, Budapest was the sixth largest city in Europe. The language of administration was Hungarian. The boom came with the Magyarisation policies of Prime Minister Kálmán Tisza (1875-90). He feared the Austrians could endanger Hungary's newly strengthened position by finding leverage among the non-Hungarian minorities of the empire, just as in 1848. His response was a programme to assimilate the assorted Croats, Slovaks and Romanians of the Hungarian realm. He declared that all schools would have to teach in Hungarian, and attempts were made to make Magyar the language of the churches. The policy laid the groundwork for the minority unrest that would cost Hungary dear in 1918 and still festers among Hungary's neighbours. Hungarian became the linguistic ticket to success in Budapest. A lively cultural life began to flourish, as artists, writers and politicians exchanged ideas.

THE GOLDEN AGE

Emperor Franz Josef, on the 25th anniversary of the 1867 agreement, decreed Budapest was to be a capital equal to that of Vienna. The city became the focus of a new sense of national pride and, to mark the millennial anniversary of Árpád's invasion, a huge fair was planned. The celebration in City Park (Városliget) incorporated continental Europe's first underground railway, which ran to a gargantuan memorial to Árpád and his chieftains: Heroes' Square (Hősök tere). An exhibition hall was built and today houses the Agriculture Museum. Nearby, at the Wampetics Gardens, famous chef Károly Gundel prepared traditional cuisine with French flair. Hungarian food was the culinary fad of the new century.

It was also the golden age of Hungarian literature and arts. Mór Jókai was one of the most widely translated novelists in the world. Endre Ady's volume of new poetry, *Új versek*, sparked a veritable literary explosion. Béla Bartók and Zoltán Kodály created the study of ethnomusicology, composing masterpieces of modern music based on Magyar folk traditions, while architects such as Ödön Lechner drew on Magyar motifs for the art nouveau buildings sprouting up around the city. Budapest was also at the forefront of cinema and photography, and became the destination of choice for the holiday-making aristocracy of Europe.

The new Parliament building, opened in 1902, was the largest in the world, naively anticipating a long and prosperous rule. Politics, however, began to take an ominous

IN CONTEXT

Centrál Kávéház, circa 1910.

turn. Working-class unrest first asserted itself in the great May Day demonstration of 1890, and its influence grew over the next decade. Ageing Liberals were challenged by newer right-wing elements, who introduced Austrian-influenced anti-Semitism – previously alien to Hungarian life – into political dialogue. Meanwhile, Hungary's high-handed administration of non-Magyars fuelled resentment and nationalism. Slavs and Romanians headed in droves for Paris or America, where their modest political voice could be heard. To the south, the idea of a South Slav ('Yugoslav') nation gained credence. The edifice of the revived Hungarian kingdom rested on rotten foundations.

After the assassination of Archduke Franz Ferdinand in Sarajevo, Austria-Hungary gave Serbia the ultimatum that would make World War I inevitable. Budapest, initially opposed to the ultimatum, changed tack when Germany supported Austria-Hungary. While no fighting took place on its soil, Hungary suffered enormously. Rampant inflation, food shortages and high casualties among the 3.5 million soldiers sent to fight brought the nation to its knees. Worse was to follow.

THE SILVER AGE

As World War I came to an end, so did the Austro-Hungarian Empire. When Hungary declared its independence as a republic on 16 November 1918, the country was faced with unsympathetic neighbours aligned with France. No clear lines existed at the border, policed by Serbian and Romanian troops from the 'Little Entente' masterminded by Czech foreign minister Edvard Benes and supported by France.

At the post-war negotiations outside Paris, Hungarian diplomatic efforts fell on deaf ears. Hungary's poor treatment of minorities was a perfectly good argument for ethnic self-determination, the guiding principle behind the redrawing of Europe.

On 21 March 1919, a Hungarian Soviet Republic was declared by Béla Kun, who formed a Red Army and sent emissaries to the new Soviet Union. Moscow did nothing in response. Czech and Romanian forces entered a Hungary in chaos. As severe food shortages swept the nation, the Romanian army occupied Budapest on 3 August 1919. Kun and his ministers fled, most never to return.

Admiral Miklós Horthy entered Budapest at the head of 25,000 Hungarian troops. The weeks that followed were known as the 'White Terror', as Communists and Jews were killed for their collaboration, real or otherwise, with the Kun regime. On 25 January 1920, Hungarian national elections brought in a Christian-right coalition parliament, with Admiral Horthy as regent. Hungary was now a monarchy without a king, led by an admiral without a navy. On 4 June 1920, the Treaty of Trianon was signed at Versailles. Hungary lost 72 per cent of its territory and a third of its native population. Refugees clogged Budapest, unemployment raged and the economy came to a virtual standstill. (See p195 **The Shape of Things to Come**.)

A new political coalition came to power under Count Gábor Bethlen, a skilful conservative. He kept left and right in check and worked abroad to gain international credit and sympathy. Budapest continued to be the focus of national development. Financial stability returned, although after the crash of 1929, labour discontent rose, Bethlen resigned and Horthy appointed right-wing Gyula Gömbös as prime minister. His anti-Semitic appeals became more and more the accepted political tone.

Budapest between the wars was not quite as dark as its politics. During this so-called Silver Age, Hungary's spas and casinos became the playground of high society. The coffeehouses still provided the base for an active literary clique. Avant-gardists grouped around Lajos Kassák and his Bauhaus-influenced journal *Ma* ('Today'), while the theatre and cinema boomed. Hollywood moguls swarmed into Budapest to sign up actors, directors and cinematographers.

But society was coming apart. The Jews were the first to feel the change, when access to higher education and certain professions was curtailed under the Numerus Clausus law in 1928. Gömbös dreamed of a fascist Hungarian-Italian-German 'axis' (his term), and worked to bring Hungary closer to Nazi Germany in the hope of reversing Trianon. German investment gained influential friends and Oktogon was renamed Mussolini tér. The second Vienna Award in 1938 returned a part of Slovakia to Hungary, and in 1940 Hungary was awarded most of Transylvania. Artists and intellectuals fled to Paris and America.

THE SHAPE OF THINGS TO COME

The 1920 Treaty of Trianon still casts a shadow over Hungary.

Spend any time in Budapest and you'll soon notice an omnipresent shape on car-bumper stickers, mounted on bar walls and sold on postcards. This, nearly 100 years after the fact, is the outline of Hungary as it looked before 4 June 1920. On that day, in Versailles outside Paris, the Treaty of Trianon set in ink the borders of the new Hungarian Republic after the collapse of the Austro-Hungarian Empire. Hungarians to this day feel that they were singled out for the most punitive treatment.

As World War I ended, the victors (France, the USA and the UK) set up treaty commissions to deal with the peace settlements. Hungary was widely believed to have been one the root causes of the war. Since 1867, Hungary had controlled much of the Carpathian Basin with a repressive policy of forced Magyar education and bureaucracy that caused deep resentment among ethnic groups. Point ten of President Wilson's programme called for autonomy for the peoples of Austro-Hungary, but not for its dismemberment as a political entity. Even so, Czechoslovakia declared its independence on 26 October 1918; the South Slavs, Yugoslavia, quickly followed.

When Hungary declared its independence as a republic on 16 November 1918, no clear demarcation existed at the borders, defined by the ceasefire lines. Troops of the 'Little Entente' supported by France – Serbs, Czechs and Romanians – camped at frontier towns.

In Paris, the peacemakers were resolved to uphold promises made to bring Romania into the war. The French were intent on taking strategic rail lines out of Hungarian hands. The Magyar towns of Szatmár (Satu Mare), Nagyvárad (Oradea) and Temesvár (Timisoara) were all on a major line. The charming British-born Queen Marie of Romania also lobbied for the Romanian cause. The Treaty Commission soon assigned Romania land in the Banat, Bukovina, Bessarabia and Transylvania.

Under the new administration of Prime Minister Mihály Károlyi, Hungarians refused to accept that the dissolution of the Austro-Hungarian Empire should affect the historical notion that the nation of Hungary comprised the Carpathian Basin. When the Allies showed their resolve to give two-thirds of Hungary's territory to neighbouring states, Károlyi resigned and the Communists took over in Budapest.

After their short, disastrous rule, and the subsequent takeover of the government by Admiral Miklós Horthy, Hungary was invited to Versailles on 1 December 1919. It sent a delegation in January 1920 after elections confirming Horthy as regent. It was already too late: the de facto borders had been all but set.

As the head of the Hungarian delegation, Count Albert Apponyi was reduced to a single address to the Allies at Quay d'Orsay on 16 January – after he had been handed the dictates of the peace treaty. French leader Clemenceau, UK Prime Minister Lloyd George and other victors listened patiently to the speech (in French, English and Italian), a rhetorical masterpiece. It argued in favour of keeping the Kingdom of Hungary intact and warned against delegating powers of nation-building to 'culturally inferior' peoples such as Slovaks and Romanians.

The leaders were not impressed. Apponyi continued negotiations but his efforts, including his key demand to hold referenda in the ethnically mixed territories, proved futile. US President Woodrow Wilson argued in vain for a fairer decision. The Hungarian delegates walked out on 4 June, having failed to turn the tide. The treaty was signed on behalf of Hungary that day by Labour Minister Ágost Bénárd and envoy Alfréd Drasche-Lázár. These are the borders still in place today.

IN CONTEXT

IN CONTEXT

LIFE DURING WARTIME

When war began, all was not rosy between the Hungarians and the Germans. Gömbös had died and the new prime minister, Count Pál Teleki, who mistrusted the Nazis, worked to keep Hungary out of combat. When Hungary invaded Yugoslavia with the Germans in 1941, Teleki, an Anglophile of the old school, committed suicide.

Hungary's participation on the Russian front was disastrous. The Russians wiped out the entire Hungarian Second Army in January 1943, effectively ending Hungary's involvement in the war. German troops entered Hungary in March 1944. Officials resisted German demands for more Jewish deportations, but that became harder when Adolf Eichmann moved his SS headquarters to Buda. Jews were herded into the Ghetto in District VII, while the nearby Astoria Hotel served as Nazi headquarters.

In October 1944, Admiral Horthy made a speech calling for an armistice. The SS responded by kidnapping his son. After Horthy had been ousted, German troops occupied Buda Castle. Nazi puppet Ferenc Szálasi and his fascist Arrow Cross Party took control of Hungary. Extra trains were put on to take Budapest's Jews to Auschwitz. Arrow Cross thugs raided the ghettos, marched Jews to the Danube and shot them. Many survivors owed their lives to Raoul Wallenberg, a Swedish diplomat posted in Budapest. He had safe houses set up and issued fake Swedish passports. He negotiated with German officers and pulled Jews off trains bound for Auschwitz. When the Soviets surrounded Pest, Wallenberg drove to meet them. He was never seen again. Moscow claimed he died in 1947, but Gulag survivors reported seeing him in the 1970s. Two memorials stand to him in Budapest.

The Russians closed in on Budapest. Allied bombing levelled industrial Angyalföld and Zugló in Pest. The Germans made a stand in November 1944. Citizens were caught in an artillery battle that lasted months, killing more civilians than combatants. The Russians advanced in bloody door-to-door fighting – bullet holes can still be seen on some Pest buildings. By the time the Russians took control of Pest – raping as they went – the Nazis had entrenched themselves around Castle Hill. While Russian tanks could control Pest's boulevards, fighting in Buda's twisting streets was hellish. When the Germans finally surrendered on 4 April 1945, and citizens emerged from their cellars, Buda Castle was in ruins, and not one bridge was left standing over the Danube. Budapest was a scene of utter devastation.

STALIN AND RÁKOSI

Rebuilding the capital would occupy its citizens for 30 years. The task of restoring order fell to the Soviet military government, which placed loyal Hungarian Communists in all positions of power. Nevertheless, the election of November 1945 was won by the Smallholders, the only legitimate pre-war political party still in existence. Even with blatant vote-rigging, the Communists only garnered 17 per cent, but Soviets insisted they remain in power. The monarchy was abolished and a Hungarian Republic was proclaimed. The Paris Peace Treaty was signed in 1947, compounding the loss of land under Trianon by granting a slice of eastern Hungary to the USSR. Communist authorities controlling the Interior Ministry set up a secret police force, the ÁVH (later ÁVO), run by László Rajk, to root out dissent. Many people were picked up off the streets, sent to the Soviet Union and never heard from again.

Changes in the social fabric of Budapest were also part of post-war city planning. Budapest neighbourhoods lost some of their social identity as the Communists tried to homogenise areas in the pursuit of a classless society. Flats went to whoever the local council chose. Schools and factories were nationalised. A plan was put forward to collectivise landholdings, neutralising the Smallholders Party. The Communist hold on Hungary was complete.

In 1949, the scales of power tipped in favour of Moscow loyalists, led by Mátyás Rákosi. Old-time party members – among them László Rajk – were tried as spies and executed. Rákosi fostered a cult of personality. By the early 1950s, Hungary was one of the dimmest lights along the Iron Curtain. Informers were everywhere, classic Hungarian books were banned, church leaders imprisoned and middle-class families persecuted as class enemies.

A brief respite came with Stalin's death in 1953. Rákosi was removed from office and replaced with Imre Nagy, a more humane

Communist with a sense of sympathy for Hungarian national ideals. It didn't last long. Rákosi, backed by Moscow, accused Nagy of 'deviationism' and came back into power in 1955.

NEW DAWN FADES

In June 1956, intellectuals began to criticise the Rákosi regime, using the forum of the Petőfi Writers' Circle for unprecedented free debate. The Kremlin, now led by Khrushchev, recalled Rákosi to Moscow 'for health reasons', but replaced him with the equally despicable Ernő Gerő. The breaking point came in October.

The Uprising that erupted on Tuesday 23 October had been brewing but wasn't planned. Students had gathered at Petőfi tér and at the statue of the 1848 Polish General Bem to express solidarity with reforms in Poland and to demand change in Hungary. Thousands of workers joined in. An angry crowd pulled down a statue of Stalin near the City Park. Others gathered at the radio building on Bródy Sándor utca to broadcast their demands. The ÁVH began shooting from the roof. Police and soldiers then attacked the ÁVH, and fighting broke out. The Uprising had begun.

In response, Imre Nagy was reinstated as prime minister. Addressing a crowd of 200,000 outside Parliament, he gave a cautious speech that didn't curtail the rising tide. Fighting continued, political prisoners were freed and General Maléter pledged army loyalty to the new government. Confusion reigned. Nagy declined Soviet help and called the Uprising 'democratic'. Soviet troops pulled out of Hungary.

For the next five days Hungary floated in the euphoria of liberation. Daily life assumed a kind of normality and Radio Free Europe promised Western aid.

With the distraction of the Suez Crisis, Moscow retaliated. On 1 November, Soviet forces entered Hungary. General Maléter was arrested, sidelining the army, and Soviet tanks re-entered Budapest. Civilians defended gallantly at the Kilián barracks at Üllői út and the Corvin Passage nearby. In Buda, students spread oil on the cobbled streets and pulled grenades on strings underneath the stalled tanks. Resistance proved futile. Nagy took refuge in the Yugoslav Embassy, but was later handed over to the Soviets. Thousands were

sent to prison and 200,000 fled Hungary. Nagy was executed in secret in 1958 and buried in a hidden grave at Plot 301 of Új köztemető Cemetery.

MARKET SOCIALISM

The stranglehold that followed the suppression of the 1956 Uprising lasted until the 1960s, when amnesties were granted and János Kádár, the new man installed by the Soviet Union, began a policy of reconciliation. His was a tricky balancing act between hard-line Communism and appeasing the population. Abroad, Hungary maintained a strong Cold War stance and toed the Moscow line; at home, Hungarians enjoyed a higher standard of living than most of Soviet Eastern Europe. Life under Kádár meant food in the shops but censorship and 'psychological hospital' for dissenters.

By the 1960s, the aftermath of World War II and 1956 had been cleared away. Historic buildings were restored, museums replaced ministerial buildings in Buda. Tourism began to grow, although Western visitors were still followed by government spies after dinner.

Kádár's balancing act reached giddy heights in 1968. When Czechoslovakia irked the Soviets with the reforms of the Prague Spring, Hungarian troops loyally participated in the invasion. At the same time, Kádár introduced his 'New Economic Mechanism', a radical reform that broke with previous hard-line communist theory and laid the ground for modest entrepreneurship.

By the 1980s, flaws in 'Goulash Communism' grew harder to ignore. Hungary became more dependent on foreign trade and inflation rose. Hungary's relationship with its Warsaw Pact neighbours was beginning to show signs of strain. A number of writers started to test the limits of open criticism, and Hungary became the centre of Eastern Europe's boom in banned samizdat literature. Younger party members began to take positions of power. Known as the 'Miskolc Mafia', after the town where they'd begun their political careers, many, such as Prime Minister Károly Grósz and his successor Miklós Németh, openly tolerated debate and 'market socialism'.

CHANGE OF SYSTEM

With the opening of the border with Austria, Hungary tipped over the first domino, bringing about the collapse of Communism in Eastern Europe. The Communist Party changed its name to the Hungarian Socialist Party and declared that it was running in the elections. All talk was focused on new-found freedoms, democracy and market capitalism. Many were quick to position themselves in the emerging economic picture. Others found themselves confused by yet another upheaval in history. The elections of March 1990 brought in a coalition led by the Hungarian Democratic Forum (MDF), a mix of nationalist and conservative views. The 'change of system' (*rendszerváltás*) saw the face of Budapest alter as new businesses opened and the city's classy old neon disappeared. Street names were changed; Lenin Boulevard and Marx Square were no longer, and their respective statues and monuments were removed out to Statue, now Memento, Park (see *p56*). A law forbade the public display of 'symbols of tyranny', such as red stars or swastikas.

Many found opportunities working in Western businesses. But the boom didn't materialise. Unemployment rose as state industries were privatised or shut down; inflation ruined savings and incomes; and people were made homeless. For many, the standard of living dropped below pre-1989 levels, when prices had been fixed and services subsidised by the state.

EU ACCESSION AND POLARISATION
Nostalgia for more stable and affordable times helped the 1994 election triumph of the Socialist Party, led by Gyula Horn, the man who, as Communist foreign minister, had opened the borders in 1989. The Socialists, along with their coalition partners the Free Democrats, prescribed belt-tightening: more privatisation and devaluations. They slashed social funding and hiked energy prices to set Hungary up for EU membership.

Foreign investors loved it, and the revived Budapest stock exchange enjoyed two years as the world's fastest-growing stock market. As the currency and the banks were stabilised, many companies made Budapest their regional centre. Shiny office blocks and business centres, rendered less intrusive by height restrictions, settled among their crusty brick-and-plaster elders. New malls saw off the corner shop.

Hungarians, particularly those in the countryside, baulked. In 1998, the country's voters turned to a third party, the Young Democrats (Fidesz), founded and led by the charismatic Viktor Orbán. Born out of a late-1980s student activist group, this party initially adopted a liberal stance, then swung right as the Democratic Forum party splintered. Orbán began promoting pre-war Christian-national values, taking the crown of St Stephen out of the National Museum, floating it up the Danube for a consecration ceremony in Esztergom Cathedral, then installing it in Parliament.

Fidesz reordered the political landscape in a starkly polarised manner, bringing a new level of bitterness to debate ahead of the 2002 elections. The divisive strategy backfired, and voters reinstated the Socialists, under the leadership of Prime Minister Péter Medgyessy, a former banker and finance minister in the old regime. He was in charge when Hungary joined the European Union on 1 May 2004, a change that brought some stability to Hungary's economic affairs. However, it could not stabilise Hungarian politics. After the revelation that he had worked as a counter-espionage agent for the Communist-era Ministry for Internal Affairs, Medgyessy was replaced by Ferenc Gyurcsány, a former Young Communist turned billionaire. Socialists hoped that one of the richest people in Hungary would have the appeal needed to win the 2006 elections.

Fidesz suffered a setback in December 2004 when the public did not support its referendum to give citizenship to people with Hungarian ancestry who were born beyond Hungary's borders. Despite Fidesz gaining a slim majority in the first round of the 2006 elections, the Socialists surprised everyone by narrowly winning the second. They entered into a coalition with the liberal Alliance of Free Democrats (SZDSZ) and proceeded to plan public-sector and welfare reform along Blairite lines. Faced with grave foreign-debt and trade-deficit levels, and a deeply polarised electorate, the government's hand was tied by EU and IMF demands for frugality.

EXIT GYURCSÁNY, ENTER ORBÁNISTAN
The salami really hit the fan in September 2006, when a private speech given in May by Gyurcsány to party members was leaked to the

Viktor Orbán votes in the 2014 national election.

press. In his frank talk, Gyurcsány admitted that the party had 'lied morning, noon and night' about policy in order to win a second term. Peaceful demonstrations became ugly almost overnight, resulting in riots in Budapest and elsewhere. Demonstrators called for Gyurcsány's resignation and a fresh round of national elections.

The Socialists got a sound beating at the October municipal elections, but Gyurcsány won a parliamentary vote of confidence on 6 October. Downtown was cleared for the 50th anniversary commemorations of the 1956 Uprising on 23 October, but not before protestors had managed to commandeer a tank and chug off around Deák tér until they ran out of petrol. Orbán, who had not endorsed the riots, led Fidesz supporters in a series of mass rallies and candlelit vigils on 4 November, the anniversary of the invasion of the Soviet troops. Order was restored but tensions did not dissipate. Gyurcsány's government set in motion plans to introduce university tuition fees and selected health service charges.

With the severe economic downturn of 2008, the forint lost ten per cent of its value and the government agreed a rescue package with the IMF and EU. Across-the-board discontent saw the rise of the extreme right-wing Jobbik party, which shocked many observers by taking three seats at the 2009 European elections. The time was right for Fidesz to storm the national elections of April

2010, gaining the two-thirds majority needed to modify major laws and the national constitution. Quickly taking control of former independent institutions, Orbán's Fidesz government set up a new media council to impose draconian fines on print, online and broadcast media for vague 'transgressions'. Many national newspapers printed a blank front page in protest and Hungary came under fire in many international forums.

With the local elections later that year, Fidesz gained control of 22 of Hungary's 23 cities and towns, including Budapest. After more than a decade of liberal leadership, Hungary's capital now had its first right-wing mayor, István Tarlós. While Fidesz promised to bring down the budget deficit, many households and family businesses felt the pinch as their debts spiralled against the strong Swiss franc.

Hungarians left the country in droves, mainly for the UK, where 70,000 were based in 2013 – according to official records. Thousands more live there unofficially. With the new electoral laws granting the vote to ethnic Hungarians in Slovakia and Romania, and with a weak, divided opposition, Fidesz walked the national election of April 2014.

With a clear two-thirds majority gained from less than 45 per cent of the vote, and the forint dropping rapidly against the euro and the Swiss franc, in October 2014 Orbán set to introduce the world's first tax on the internet. In days, a popular movement against it garnered nearly a quarter of a million likes on Facebook and encouraged up to 100,000 to march in the biggest of a series of demonstrations in Budapest.

Orbán was forced to pull back, though more protests broke out in January 2015 with a redrawing of motorway toll zones. In February, a by-election in Veszprém was won by a leftist-supported independent. Now without its super majority, the government can no longer make unchallenged changes to the constitution or pass major legislation. It was a serious blow to the increasingly embattled ruling party: reeling from corruption scandals, flat-lining in the polls, and with Orbán's open courting of Vladimir Putin generating opprobrium from Hungary's allies in the EU and NATO, further flashpoints seem a certainty in Strasbourg, in Parliament, and on the streets of Budapest.

IN CONTEXT

Baths & Spas

Budapest's best-loved attractions.

TEXT: PETERJON CRESSWELL & MATTHEW HIGGINSON

Budapest's healing waters are its most lucrative resource and reason alone to visit. Over the course of nearly 2,000 years, the Romans, Turks and Habsburgs all enjoyed the benefits of the 120 thermal springs gushing from Buda's limestone bedrock. These days, two dozen baths are in daily public use around this hub of healthy waters. While canny private investors try to reinvent the capital as an upmarket thermal bathing destination, its clutch of historic state-run baths has also been given a serious upgrade in the last decade.

Of these, the most sparkling is the Széchenyi Baths – ornate, luxurious and one of Budapest's busiest tourist attractions. But almost every year, another site is significantly modernised or added to the city's watery attractions. The most recent, Veli Bej, with historic links to its Turkish past, opened in 2014, while the Rudas Baths has recently acquired a rooftop pool and sun terrace. And from 2015, the Dagály, the Paskál and the Palatinus spearhead a Ft15-billion, five-year development that will also affect the Gellért and Király Baths.

IN CONTEXT

OTTOMAN HERITAGE

The pull of the mineral-rich waters is one of the reasons a settlement developed here in the first place. Evidence suggests that Neolithic peoples were drawn to Buda's warm springs; later, the Romans brought in bathing customs. The Magyars continued the tradition from the ninth century, but it was under the Ottomans in the 16th and 17th centuries that bathing in Buda reached its zenith.

The demands of Islam that its followers adhere to strict rules for ablutions before praying five times a day inspired an aquatic culture that still thrives. The Ottoman mosques, along with the monasteries and schools that once filled the streets of Buda, are long gone. But centuries later it's still possible to bathe under an original Ottoman dome in the **Király Baths** or **Rudas Baths** – which, alongside the Tomb of Gül Baba, are the only significant architectural remains from the period. Unlike most evidence of the Ottoman occupation, the Hungarians didn't build over the Turkish baths – they built around them.

With so much history involved, it's no wonder that Budapest's bathers held their collective breath when extensive renovations started on both the Rudas and the **Rácz Baths**, the most ambitious of the projects. The revamp of the Rudas is now finished, but the potentially fabulous Rácz, although it's been faithfully reconstructed around the original Ottoman and Habsburg baths complex as part of a five-star hotel, is mired in red tape and has yet to reopen.

The Rácz was the most modest of the 16th-century Ottoman spas, hence their Turkish name, *Küçül ilica*, 'small baths'. As the archaeological team attached to the nearby Budapest History Museum discovered during its long dig, the Turks were not the first here. They found evidence – 130 pieces of ceramic, including a whole dish – of Celtic activity from the first century BC. The Romans, whose camp further north was named Aquincum after the Celtic *ak-ink* ('much water'), did not settle this far. There was a stream here, and recorded bathing of sorts, but no evidence of any medieval spa.

Nearby, at today's **Lukács Baths**, Magyars arriving in the late ninth century set up a 'sick house' around a thermal spring. After the Ottomans were chased out in 1686, the Hungarians came to enjoy the facilities so

Rudas Baths.

expertly put in place. Being Christian, they didn't follow Islamic washing rituals with connecting halls – they simply built as many bathing rooms on the one site as possible.

WATCHES, LOCKERS AND KIDS

If your knowledge of Hungarian is limited, entering a bathhouse can be baffling. Long menus offer ultrasound and pedicures, as well as various massages. In addition, there is a confusing electronic entry system, activated by the plastic watch that you will receive upon paying the admission fee. To enter, press the watch face against the scanner on the turnstile. Then choose any free locker. Once you've changed, press the watch face against the little knob on the locker door, so that it clicks in. For the duration of your stay, only you can now unclick the knob – make a mental note of your locker number. Cabins are also available: larger and private, but more expensive, they're ideal for couples.

Valuables should be left at the entrance, where they're kept in a locked drawer along with your ID – though it may be wise to bring only what you need for the visit. Flip-flops are handy; in winter, when snow falls over outdoor Széchenyi, bring a dressing gown too. A cap is usually required to use the swimming lanes.

Most of the baths are now mixed, with similar changing and bathing routines. Each site usually has one or two main pools, plus a series of smaller ones around the perimeter, of temperatures ranging from dauntingly hot to icy cold. The precise drill depends on preference, but involves moving between different pools, as well as taking in the dry heat of the sauna and the extreme humidity of the steam rooms, alternating temperatures and finally relaxing in gentle warm water.

A couple of hours' bathing is usually sufficient; it's extremely relaxing and good for relieving aches and pains. Then you shower (bring your own soap and a towel). Most baths have a resting room, so that you can take a short nap before changing back into your street clothes. Most also have bars – you can enjoy a beer between soaks and swims.

Most sites offer massages: *vízi* (water) and *orvosi* (medical), the latter more gentle. Pay for the massage when you get your entrance ticket. The attendant will give you a small metal token with a number on it. Upon entering the baths area, go to the massage room and give your token to a masseur with a tip of Ft100 or so. Also let him know you don't speak Hungarian (otherwise he'll just call out your number when it's your turn and get angry when you don't run over); keep an eye out and he'll wave for you when your time has come.

Don't expect to have the energy to do very much after a visit, except settle down for a long lunch and/or stretch out for a doze. Do remember to drink lots of water to rehydrate. Drinking-water fountains are provided inside most baths too.

Apart from the baths listed here, there are thermal facilities at many high-end hotels – the **Corinthia Grand Hotel Royal** (see p221) is recommended. Day spas include the **Isis** (VIII. Üllői út 14, 266 7788, www.isisdayspa.hu) and the **Mandala** (XIII.Ipoly utca 8, 491 0078, www.mandaladayspa.hu). Finally, some baths, particularly the Széchenyi, double up as lidos (aka beach; *strand* in Hungarian) in summer.

Note that spa baths such as the Széchenyi don't offer discounts for children (and the Király doesn't even permit under-14s). Those classed as lidos do. So, at the most popular lido, the **Palatinus** (www.palatinusstrand.hu) on Margaret Island, children's admission at weekends is two-thirds of the adult price. Lidos generally operate summer only.

For more information on the city-run spa network, visit www.spasbudapest.com.

Veli Bej. See p205.

WATERY DELIGHTS

The main baths for health and relaxation.

Gellért Baths

Gellért Gyógyfürdő és Uszoda
XI.Kelenhegyi út 4 (466 6166, www.gellert furdo.hu). M4 Gellért tér, or tram 18, 19, 47, 49. **Open** 6am-8pm daily. **Admission** *Locker* Ft4,900 Mon-Fri; Ft5,100 Sat, Sun. *Cabin* Ft5,300 Mon-Fri; Ft5,500 Sat, Sun. **Map** p249 E7.

The most expensive of all the baths, but it does have an art nouveau pool. In summer, you get access to several outdoor pools (one with a wave machine) and sunbathing areas, plus a terrace restaurant. The separate thermal baths lead from the main pool, which also has its own small warm-water pool.

Király Baths

Király Gyógyfürdő
II.Fő utca 84 (202 3688, www.kiralyfurdo.hu). M2 Batthyány tér, or bus 86. **Open** 9am-9pm daily. **Admission** *Locker* Ft2,300 (until noon Ft1,300). *Cabin* Ft2,600 (until noon Ft1,500). **Map** p245 C3.

A significant Ottoman monument, this takes its name from the 19th-century owners, the König (King) family, who changed their name to its Hungarian equivalent: Király. Construction of the Turkish part began in 1566 and was completed by Pasha Sokoli Mustafa in 1570. Located within the Viziváros town walls, it meant the Ottoman garrison could enjoy a soak even during the siege. Three Turkish-style reliefs mark the entrance corridor. Note the significant discount for morning use.

Lukács Baths

Lukács Gyógyfürdő és Uszoda
II.Frankel Leó út 25-29 (326 1695, www. lukacsfurdo.hu). Tram 4, 6, or bus 86. **Open** 6am-10pm daily. **Admission** *Locker* Ft3,100 (after 6pm Ft2,700) Mon-Fri; Ft3,200 Sat, Sun. *Cabin* Ft3,500 (after 6pm Ft3,100) Mon-Fri; Ft3,600 Sat, Sun. **Map** p245 C1. These baths have been in use since the time of the Crusades. Few features have carried over from the Ottoman era, so the layout is different from the other Turkish places. By day, there's something of an institutional feel to the warren-like facility, not least because a main hospital for rheumatism and arthritis is next door. The wall by the entrance is lined with testimonials from satisfied customers.

A recent upgrade – renovated bath sections, mud bath and sunbathing roof – has brought in Sauna World (Ft600-Ft800), a separate area of salt, naturist and igloo saunas, plus heated roman seats. The Lukács is also the current setting for Magic Bath (9.30pm-3am Sat; admission Ft10,000 in advance, Ft12,000 on the night), the latest in the city's spa DJ parties.

Rudas Baths

Rudas Gyógyfürdő és Uszoda
I.Döbrentei tér 9 (356 1010, www.rudasfurdo. hu). Tram 18, 19, or bus 7. **Open** 6am-8pm Mon-Thur, Sun; 6am-8pm, 10pm-4am Fri, Sat. *Men only* Mon, Wed-Fri. *Women only* Tue. *Mixed* Sat, Sun. **Admission** Ft3,100 (with pool Ft3,800) Mon-Fri; Ft3,400 (with pool Ft4,100) Sat, Sun. *Night rate* Ft4,400 from 10pm Fri, Sat. **Map** p249 D7.

Gellért Baths.

Rudas Baths.

Having recently deigned to allow women bathers in for the first time in more than four centuries, the Rudas is currently the only state-run bath with separate days for men and women (except at the weekends). In autumn 2014, a new spa section opened with a 42°C/107°F thermal pool and 11°C/52°F plunge one, a panoramic rooftop sun terrace and pool, and restaurant. The Rudas also now throws open its doors (though not the new rooftop) at night on Fridays and Saturdays.

Inside, this is the most atmospheric of the original Turkish baths, especially when rays of sunlight stab through windows in the dome's roof and fan out through the steam above the central pool. The original cupola, vaulted corridor and main octagonal pool remain, and have been restored.

Széchenyi Baths

Széchenyi Gyógyfürdő és Strandfürdő XIV.Állatkérti körút 9-11 (363 3210, www. szechenyifurdo.hu). M1 Széchenyi fürdő. **Open** 6am-10pm daily. **Admission** Locker Ft4,500 Mon-Fri; Ft4,700 Sat, Sun. Cabin Ft4,700 Mon-Fri; Ft5,200 Sat, Sun. **Map** p247 J1.

Located in the City Park, this large, ornate complex of pools and thermal baths, both outdoors and in, is Budapest's most popular spa. Although pricey, it's the best choice for a day of relaxation – guests can exercise, laze and sunbathe all on one site, which fosters an endearing holiday atmosphere encouraged by indoor and outdoor whirlpools and a terrace café. This is where you'll see those classic images of bathers playing chess while chest-deep in the water, or of steam rising as bathers take a dip outside during the icy winter.

Veli Bej

II.Árpád fejedelem útja 7 (438 8641). Bus 86. **Open** 6am-noon, 3-9pm daily. **Admission** (3hrs only) Ft2,800. **Map** p245 C1.

Budapest's newest baths was also used in Ottoman times. Modernised and attached to a hospital built in the 1960s – look for the glass-fronted building on the Margaret Bridge side of the Komjádi Béla pool – the Veli Bej operates in the mornings and from mid afternoon, allowing bathers in for three-hour periods. Fines are imposed for longer stays, but three hours should be long enough to enjoy the intimate thermal pool, saunas (including infra-red) and whirlpool. Veli Bej – not part of the city's spa network, and noticeably cheaper – also keeps visitor numbers down to 80 at any one time: something to bear in mind when you're elbowing for space at the Széchenyi. The Turkish cupola and pool lighting help make for a memorable experience. Photo p203.

Essential Information

Hotels

Visitors to Budapest are spoiled for choice when it comes to finding somewhere to stay. Thanks to the superb renovation of many of the capital's splendid fin-de-siècle buildings, Budapest now offers a healthy choice of high-end options – with spa treatments to match. Luxury landmarks such as the neoclassical Corinthia Grand Hotel Royal, the deservedly hyped Four Seasons Gresham Palace and the neo-Baroque Boscolo Budapest have brought genuine opulence to the Hungarian capital for the first time in a century. Those on a tighter budget can pick from a wide array of major mid-range and budget chains, plus hostels and short- and long-term apartment rentals. With such strong competition in all price brackets, establishments are falling over themselves to attract custom, offering airport transfers for direct booking and three-nights-for-two longer-stay deals. So it's definitely worth hunting around.

STAYING IN BUDAPEST

The new millennium was marked by a wave of impressive reconstructions and conversions of fin-de-siècle Pest landmarks into high-end hotels. It left in its wake three spectacular five-star properties in particular – one a former insurance office (**Four Seasons Gresham Palace**), one a former coffeehouse (**Boscolo Budapest**) and one a former cinema (**Corinthia Grand Hotel Royal**). But this devil-may-care approach to expenditure and architecture – the Corinthia simply added an extra floor when it found out it couldn't call itself 'Grand' otherwise – belongs to the pre-crisis days. Slated to join this trio of luxury lodgings recreated from the Habsburg era, the Rácz now stands empty and forgotten. These former baths by Elizabeth Bridge were converted into a high-end hotel, but the project has since foundered. We may have seen the last of the spectacularly reconfigured five-star in Budapest for a while. On the plus side, the choice at mid-range and budget level has expanded beyond all recognition. Walk around Pest and it's almost as if every other building is some kind of guesthouse, hostel or B&B.

Budapest is compact enough that its sights and attractions are within a few transport stops of any city hotel. Location is only really important if you insist on a Danube view, or you're here for a relentless bar crawl (choose Pest) or quiet relaxation (choose Buda).

Information and prices

High season runs from late spring to early autumn, with rates set accordingly. The Grand Prix in late July and the Sziget music festival in early August tend to do terrible things to rates and availability, and in recent years New Year's Eve has seen many of the city's hotels full up.

In winter, occupancy levels in Budapest hit rock bottom, hence the many offers by local hotels to encourage you to book directly on their website, with airport transfers and three-for-two deals. Smoking rooms are now rarer, while international TV stations, Wi-Fi and air-conditioning are now standard. English-speaking service is another given.

Prices are usually quoted in forints, euros or dollars. Price ranges below have been worked out in euros, though rates fluctuate considerably according to season and demand. In January, with a bit of shopping around online, you could possibly snag a room in a five-star for less than €100. The four average price categories for a double room in the hotels listed below are:

Deluxe – above €200
Expensive – €150-€200
Moderate – €100-€150
Budget – below €100

DANUBE & BRIDGES

Expensive

Danubius Health Spa Resort Margitsziget

XIII. Margitsziget (889 4700, www.danubius hotels.hu). M3 Nyugati pu or tram 4, 6, then bus 26. **Rooms** 267.

At the northern tip of Margaret Island and fed by three of its thermal springs, this is more modern than the nearby Grand thanks to its high-quality medical and spa services. The Danubius offers curative reflexology as well as hydromassage, electrotherapy, mud body wraps and rheumatic treatments, alongside 267 rooms, all with a balcony. There are all kinds of leisure activities close by, including tennis, rowing and cycling.
► *Under the same umbrella and on the same island, the Danubius Grand Hotel Margitsziget (889 4700) recalls a more elegant era.*

CASTLE DISTRICT

Deluxe

Hilton Budapest Hotel

I. Hess András tér 1-3 (889 6600, www.hilton.com). Várbusz from M2 Széll Kálmán tér, or bus 16. **Rooms** 331. **Map** p245 B4.

With spectacular views over the Danube and the old quarter, the Hilton is located in the heart of the Castle District. One of Budapest's first high-end hotels, it's designed around a 17th-century façade (once part of a Jesuit cloister) and the remains of a 13th-century Gothic church, with a small, open-air stage between the two wings for summer opera performances. All rooms have been refurbished; the quieter ones have courtyard views. The foyer is decked out with sleek Canadian maple, with a bar and restaurant alongside and disabled access throughout.
Other location Hilton Budapest City, VI. Váci út 1-3 (288 5500).

Expensive

Buda Castle Fashion Hotel

I. Úri utca 39 (224 7900, www.budacastlehotel budapest.com). Várbusz from M2 Széll Kálmán tér, or bus 16. **Rooms** 25. **Map** p245 B4.

This four-star in a former merchant's house provides welcome contemporary design in the otherwise twee Castle District. Drenched in macchiato shades, all rooms and suites are spacious and provide easy

ESSENTIAL INFORMATION

Buda Castle Fashion Hotel.

Baltazár.

access to the city's main sights. One of several so-called 'fashion hotels' in Budapest and Vienna in the Mellow Mood group, the BCFH contains several varieties of room, including four duplexes. A pretty courtyard opens for breakfast in the warmer months.

St George Residence

I.Fortuna utca 4 (393 5700, www.stgeorgehotel budapest.co.uk). Várbusz from M2 Széll Kálmán tér, or bus 16. **Rooms** 26. **Map** p245 B4.

This beautifully restored boutique hotel was once home to the popular Fortuna Inn and café, and it still contains frescoes dating back to the 18th century. Each of the 26 spacious suites are equipped with a kitchen and decorated with antique furnishings. The courtyard is an oasis of calm where guests can sip afternoon tea or tuck into classic Hungarian dishes.

Moderate

★ Baltazár

I.Országház utca 31 (300 7051, baltazarbudapest. com). Várbusz from M2 Széll Kálmán tér, or bus 16. **Rooms** 11. **Map** p245 B4.

This stylish boutique hotel/restaurant, opened in 2013, is becoming better known for its 11 individually styled rooms than for its gourmet street food and quality wines. Inspired by Warhol, Vivienne Westwood and other style icons, designers Tibor Sómlai and Géza Ipacs have created a striking, contemporary hotel. Vintage furniture and historic iconography are nicely complemented by modern rain showers and L'Occitane toiletries. The setting, of course, is perfect, and the view from the suites panoramic. Direct booking is rewarded with continental breakfast thrown in. For the restaurant, see p53.

Burg Hotel

I.Szentháromság tér 7-8 (212 0269, www. burghotelbudapest.com). Várbusz from M2 Széll Kálmán tér, or bus 16. **Rooms** 26. **Map** p245 B4.

A relative bargain for the Castle Hill district, the Burg Hotel skimps on design but offers clean, basic accommodation. With an entrance just off the main square, the hotel is within easy walking distance of many of the city's major historical sites and a handful of good restaurants. Most rooms even have a view of Matthias Church and the Fishermen's Bastion.

RIVERSIDE & GREEN BUDA

Deluxe

Art'otel Budapest

I.Bem rakpart 16-19 (487 9487, www.artotels. com). M2 Batthyány tér, or tram 19, or bus 86. **Rooms** 174. **Map** p245 C4.

Budapest's original boutique hotel glides between the 18th and 21st centuries, with superb views of the Danube below and Castle Hill above. Urban at the front, baroque at the back, this is the Budapest branch of a concept chain started in Berlin in 1990. At the rear are four 18th-century fishermen's houses, where tastefully furnished rooms are graced with period fixtures and fittings – authentic down to the door handles – as well as arches and passageways. The huge rooms open on to the tiny romantic streets of Víziváros, which curve all the way up to the top of Castle Hill. The Danube-facing modern wing displays the abstract expressionist art of maverick New Yorker Donald Sultan. Those staying three floors up enjoy a castle vista as well as a riverside one.

Expensive

★ Lánchíd 19

I.Lánchíd utca 19 (457 1200, 419 1900, www. lanchid19hotel.hu). Tram 19, or bus 16, 86, 105. **Rooms** 48. **Map** p245 C5.

Lánchíd 19 is the most splendid boutique hotel in town, its design inspired by the Danube. The building is clad in a veil of accordion-like glass panes, their tiny decorative, hand-painted graphics chronicling the river's ecosystem; when closed, the panes morph into little waves. Set in riverside Víziváros, L19 glistens in the sun; the panes backlit, it shines kaleidoscopically at night. Staff uniforms are by up-and-coming local designers, and cutlery is more award-winning Hungarian handiwork. Overlooking the Chain Bridge (Lánchíd), it enjoys a Danube vista enhanced by a tender curve in the river, best enjoyed from the top-floor terrace suites.

Moderate

Danubius Hotel Gellért

XI.Szent Gellért tér 1 (889 5500, www.danubius group.com/gellert). M4 Szent Gellért tér, or tram 18, 19, 47, 49. **Rooms** 234. **Map** p249 E8.

This historic art nouveau gem overlooking the Danube basks in luxurious illumination at night, but many of its rooms are in urgent need of refurbishment and not all have air-conditioning. The striking architecture, terrace, and renovated spa and outdoor wave pool perched halfway up Gellért Hill provide plenty of compensation.

Novotel Budapest Danube

II.Bem rakpart 33-34 (458 4900, www.accorhotels. com). M2 Batthyány tér, or tram 19, or bus 86. **Rooms** 175. **Map** p245 C3.

This property on the Buda bank, right across from the Parliament, features 175 rooms, 36 of them facing the river. They're bedecked in beige and burgundy, yet modern design eloquently surfaces in the common areas, giving this place an edge over some of Budapest's older and dustier four-stars. The gym and conference rooms encourage business trade, while Café Danube is a destination cocktail bar and restaurant in its own right.

Other locations Novotel Budapest City, II.Alkotás utca 63-67 (372 5400); Novotel Budapest Centrum, VIII.Rákóczi út 43-45 (477 5300).

Budget

Ábel Panzió

XI.Ábel Jenő utca 9 (209 2537, www.abelpanzio. hu). Tram 61. **Rooms** 10. **Map** p248 B8.

Ábel is probably the most beautiful *panzió* in Budapest, set in an ivy-covered 1920s villa on a quiet side street and fitted out with period furniture in the common areas. The ten air-conditioned rooms are all light and clean, with antique furniture, although those on the ground floor are slightly bigger and come with bathtubs. Breakfast takes place around a pleasant common dining table overlooking a terrace and well-kept garden. This is a summer favourite, so be sure to reserve. Discounts for cash payments.

Hotel Császár

II.Frankel Leó út 35 (336 2640, www.csaszar hotel.hu). Tram 17. **Rooms** 45. **Map** p245 C2.

Hotel Császár offers excellent value. Its 45 rooms are housed in a former convent. Built in the 1850s, the building has been beautifully renovated, combining monastic simplicity with modern amenities such as air-conditioning. The hotel shares walls with the Komjádi baths, and guests have access to the outdoor pools – the room rate includes one entry per day.

Danubius Hotel Gellért.

The adjacent hospital specialises in thermal water treatments, and you can arrange appointments. The location is a winner too: it sits within easy reach of sights on both embankments.

Hotel Victoria

I.Bem rakpart 11 (457 8080, www.victoria.hu). *M2 Batthyány tér, or tram 19, or bus 86.* **Rooms** 27. **Map** p245 C4.
One of Budapest's first private hotels occupies a townhouse below the castle, facing the Danube and within easy reach of the main sights. The 27 rooms are simple but comfortable, commanding a view of the river, and garden rooms offer pleasant patios at no extra charge. Excellent value for the location, size of rooms and services offered.

Hotel Villa Korda

II.Szikla utca 9 (325 9123, www.villakorda.com). *Bus 29, 65.* **Rooms** 21.
Yellow and white dominate this purpose-built villa, owned by an evergreen couple of ex-stage singers, with rustic antique furniture testifying to a higher style. Fine views can be enjoyed from this quiet spot in the rich heartland of the Buda hills: half the rooms have a city vista, the other half overlook the woods.

Hostels

Grand Hostel

II.Hűvösvölgy út 69 (274 1111, www.grand hostel.hu). *Tram 61.* **Open** *Reception* 24hrs. No curfew.

ÓBUDA

Deluxe

Aquincum Hotel

III.Árpád fejedelem útja 94 (436 4100, www. aquincumhotel.com). *HÉV Szentlélek tér,* *or tram 1.* **Rooms** 310.
This former Ramada Hotel attracts considerable business trade thanks to its conference facilities and Aphrodite Spa & Wellness Centre. Located in Óbuda near Árpád Bridge, it allows swift access to Margaret Bridge and Batthyány tér, but in reality few guests venture further than the Ambrosia restaurant, River Bar or spa.

BELVÁROS

Deluxe

Kempinski Hotel Corvinus Budapest

V.Erzsébet tér 7-8 (429 3777, www.kempinski-budapest.com). *M1, M2, M3 Deák tér.* **Rooms** 366. **Map** p246 E5.
Built in 1992, the glass-laden Kempinski offers the biggest rooms in the heart of Budapest. Pop stars and movie stars seem to like it, especially

after the high-profile opening of a Nobu restaurant in 2010, De Niro and all. The rooms come in 70 different shapes and some have views over a small courtyard. The spacious but somewhat cold lobby is a popular meeting point, as is the Kempinski Terrace in summer. The Asian-inspired spa features an extensive variety of massage treatments, some especially designed for couples.

Le Méridien Budapest

V.Erzsébet tér 9-10 (429 5500, www.lemeridien-budapest.com). *M1, M2, M3 Deák tér.* **Rooms** 218. **Map** p246 E5.
Once the Adria Palace apartment and office block, Le Méridien meticulously adopted clear millennial minimalism when it set to work on this 1918 building. The white austerity of the exterior is ornamented with wrought-iron balconies and statuettes, while the beige-and-burgundy rooms are adorned with high ceilings, French windows and oriental rugs. The top-floor health club features a pool bathed in natural light. Destination restaurant Le Bourbon sparkles under a stained-glass dome.

Sofitel Chain Bridge

V.Széchenyi tér 2 (235 1234, www.sofitel.com). *M1 Vörösmarty tér, or tram 2.* **Rooms** 350. **Map** p246 D5.
The renovated Sofitel has a prime location near the banks of the Danube by the Chain Bridge – and views to match. Many of the 350 rooms and suites open out on to an imposing multi-storey lobby. The breakfast buffet is lavish and the Paris Budapest is a better class of hotel bar.

Expensive

Buddha-Bar Hotel Budapest
Klotild Palace

V.Váci utca 34 (799 7300, www.buddhabarhotel budapest.com). *M3 Ferenciek tere, or bus 7.* **Rooms** 102. **Map** p249 E6.

The jewel in the crown of diverse local hotel group Mellow Mood, the Buddha-Bar brings high-end, Asian colonial style to one of the last great Pest edifices to undergo a 21st-century makeover. The Klotild Palace is one of a facing pair of towering Habsburg creations that provided a sweeping gateway to Elizabeth Bridge. Significantly damaged after 1945 and 1956, the buildings housed a bank and post office before this lengthy conversion. Done out in luxurious red and gold, this welcome addition to Budapest's five-star stable also features the glass-roofed, panoramic Klotild Bar & Lounge, Asian fusion cuisine in the Buddha-Bar Restaurant and customised treatments in the Buddhattitude Spa. DJ sounds, as befits the Buddha-Bar concept created 20 years ago in Paris, complement the stand-out Sunday brunch.

InterContinental Budapest
V.Apáczai Csere János utca 12-14 (327 6333, www.ihg.com). M1 Vörösmarty tér, or tram 2. **Rooms** 418. **Map** p249 D6.

The vast InterContinental boasts 418 newish rooms and one of the town's biggest conference facilities. Don't let the lugubrious brown façade discourage you: beyond, you'll find a buzzing lobby with live music at the bar, and dramatic views from the Danube-facing rooms (well worth the surcharge) – the angle beautifully integrates the Chain Bridge with the river and Castle District. Excellent service spoils guests, coupled with what the InterContinental calls 'icons': massage, jetlag recovery kit, instant money pack for tipping and international newspapers.

Marriott Hotel Budapest
V.Apáczai Csere János utca 4 (486 5000, www.marriott.com). M1 Vörösmarty tér, or tram 2. **Rooms** 364. **Map** p249 D6.

Celebrity-spotting? The surprisingly low-cost Marriott is your patch. Hollywood seems to love this burgundy-and-brass old-timer – almost all the visiting film crews seem to stay here. Marriott found that guests weren't using the balconies and built

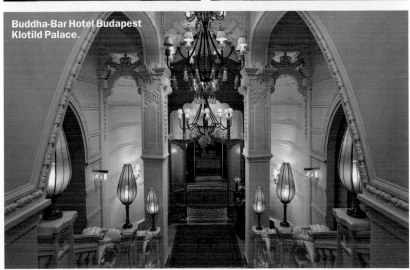
Buddha-Bar Hotel Budapest Klotild Palace.

ESSENTIAL INFORMATION

24-HOUR PARTY PEOPLE

Boozing with the backpackers.

Spend a long summer night with the hard-drinking backpackers of Budapest and you'll realise that hostelling has come a long way since German schoolteacher Richard Schirrmann conceived of cheap lodgings for his charges to yomp merrily around the dales of Westphalia.

Just a quick glance at the hostel names – **Instant Groove! Party Hostel** (see p219), **Njoy Budapest** (see p222), **Wombat's Budapest** (see p219) and **Retox Party Hostel** (see p219) – shows that today's hostellers haven't come to the Hungarian capital to yomp.

Location is another factor. Budapest's busiest hostels aren't set a steady climb from the Buda Hills or in the fresh pastures of Budakeszi. No, the party-seekers who fall off the train from Prague or budget flight from Luton make a beeline straight for the nightlife hubs of Pest, Districts VI, VII and VIII. And not for sad gatherings of spin-the-bottle games

in empty communal areas after all the bars have closed at midnight. Places such as the **Grandio Party Hostel** (see p221) are home to destination bars, part of a network of Budapest Party Hostels (www.budapest partyhostels.com) whose motto reads: 'For those who like to drink outside the box'. Self-awarded ratings for 'craziness' count above those for 'comfortability'. That's not to say that such venues are uncomfortable. The award-winning, high-design **Aventura Boutique Hostel Budapest** (see p217) has individually decorated rooms ('Afrika', 'Japan', 'India') and even offers in-room Swedish massage. The funky **11th Hour Cinema Hostel** (see p217) offers just that, a cinema room, plus help-yourself coffee and tea and, inevitably, guided crawls of nearby ruin bars. Finally, **Casa de la Música Hostel** (see p222), in business since 2006, has gained regular return custom thanks to its Bikini Beach terrace bar and summer pool.

Aventura Boutique. Inset: **Instant Groove! Party Hostel.**

Four Seasons Gresham Palace.
See p217.

them back into the rooms, boosting their size to a comfortable 30sq m (300sq ft). The facelift gave the 1960s façade a softer look, and the room overhaul brought with it super-soft bedding and ergonomic work stations. All rooms have a river view. For all its comings and goings, the buzzing lobby is always welcoming and cosy. The upstairs gym is popular with the expat crowd.

Other locations Courtyard Budapest City Center, VIII.József körút 5 (327 5100); Millennium Court, Budapest – Marriott Executive Apartments, V.Piarista utca 4 (235 1800).

Moderate

City Hotel Pilvax
V.Pilvax köz 1-3 (266 7660, www.cityhotel.hu). M3 Ferenciek tere, or bus 7. **Rooms** 32. **Map** p249 E6.
Laden with history, the Pilvax café played host to the revolutionaries of 1848 – although its existence as a hotel goes back less than two decades. The common areas pay some homage to the building's Biedermeier past, while rooms are light and done out in standard pastel shades.
▶ *The Pilvax is one of three in a chain that also includes the City Hotel Mátyás (V.Március 15. tér 7-8, 318 0595) and the City Hotel Ring (XIII.Szent István körút 22, 340 5450).*

Danubius Hotel Astoria City Centre
V.Kossuth Lajos utca 19-21 (889 6000, www. danubiusgroup.com/astoria). M2 Astoria, or tram 47, 49, or bus 7. **Rooms** 138. **Map** p249 F6.
Opened in 1914 and lending its name to the busy junction (and metro station) on which it stands, the landmark Astoria was where the first Hungarian government was formed in 1918. The hotel was popular with Nazi officials in World War II, before housing the famous Pengő jazz club. It became the Soviet headquarters during the 1956 Uprising. The chandeliered, art nouveau Mirror coffee lounge and restaurant recall the elegant atmosphere of pre-war Budapest. All rooms are air conditioned and soundproofed, and some have been refurbished in Provençal style. A plaque in the lobby boasts of past guests such as Larry Hagman from *Dallas*, while the one outside marks the historic date in 1918.

Budget

Hotel Erzsébet City Center
V.Károlyi Mihály utca 11-15 (889 3700, www. danubiusgroup.com/erzsebet). M3 Ferenciek tere, or bus 15. **Rooms** 123. **Map** p249 E6.
The original hotel on this site was christened Erzsébet (Elizabeth) in honour of Empress Sissi (and with her permission). Unfortunately, that building was demolished, with not so much as a ghost remaining in this modern construction. The good news is that a refurbishment has ripped off the staple dark wood, replacing it with lighter shades and a fresher feel. The main draw is still the downtown location, and while the street is one-way and congested, the precious pocket park of Károlyi kert nearby offers an oasis of calm. The higher rooms offer a view to Gellért Hill.

Leó Panzió-Hotel
V.Kossuth Lajos utca 2A (266 9041, www. leopanzio.hu). M3 Ferenciek tere, or bus 7. Closed 1-15 Feb. **Rooms** 14. **Map** p249 E6.
Budget meets excellent location here – as well as city traffic. But the rooms are tastefully furnished, even if the interior decorators went a bit overboard

Made with

Marrakech

2015 guidebook on sale now
Written by local experts

100% locally sourced ingredients

on blue, mahogany and yellow touches in an effort to recreate some of the building's Habsburg history and grandeur. It's a convenient option, with great views over this main downtown artery.

Promenade City Hotel
V. Váci utca 22 (799 4444, www.promenadehotel budapest.com). M3 Ferenciek tere. **Rooms** 45. **Map** p249 E6.
All 45 rooms at this budget hotel are decorated in rather uninspiring brown and beige tones, but they're modern, clean and remarkably spacious for the wonderfully central location on Budapest's main pedestrian drag. The main downside is that they all face the atrium and reception area of the hotel, which can be noisy.

Hostels

11th Hour Cinema Hostel
V. Magyar utca 11 (266 2153, www.11thhour cinemahostel.com). M2 Astoria, or M3, M4 Kálvin tér, or tram 47, 49. **Open** *Reception* 24hrs. No curfew. **Map** p249 F6.
See p214 **24-Hour Party People**.

LIPÓTVÁROS & ÚJLIPÓTVÁROS

Deluxe

★ Four Seasons Gresham Palace
V. Széchenyi tér 5-6 (268 6000, www.fourseasons com/budapest). M1 Vörösmarty tér, or tram 2. **Rooms** 179. **Map** p246 D5.
The Four Seasons, opened in 2004, still sets the standard for five-stars. The keenest eye for architectural detail and impressive service make the glitzy Gresham a destination in itself – and there are surprising seasonal deals to be had. Created in art nouveau style by Zsigmond Quittner and the Vágó brothers in the early 1900s, the building was ruined in the war and left to fade. It was then acquired by Canadian investment company Gresco, which raised $85 million to restore it. While 90 per cent of the marble was still intact, the specially glazed Zsolnay tiles were pieced together from memory by workers from the old Zsolnay factory. Modern design touches embellish a hugely impressive lobby space, and floors flooded with natural light have a Central European ambience. Danube-facing rooms come at a hefty price, while courtyard-facing rooms offer views of the building's stunning stained glass. There's a spa on the fifth floor, just under the roof. *Photo p215.*

Moderate

Hotel President
V. Hold utca 3-5 (373 8200, www.hotelpresident.hu). M3 Arany János utca. **Rooms** 118. **Map** p246 E4.

Located at the centre of Budapest's business district, Hotel President features fabulous views from its panoramic terrace. Travelling in style? You can even opt to arrive via the hotel's own helipad. For lesser mortals, the smaller rooms are pretty small, making the rack rate a steep proposition given the five-star competition nearby. Grab yourself an internet deal and wallow in the beautiful spa area.

Hostels

Aventura Boutique Hostel Budapest
XIII. Visegrádi utca 12, 1st floor (239 0782, www.aventurahostelbudapest.com). M3 Nyugati pu, or tram 4, 6. **Open** *Reception* 24hrs. No curfew. **Map** p246 E2.
See p214 **24-Hour Party People**.

Hotel President.

Casati Budapest Hotel.

DISTRICT VI & ANDRÁSSY ÚT
Moderate

Casati Budapest Hotel

VI.Paulay Ede utca 31 (343 1198, www.casati budapesthotel.com). M1 Opera. **Rooms** 25. **Map** p246 F4.

The former Hotel Pest, renamed and overhauled, retains its attractive 1790 façade, but the interior is thoroughly 21st-century. The 25 rooms, set back on a quiet street near the Opera House, are now themed around four concepts. Whether it's Classic, Heaven, Cool or Natural, your room will feature original art and striking design touches. This has all been done for grown-ups, either couples on a weekend away or business travellers – it's not really child-friendly. An ivy-clad inner courtyard, sauna and gym complete the picture.

Hotel Benczúr

VI.Benczúr utca 35 (479 5650, www.hotelbenczur. hu). M1 Bajza utca or Hősök tere. **Rooms** 160. **Map** p247 H2.

Located in a concrete cube, the Benczúr's 160 rooms still manage a bucolic atmosphere, tucked away from the quiet street in a pristine garden. Renovated in pastels and light wood, they offer great value in the diplomatic quarter off Andrássy út, near Városliget. The hotel's most famous guest was none other than Pope John Paul II.

Mamaison Andrássy Hotel Budapest

VI.Andrássy út 111 (462 2100, www.mamaison. com). M1 Bajza utca. **Rooms** 68. **Map** p247 H2.

Renovated in 2007, 70 years after its construction as a city hotel, the Andrássy is now under the Mamaison umbrella. The 61 bedrooms and seven suites are graced with warm beige and red tones, and reflect much of the lobby's serene elegance. The in-house restaurant, La Perle Noire, is a destination in its own right.

Other location Mamaison Residence Izabella Budapest, VI.Izabella utca 61 (475 5900).

Radisson Blu Béke Hotel, Budapest

VI.Teréz körút 43 (889 3900, www.radissonblu. com/hotel-budapest). M3 Nyugati pu, or tram 4, 6. **Rooms** 247. **Map** p246 F3.

While the Béke boldly oozes Viennese airs and graces on the outside, refurbishment has dragged the interior into the standard light-wood world of affordable four-star business hotels. Built with all the trappings as the Hotel Britannia in 1912, the Béke ('Peace') housed a famous jazz club in the 1950s, and footballer Ferenc Puskás was among the many Magyar personalities to live here for a while – though, in truth, it has been refurbished so many times that there's little to show for its eventful 80-year history. These days, non-guests come here for afternoon tea and gooey cakes at the old-world Zsolnay Café – for guests, *béke* is best found in the quieter rooms away from the busy ring-road traffic.

Budget

Medosz Hotel

VI.Jókai tér 9 (374 3000, www.medoszhotel.hu). M1 Oktogon, or tram 4, 6. **Rooms** 69. **Map** p246 F4.

One of the least expensive – and certainly one of the best located – choices in Pest, this is a gradual but optimistic renovation of a former party workers' hostel. Rooms are simple but comfortable. In-room Wi-Fi and proximity to the nightlife options of

Districts VI and VII make up for any drabness – this is an affordable base for those looking to go out and enjoy Budapest to the full.

Hostels

Instant Groove! Party Hostel

VI.Nagymezö utca 28 (269 4871, www.instant groovehostel.com). M1 Oktogon, or tram 4, 6. **Open** *Reception* 24hrs. No curfew. **Map** p246 F4. *See p214* **24-Hour Party People**.

Retox Party Hostel

VI.Ó utca 41 (06 70 670 0386, www.retoxparty hostel.com). M1 Oktogon, or tram 4, 6. **Open** *Reception* 24hrs. No curfew. **Map** p246 F4. *See p214* **24-Hour Party People**.

Wombat's Budapest

VI.Király utca 20 (883 5005, www.wombats-hostels.com/budapest). M1, M2, M3 Deák tér. **Open** *Reception* 24hrs. No curfew. **Map** p246 F5. *See p214* **24-Hour Party People**.

DISTRICT VII

Deluxe

Boscolo Budapest

VII.Erzsébet körút 9-11 (886 6111, www.budapest. boscolohotels.com). M2 Blaha Lujza tér, or tram 4, 6. **Rooms** 112. **Map** p247 G5.

This abused gem has finally received some decent treatment at the hands of the Boscolo group, with New York-based interior designer Adam D

Boscolo Budapest.

THE BRODY BUNCH

Award-winning stylish lodging with an arts agenda.

The brainchild of start-up gurus Will Clothier and Peter Grundberg, **Brody House** (see p221) is the hippest place to stay in Budapest and a real hub for the creative arts. Part of a network of arts and private members' clubs around the world – others include the Lansdowne in London's Mayfair and Norwood House in New York – Brody House exudes exclusivity while retaining a quirky credibility.

Its 11 guestrooms, set behind a heavy wooden door across the street from the neoclassical grandeur of the National Museum, have been inspired by, and named after, the artists-in-residence who once worked in them. They were artist's studios before Clothier and Grundberg, former residents themselves, decided to convert them. From the top floor down, the pair set about creating a unique residence less than ten minutes' walk from the centre of Budapest in this former doctor's practice dating back to 1896.

Each room is wonderfully individual. Moldovan Alexander Tinei, who has exhibited in London, Berlin and New York, is celebrated with a riot of colour on the walls and a gold-tinted, stand-alone bath. The spacious Printa Studio, linked with a nearby workshop and design outlet, displays retro touches of Sputnik-era Budapest.

Guests, housed on the hallowed top floor or around a pretty interior courtyard, have access to a well-stocked honesty bar and a lounge area, each flooded – floor to high ceiling – with plenty of natural light. These communal areas have a relaxing, stripped-back, bohemian feel – guests gather around a traditional stove in winter before heading out to the many nearby bars and clubs.

Live music, DJ sessions, literary evenings and cabaret are also laid on four nights a week at the members-only **Brody Studios** (VI. Vörösmarty utca 38, 266 3707), a short taxi ride away. Hotel guests are allowed access, and the agenda is posted up by the reception area at Brody House.

Nearby, the **Brody ArtYard** (VI.Vasvari Pal utca, 708 5130, www.brodyartyard.com, open 11am-7pm Mon-Fri, noon-6pm Sat) has monthly exhibitions in its gallery space, runs a print studio and publishes limited-edition art books.

The whole package earned Brody House 'Best Budget Boutique' in the Smith Hotel Awards and ensured a full house of bookings every weekend for the first half of 2015.

Tihany adding his own Italianate touches to the building's illustrious history. The treasure remains its Baroque café, while more updated Baroque awaits in the rooms: silk and leather wallpaper, metallic drop curtains in the bathrooms, beige tones with splashes of red and blue. In the suites, Murano glass chandeliers crown the living rooms. There's also an ultra-modern spa and fitness facility. Dining has been significantly improved with the arrival of András Wolf as head chef at the Salon restaurant.

Continental Hotel Budapest

VII.Dohány utca 42-44 (815 1000, www.continental hotelbudapest.com). M2 Blaha Lujza tér, or trolleybus 74. **Rooms** 281. **Map** p249 G5.

Reborn from the ruins of the historic Hungária Baths, the Continental Hotel Budapest (formerly Zara) preserves many original Secessionist-era details, from the imposing façade to the famous glass cupola. The 272 rooms and nine suites, though somewhat compact, are rated four-star superior. The rooftop spa is well worth a visit: views stretch as far as the hills of Buda – not bad for a terrace in the heart of the Jewish quarter. There are great lunchtime deals at the Araz restaurant and cocktail bar.

Corinthia Grand Hotel Royal

VII.Erzsébet körút 43-49 (479 4000, www.corinthia hotels.com/hotels/budapest). M1 Oktogon, or tram 4, 6. **Rooms** 414. **Map** p246 G4.

The Royal, as it was christened when it was built for the 1896 millennial celebrations, was the Queen of the Boulevard, with cast-iron statues from Paris, a tropical garden, concert and banqueting halls, plush restaurants and cafés. Destroyed in the war, this vast warren of a hotel led a patchwork existence before Malta-based Corinthia Hotels reopened it in 2002. Modern twists embellish this majestic icon of Hungarian hospitality. An exquisite lobby features original fittings, set under a glassed-in triple atrium. The rooms combine historic grandeur with tasteful contemporary furniture – marble bathrooms, South African carpets, cherrywood headboards and modern artworks. The Grand Ballroom is beautifully restored and lined with portraits of Hungary's cultural giants. Six eating options include the Asian Rickshaw and high-class Bock Bisztró. A spacious spa downstairs features a sizeable pool.

Moderate

Soho Boutique

VII.Dohány utca 64 (872 8292, www.sohoboutique hotel.com/hu). M2 Blaha Lujza tér, or tram 4, 6. **Rooms** 68. **Map** p249 G5.

The smart urban design begins with the images of Davids Lynch and Bowie in the bar that fills most of the ground floor. With an eminently central location close to Budapest's bar vortex, the Soho is affordable – though rooms are on the small side. A plentiful breakfast buffet is served in a small dining room.

Hostels

Grandio Party Hostel

VII.Nagy Diófa utca 8 (06 70 670 0390, www. aventurahostelbudapest.com). M2 Blaha Lujza tér, or tram 4, 6. **Open** *Reception* 24hrs. No curfew. **Map** p249 G5.

See p214 **24-Hour Party People.**

Hostel Marco Polo

VII.Nyár utca 6 (413 2555, marcopolohostel.com). M2 Blaha Lujza tér, or tram 4, 6, or bus 7. **Open** *Reception* 24hrs. No curfew. **Map** p249 G5.

DISTRICTS VIII-X & XIII

Moderate

Atrium Fashion Hotel

VIII.Csokonai utca 14 (299 0777, www.atrium hotelbudapest.com). M2 Blaha Lujza tér, or tram 4, 6. **Rooms** 57. **Map** p250 H5.

The inventive Atrium Fashion Hotel houses 57 rooms in a superbly refurbished, light-filled building topped by a glass roof. The seven-storey atrium is graced with an oversized pendulum sweeping above the bar and restaurant. The colour scheme and design of the comfortable rooms, all soundproofed and air-conditioned, follow the airy feel of the common areas. *Photos p222.*

★ Brody House

VIII.Bródy Sándor utca 10 (266 1211, www. brodyhouse.com). M2 Astoria, or M3, M4 Kálvin tér, or tram 47, 49. **Rooms** 11. **Map** p249 F6.

See p220 **The Brody Bunch.**

Hotel Nemzeti Budapest – MGallery Collection

VIII.József körút 4 (477 4500, www.accorhotels. com). M2 Blaha Lujza tér, or tram 4, 6. **Rooms** 80. **Map** p250 G5.

Reopened by the Accor Group in December 2012, the Hotel Nemzeti clings on to its fin-de-siècle glory days while offering affordable, comfortable lodgings in prime Blaha Lujza tér. Unveiled for the Magyar millennial celebrations of 1896, the 'National' had in-room electricity and en-suite bathrooms. Then close to the old National Theatre, it attracted a cultured crowd through its doors, a tradition not lost on the MGallery designers, who have added their own touches of cultural heritage – the Venetian mirrors and contemporary paintings tastefully blend in with features such as the original Habsburg staircase.

Hotel Palazzo Zichy

VIII.Lőrinc pap tér 2 (235 4000, www.hotel-palazzo-zichy.hu). Tram 4, 6. **Rooms** 80. **Map** p249 G6.

This former residence of Count Nándor Zichy in the increasingly desirable Palace Quarter features an exterior, main foyer and courtyard that reflect the

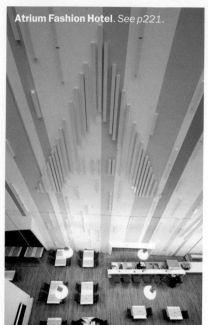

Atrium Fashion Hotel. *See p221*.

Baroque grandeur of the original building. Within, all 80 rooms are ultra-modern with sleek design details leaning towards cool tones of grey and silver. A delicious breakfast buffet is served in the glass-domed restaurant, and free water, coffee and snacks are available in the lounge every day until 5pm. Set off the main drag on a quiet square in the centre of District VIII, prices are remarkably affordable given the quality and level of service.

Budget

Central Hotel 21

VIII.Mária utca 10 (668 2808, www.central hotel21.hu). Tram 4, 6. **Rooms** 26. **Map** p249 G6.
Difficult to spot from the street, Central 21 is housed within a private apartment building. It occupies the second floor and offers 26 rooms and three apartments, all of which are modern and quite compact. For more breathing space, book the family room if it's available.

Kálvin Ház

IX.Gönczy Pál utca 6 (216 4365, www.kalvin house.hu). M3, M4 Kálvin tér, or tram 47, 49. **Rooms** 30. **Map** p249 F7.
Kálvin Ház harks back to the Budapest of the late 19th century. The location is brilliant – at the gateway to Ráday utca's bars – and the 30 rooms are all different, featuring parquet flooring and antique furniture. A buffet breakfast is included in the price.

Sissi

IX.Angyal utca 33 (215 0082, www.okhotels.cz/ en/hotel-sissi). M3 Corvin-negyed, or tram 4, 6. **Rooms** 44. **Map** p250 G8.
Situated in the up-and-coming IX District, Sissi opens a little gateway to the various regeneration projects in the area – from the busy bar zone of Ráday utca to the colourful residential revival of the hotel's surroundings. No allusion is made to the simplicity of the 44 rooms by the terraced façade. The tacky influence of Habsburg namesake legend Sissi surfaces in pleasingly modest attempts at antique decoration and the unassuming Sissi Room.

Hostels

Casa de la Música Hostel

VIII. Vas utca 16 (06 70 373 7330, www.casa delamusicahostel.com). M2 Blaha Lujza tér, or bus 5, 7. **Open** *Reception* 24hrs. No curfew.
Map p249 G6.
See p214 **24-Hour Party People**.

Njoy Budapest

VIII.Rákóczi út 9 I/3 (266 1900, www.njoy budapest.hu). M2 Astoria, or bus 7. **No credit cards. Open** *Reception* 24hrs. No curfew.
Map p249 F6.
See p214 **24-Hour Party People**.

Getting Around

ARRIVING & LEAVING

By air

Liszt Ferenc Airport, still commonly referred to by its old name of Ferihegy, is 20km (12.5 miles) south-east of Budapest. It now only consists of adjacent Terminals 2A and 2B. Terminal 1, closer to town with its own railway station, is no longer operational.

A Sky Court connects Terminals 2A and 2B, with shops, fast-food outlets and a children's play area. Departure gates are divided into border-free Schengen and non-Schengen flights, such as the UK and Ireland, that require passport control. For details on arrivals and departures, call 296 7000 or check www.bud.hu.

Airport train

The service between Terminal 1 and Nyugati Station (20mins) is still running, though you have to take the 200E bus from Terminal 2 five stops to Ferihegy vasútállomás.

AirportShuttle-Minibus

As you stride through baggage collection in Arrivals, a line on the floor directs you through to the **AirportShuttle-Minibus** desk (www.airportshuttle.hu) in the terminal. This is a shared-ride, door-to-door service – give your destination and wait for 10-15mins while a communal route is drawn up. Your driver will collect you and your fellow passengers and lead you outside to his waiting minibus.

The fare for a central destination is Ft3,200 – for two people, a taxi (*see right*) is only slightly pricier and makes more sense. A return ticket costs Ft5,500 –call the number (296 8555) at least 12 hours before you wish to be picked up from any address in town.

Public transport

Bus 200E runs from outside Terminal 2 (veer left as you exit the building) to Kőbánya-Kispest station at the end of the M3 metro line. Buses run every 7-10mins, 4am-midnight, and take 20mins to reach Kőbánya-Kispest. A BKK transport ticket (Ft350) is required for the bus, then another for the onward metro journey. For more information, *see right*.

Taxis

Főtaxi (222 2222, www.fotaxi.hu) has a stand outside Arrivals. Give your destination to the English-speaking receptionist, who will give you a receipt. Within a couple of minutes, you'll be ushered into a car as it pulls up – show the driver your receipt. Fares are calculated by the meter; there are no more fixed rates. A journey to the city centre should cost around Ft6,000-Ft7,000.

Airlines

Aer Lingus *999 1430, www.aerlingus.com.*
Air France *483 8800, www.airfrance.hu.*
British Airways *777 4747, www.britishairways.com.*
EasyJet *+44 330 365 5454, www.easyjet.com.*
Emirates *777 7525, www.emirates.com.*
Jet 2 *+44 20 3059 8336, www.jet2.com.*
KLM *373 7737, www.klm.hu.*
Lufthansa *429 2200, www.lufthansa.hu.*
Ryanair *06 90 982 213, www.ryanair.com.*
Wizz Air *06 90 181 181, www.wizzair.com.*

By bus

If you're arriving by international or major national bus, you'll be dropped at the **Népliget** terminal by the metro station of the same name.

Népliget bus terminal *Üllői út 131 (219 8086, international 219 8040, www.volanbusz.hu). M3 Népliget.* **Open** *Ticket office* 6am-6pm Mon-Fri; 6am-5pm Sat, Sun.

By train

Budapest has four main train stations: **Déli** (south), **Keleti** (east), **Nyugati** (west), plus **Kelenföld**, all with metro stops of the same name. The Hungarian for a main station is *pályaudvar*, often abbreviated to *pu.* Keleti serves most trains to Vienna, Bucharest, Prague, Poland and north-eastern Hungary. Déli also serves Austria as well as Croatia, Slovenia and south-eastern Hungary. Nyugati is the main point of departure for Transylvania and Bratislava. Most trains heading

west to Vienna, or south to Zagreb, stop at Kelenföld.

Trains are affordable and reliable. The fastest, InterCity, require a seat reservation (from Ft450 for domestic trains; international trains vary). Avoid *személy* trains, which stop at all stations. *Gyors* ('fast') trains are one class down from InterCity.

MÁV Information *06 40 49 49 49, from abroad +36 1 444 4499, www.mav-start.hu.*
Déli Station *I.Alkotás út. M2 Déli pu, or tram 18, 59, 61.* **Map** p245 A5.
Kelenföld Station *XI.Etele tér. M4 Kelenföld pu, or tram 19, 49.*
Keleti Station *VIII.Baross tér. M2, M4 Keleti pu, or bus 7.* **Map** p247 J5.
Nyugati Station *VI.Nyugati tér. M3 Nyugati pu, or tram 4, 6.* **Map** p246 F3.

PUBLIC TRANSPORT

Budapest's cheap, efficient public transport system is run by **BKK** (325 5255, www.bkk.hu). The network consists of four metro lines, plus trams, buses, trolleybuses and local trains. There are also BKK ferries in summer. Maps of the system are available at main metro stations. Routes and timetables are put up at bus and tram stops; or see BKK's website. Services start around 4.30am and finish around 11pm; there's a limited night bus network.

Tickets

Tickets can be bought at metro stations, and some tram stops and newsstands. A single ticket (*vonaljegy*, Ft350) is valid for one journey on one type of transport, including changing metro lines, within the city boundary. If you're only going three stops on the metro, there's the reduced *metrószakaszjegy* (Ft300).

To change transport en route, punch a new ticket or get a transfer ticket (*átszállójegy*, Ft530). If you're here for more than a day, the easiest option is to buy ten tickets (*tíz darabos gyűjtőjegy*, Ft3,000). There are also one-day (*napijegy*, Ft1,650), three-day (*72 órás jegy*, Ft4,150) and weekly (*hetijegy*, Ft4,950) tickets. Inspectors guard most metro station entrances, where you must stamp your ticket or show your pass. On buses, trams and trolleybuses, stamp on board – inspectors in blue armbands are common and can levy on-the-spot fines of Ft8,000.

Budapest Card

One-, two- and three-day cards (Ft4,500/Ft7,500/Ft8,900) work as transport passes, as well as providing free or discounted admission to museums and attractions. There's a five per cent discount if you purchase the card online (www.budapest-card.com).

Metro

The Budapest metro is safe, clean, regular and simple. There are four lines: yellow M1, red M2, blue M3 and green M4. These connect the main rail stations and three intersect at central Deák tér. In rush hour, trains run every two to three minutes – the time until the next train is shown on a digital clock on the platform.

Buses, trams & trolleybuses

There's a comprehensive bus, tram and trolleybus network. The main bus route is line 7, connecting Bosnyák tér, Keleti Station, Blaha Lujza tér, Astoria, Ferenciek tere and Móricz Zsigmond körtér. The Castle bus (Várbusz) goes from Széll Kálmán tér round the Castle District and back. Buses labelled E are expresses that miss certain stops.

Night buses have three-digit numbers starting with 9; a reduced but reliable service follows the main daytime routes. Note that the 6 tram along the Nagykörút is now 24hrs. The 4 follows a similar route from 5am until 11.30pm. The 2 tram runs up the Pest side of the Danube, and trams 47 and 49 run from Deák tér to Buda.

Suburban trains (HÉV)

There are five HÉV lines. The main one runs from Batthyány tér via Margaret Bridge to Szentendre. A normal BKV ticket is valid as far as the city boundary at Békásmegyer, with an extra fee thereafter. First and last trains from Batthyány tér are at 4.18am and 11.48pm, and from Szentendre at 3.53am and 11.03pm. Other lines run from Örs vezér tere to Gödöllő, Közvágóhíd to Ráckeve, and Boráros tér to Csepel.

Ferries

BKK also operates a ferry service, which is cheap when compared with the various organised tours. The main service runs year-round from

Kopaszi-gát to Újpest via the A38 boat, Kossuth tér and Batthyány tér. Boats are hourly and take 1hr 15mins to run the whole route. A boat ticket (*hajó vonaljegy*) is Ft750, Ft550 for under-15s. There's also a summer-only service between Pünkösdfürdő in the north of the city and Boráros tér at the Pest foot of Petőfi Bridge, stopping at most of the bridges, Vigadó tér and Margaret Island. See www.bkk.hu for details.

The main boat terminal is situated at Vigadó tér in downtown Pest. Boats to Szentendre, Visegrád and Esztergom on the Danube Bend, as well as Vienna and Bratislava, are run by **Mahart Passnave** (www.mahartpassnave.hu). There are also any number of sightseeing tours down the Danube, by day and night, with commentaries, gypsy bands or dinner-and-dance.

Vígadó tér terminal *V. Vigadó tér, 484 4013. Tram 2.* **Map** p249 D5.

Eccentric conveyances

Budapest has a bizarre range of one-off forms of public transport. For the price of a BKK ticket, the **cog-wheel railway** (*fogaskerekű*) runs up Széchenyi-hegy. It starts at Városmajor, two stops from Széll Kálmán tér on the 61 tram.

Across the park from the cog-wheel railway is the terminal of the narrow-gauge **Children's Railway** (397 5394, 395 5420, www.gyermekvasut.hu), which wends its way through the wooded Buda Hills. Trains leave every hour between 9am and 4pm Tue-Sun; tickets cost Ft700 each way for adults, Ft350 under-14s.

Another way up into the hills is the **chairlift** (*libegő*) up to János-hegy – at 520 metres (1,706 feet) the highest point in Budapest. Take the 102 bus from Széll Kálmán tér to the terminus at Zugliget. The chairlift (Ft1,000 one-way/Ft1,400 return; Ft600/Ft800 reductions) runs 10am-5pm Mon-Fri, 10am-6pm Sat, Sun – and less often in winter. You can walk to the Erzsébet lookout tower or to the János-hegy stop on the Children's Railway.

The **funicular** (*sikló*) takes a minute to climb up from Clark Ádám tér to the Castle District. It runs from 7.30am to 10pm. A one-way ticket for adults is Ft1,200 (return Ft1,800); for under-14s Ft700 (return Ft1,100).

The **Nostalgia Train**, an old-fashioned steam engine, chuffs from Nyugati Station up the Danube Bend in summer. See www.mav nosztalgia.hu for details. The ticket office (269 5242) is next to platform 10 at Nyugati Station.

TAXIS

Taxis in Budapest have recently standardised their rates: Ft450 setting-off fee, Ft280 per km and Ft70/min waiting time. An average journey across town with a reliable company should cost no more than Ft2,000. Try to stick to cabs displaying the logo of one of the companies mentioned below. Despite the 2014 standardisation, sharks still operate. Be wary at Keleti or Nyugati Stations. For a taxi to or from Liszt Ferenc Airport, *see p223*.

In general, calling a taxi is the safest and easiest method. Most dispatchers can speak English and the cab will usually be there in five to ten minutes. A receipt should be available on request (*számlát kérek*). A small tip (rounding up to the nearest Ft100-Ft200) is customary but not compulsory.

Reliable companies include **City Taxi** (211 1111), **Főtaxi** (222 2222) and **Rádió Taxi** (777 7777).

DRIVING

Budapest has all the road problems of most modern European cities with a few extra ones thrown in. Local driving isn't good. Many roads and vehicles are of poor quality.

When driving, be aware that:

● Seatbelts must be worn at all times by everyone in the car.

● Children under eight must be in a child car seat. If a child can't be fitted into a car seat, special cushions (*ülésmagasító*) should be used, so the child is lifted up enough to fasten the seatbelt. Children under 12 or under 150cm aren't allowed to travel in the front seat without a child car seat.

● Always make sure you carry your passport, driving licence, vehicle registration document, motor insurance and *zöldkártya* (exhaust emissions certificate) for cars that have been registered in Hungary. Don't leave anything of value in an unattended car.

● Headlights are compulsory by day when driving outside built-up areas. It's also recommended that you use them in the city at all times.

● Priority is from the right except on a priority road, signified by a yellow diamond on a white background.

● Watch out for trams in places such as the Nagykörút where passengers alight in the middle of the road.

● Speed limit on motorways is 130km/h, on highways 110km/h, on all other roads 90km/h unless otherwise indicated, and 50km/h in built-up areas. Speed traps abound, with on-the-spot fines.

- The alcohol limit is zero and there are plenty of spot checks, with severe penalties.
- You're not allowed to speak on a mobile phone while driving unless you're using a speakerphone or hands-free set.

Breakdowns

A 24-hour breakdown service is provided by the **Magyar Autóklub** (345 1800, 24hr emergency 188), which has reciprocal agreements with many European associations. English is usually spoken, but if not they'll ask you for the model (*típus*), colour (*szín*) and number plate (*rendszám*) of the vehicle, and also the location. Just dial 188 from any phone in Hungary.

Motorway tolls

Fees for using Hungary's motorways are levied by means of e-vignettes (*e-matrica*), a computerised system that registers number plates and toll payments.

Currently, the minimum tariff for a family sized car on Hungarian motorways is Ft2,975 for ten days. There are also e-vignettes for one month (Ft4,780) and one year (Ft42,980). E-vignettes are available online (www.toll-charge.hu) or at most petrol stations. Many also stock Austrian e-vignettes for those driving to Vienna.

A controversial redrawing of the toll network, introduced in January 2015, is currently under review. It raises levies on sections of the M0 ring road close to Budapest, where several hypermarkets and warehouses are located. A complete map can be found at www.toll-charge.hu/road-network. The customer service number is +36 36 587 500 (Hungarian 24hrs, English 8am-4pm daily).

Car hire

It's advisable to arrange car hire in advance. When asking for a quote, check whether the price includes *ÁFA* (VAT). You have to be over 21 with at least a year's driving experience. A valid driver's licence is required and a credit card is usually necessary for the deposit. Many companies have desks at both airport terminals.

Avis *Bank Center, V.Arany János utca 26-28 (318 4240, www.avis.hu). M3 Arany János utca.* **Open** 7am-6pm Mon-Fri; 8am-2pm Sat, Sun. **Map** p246 E4.

Other location Liszt Ferenc Airport, Terminal 2B Arrivals (296 6421).
Budget *I.Krisztina körút 41-43 (06 70 931 8010, www.budget.hu). M2 Déli pu.* **Open** 8am-8pm Mon-Fri; 8am-6pm Sat, Sun.
Other location Üllői út 809A, Vecsés (06 70 931 8001).
Europcar *V.Erzsébet tér 7-8 (505 4400, www.europcar.hu). M1, M2, M3 Deák tér.* **Open** 8am-6pm Mon, Fri; 8am-4.30pm Tue-Thur; 8am-noon Sat. **Map** p249 E5.
Other location Liszt Ferenc Airport, Terminal 2 Arrivals (421 8370).
Hertz *V.Apáczai Csere János utca 4 (266 4361, www.hertz.hu). M1 Vörösmarty tér, or tram 2.* **Open** 7am-7pm daily.
Other locations BSR Center, XIII. Váci út 135-139 (06 30 420 2157); Liszt Ferenc Airport, Terminal 2 (296 7171).

Parking

Many areas have parking meters, so look for the signs that show you've entered a pay zone. Little red bags placed behind the windscreen wipers of other cars are another indication – these will be vehicles that have already received a fine.

Check signs for hours (usually 8am-8pm Mon-Fri, 8am-noon Sat); after that, parking is free. Tickets are valid for up to two or three hours and can be purchased at meters (you'll need change). Parking can also be paid for with a Hungarian mobile or SIM card – on top of the meter will be a four-character code. Simply text your registration number to 06 30 763 + meter code. If you have a foreign-registered car, then text 06 30 763 + meter code, GB (or its particular country code – don't forget the comma). You'll then receive a text acknowledgement that the fee has been taken from your mobile phone account and you're OK to park. For those with a foreign mobile, there's a complicated system of payment – in practice it's easier just to throw coins into the meter.

If you forget to buy a ticket or it exceeds the time limit, you might find a red bag under your wiper, with details of the fine within. This varies from district to district, but usually starts around Ft4,500 and increases after 15 days. You can pay it at parking meters in the same district, remembering to gather enough change first. Find 'extra fee' and 'paying the demanded amount' in the menu and you'll get a receipt. You must then forward the copy of the receipt via fax or post to the district office indicated on the fine document. It might be easier to pay

the fine at any post office – simply hand over the money with the yellow payment cheque also contained in the red bag.

In more serious cases, you might find your car clamped or towed. For wheel-clamping release (about Ft15,000), call the number displayed. If your car has been towed, type your registration number into www.fori.hu/elszallitott-jarmuvek or call 796 3122 and give the address to find the nearest police station.

Alternatively, there are park-and-ride areas by Örs vezér tere, Etele tér and other transport hubs, or 24-hour car parks at V.Szervita tér 8, V.Sas utca, VIII.Futó utca 52 and other locations given at www.budapest.com/travel/getting_around/parking_in_budapest.en.html.

Petrol stations

Most filling stations are open 24 hours a day. Unleaded petrol is *ólommentes*. Fuel marked with a 'K' is for lawnmowers and Trabants. Nearly all petrol stations accept credit cards.

CYCLING

Budapest is becoming more cycle-friendly, with more than 200km of designated lanes, particularly along the Danube in Buda. Several firms can rent you a bicycle and/or give you a tour. These include:

Bikebase *VI.Podmaniczky utca 19 (06 70 625 8501, www.bikebase.hu). M3 Nyugati pu, or tram 4, 6.*
Budapest Bike *VII.Wesselényi utca 13 (06 30 944 5533, www.budapestbike.hu). M2 Astoria, or tram 47, 49, or bus 7.* **Open** 9am-6pm daily.

Bike share

A city-wide bike-sharing scheme, **BuBi** (325 5255, molbubi.bkk.hu), was introduced in 2014. Register a bank card, either at one of the lime-green docking stations or online, and you can use a bike for up to 30mins free of charge. The BuBi system automatically blocks a Ft25,000 deposit on your card, unblocked within 4-15 working days, plus takes off any subsequent access fee (24hrs/Ft500, 72hrs/Ft1,000, 1wk/Ft2,000 plus usage fee (eg 3hrs/Ft2,000) after the initial 30mins. A pin code sent to your mobile allows you to access your bike. Longer-term users can invest in half-year or annual cards, with discounted schemes available on the website.

Resources A-Z

ESSENTIAL INFORMATION

ADDRESSES

When addressing an envelope in Hungarian, write the name of the street first, followed by the house number. Street is *utca*, abbreviated to *u* on street plates, envelopes and maps. This shouldn't be mixed up with *út* (*útja* in the genitive): road or avenue – unless it's *körút*, ring road. *Tér* (genitive *tere*) is a square; *körtér* is a roundabout. Other possibilities include *köz* (lane), *fasor* (boulevard), *udvar* (passage/courtyard), *sétány* (parade) and *rakpart* (embankment).

Envelopes should show the four-figure postcode; the middle numbers stand for district. For flats, the floor number is given in Roman numerals, followed by the flat number. On street signs, the district is in Roman numerals, along with (handily) the building numbers within the block/s in that stretch, so you know exactly which houses are in which block.

AGE RESTRICTIONS

The age of consent is 14. You need to be 18 to buy cigarettes and alcoholic drinks, or to get a driving licence without parental permission.

ATTITUDE & ETIQUETTE

Hungarians are very formal, greeting strangers with a *'jó napot kívánok'* ('good day'), before introducing themselves by their full name, *'Kovács Péter vagyok'* ('I am Péter Kovács'), and a handshake. For acquaintances (even men), a kiss on each cheek may be required. Hungarians are also impeccably tidy – inside the front door, coats must be hung rather than slung over a chair, and shoes removed. Importantly, when you greet or clink glasses, look your addressee in the eye.

BUSINESS

The Hungarian market has long been liberalised, with foreign-owned companies and individuals able to buy property. Local business revolves around personal contacts.

Conventions & conferences

Major hotels (*see pp208-222*) offer conference facilities too.

Budapest Congress Centre
Budapest Kongresszusi Központ
XII.Jagelló utca 1-3 (372 5400, www.bcc.hu). Tram 61, or bus 8, 12, 112. **Open** varies. **Map** p248 A7.
Regus Business Center *Regus House, V.Kálmán Imre utca 1 (475 1100, www.regus.com). M2 Kossuth tér, or tram 2.* **Open** 8.30am-6pm Mon-Fri. **Map** p246 E3.
Other locations Bank Center, V.Szabadság tér 7 (474 8100); V.Kossuth Lajos utca 7-9 (810 1100).

Couriers & shippers

DHL Hungary *XI.Fehérakác utca 3 (06 40 454 545, www.dhl.hu). Tram 3.* **Open** 7am-6pm Mon-Fri. More than 20 service points citywide.
Federal Express *Airport Business Park Building C5, Vecsés, Lőrinci utca 59 (06 40 980 980, 06 29 558 760, www.fedex.com/hu).* **Open** 8am-6pm Mon-Fri.
Hajtás Pajtás Bicycle Messenger *VII. Vörösmarty utca 20, entrance on Király utca (327 9000, www.hajtas pajtas.hu). Trolleybus 70, 78.* **Open** 9am-5pm Mon-Fri. **No credit cards**. **Map** p247 G4.

Office services

In early 2015, top-quality office space in Budapest cost €12-€18 per square

metre per month. The following offices have English-speaking staff. The **Regus Business Center** (*see left*) also rents offices.

Colliers International *MOM Park, XII.Csörsz utca 41 (336 4200, www.colliers.hu). Tram 61.* **Open** 8am-6pm Mon-Fri.
Cushman & Wakefield *Deák Palota, V.Deák Ferenc utca 15 (268 1288, www.cushwake.com). M1, M2, M3 Deák tér.* **Open** 8.30am-6.30pm Mon-Fri. **Map** p249 E5.
Jones Lang LaSalle *V.Szabadság tér 14 (489 0202, www.jll.hu). M2 Kossuth Lajos tér, or M3 Arany János utca.* **Open** 9am-6pm Mon-Fri. **Map** p246 E4.

Useful organisations

American Chamber of Commerce *V.Szent István tér 11 (266 9880, www.amcham.hu). M1 Bajcsy-Zsilinszky út.* **Consultations** by appt. **Map** p249 E5.
British Chamber of Commerce *Eiffel Palace, V.Bajcsy-Zsilinszky út 78 (302 5200, www.bcch.com). M1 Bajcsy-Zsilinszky út.* **Consultations** by appt. **Map** p246 E3.
British Trade & Investment Section *V.Harmincad utca 6 (266 2888). M1 Vörösmarty tér, or M1, M2, M3 Deák tér.* **Open** 9am-5pm Mon-Fri. **Consultations** by appt. **Map** p249 E5.
Budapest Stock Exchange (Budapesti Értéktőzsde) *H-1364 Budapest Pf 24 (429 6857, www.bse.hu).*
Hungarian Investment & Trade Development Agency (Magyar Befektetési és Kereskedelemfejlesztési Kht) *www.itd.hu.*
Hungarian National Bank (Magyar Nemzeti Bank) *V.Szabadság tér 8-9 (428 2600, www.mnb.hu). M2 Kossuth Lajos tér, or M3*

Arany János utca. **Open** 8am-4pm Mon-Thur; 8am-3pm Fri. **Map** p246 E4.

Ministry for the National Economy (Nemzetgazdasági Minisztérium) *V.József Nador tér 2-4 (795 1400, www.kormany.hu/en/ministry-for-national-economy)*. M1 Vörösmarty tér, or bus 15. **Map** p246 D5.

US Embassy Commercial Service *Bank Center, Granite Tower, V.Szabadság tér 7 (475 4090, www.export.gov/hungary)*. M3 Arany János utca, or M2 Kossuth Lajos tér. **Open** 8am-5pm Mon-Fri. **Map** p246 E4.

CONSUMER

Some shops and restaurants in more touristy areas treat foreigners as one-off customers, overcharging shamelessly. The attitude is 'buyer beware', though the European Consumer Centre can sometimes help. It's best to phone rather than drop in.

European Consumer Centre (Hungary Európai Fogyasztói Központ Magyarország) *VIII.József körút 6 (459 4832, www.magyarefk.hu)*. M2 Blaha Lujza tér, or tram 4, 6. **Open** 9am-4pm Mon-Thur; 9am-1pm Fri. **Map** p249 G5.

CUSTOMS

When entering Hungary, items of clothing or objects that could be deemed to be for personal use remain exempt from duties.

Arriving from an EU country, apart from Romania and Bulgaria, over-17s are allowed to bring in 800 cigarettes, 200 cigars, 400 cigarillos or 1,000 grams of tobacco, as well as 90 litres of wine, ten litres of spirits, 110 litres of beer, and 250ml of perfume.

Arriving from Romania, Bulgaria and outside the EU, over-17s are allowed to bring in 200 cigarettes, 50 cigars, 100 cigarillos or 250 grams of tobacco, as well as one litre of wine, one litre of spirits, five litres of beer, and 250ml of perfumes.

Merchandise up to a value of €175 is allowed in duty-free. On exit, the limits are one litre of wine; one litre of spirits; 100 cigars, 250 cigarettes or 250 grams tobacco

Those entering, leaving or travelling within the EU must declare any cash sum they are holding above the limit of €10,000.

When leaving the country, non-EU citizens can reclaim value-added tax on most items bought in Hungary. The total value of the items should exceed €175 and the goods should be taken out of the country within three months of purchase. You must collect a VAT receipt (ask for an *ÁFAs számla*) and two copies of a tax refund form (*ÁFA visszaigénylő lap*) from the store where you made the purchase. The receipt and form must be shown to the customs officer, who will keep one copy. You can then mail in for a refund, using the instructions on the form. For further information, contact the **Customs Office** (301 6950, www.nav.gov.hu, open 8.30am-4pm Mon-Thur, 8.30am-1.30pm Fri).

DISABLED

On public transport, many older buses have been replaced by low-floored ones, as have most trams on the busiest lines 4 and 6. The M1 metro line is also accessible, as is the airport minibus. A special transport bus can be arranged by the Hungarian Disabled Association, which can also provide a helper. Many main museums in the city are now accessible, and new buildings and street sections are designed with the disabled in mind. There are also a limited number of special trips available. For details contact:

Hungarian Disabled Association (MEOSZ) *III.San Marco utca 76 (transport bus 06 70 390 3414, www.meosz.hu)*. Tram 1.

DRUGS

If caught with a small amount of drugs, you can be sentenced to several years' imprisonment. If it's a first-time offence and you're not dealing to minors, you might only get a fine, a compulsory rehabilitation treatment or a warning. For a large amount of drugs, the punishment is anything from five years to life, depending on whether the drugs were for sale or personal use. Small amounts are defined as: amphetamine 1-10g; cocaine 3-8g; ecstasy 10-20 tablets; grass or hashish 10-100g; heroin 1-6g; LSD 5-15 pieces; methadone 200 pieces. Large amounts are defined as 20 times the small amounts.

If the police consider you suspicious, they have the right to stop and search; if you're driving, they can give you a compulsory urine and blood test. You have the right to ask for a lawyer or call your own. In a drug-related emergency, call 104. Doctors must observe laws of confidentiality. For more details and drug-related legal advice, contact the Hungarian Civil Liberties Union (209 0046, www.tasz.hu/en) or www.drogriporter.hu.

Drog-Stop Hotline *06 20 223 7253, www.drog-stop.hu*. **Open** 10am-3pm Mon, Wed; 10am-6pm Tue, Thur.

ELECTRICITY

The voltage is 230V, which works with UK 240V appliances – bring a two-pin adaptor. If you have US 110V gadgets, bring transformers.

EMBASSIES & CONSULATES

American Embassy *V.Szabadság tér 12 (475 4400, http://hungary. usembassy.gov)*. M2 Kossuth Lajos tér, or M3 Arany János utca. **Open** 8am-5pm Mon-Fri. **Map** p246 E4.

Australian Embassy *Mattiellistrasse 2-4, Vienna, Austria (+43 1 506 740, www. austria.embassy.gov.au)*. **Open** 8.30am-4.30pm Mon-Fri.

British Embassy *V.Harmincad utca 6 (266 2888, www.gov.uk/government/world/organisations/british-embassy budapest)*. M1 Vörösmarty tér, or M1, M2, M3 Deák tér. **Open** June-Aug 8am-4.30pm Mon-Thur; 8am-1pm Fri. Sept-May 9am-5pm Mon-Fri. **Map** p249 E5.

Canadian Embassy *II.Ganz utca 12-14 (392 3360, www.canada international.gc.ca/hungary-hongrie)*. Bus 11, 86. **Open** 8am-4.30pm Mon-Thur; 8am-1.30pm Fri. **Map** p245 C3.

Irish Embassy *Bank Center, Platina Tower, V.Szabadság tér 7 (301 4960, www.dfa.ie)*. M2 Kossuth Lajos tér, or M3 Arany János utca. **Open** 9.30am-1pm, 2.30-4.30pm Mon-Fri. **Map** p246 E4.

New Zealand Consulate *VI.Nagymező utca 47 (302 2484, www.hungarianconsulate.co.nz)*. M1 Opera/Oktogon. **Open** 8.30am-1pm, 1.45-5pm Mon-Fri. **Map** p246 F4.

EMERGENCIES

There should be English speakers available on all these numbers. If not, the 24-hour emergency line for English speakers is 112. For hospitals, *see p228* **Health**. For helplines, including poisoning, *see p229*.

Ambulance **104**, **350 0388**
Emergency breakdown **188**
Fire **105**
General emergencies **112**
Police **107**

GAY & LESBIAN

For more detailed information and listings, *see pp148-151* **Gay & Lesbian**. The following is a list of helplines and community organisations:

Háttér Baráti Társaság a Melegekért *Office 238 0046, 329 2670; helplines 329 3380, 06 80 505 605; www.hatter.hu.* **Open** 6-11pm daily.
Hungary's main gay and lesbian organisation, offering information and counselling.
Labrisz Lesbian Society *VIII.Szentkirályi utca 22-24 (06 30 295 5415, www.labrisz.hu). M2 Astoria, or M4 Rákóczi tér.* **Map** p249 G6.
The city's main lesbian group runs a range of meetings and educational programmes, and organises parties.
Mozaik *www.mozaikkozosseg.hu.*
Christian gay group with weekly meetings, discussion and prayer.

HEALTH

Most doctors in Budapest speak some English. Emergency care is provided free to EU citizens, but it's wise to take out medical insurance. Those working here should get a **TAJ** (Social Security) card through their employer, and register with a local GP.

Accident & emergency

In an emergency, go to the nearest hospital casualty department. There are close to 20 hospitals in Budapest that can take in emergency patients; an ambulance or cab driver can take you to the nearest. Take a Hungarian speaker and some ID. For emergency numbers, *see p227*.

Complementary medicine

Dr Funan Yu *II.Pasaréti út 1 (201 1116, www.akupunktura-prof.hu). Tram 61, or bus 5.* **Open** 2-6pm Mon, Fri; 7am-noon Wed.
Chinese acupuncture at a fraction of Western prices.
Other location VII.Bethlen Gábor utca 8 (342 2772).
Homeopathic Doctors' Association *XI.Bocskai út 77-79 (225 3897, www.homeopata.hu). Bus 88, 140, 239.* **Open** 2-6pm Mon; 9am-1pm Wed. **No credit cards**. **Map** p248 A8.
The website has a list of English-speaking practitioners.

Contraception & abortion

Condoms are available at pharmacies, supermarkets and 24-hour corner shops. Abortion is legal and widely used. Birth-control pills can be bought at pharmacies with a local prescription. To avoid pregnancies, medicinal treatment is available within 72 hours after conception – though there's still no over-the-counter morning-after pill. For 24-hour advice, call 06 30 832 6260.

Dentists

Quality dentists are cheap, so many Westerners come here for treatment. English is spoken in these clinics:

Dental Co-op *XII.Zugligeti út 60 (398 1028, 06 30 228 3199, www. dentaltourist.co.uk). Bus 102.* **Open** 8am-8pm Mon, Wed, Thur; 10am-6pm Tue; 9am-5pm Fri.
SOS Dental Clinic *VI.Király utca 14 (269 6010, 06 30 383 3333, www.sosdent.hu). M1, M2, M3 Deák tér.* **Open** 8am-8pm Mon-Sat. **Map** p249 E5.
Super Dent *XIII.Botond utca 10 (451 0506, 06 30 845 1922, www. superdent.hu). M3 Dózsa György út.* **Open** 9am-7pm Mon-Fri.

Hospitals

Heim Pál Gyermekkórház *VIII.Üllői út 86 (459 9100, heimpalkorhaz.hu). M3 Nagyvárad tér.* **Map** p250 K9.
Major paediatric hospital providing emergency care, surgery, psychiatry and more.
National Cancer Institute (Országos Onkológiai Intézet) *XII. Ráth György utca 7-9 (224 8600, www.onkol.hu). M2 Déli pu.* **Map** p245 A5.
Adult oncology, surgery, laser-based cosmetic surgery and dermatology.
Nyiro Gyula Kórház *XIII.Lehel út 59 (451 2600, nygy-opai.hu). Tram 1, 1A, 14.*
Specialising in adult psychiatry, drug rehabilitation and diabetes.
National Accident & Emergency Institute (Országos Baleseti és Sürgősségi Intézet) *VIII.Fiumei út 17 (299 7700, www. peterfykh.hu). M2, M4 Keleti pu.* **Map** p250 J5.
This trauma centre is the best place for victims of accidents and injuries.
National Cardiological Institute (Országos Kardiológiai Intézet) *IX. Haller utca 29 (215 1220, www.kardio.hu). M3 Nagyvárad tér.*
The main cardiology centre.

Péterfy Sándor utcai Kórház *VII. Péterfy Sándor utca 8-20 (461 4700, www.peterfykh.hu). M2 Keleti pu.* **Map** p247 H5.
Obstetrics and gynaecology, urology and neurology. Affiliated with the National Accident & Emergency Institute (*see left*).
Szent Imre Kórház *XI.Tétényi út 12-16 (464 8600, www.szentimre korhaz.hu). Bus 7.*
This is the main hospital in Buda for gynaecology, urology and neurology.
Szent István és Szent László Kórház *IX.Nagyvárad tér 1 (455 5700, 455 8100, www.eszszk.hu). M3 Nagyvárad tér.* **Map** p250 K8.
Two south Pest hospitals now merged for treatments of ear, nose and throat ailments and internal problems.
Szent Margit Kórház *III.Bécsi út 132 (250 2170, www.szent margitkorhaz.hu). Bus 17, 160, 260.*
The main hospital in Óbuda for internal medicine and oncology.

Pharmacies

Pharmacies (*gyógyszertár/patika*) are marked with an illuminated green cross. They're generally open from 8am to 6pm or 8pm Mon-Fri; some also open on Saturday mornings. Some English should be spoken. The following pharmacies in Buda and Pest are open late:

Déli Gyógyszertár *XII.Alkotás út 1B (355 4691, www.deligyogyszertar. hu). M2 Déli pu, or tram 59, 61.* **Open** 8am-8pm Mon-Fri; 8am-2pm Sat; duty rota from 2pm Sat & all Sun. **Map** p245 A4.
Teréz Patika *VI.Teréz körút 41 (311 4439, www.terezpatika.hu). Tram 4, 6.* **Open** 24hrs daily. **Map** p246 F3.

STDs, HIV & AIDS

You can have an anonymous HIV test. If it's positive and a second test is required, you can opt to go to Szent László Hospital – if so, you give up your anonymity to get a health insurance number.

Anonymous AIDS Advisory Service (Anonim AIDS Tanácsadó Szolgálat) *XI.Karolina út 35B (466 9283, www.anonimaids.hu). Bus 212.* **Open** *Blood tests* 5-8pm Mon, Wed; 9am-noon Tue. *Counselling only* 5-8pm Thur; 9am-noon Fri. **Map** p248 A6.
Free anonymous AIDS and STD tests. English spoken.

Szent László Kórház *IX.Gyáli út 5-7 (455 8100, www.eszszk.hu).* **M3** *Népliget.* Main hospital for secondary HIV testing and HIV/AIDS treatment.

HELPLINES

Alcoholics Anonymous *06 20 802 0262, www. anonimalkoholistak.hu/en.* **Heim Pál Gyermekkórház** *459 9100, www.heimpal korhaz.hu.* Treatment for poisoning in children. **NaNE – Women United Against Violence** *06 80 505 101, www. nane.hu.* **Open** 6-10pm daily. **Péterfy Sándor Kórház** *461 4700, www.peterfykh.hu.* Treatment for poisoning in adults.

ID

You're legally obliged to carry photo ID or a passport at all times – but it will rarely be checked. If you lose your passport, report it to the nearest police station, then go to your embassy for an emergency replacement. For police stations, *see p231.*

INSURANCE

All EU citizens are entitled to free emergency treatment – make sure you carry a valid European Health Insurance Card – but it's wise to have medical cover on your travel insurance as well.

INTERNET

Many bars and restaurants now have free Wi-Fi available. For select web resources about Budapest and Hungary, *see p236.*

Internet cafés

Vist@NetCafe *XII.Váci út 6 (06 70 585 3924, www.vistanetcafe.com). M3 Nyugati pu, or tram 4, 6.* **Open** 24hrs daily. **Map** p246 E2. **Király Internet Kávézó** *VI.Király utca 54 (321 0106). Tram 4, 6.* **Open** 9am-10pm daily. **Map** p246 F4.

LANGUAGE

Many local under-40s can speak some English. The older generation will have a smattering of German. Signs in the metro stations have English translations, but you'll have to learn as you go in shops, restaurants, places of entertainment and offices. *See also p231* **Study** and *p234* **Vocabulary.**

LEFT LUGGAGE

There are 24-hour left-luggage facilities at **Nyugati** and **Keleti** stations, and **Népliget** bus terminal (for all, *see p223*). Lockers are also provided. **Liszt Ferenc** airport also has 24-hour left-luggage facilities (*see p223*).

LEGAL HELP

For legal assistance, contact your embassy (*see p227*) for English-speaking lawyers or try these:

Allen & Overy *Madách Trade Center, VII.Madách Imre út 13 (483 2200, www.allenovery.com). M1, M2, M3 Deák tér.* **Open** 8am-8pm Mon-Fri. **Map** p249 E5. **CMS Cameron McKenna/ Ormai & Partners** *Ybl Palace, V.Károlyi Mihály utca 12, 3rd floor (483 4800, www.cms-cmck.com/ Budapest-Hungary). M3 Ferenciek tere.* **Open** 9am-6pm Mon-Fri. **Map** p249 E6. **Kajtár Takács Hegymegi-Barakonyi Baker & McKenzie** *V.Dorottya utca 6 (302 3330). M1 Vörösmarty tér, or bus 15.* **Open** 9am-5.30pm Mon-Fri. **Map** p246 D5.

LIBRARIES

Municipal Ervin Szabó Library (Fővárosi Szabó Ervin Könyvtár) *VIII.Reviczky utca 1 (411 5000, www.fszek.hu). M3 Kálvin tér.* **Open** 10am-8pm Mon-Fri; 10am-4pm Sat. **Map** p249 F7. Located in a gorgeous old villa, the city's main public library contains nearly 50,000 titles in English, as well as English-language DVDs, audio books and periodicals. Membership (Ft3,600/yr; Ft2,400/6mths) offers access to good periodical and English-teaching sections, plus a huge video library. **National Foreign-Language Library** *V.Molnár utca 11 (318 3688). Tram 2.* **Open** 10am-8pm Mon, Tue, Thur, Fri; noon-8pm Wed. Closes 4pm in summer. **Map** p249 E6. Extensive English-language holdings, many periodicals and helpful staff. Day membership (or longer) required. **National Széchényi Library** *Buda Palace Wing F, I.Szent György tér 4-5-6 (224 3700, www.oszk.hu). Várbusz from M2 Széll Kálmán tér.* **Open** 9am-8pm Tue-Sat. **Map** p248 C5. Hungary's biggest public library claims to have every text written in Hungarian, about Hungary or

translated from Hungarian. With periodicals and academic texts, it's useful for research, but you can't check books out. Take ID to enter.

LOST PROPERTY

If you lose something, enquire at the police station in the area where you lost it (*see p231* **Police**). Take along a Hungarian speaker, especially if you need to obtain a statement for insurance purposes.

Airport

Liszt Ferenc airport lost luggage *Terminal 2 (06 70 332 4006, 06 70 332 4007, www.bud.hu).* You can try tracing your luggage online at www.sita.aero/product/ worldtracer.

Public transport

BKK Lost Property Office (Talált Tárgyak Osztálya) *VII.Akácfa utca 18 (258 4636 option 3). M2 Blaha Lujza tér.* **Open** 8am-8pm Mon; 8am-5pm Tue-Thur; 8am 3pm Fri. **Map** p249 G5.

Rail

Each main station in Budapest has a lost-property office, where items are kept for three months. **Déli Station** *I.Krisztina körút 37A. M2 Déli pu, or tram 18, 59, 61.* **Open** 7.30am-3pm Mon-Thur; 7.30am-noon Fri. **Map** p245 A5. **Keleti Station** *VIII.Kerepesi út 2-5. M2, M4 Keleti pu, or bus 7.* **Open** 4am-11.30pm daily. **Map** p247 J5. **Nyugati Station** *Platform 10, VI.Nyugati tér. M3 Nyugati pu, or tram 4, 6.* **Open** 24hrs daily. **Map** p246 F3.

MEDIA

With the exception of RTL Klub TV, the news media is almost entirely state-dominated.

English-language

Budapest Business Journal *www.bbj.hu.* Fortnightly coverage of national corporate and economic news, in place since 1992, with a recently improved and regularly updated website. **Hungary Around the Clock** *www. hatc.hu.* Digest of each day's political and financial news, compiled from the Hungarian press for subscribers by 7am Mon-Fri.

ESSENTIAL INFORMATION

Magazines

168 Óra *www.168ora.hu*. Liberal weekly that has enraged every government since its foundation in the 1980s.

Figyelő *www.figyelo.hu*. Respected news and business weekly, best known for breaking the Tocsik corruption scandal of the 1990s.

Forbes Magyarország *www.forbes. hu*. Highly successful Budapest-based Hungarian edition of the US heavyweight, launched in 2014 as a monthly.

Heti Világgazdaság (HVG) *www. hvg.hu*. Hungary's *Economist* is the country's most influential weekly. Owned by its employees, HVG is largely independent, aspiring to non-partisan, hard-hitting journalism.

Magyar Narancs *www. magyarnarancs.hu*. Leading alternative newspaper with broad coverage of minority issues, in-depth features and extensive listings.

Newspapers

Blikk *www.blikk.hu*. Top-selling daily tabloid with more than 100,000 readers. Crime, celebrity and scandal.

Magyar Hírlap *www.magyarhirlap. hu*. A centre-right mainstream paper that has long lost its mojo.

Magyar Nemzet *www.mno.hu*. Right-wing daily said to have close links with the ruling Fidesz party.

Nemzeti Sport *www.nemzetisport. hu*. Leading daily sports paper – its international results coverage is second to none.

Népszabadság *www.nol.hu*. The closest thing Hungary has to a paper of record. Second to *Blikk* in terms of overall readership.

Népszava *www.nepszava.hu*. Old organ of the Communist trades unions.

Világgazdaság *www.vg.hu*. Daily coverage of business, economic and financial news.

Radio

There are three big state-run stations: **Kossuth Rádió** (540 AM) is the national station, offering a gabby yet informative mix of talk and music; **Petőfi Rádió** (98.4 FM) provides a regular background of inane Hungaropop, sport and the occasional political discussion; **Bartók Rádió** (105.3 FM) plays the highbrow card, with classical music, poetry and drama. Apart from broadcasters propped up by the state, almost every local station plays commercial pop. The main

alternative station is **Tilos Rádió** (90.3 FM), which began as an anti-regime pirate under Communism. Today, it's still non-profit with no ads, surviving on listener donations. Another alternative is **Rádió C** (88.8 FM), the radio station for Roma, with music and talk shows of interest to the Roma community.

BBC World Service frequencies change every six months; www.bbc. co.uk/worldserviceradio has the latest information.

Television

Cable TV Each city district has separate arrangements for cable TV, but UPC from the Netherlands dominates the market. Packages tend to include some English-language channels, such as CNN, BBC World and Eurosport.

Duna TV Satellite channel aimed at the substantial ethnic Hungarian minorities in neighbouring countries. Heavy on culture and documentaries.

MTV1 The flagship of state-owned broadcasting spreads propaganda for the current government.

MTV2 Offers more documentaries, culture and public service shows, but often just rebroadcasts MTV1.

RTL Klub Majority-owned by Luxembourg/Germany-based CLT-UFA. Launched as a rival to TV2 but with higher local production quality. Home of *Való Világ*, Hungary's *Big Brother*. Its news programme is the only one to take a critical stance against ruling party Fidesz – giving rise to a controversial tax on TV advertising.

TV2 Airs a predictable mix of news, mostly dismal foreign films and locally produced trash, including the latest game shows and voyeur TV. Current home of *Rising Star*, a kind of *Hungary's Got Talent*.

MONEY

The Hungarian unit of currency is the forint, usually abbreviated as HUF or (as in this guide) Ft. Forint coins come in denominations of Ft5, Ft10, Ft20, Ft50, Ft100 and Ft200, notes in Ft500, Ft1,000, Ft2,000, Ft5,000, Ft10,000 and Ft20,000.

Hungary is not in the euro zone and the country's struggle to rein in government debt following a 2008 IMF bailout means the forint will probably be the local currency for a few more years. During 2014 and early 2015, the forint fell significantly against major currencies. In February 2015, the forint was trading at Ft310 to the euro, Ft415 to the pound.

Credit and debit cards connected to half-a-dozen global clearance systems can be used to withdraw forints at thousands of ATMs around Hungary. Wire transfers are easily arranged, but expect a one-day delay.

Cheques (except travellers' cheques) are pretty much non-existent in Hungary and take weeks to clear. Foreigners are free to open a bank account in Hungary in almost any currency with little hassle.

Banks & ATMs

Most banks open at 8am and close at 3pm, 4pm or 5pm Monday to Friday; some are open on Saturday morning. Apart from cash and travellers' cheques, banks can advance money on a credit card. ATM and exchange machines are available at most banks all across town.

Banks may give better rates than change kiosks, but do shop around – rates can vary. Travellers' cheques can be changed at banks and change kiosks, though often at a lower rate than the cash equivalent.

Bureaux de change

Exclusive Change *V. Váci utca 12 (06 70 383 0654, www.exclusive.hu). M1 Vörösmarty tér, or M1, M2, M3 Deák tér.* **Open** 9am-7.30pm Mon-Fri; 9am-4.30pm Sat, Sun. **Map** p249 E5. **Other locations** throughout the city.

Credit cards

Credit cards are accepted in most outlets. The most widely accepted are American Express (AmEx), Diners Club, MasterCard and Visa. For lost/stolen credit cards call:

American Express *235 4300, www.americanexpress.com.*
Diners Club *+44 1244 470 910, www.dinersclub.com.*
MasterCard *+44 1525 402 184, www.mastercard.com.*
Visa *06 800 17682, www. visaeurope.com.*

OPENING HOURS

Hours vary according to the type of shop, but most are open from 10am to 6pm Monday to Friday, and 10am to 1pm on Saturday. Shopping malls usually open daily at 10am and close at 9pm. Supermarkets, greengrocers and bakeries usually open at 7am and close between 6pm and 8pm Monday to Friday, and 1pm and 3pm on Saturdays. '*Rögtön jövök*' means that the owner will be back in five minutes

– maybe. Many shops stay open later on Saturdays and on Thursday evenings. Non-stops are small 24-hour corner shops where you can buy basics and booze; almost every district will have one. Most restaurants close by 11pm or midnight; bar closing times vary. For public holidays, *see p233*.

POLICE

Unless you commit a crime, you shouldn't have much contact with the police, but they can stop you and ask for ID. If you're robbed or lose something, report it to the police station nearest the incident. Take a Hungarian speaker. It's only worth it if the item was valuable, or your insurance company needs the forms.

You can report a crime on the Central Emergency Number (112) or to the police (107).

Police headquarters *XIII.Teve utca 4-6 (443 5500, www.police.hu). M3 Árpád-híd, or tram 1.*

Police stations

V.Szalay utca 11-13 (373 1000). M2 Kossuth tér, or bus 15. **Map** p246 E3.
VII.Dózsa György út 18-24 (461 8100). M2, M4 Nyugati pu, or bus 7, 30. **Map** p247 K4.
VIII.Vig utca 36 (477 3700). M2 Rákóczi tér, or tram 4, 6. **Map** p249 H6.

POSTAL SERVICES

Most post offices are open from 8am to 7pm on weekdays. There are no late-night branches in central Budapest, but the one at Keleti Station (VIII.Baross tér 11C) is open 7am to 9pm Monday to Friday. There's a 24-hour post office at the Fogarasi út branch of Tesco (XIV.Pillangó utca 15).

Letters weighing up to 30g cost Ft90 to send within Hungary. A letter weighing up to 20g costs Ft280 to European countries, and Ft310 to anywhere else in the world. Priority postage (*elsőbbségi*) brings an extra fee depending on weight. Postcards (*képeslap*) cost Ft220 to European countries; Ft250 to anywhere else.

Poste restante letters go to the office at Nyugati Station. For courier services and express mail, *see p226* **Business**.

Sending packages

You can send a package weighing up to 2kg as a normal letter, which is cheaper than sending a package.

Otherwise, a package weighing up to 5kg costs Ft11,250 overland to European countries; overseas ranges from Ft15,675 to Ft22,400 depending on how quickly you want it delivered. Tie your package with string and fill out a blue customs form (*vámáru nyilatkozat*) from the post office. Special boxes are sold at the post office. Post offices provide a booklet in English detailing charges; otherwise try www.posta.hu.

RELIGION

The following places of worship all have services in English.

Protestant services

International Baptist Church of Budapest (Móricz Zsigmond Gimnázium) *II. Törökvész út 48-54 (www.ibcbudapest.org). Bus 11.* The English service is held on Sundays at 10.30am.
International Church of Budapest (Óbudai Társaskor) *III.Kis Korona utca 7 (06 30 269 9730, www.church.hu). HÉV Szentlélek tér, or tram 1.* Multi-denominational English-language services are held every Sunday at 10.30am.
Presbyterian Church of Scotland *VI.Vörösmarty utca 51 (06 70 615 5394, www.reformatus.hu/mutat/6861). M1 Vörösmarty utca.* **Map** p246 F3. There's an English service on Sundays at 11am.
St Margaret's Anglican/Episcopal Church *VII.Almássy utca 6 (no phone). Tram 4, 6.* **Map** p247 H4. The English service is on Sundays at 10.30am.

Catholic services

Jézus Szíve templom *VIII.Mária utca 25 (318 3479, www.jezusszive.jezsuita.hu). M4 Rákóczi tér, or tram 4, 6.* **Map** p249 G7. Catholic mass is held in English on Saturdays at 5pm.

Jewish services

Dohány Street Synagogue (Dohány utcai Zsinagóga) *VII. Dohány utca 2 (462 0477, www.dohanyutcaizsinagoga.hu). M2 Astoria, or tram 47, 49, or bus 7.* **Map** p249 F5. Services in Hebrew.
Pesti Shul Synagogue (Orthodox) *XIII. Visegrádi utca 3. M3 Nyugati pu, or tram 4, 6.* **Map** p246 E2.

SAFETY & SECURITY

Budapest is a relatively safe city. Look out for pickpockets and purse-snatchers around the tourist spots of Váci utca, the Castle District, Heroes' Square and at stations. Be careful if walking alone at night around the ill-lit outlying areas of town or District VIII behind Rákóczi tér; phone a taxi (*see p224*) if necessary.

SMOKING

Smoking is banned in bars, restaurants, on all public transport, on trains, and in theatres and cinemas. Cigarettes and tobacco are now only sold at specified shops, marked with a brown circular logo with the words '*Nemzeti Dohánybolt*' ('National Tobacco Shop').

STUDY

The main university in the city, with faculties around town, is **Eötvös Loránd Tudományegyetem** (ELTE; V.Egyetem tér 1-3, 411 6500, www.elte.hu). Other major institutions include the **Budapest Technical & Economic Sciences University** (BME; XI.Műegyetem rakpart 3, 463 1111, www.bme.hu), the **Corvinus University of Budapest** (Economics and Public Administration; IX.Fővám tér 8, 482 5000, www.bke.hu) and the **Semmelweis University of Medicine** (SOTE; VIII.Üllői út 26, 459 1500, www.semmelweis.hu). **Central European University** (CEU; V.Nádor utca 9, 327 3000, www.ceu.hu), founded by philanthropist financier George Soros, has developed an excellent reputation for its faculties of international policy, business and medieval studies.

Language classes

The schools below offer foreigners Hungarian classes that range in intensity and frequency:

Balassi Bálint Institute (BBI) *I.Somlói út 51 (381 5160, www.balassiintezet.hu). Bus 8, 27, 112.* **Map** p248 B7. One of the city's most highly rated schools for foreign students learning Hungarian.
Debreceni Nyári Egyetem *H-4010 Debrecen Pf35 (06 52 532 594, www.nyariegyetem.hu).* This summer school in Debrecen has a reputation as the best place for foreigners to learn Hungarian.
ELTE Idegennyelvi Továbbképző Központ *VIII.Baross utca 26 (459*

9614, www.itk.hu). Tram 4, 6.
Map p250 H6.
Independent, non-profit institution organised under the Eötvös Lóránd University. It assesses knowledge of Hungarian language and culture for examinations.
Hungarian Language School
VIII.Bródy Sándor utca 4 (266 2617, www.magyar-iskola.hu). M2 Astoria, or M3, M4 Kálvin tér, or tram 47, 49.
Map p249 F6.
The Hungarian Language School specialises in Hungarian courses for foreigners.
Hungarolingua Language School
VIII.Rákóczi tér 10 (337 4742, www.hungarolingua.hu). M4 Rákóczi tér.
Map p249 G6.

TELEPHONES
Dialling & codes

To make an international call, dial 00, wait for the second purring dial tone, then dial the country code and number: Australia 61, Canada 1, Ireland 353, New Zealand 64, UK 44, USA 1.

To call other places around Hungary from Budapest, or to call Budapest from the rest of the country, you have to dial 06 first, wait for the second tone, and then follow with the code and number. You also have to dial 06 before calling mobile phones.

To call Hungary from abroad, dial 36 and then 1 for Budapest. For a provincial Hungarian town or a Hungarian mobile from abroad, dial 36 then the number with no initial 06.

Mobile phones

The three main mobile phone companies in Budapest – **T-Mobile**, **Telenor** and **Vodafone** – have branches all over town, including in all the malls.

Telenor *06 20 200 0000, www.telenor.hu.*
T-Mobile Magyarország *458 0000, 458 7000, www.t-mobile.hu.*
Vodafone *288 3288, www.vodafone.hu.*

Operator services

English-language enquiries **197**

Public phones

Public phones can be found around busy squares, in malls, at the airport and at train and bus stations. Most public phones take a card called a

barangoló hívókártya, which are sold in units of Ft1,000, Ft2,000 and Ft5,000 at post offices, newsagents or offices of the T-Com phone company. Coin phones in bars take Ft10, Ft20, Ft50 and Ft100 units; a local call costs Ft60.

TIME

Hungary is on Central European Time, which means that it's one hour ahead of GMT, six ahead of US Eastern Standard Time and nine ahead of US Pacific Standard Time. As elsewhere in Europe, Hungary changes the clocks in late March then back again in late October.

TIPPING

There are no fixed rules about tipping but it's customary to leave about ten to 15 per cent for waiters in cafés and restaurants. Round up the amount to the nearest couple of hundred forints. Simply tell the waiter as you pay either how much your rounded-up amount comes to or how much change you'd like back. Saying *köszönöm* ('thank you') as you hand over a note means you're expecting them to keep all the change. The same rule applies to taxi drivers. It's also customary to tip hairdressers, beauticians, car mechanics, cloakroom attendants, repairmen, doctors and dentists.

Some restaurants now add a ten per cent service charge, in which case don't feel obliged to give any tip.

TOILETS

There are public toilets at various locations around town, for which you'll have to pay a small fee (usually Ft100-Ft150) to an attendant. Look for *Nő/k* or *Hölgyek* (Ladies) and *Férfi/ak* or *Úrak* (Gents).

TOURIST INFORMATION

The best place for tourist information is **Tourinform**, with terminals around town. **IBUSZ** is the most useful for accommodation.

IBUSZ *V.Ferenciek tere 2 (501 4908, http://ibusz.hu). M3 Ferenciek tere.* **Open** 9am-6pm Mon-Fri; 9am-1am Sat. **Map** p249 E6. Hungary's oldest tourist agency can book rooms, organise tours and provide information, plus offers the usual travel agency services. **Other locations** throughout the city.
Tourinform *V.Sütő utca 2 (438 8080, www.tourinform.hu). M1, M2, M3 Deák tér.* **Open** 8am-8pm daily. **Map** p249 E5. Staff are helpful and multilingual, and can provide details of travel, sightseeing and leisure options. **Other locations** Liszt Ferenc airport, Terminals 2A/2B (438 8080).

VISAS & IMMIGRATION

Nationals of EU member countries can enter Hungary with their valid national passport or national ID card. Those wishing to stay longer than three months should register with the Hungarian Immigration and Nationality Office for a European Economic Area Residents' Permit for Citizens. More details can be found at www.bmbah.hu.

Citizens of the United States, Canada, Australia, New Zealand and most non-EU European countries can stay in Hungary for up to 90 days with only a passport. Citizens of South Africa require a visa. In theory, non-EU citizens who wish to stay longer than 90 days need a residence visa. In practice, they can skip into a neighbouring country and get their passport stamped for another three

LOCAL CLIMATE

Average temperatures and monthly rainfall in cm.

	High (°C/°F)	Low (°C/°F)	Rainfall
Jan	7 / 45	2 / 36	53cm
Feb	10 / 50	2 / 36	43cm
Mar	13 / 55	4 / 39	49cm
Apr	17 / 63	6 / 43	53cm
May	20 / 68	9 / 48	65cm
June	23 / 73	12 / 54	54cm
July	25 / 77	15 / 59	62cm
Aug	26 / 79	16 / 29	42cm
Sept	23 / 73	12 / 54	54cm
Oct	20 / 68	8 / 46	60cm
Nov	14 / 57	4 / 39	51cm
Dec	7 / 44	3 / 37	59cm

months, though anyone who uses this trick repeatedly may eventually be refused entry.

Residence visas are obtained from the Hungarian consulate in your country. The issuing process may take up to two months. Residence visas are usually valid for one year and must be renewed prior to the expiration date. Applying requires a work permit, a legal permanent residence, an AIDS test, a chest X-ray, several forms and passport photos, your passport and official translations of every foreign language document with stamps on them.

If you're not working in Hungary but would like a residence visa, you'll need to prove, with the assistance of a recent bank account statement, that you have the wherewithal to reside in Hungary without having recourse to work.

Obtaining Hungarian citizenship can take up to eight years, and starts with successful receipt of a residence visa for one year and a residence permit for two years. If you have Hungarian parents, you can apply for a local passport immediately. If you're married to a Hungarian, you can apply for an immigration certificate after you've lived in Hungary with a residence permit or visa for three years, and have been married to the Hungarian person for three years. *See also right* **Working in Budapest**.

WEIGHTS & MEASURES

Hungary has its own system for measuring out solids and liquids. A *deka* is ten grams; a *deci* is ten centilitres. In a bar, for example, you might be asked whether you want *két deci* or *három deci* (0.2 or 0.3 litres) of whatever drink you've just ordered. Wine in bars, and often in restaurants, is priced by the *deci*. At a delicatessen, if you want 300 grams of ham, you'd ask for 30 *deka* – *harminc (30) deka sonkát*.

WHEN TO GO

Spring
May is probably the most pleasant month in the city, before the influx of tourists begins. Winter attire gets discarded, though rain showers can sometimes dampen spirits.

Summer
Most Hungarians leave Budapest for the Balaton or their weekend house. It can get very hot, especially during July. If there's a breeze off the

Danube, it's pleasant – if there isn't, you can expect a pall of pollution.

Autumn
The weather is lovely in September, but it starts to get cold in October when everything moves inside and the heating gets turned on.

Winter
Winters are cold and quite long, but not unbearably so: the air is very dry and central heating is good. Snow falls a few times. Smog can descend if there's no breeze.

Public holidays

There's usually something open on most holidays apart from the night of 24 December, when even the non-stop shops stop. New Year's Eve is very lively, as is St Stephen's Day on 20 August, with fireworks launched over the Danube.

New Year's Day
Revolution Day (15 March)
Easter Sunday
Easter Monday
May Day (1 May)
Whit Monday
St Stephen's Day (20 Aug)
Remembrance Day (23 Oct)
Christmas (25-26 Dec)

WOMEN

Men and women are legally equal in Hungary, but in reality women face wage differentials, harassment at work, unfair division of labour and domestic violence. Values imposed on the traditional division of labour by the old regime meant that women kept their homemaker roles while being expected to work eight hours a day outside the home. This situation is changing slowly. Abortion is now legal and accessible, women's wages are edging up, sexual harassment and wife beating are more often reported and punished, and more men do the housework. But the old values still surface, as do sexist jibes.

Association of Hungarian Women (Magyar Nők Szövetsége) *VI.Andrássy út 124 (331 9734, www.nokszovetsege.hu). M1 Hősök tere.* **Open** 11am-4pm Mon-Fri. **Map** p247 H2.
Now independent, this was the original Communist-era association, so don't expect it to be particularly radical. It has a membership of 45 organisations and 10,000 individuals, all striving for equal opportunity and participation.

NaNE – Women United Against Violence (Nők a Nőkért Együtt az Erőszak) *Helpline 06 80 505 101, www.nane.hu.* **Open** 6-10pm daily.
Rape and domestic violence are low-profile issues in Hungary. There's no law against marital rape and little sympathy for rape victims. NaNE gives information and support to battered and raped women and children, campaigns for changes in the law, and challenges social attitudes to violence.

WORKING IN BUDAPEST

UK, Irish and certain EU nationals have the right to live and work in Hungary without a permit. For more information, check the Hungarian embassy website in your home country or visit www.ec.europa.eu.

Non-EU citizens coming to Hungary to work must already have a work permit and a residence visa, except for company directors, who only need the relevant Hungarian corporate documents. You must start the process in your home country, because you'll need to obtain a residence visa from the Hungarian embassy there.

A work permit is your employer's responsibility. You need to provide translated certificates and diplomas, and a translated medical certificate. Only documents translated by the National Translation Office are accepted. The medical certificate involves having a chest X-ray and a blood test. The employee submits the work permit to the Hungarian embassy in his or her home country. *See also p232* **Visas & immigration**.

National Labour Service *VIII.Kisfaludy utca 11 (477 5700, kmrmk.afsz.hu). Tram 4, 6.* **Open** 8.30am-2pm Mon-Wed; 8.30am-1pm Thur, Fri. **Map** p250 G7.
National Translation Office (Országos Fordító Iroda) *VI.Bajza utca 52 (428 9600, www.offi.hu). M1 Bajza utca.* **Open** 8am-7pm Mon; 8am-4pm Tue, Thur; 8am-6pm Wed; 8am-2pm Fri. **Map** p247 G2.
Settlers Hungary *XII.Maros utca 12 (212 5017, www.settlers.hu). M2 Déli pu, or tram 59, 61.* **Open** 8.30am-5pm Mon-Thur; 8.30am-3pm Fri.
State Public Health & Medical Administration (Állami Népegészségügyi és Tisztiorvosi Szolgálat – ÁNTSZ) *XIII.Váci út 174 (465 3800, www.antsz.hu). M3 Gyöngyösi utca.* **Open** 8am-3pm Mon-Thur; 8am-noon Fri.

Vocabulary

Nowhere else in Europe will the traveller be confronted with as great a linguistic barrier as in Hungary. Basic words bear no resemblance to equivalents in any major European language.

The good news is pronunciation of common words is easy – and the long ones can be shortened: *viszlát* for *viszontlátásra* ('goodbye'), for example, or *köszi* for *köszönöm* ('thank you'). *Szervusz* is an all-purpose greeting, more formal than *szia*, for both hello and goodbye. For menu terms, *see p235*.

PRONUNCIATION

The stress is always on the first syllable. Accents denote a longer vowel. Double consonants are pronounced longer (*kettő, szebb*). Add 't' to nouns if they are the object of the sentence: 'I would like a beer' is *egy sört kérek* (sör + t).

a – like 'o' in hot
á – like 'a' in father
é – like 'a' in day
í – like 'ee' in feet
ö – like 'ur' in pleasure
ü – like 'u' in French tu
ő, ű – similar to ö and ü but longer
sz – like 's' in sat
cs – like 'ch' in such
zs – like 's' in casual
gy – like 'd' in dew
ly – like 'y' in yellow
ny – like 'n' in new
ty – like 't' in Tudor
c – like 'ts' in roots
s – like 'sh' in wash

USEFUL EXPRESSIONS

yes *igen*; no *nem*; maybe *talán*
(I wish you) good day *jó napot (kívánok)* (formal)
hello *szervusz*; *szia* (familiar)
goodbye *viszontlátásra*
how are you? *hogy van?* (formal); *hogy vagy?* (familiar)
I'm fine *jól vagyok*
please *kérem*
thank you *köszönöm*
excuse me *bocsánat*
I would like *kérek…* (an object)
I would like (to do something) *szeretnék…* (add infinitive)
where is…? *hol van…?*
where is the toilet? *hol van a wc?* (wc = *vay tzay*)
where is a good (not too expensive) restaurant? *hol van egy jó (nem túl drága) étterem?*

when? *mikor?* who? *ki?*
why? *miért?* how? *hogyan?*
is there…? *van …?*
there is none *nincs*
how much is it? *mennyibe kerül?*
we're paying separately *külön-külön fizetünk*
open *nyitva*; closed *zárva*
entrance *bejárat*; exit *kijárat*
push *tolni*; pull *húzni*
men's *férfi*; women's *női*
good *jó*; bad *rossz*
I like it *ez tetszik*
I don't like it *ez nem tetszik*
I don't speak Hungarian *nem beszélek magyarul*
do you speak English? *beszél angolul?*
what is your name? *mi a neve?*
my name is… *a nevem…*
I am (English/American) *(angol/amerikai) vagyok*
I feel ill *rosszul vagyok*
doctor *orvos*; pharmacy *patika/gyógyszertár*; hospital *kórház*;
ambulance *mentőautó*
police *rendőrség*

GETTING AROUND

railway station *pályaudvar*
airport *repülőtér*
arrival *érkezés*
departure *indulás*
inland *belföldi*
international *külföldi*
ticket office *pénztár*
I would like two tickets *két jegyet kérek*
when is the train to Vienna? *mikor indul a bécsi vonat?*
here *itt*
there *ott*
towards *felé*
from here *innen*
from there *onnan*
to the right *jobbra*
to the left *balra*
straight ahead *egyenesen*
near *közel*; far *messze*

ACCOMMODATION

hotel *szálloda*
a single room *egyágyas szoba*
a double room *kétágyas szoba*
per night *egy éjszakára*
shower *zuhany*
bath *fürdőkád*
breakfast *reggeli*
do you have anything cheaper? *van valami olcsóbb?*
air-conditioning *légkondicionálás*

TIME

now *most*; later *később*
today *ma*; tomorrow *holnap*
morning *reggel*; late morning *délelőtt*; early afternoon *délután*;
evening *este*; night *éjszaka*
(at) one o'clock *egy óra (kor)*

NUMBERS

zero *nulla*
one *egy*
two *kettő* (note *két*, used with an object: *két kávét* two coffees)
three *három*
four *négy*
five *öt*
six *hat*
seven *hét*
eight *nyolc*
nine *kilenc*
ten *tíz*
eleven *tizenegy*
twenty *húsz*
thirty *harminc*
forty *negyven*
fifty *ötven*
sixty *hetven*
eighty *nyolcvan*
ninety *kilencven*
one hundred *száz*
one thousand *ezer*

DAYS OF THE WEEK

Monday *hétfő*
Tuesday *kedd*
Wednesday *szerda*
Thursday *csütörtök*
Friday *péntek*
Saturday *szombat*
Sunday *vasárnap*

MONTHS OF THE YEAR

January *január*
February *február*
March *március*
April *április*
May *május*
June *június*
July *július*
August *augusztus*
September *szeptember*
October *október*
November *november*
December *december*

HOLIDAYS

New Year *szilveszter*
Easter *húsvét*
Christmas *karácsony*

EATING OUT
Useful phrases

are these seats taken? *ezek a helyek foglaltak?*
bon appétit! *jó étvágyat!*
do you have…? *van…?*
I'm a vegetarian *vegetáriánus vagyok*
I'd like a table for two *két fő részére kérek egy asztalt*
I'd like the menu, please *kérem az étlapot*
I didn't order this *nem ezt rendeltem*
thank you *köszönöm*
the bill, please *számlát kérek*

Basics (alapok)

ashtray *hamutartó*
bill *számla*
bread *kenyér*
cup *csésze*
fork *villa*
glass *pohár*
knife *kés*
milk *tej*
napkin *szalvéta*
oil *olaj*
pepper *bors*
plate *tanyér*
salt *só*
spoon *kanál*
sugar *cukor*
teaspoon *kiskanál*
vinegar *ecet*
water *víz*

Meat (húsok)

bárány lamb
bográcsgulyás thick goulash soup
borjú veal
comb leg
jókai bableves bean soup with pork knuckle
kacsa duck

liba goose
máj liver
marha beef
mell breast
nyúl rabbit
pulyka turkey
sonka ham
szarvas venison

Fish & seafood (hal & tengeri gyümölcs)

halfilé roston grilled fillet of fish
harcsa catfish
homár lobster
kagyló shellfish, mussels
lazac salmon
pisztráng trout
ponty carp
rák crab, prawn
tonhal tuna

Accompaniments (köretek)

burgonya (or **krumpli**) potatoes
galuska noodles
hasábburgonya chips
rizs rice
tészta pasta

Salads (savanyúság)

cékla beetroot
fejes saláta lettuce salad
paradicsom tomato
uborka cucumber

Vegetables (zöldség)

gomba mushrooms
karfiol cauliflower
kukorica sweetcorn
lencse lentils
paprika pepper
sárgarépa carrot
spárga asparagus(white/*fehér*, green/*zöld*)
spenót spinach
zöldbab green beans
zöldborsó peas

Fruit & nuts (gyümölcs & dió)

alma apple
cseresznye cherry
dinnye melon
dió nut, walnut
eper strawberry
gesztenye chestnut
málna raspberry
narancs orange
őszibarack peach
sárgabarack apricot
szilva plum

Drinks (italok)

ásványvíz mineralwater
bor wine
édes bor sweet wine
fehér bor white wine
kávé coffee
narancslé orange juice
pálinka fruit brandy
pezsgő sparkling wine
sör beer
száraz bor dry wine
vörös bor red wine

Further Reference

BOOKS

Biography, memoir & travel

Leigh Fermor, Patrick *Between the Woods and the Water; A Time of Gifts* In the 1930s, Fermor hiked from Holland to Istanbul, stopping off in Hungary on the way. These evocative memoirs are the result.
Márai, Sándor *Memoir of Hungary 1944-48* Insightful memoir by exiled Magyar author.
Pressburger, Giorgio & Nicola *Homage to the Eighth District* Authentic and touching recollections of Jewish society before and during World War II.

Children

Gárdonyi, Géza *Eclipse of the Crescent Moon* Boy's-own adventure about the 1552 Turkish siege of Eger.
Molnar, Ferenc *The Paul Street Boys* Juvenile classic of a boys' gang on a District VIII building site.

Food & drink

Banfalvi, Carolyn *Food Wine Budapest* A practical, informative guide to Hungarian cuisine, and where to enjoy it.
Gundel, Károly *Gundel's Hungarian Cookbook* The best Hungarian cookbook, by the man who modernised Magyar cuisine.
Lang, George *The Cuisine of Hungary* Detailed study of local gastronomic development.
Liddell, Alex *The Wines of Hungary* A useful introduction to the art of Hungarian viticulture.

History, art & architecture

Búza, Péter *Bridges of the Danube* Budapest's famous river crossings.
Crankshaw, Edward *The Fall of the House of Habsburg* Solid and solidly anti-Hungarian account of the dynasty's demise.
Dent, Bob *Budapest 1956 – Locations of Drama* Detailing the Uprising – what happened where.
Éri, Gyöngyi et al *A Golden Age: Art & Society in Hungary 1896-1914* Colourful compendium, including works by the greats.
Garton Ash, Timothy *We the People* An instant history by this on-the-spot Oxford academic.

Gerő, András *Modern Hungarian Society in the Making* Collection of essays on the last 150 years of Hungarian political, social and cultural history.
Heathcote, Edwin *Budapest: A Guide to 20th Century Architecture* Portable, clear and concise guide.
Jones, Gwen *Chicago of the Balkans: Budapest in Hungarian Literature 1900-1939* Entertaining analysis of the competing narratives in pre-war Hungarian literature.
Kontler, László *Millennium in Central Europe: A History of Hungary* The most thorough account in English of the Magyars.
Lendvai, Paul *The Hungarians: A Thousand Years of Victory in Defeat* Not as comprehensive as Kontler, but a great read.
Litván, György *The Hungarian Revolution of 1956: Reform, Revolt and Repression 1953-1963* Blow-by-blow accounts of the 1956 Uprising.
Lukács, John *Budapest 1900* Extremely readable literary and historical snapshot of Budapest at its height. The best book about the city's history and culture currently in print.
Taylor, AJP *The Habsburg Monarchy 1809-1918* Terse history of the Habsburg twilight.
Ungváry, Krisztián *The Siege of Budapest: 100 Days in World War II* Fine chronicle of a city under siege.

Language

Payne, Jerry *Colloquial Hungarian* Entertaining primer, witty dialogues.

Literature

Ady, Endre *Neighbours of the Night: Selected Short Stories* Prose pieces stiffly rendered in English, but at least they translate – unlike his gloomy but stirring poetry.
Bánffy, Miklós *They Were Counted; They Were Found Wanting; They Were Divided* Acclaimed Transylvanian trilogy recalls the lost world of Hungarian aristocracy as it falls apart.
Bierman, John *The Secret Life of Laszlo Almasy* True story of the Hungarian desert adventurer whose life was the basis for Michael Ondaatje's *The English Patient*.
Eszterházy, Péter *A Little Hungarian Pornography; Helping Verbs of the Heart; The Glance of Countess Hahn-Hahn; She Loves Me;*

Celestial Harmonies One of Hungary's most popular contemporary writers, Eszterházy's postmodern style represents a radical break with the country's literary tradition.
Fischer, Tibor *Under the Frog* Seriously funny and impeccably researched Booker-nominated romp through Hungarian basketball, Stalinism and the 1956 revolution.
Kertész, Imre *Fateless; Kaddish for a Child Not Born* Accounts of the Holocaust and its effects by the 2002 Nobel Laureate for Literature.
Konrád, George *A Feast in the Garden* Highly autobiographical novel leading from village to Holocaust to Communist tyranny.
Kosztolányi, Dezső *Skylark; Anna Édes; Darker Muses, The Poet Nero* Kosztolányi, who wrote these novels in the 1920s, was probably the best Magyar prose writer of the last century.
Krasznahorkai, László *The Melancholy of Resistance* This tale of events in a tiny village is the basis for the film *Werckmeister Harmonies*.
Örkény, István *One Minute Stories* Vignettes of contemporary Budapest: absurd, ironic, hilarious.
Rubenstein, Julian *Ballad of the Whisky Robber* Punchy crime fiction based on the true story of the whisky-sodden folk hero Attila Ambrus, set in 1990s Budapest.

WEBSITES

www.budapest.com
Travel site for tourists and business people, with hotel-booking function.
www.lovebudapest.com
Excellent, regularly updated resource for diners, bar-hoppers and shoppers.
www.caboodle.hu
News of Hungary in English.
www.gotohungary.co.uk
Tourist-oriented site run by the UK office of the national tourist board, with regular holiday suggestions.
www.bbj.hu
Consistently updated financial and political news.
www.budapest100.hu/fooldal
Fascinating project to bring all of the city's 100-year-old houses to life.
www.hlo.hu
Hungarian literature online.
www.yellowstarhouses.org
Details the 1,944 buildings designated by the mayor of Budapest in 1944 to house 220,000 Jews forcibly removed from their homes.

Index

INDEX

INDEX

Bags packed, milk cancelled, house raised on stilts.

You've packed the suntan lotion, the snorkel set, the stay-pressed shirts. Just one more thing left to do – your bit for climate change. In some of the world's poorest countries, changing weather patterns are destroying lives.

You can help people to deal with the extreme effects of climate change. Raising houses in flood-prone regions is just one life-saving solution.

**Climate change costs lives.
Give £5 and let's sort it** *Here & Now*

www.oxfam.org.uk/climate-change

Be Humankind 🛇 Oxfam

INDEX

Maps

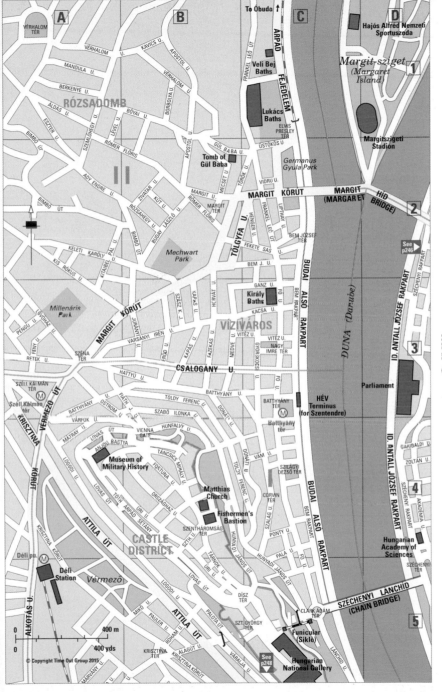

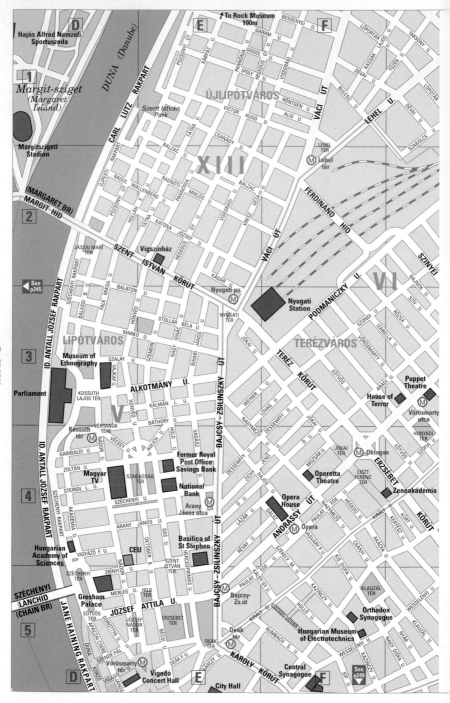

MAPS

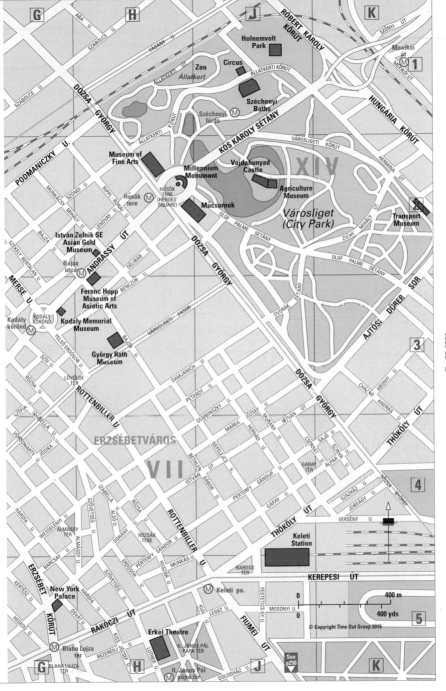

MAPS

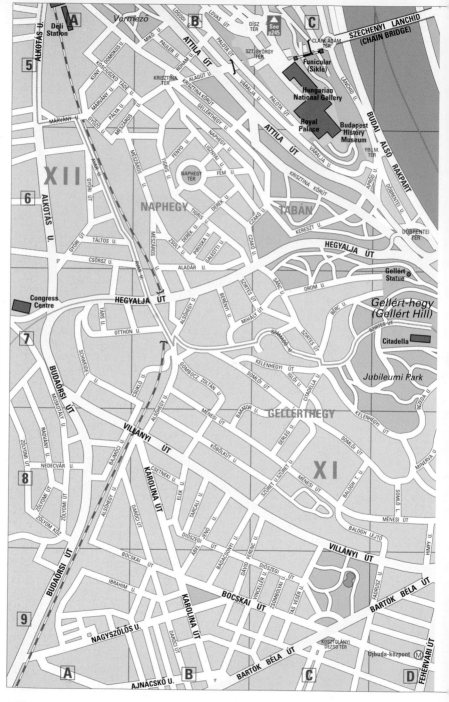

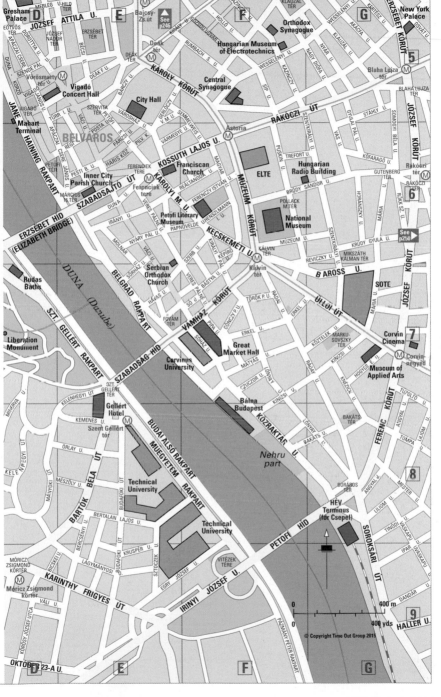

MAPS

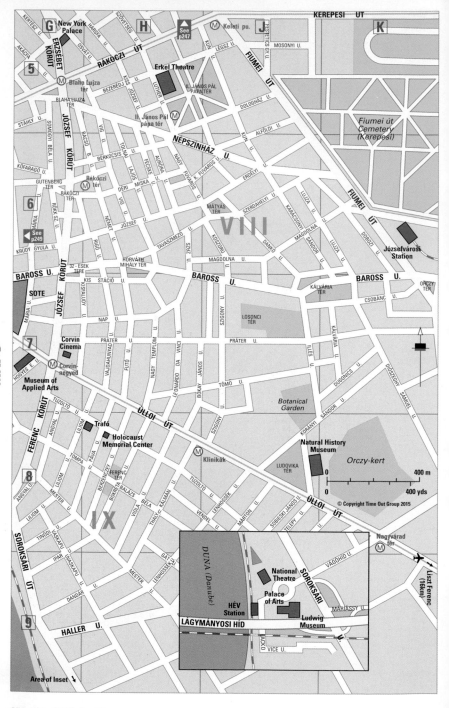

Street Index

STREET INDEX

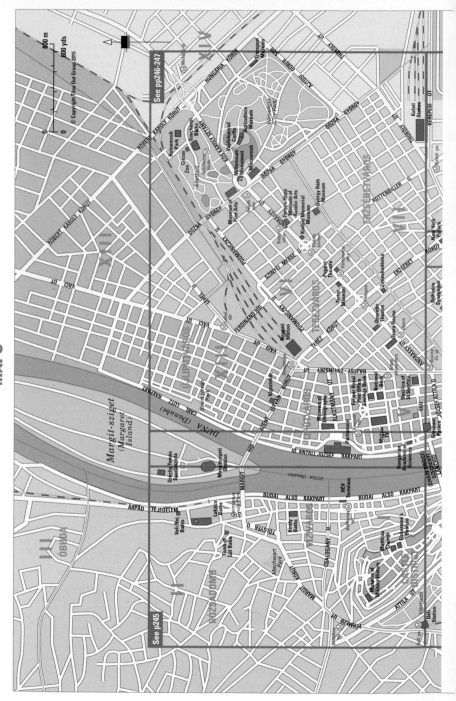

MAPS

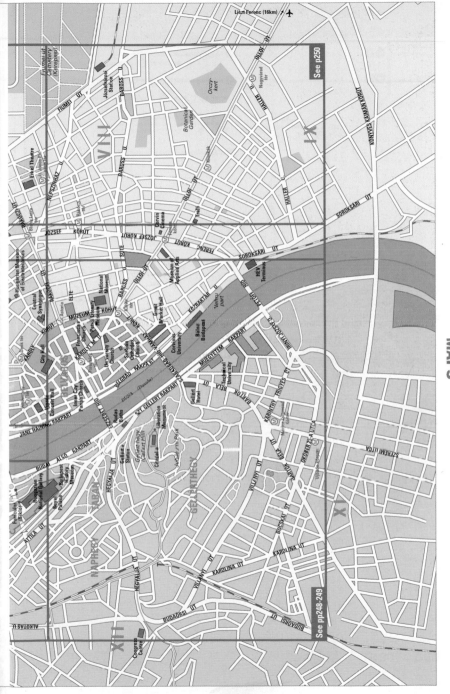

Liszt Ferenc (16km)

See p250

See pp248-249

MAPS

Time Out Budapest **255**

Budapest metró- és hév-hálózata
Metro and Suburban Railway Network in Budapest

Metróvonalak / Metro lines
1   2   3   4

Hév-vonalak / Suburban Railway lines
Szentendrei 5   Ráckevei 6   Csepeli 7   Gödöllői 8   Csömöri 9

Átszállóhely / Transfer point
Metróvonalak közötti átszálláskor nem szükséges új vonaljegyet érvényesíteni.
On the metro network single tickets allow transfers between the lines.

Vasútállomás / Railway station

Szentendre
Békásmegyer
Csillaghegy
Rómaifürdő
Aquincum
Kaszásdűlő
Filatorigát
Szentlélek tér
Tímár utca
Szépvölgyi út
Margit híd, budai hídfő
Batthyány tér
Széll Kálmán tér
Déli pályaudvar

Újpest-Városkapu
Gyöngyösi utca
Forgách utca
Árpád híd
Dózsa György út
Lehel tér
Nyugati pályaudvar
Arany János utca
Kossuth Lajos tér
Vörösmarty tér
Deák Ferenc tér

Újpest-Központ
Mexikói út
Széchenyi fürdő
Hősök tere
Bajza utca
Kodály körönd
Vörösmarty utca
Oktogon
Opera
Bajcsy-Zsilinszky út
Blaha Lujza tér
Keleti pályaudvar
Astoria
Ferenciek tere
Kálvin tér
Szent Gellért tér
Móricz Zsigmond körtér
Fővám tér
Újbuda-központ
Boráros tér
Közvágóhíd
Bikás park
Kelenföld vasútállomás

Pillangó utca
Örs vezér tere
Rákosfalva

Puskás Ferenc Stadion
II. János Pál pápa tér
Rákóczi tér
Corvin-negyed
Klinikák
Nagyvárad tér
Népliget
Ecseri út
Pöttyös utca
Határ út
Kőbánya-Kispest

Szabadságtelep
Árpádföld
Cinkota alsó
Csömör
Gödöllő
Ilonatelep
Cinkota
Mátyásföld alsó
Mátyásföld, Imre utca
Mátyásföld, repülőtér
Sashalom
Nagyicce

Közvágóhíd
Beöthy utca
Kén utca
Timót utca
Pesterzsébet felső
Torontál utca
Soroksár felső
Soroksár, Hősök tere
Szent István utca
Millenniumtelep
Szabadkikötő
Szent Imre tér
Karácsony Sándor utca
Csepel

Dunaharaszti, Tököl, Ráckeve